# The Diseases of Civilisation

# The Diseases of Civilisation

## Brian Inglis

HODDER AND STOUGHTON
LONDON SYDNEY AUCKLAND TORONTO

British Library Cataloguing in Publication Data
Inglis, Brian
  The diseases of civilization.
  1. Epidemiology
  2. Medical geography
  I. Title
  614.4'2        RA651
  ISBN 0 340 21717 0

# Contents

# Introduction

Until recently it was widely believed that medical science has been gradually but systematically banishing civilisation's diseases. For centuries, the assumption ran, mankind had been the victim of scourges such as the great plagues, which ignorance and superstition combined to permit, and even encourage. Gradually, however, medicine and science threw off these encumbrances, until in the second half of the nineteenth century the achievements of the bacteriologists finally pinned down the causes of infectious diseases, still the greatest threat, enabling work to begin on finding ways to prevent them by immunisation, and to cure them with drugs – 'magic bullets', as Paul Ehrlich called them. At the same time, improved technology was facilitating more accurate diagnosis, and advances in anaesthesia were enabling surgeons to carry out more sophisticated operations. The steady rise in life expectation in the West reflected the pace of the advance, and with the introduction of the sulpha drugs in the 1930s, and later of penicillin and the antibiotics, medical science enjoyed its most resounding triumph.

Occasionally, though, warning voices were raised, and one from within orthodoxy's camp was René Dubos's *Mirage of Health*, published in 1959. As an eminent bacteriologist – discoverer of an antibiotic, biographer of Pasteur, and holder of a Chair at the Rockefeller University, New York – Dubos could not be accused of hostility to the medical establishment, but he felt compelled to point out that its achievements were less spectacular than they had been cracked up to be. The chief credit for the conquest of the destructive epidemics, for example, ought to have been given to the social reformers who had campaigned for purer water, better sewage disposal and improved living standards. It had been their efforts, rather than the achievements of the medical scientists, which had been chiefly responsible for the reduction of mortality from infectious diseases; the sulpha drugs and the antibiotics had merely speeded up the process. And valuable though their contribution was, it had not appreciably lowered the level of disease in general. Although the living standards of the average American citizen were the highest in the world in material terms, he was spending ten per cent of his income on medical care. His 'ubiquitous national smile' might beam down from every poster, but one citizen in every four would spend months, sometimes years, in a mental hospital. 'Is it not a delusion,' Dubos asked, 'to proclaim the present state of health as the best in the history of the world, at a time when increasing numbers of persons in our society depend upon drugs and doctors for meeting the ordinary problems of everyday life?'

## Medical Nemesis

Dubos's warning went unheeded in the medical profession, and if doctors were not disturbed, why should the general public worry? It was not until the 1970s that critics began to insinuate, and then to claim outright, that the profession was not worried for the very reason that ill-health is its business. The most pugnacious of these critics, the former priest Ivan Illich, was preaching the gospel which he was to present in his *Medical Nemesis*: 'The medical establishment,' he asserted, 'has become a major threat to health.' In *The End of Medicine* the American lawyer Rick J. Carlson took up the theme. As a consultant to a number of medical bodies, he had begun to study the effects of medical care, and he had been disconcerted to find that it had 'very little to do with health', a statement which he was able to support with a mass of evidence.

Carlson's was the more sober appraisal, but Illich's work attracted the most attention, the world over. The medical profession, he contended, was concentrating almost all its resources on treatment, for which doctors are paid, rather than on prevention which, if it were effective, would reduce their income and their status. Not merely was this a mistake from the community's point of view, he argued; it was actually making people unhealthier, because the treatments were so often unnecessary. The surgeon was concerned less with the needs of his patients than with the size of his bank balance; the physician was actually making his patients ill by inducing iatrogenic disorders – the side-effects of the drugs used. And although Illich's style was tiresome and his approach abrasive, Franz Inglefinger, editor of the *New England Journal of Medicine*, called it 'exceptionally important'.

Illich and Carlson were chiefly concerned with what had been happening in the United States, but the same trends could be observed in Europe. This was particularly discouraging to the British, in view of the expectations aroused by the introduction of the National Health Service in 1948. It was assumed that the demand for health services would rise sharply as soon as the NHS came into being, because so many people who had lived with their lumbago or rotten teeth would now be able to have them treated. But surely, as soon as the backlog had been worked through, the Welfare State's benefits – free maternity services, free orange juice for infants, and milk for school children, free advice on prevention, linked with free immunisation procedures – would mean that fewer people would fall ill? By the mid-1950s, when the initial demands upon the NHS were expected to decline, living standards were rising more rapidly than ever before, which in itself might have been expected to lead to a considerable improvement in the nation's health.

How sadly the NHS failed to live up to expectations was to be shown in 1977, in the results of a survey undertaken by the Office of Population Censuses and Surveys, reporting on the level of health in a sample of the population. Over half the men and over two-thirds of the women interviewed considered that they had chronic or recurrent health problems – a much higher proportion than in earlier surveys. One of every three of the men who claimed to be chronically unwell, and two out of every five of the women, admitted to constant use of medicines. Assuming that the sample had been representative 'eighteen per cent of all men and twenty-eight per cent of all women were taking some prescribed medication all the time'.

That the sample had been reasonably representative was to be confirmed by surveys in connection with the NHS's thirtieth birthday, the following year. By all the standard indicators, they showed that the level of ill-health had continued to rise. More working days were being lost through sickness; more medical prescriptions were being issued; more patients were being admitted to hospitals, and the amount spent on the health services had increased by a thousand-fold – which, even allowing for inflation, was a melancholy commentary on the working of a system which had held out such promise.

What has gone wrong? There is one clue: the fact that, in spite of the differences between the way in which national health services are financed and managed, the similarities are far more striking. Allowing for certain national idiosyncrasies – such as the extensive use in France of suppositories – the kind of treatment which patients can expect, the drugs and the operations, are much the same wherever they happen to be, in Manchester or Memphis, Munich or Melbourne.

All the indications are that the medical profession as an institution straddles and transcends national boundaries.

This strongly suggests that the critics of the medical profession, *as a profession*, have a case. Halfdan Mahler, Director General of the World Health Organisation, admitted as much in the course of a lecture he gave in London in 1975. The medical profession, he feared, was in real trouble. The charge levelled against it was that 'by legislation, by training, by organisation and by the way in which health-related investigations are started and restricted, there has been a progressive "mystification" in medical care which has continued almost unchecked'. Absorbed in its own preoccupations, the profession had allowed the gap between *health* care and *medical* care to continue to widen; at the same time it had exploited its monopolistic position to create 'an unnecessary but inevitable dependency of the population upon the holders of these mysteries'.

If true, Mahler concluded, 'this is a grave charge'. Its truth has since been confirmed by a number of writers, including Thomas McKeown, Professor of Social Medicine at the University of Birmingham, in *The Role of Medicine*. Surveying the historical evidence, McKeown comes to the conclusion that 'medical intervention has made, and can be expected to make, a relatively small contribution to prevention of sickness and death'. Even the statistics purporting to show a great increase in life expectancy have been misleading, because the increase has largely been the consequence of more people surviving childbirth and infancy, chiefly the result of higher living standards. Life expectation for those who have reached adulthood is little higher today than it was at the beginning of the century.

Recently the mass media, formerly subservient to the medical profession, have become increasingly restive, and occasionally hostile. In Germany, in particular, the newspapers and television have given a great deal of space to the diatribes of Dr Julius Hackethal, the surgeon whose books denouncing his colleagues – 'murderers sitting behind desks' – have become best-sellers. In Britain the 1980 Reith Lectures on BBC radio were given by a young lawyer, Ian Kennedy, who took much the same critical line as Carlson had done; and, following complaints from the medical establishment about a television programme on transplants, the BBC did not, as so often before, climb down, but counter-attacked.

Is this antagonism to the profession justified? And if so, why? I have tried to answer that question by looking at the way it deals with some of the diseases of our civilisation, including the most lethal – heart attacks and cancer; the most disturbing – mental illness and iatrogenic disorders; and the most baffling – the neuropathies and allergies. If what emerges is often an indictment of the profession, perhaps I may be permitted to rebut, in advance, the charge that I am 'anti-doctor'. 'I honour physicians not for their services but for themselves,' Montaigne claimed in his autobiography. 'I have known many a good man among them, and most worthy of my affection. I do not attack them, but their art.' That goes for me.

# 1

# Heart Disease

Heart disease used to be regarded as a manifestation of old age. Like any mechanical pump, the assumption was, a heart must 'give out' eventually; death, in such cases, could be attributed to natural causes. Only in the 1920s did it receive more systematic study as a disease, because of the growing suspicion that it was on the increase: in particular heart attacks, which often carried off men, to outward appearances in good health, in the prime of life. Two suspects were identified: the 'furring-up' of the arteries with a fatty deposit, cholesterol, and clotting of the blood – thrombosis. Heart attacks were taken to be the end-product of processes similar to those by which the outlet pipe of a kitchen sink can become blocked: congealed grease narrowing the outlet, and insoluble objects becoming stuck fast.

Although no simple method of dissolving the fatty deposit on the artery walls presented itself, it proved a relatively easy matter to produce drugs to prevent blood from clotting, and when, after the Second World War, the mortality statistics revealed that the incidence of deaths from heart disease was growing, a flood of these anti-coagulants poured on to the market. So self-evident did it seem that they would reduce the number of heart attacks that, for a while, failure to prescribe them for patients considered to be at risk – angina sufferers, say, or people who had just survived an attack – was considered almost tantamount to professional negligence.

Their use, however, did not stem the mounting death-rate from heart attacks. In 1954 William Evans, consultant cardiologist at the London Hospital, warned that experience had shown anti-coagulant therapy to have been a costly mistake. 'Let it go soon,' he urged in a lecture at the Royal Society of Medicine; 'let it go now, before remorse weighs too heavily on those who may continue for a little time longer to advocate its use.' Remorse, it turned out, continued to weigh lightly. In a paper on 'addiction to medicines' in the *British Medical Journal* in 1962, Evans reiterated his warning. Huge amounts were still being squandered on this form of treatment, he complained, in spite of the fact that not only had it failed to save lives, it had also been known to cause deaths from internal bleeding, 'all too frequently into vital tissues like the brain'.

Little attention was paid to Evans, in spite of his high standing in the profession. Research papers continued to appear in the medical journals, citing evidence that anti-coagulant therapy worked, until in 1969 the papers were made the subject of a critical survey by R. H. Gifford and A. R. Feinstein of the Yale School of Medicine. Of the thirty-odd papers they had studied, only one, they had found, described research which could be regarded as methodologically sound. The rest were largely based on untrustworthy work and citations of the results of earlier untrustworthy work. They lent hardly more justification for using anti-coagulants to treat heart disease than there had been for the use, centuries old, of 'bleeding'.

By this time, however, cardiologists had established themselves even more securely in the hospital hierarchy through the introduction of coronary care units, in which patients who had suffered 'coronaries' – heart attacks consequent upon an artery being blocked by a blood clot (coronary thrombosis), or the death of heart muscle (myocardial infarction) owing to an inadequate blood supply – could be kept under constant round-the-clock surveillance, wired up to gadgets which would give warning of any change in their condition, such as a fall in the pulse-rate or an erratic heartbeat, alerting the nurses to take prompt action. These spawned intensive care units facilitating, among other things, heart surgery, and when in 1967 Christiaan Barnard in Cape Town carried out the first transplant of a human heart, it was widely hailed as modern medicine's supreme achievement.

The patient died not long afterwards of pneumonia, contracted because the drugs which had been used to try to prevent the rejection of his alien heart had left him more susceptible to infection, and when the results of similar operations in other parts of the world proved, on balance, disappointing, reaction set in. Even if they had a hundred per cent success rate, it was realised, their contribution to the reduction of the mortality-rate from heart attacks would be marginal. And not merely was the mortality-rate becoming alarming; so also was the proportion of men – the victims were still predominantly male – who were dying before their time. In the United States and Britain about a third of the victims were under the age of sixty-five. One American male out of five, it was calculated, would contract a heart disorder of some kind before the age of sixty, and even if he survived, his health would often be irrevocably impaired. 'Coronary heart disease has

2

reached enormous proportions, striking more and more at younger subjects,' the World Health Organisation proclaimed in 1969. 'It will result in coming years in the greatest epidemic mankind has faced, unless we are able to reverse the trend by concentrated research into its cause and prevention.'

## Framingham

Researchers had been concentrating mainly on the heart, the arteries and the blood, in the hope that they would yield up secrets which would enable physicians and surgeons to treat more effectively those patients who survived heart attacks. But one research team was pursuing a different line, using the techniques of epidemiology to try to find the cause, or causes, of heart disease.

The epidemiological method, based on the evaluation of statistics, was not new. Its most striking success had been when in 1854 the London doctor John Snow surmised from his study of the statistics showing the incidence of cholera in different parts of the capital that polluted drinking-water in certain wells, rather than bad air floating over the capital, must be responsible – a hypothesis which he was able to confirm dramatically by removing the handle of one Soho pump, compelling the locals to obtain their water from another and, as it turned out, safer source. But Snow's achievement won him little recognition (although a nearby London pub is named after him). Epidemiology continued to be regarded as a discipline of little significance to medicine, except in so far as it could plot the advance of a flu epidemic, allowing preventive measures, such as immunisation, to be taken in good time. This, it was assumed, would in any case only apply to infectious diseases. Doctors tended to mistrust statistics as a source of information, preferring to rely upon their own clinical impressions. 'I think it only fair to say,' Professor F. A. Crew remarked in a lecture on the subject in 1945, 'that by the profession as a whole, an ignorance of, and a scornful and distrustful attitude towards, statistics, are regarded as the praiseworthy attributes of a robust personality.'

It had required courage, therefore, for a group of doctors to mount an epidemiological experiment designed to investigate not patients with heart disease, but people who were healthy, to try to discover why they should develop heart disease later, if at all. The inhabitants of the small town of Framingham, Massachusetts, were invited to the local hospital, where their medical histories were recorded, and they

3

underwent various medical tests. They also filled in a questionnaire giving details of their diet, whether they smoked, what exercise they took, and so on. More than five thousand men and women participated – over a third of those who had been asked to volunteer – committing themselves to provide the team with the information required, and to come back every second year for further investigation. By this means the investigators hoped to construct a model of the heart-attack-prone individual, not unlike an identikit, or photokit, picture of a police suspect. In due course it was found that in Framingham high blood pressure, high animal fat and cholesterol intake, and cigarette smoking were significantly related to proneness to heart attacks.

These findings appeared to explain the rise in the mortality from heart disease, and in particular from heart attacks, the major cause of death. The spread of the cigarette-smoking habit had been accompanied by increased consumption of foods rich in animal fats, from hamburgers to dunked doughnuts. Other 'risk factors', as they came to be called, were found which upheld this supposition: people who were obese were more heart-attack-prone. And, in time, confirmation of these findings began to come in from further American research projects, and from other countries. Although they did not at first attract much attention within the profession, the media picked them up; so by 1969 there was a growing public awareness, at least in the United States, that a fat-laden diet might put people at risk (cigarettes were already suspect, because they had been shown to be linked with lung cancer).

## Stress

By 1969, too, another possible risk factor had emerged, although not from the Framingham investigation: psychosocial stress.

That there is a link between heart disease and the emotions is a belief of very long standing – not surprisingly, in view of the common experience of the heart pounding in tension-inducing circumstances, in love or war. In his work on the circulation of the blood William Harvey cited an example: the case of a man who suffered from 'extreme oppression and pain of the heart', arising from a thwarted desire for revenge on a rival. And the eighteenth-century surgeon John Hunter remarked that his heart and his life were at the mercy of any fool who might put him in a passion – a prognosis confirmed by his death at a hospital board meeting. But when towards the end of the nineteenth century it came to be accepted that organic disease – involving detectable structural changes, or lesions – must have some physical or chemical cause, it also came to be assumed that the emotions played no part except, perhaps, on rare occasions as a precipitant, and eventually they were disregarded altogether in diagnosis.

The first reminder that the mind might after all have a role in relation to heart disease came in 1933 from a report of the results of experiments conducted by William Evans and a colleague, Clifford Hoyle, in the cardiac department of the London Hospital. Becoming dissatisfied with the effects of the drugs then recommended for the treatment of angina, they decided to see what would happen if some patients, thinking they were being prescribed drugs, were given a placebo – bicarbonate of soda. Over a three-year period, thirteen different drugs were tested in this way, with half the group of patients getting the drug and half the placebo. At the end of the trials it was found that placebo treatment 'gave better results than most of the actual drugs, and appeared statistically to be the better form of protection'. Even standard pain-killers such as morphine were little more effective, on balance, and against their greater effectiveness had to be set the risk of addiction.

It was soon to be found that 'placebo effect', as it came to be called, was very common; suggestion (or auto-suggestion) can make a dummy drug work as well as the real drug. Surveying the literature on the subject thirty years later, Henry K. Beecher, Professor of Research in Anesthesia at the Harvard Medical School, described the Evans/Hoyle report as the pioneer study in this field, 'a milestone in clinical sophistication in studies of subjective responses'. It provided the explanation for the phenomenon known to generations of doctors from the old tag, 'Use your new drugs quickly, while they still have the power to heal', and it marked the beginning of a new era in drug testing, in which no drug could be considered effective unless controlled trials demonstrated that it gave better results than a placebo. But it did not lead to any re-appraisal in orthodox cardiological circles of the role of the mind, or to any investigation of the possibility that the mind might have some responsibility for the onset of angina, or of heart disease in general.

This exploration was left to the early investigators, chiefly Freudian-orientated physicians and psychiatrists, of what came to be known as psychosomatic medicine. A number of them reported that fluctuations of blood pressure were related to emotional states; it could be raised, for example, by introducing topics calculated to arouse feelings of irritation in the patient. A survey of the evidence up to 1939 suggested to Franz Alexander, Professor of Psychiatry at the University of Illinois, that 'essential' hypertension – the condition where blood pressure remained persistently above normal levels, for no identifiable reason – was 'based on excessive and inhibited hostile impulses'; that is to say, on how certain people reacted subjectively to emotional pressures put on them, rather than on the objective severity of the pressures themselves.

The believers in the psychosomatic theory did not regard suppressed emotions as the *cause* of heart disease. They suggested rather that some categories of people are at risk because of their personality structure. 'It is characteristic of people who suffer from heart disease that they are hard workers,' Flanders Dunbar claimed in her *Mind and Body*, published in 1947, 'driving themselves without mercy and apparently enjoying it.' Such speculation, however, was ignored by cardiologists, and derided as 'notional' by the behaviourists (who had joined battle with the Freudians for a role in psychiatry) on the ground that it could not be statistically demonstrated. Occasionally a cardiologist whose reputation was sufficiently well established would take the mind/body link seriously. In 1951 Paul Dudley White in a paper 'Psyche and soma' agreed that their interaction 'could precipitate angina, and death'. Occasionally attempts were made to provide some statistical evidence. In 1952 two University of Cincinnati researchers reported that three out of four patients brought to their hospital following a heart attack had recently suffered an emotionally stressful event which appeared to have been 'the straw which broke the camel's back'. But a report of this kind was rarely seen in any of the orthodox medical journals; the *Journal of Psychosomatic Medicine*, in which it appeared, reached only the converted. Psychosomatic theory hardly impinged upon cardiology, except as an irritant, until the appearance in 1956 of *The Stress of Life* by Hans Selye, Professor of Experimental Medicine at McGill University, Montreal.

Selye described experiments in which laboratory rats had been given a drug in doses small enough to have no observable effects. 'However, when those animals were subsequently strapped to a board (a frustrating experience which leads to nervous excitement and struggle) large patches of their heart muscle underwent acute disintegration and all the animals died within a few hours.' The damage caused by the combination of the drug and stress, it was found, was very similar to that which had been found in autopsies of individuals who had died of heart attacks following exposure to stress.

Although Selye's theory of the way in which stress worked could not

6

so easily be discounted as its psychosomatic predecessor had been, it failed to convince cardiologists. Partly this was because the effect of exposure to stress, though it could be demonstrated, was still not quantifiable – even less so in humans than in rats. But chiefly it was because of confusion over the meaning of the term 'stress', which colloquially had come to be used in two different senses – as both cause and effect. Selye himself distinguished between stressors, which impose strain, and stress, the animal or human reaction to them. Stressors, he pointed out, can be stimulating; they can actually speed up cure. But if they become too overwhelming, or if the rat (or patient) is under some other pressure, the resultant stress can kill.

This distinction was rarely grasped by Selye's critics. Medical lecturers, sceptical of the stress theory without having studied it, used to dismiss it on the ground that our ancestors, never far removed from visits by the horsemen of the Apocalypse, must have suffered more from stress than does twentieth-century man, cocooned with his central heating and antibiotics. A derisive commentary on disease and stress which won much approval at the time was H. R. Sprague's editorial in the medical journal *Circulation* in 1958. Why, Sprague asked, was suicide – surely an indication of stress – common in Japan, where heart disease was relatively rare? Why should heart disease tend to diminish in wartime? Why were manic depressives not more at risk than the rest of the population? Almost as an afterthought – as if somebody had suggested he ought to mention *The Stress of Life* before having the editorial printed – Sprague suggested that people who believed in the stress link ought to read what Selye had to say on the subject, evidently unaware that it undermined his own criticism.

Two years later an explanation in evolutionary terms of the relationship between stress and physiological reactions leading to disease was put forward by A. T. W. Simeons in his *Man's Presumptuous Brain*, a work which deeply impressed two such different intelligences as Aldous Huxley and Bertrand Russell. Man, Simeons argued, has not fully resolved the conflict between instinct and reason. He still feels the primitive urge either to fight or to fly, in difficult situations. This automatically pushes up his blood pressure, and generally alerts his autonomic nervous system. But because today he cannot, as a rule, either fight or fly, the release-mechanism cannot come into action. People who experience a state of tension because of the demands of their work or the vagaries of their home life may consequently put too prolonged a strain on their homeostatic mechanism, which eventually goes out of order.

Finding methods of testing the stress theory which would satisfy

7

medical scientists remained a problem. The initial break-through came in a report in 1962 of research among the inhabitants of Roseto, a small Italian community in Pennsylvania, in which the immigrants had managed to preserve much of their traditional Italian way of life unchanged for more than half a century. Although they had a high animal-fat intake and a tendency towards obesity, it was found that they had far less heart disease than the inhabitants of neighbouring towns, and less than half their mortality-rate from heart attacks. By contrast, those Rosetans who had left to work in other cities had mortality-rates closer to the general average. The most likely explanation was that the Rosetans had managed to insulate themselves from psychosocial stresses operating in the world around them. And soon this finding was supplemented by similar reports: an investigation of social and cultural factors associated with heart disease in North Dakota, described in the *Journal of Chronic Diseases* in 1964, disclosed that, independently of established risk factors such as smoking and consumption of fat, citizens who frequently moved their homes ran a greater risk. For urban dwellers, too, the risk was three times as high as for those who lived in the country.

Another method of measuring stress, the 'Social Readjustment Rating Scale', was devised in the 1960s by Thomas H. Holmes and Richard H. Rahe. They listed life-events likely to be stressors, and allotted to each a figure on a scale from one to a hundred, according to its estimated impact. At the head of the list came 'death of spouse' (100), followed by 'divorce' (73), 'marital separation' (65), 'jail term' (63), and so on down to 'minor violation of the law' (11).

Ordinarily such a list would have attracted only derision, with little prospect of securing funds to test it. Rahe, however, was a naval officer at the San Diego Neuropsychiatric Research Unit, and the naval authorities, anxious to find ways to reduce the time lost through sickness, were intrigued by the idea, particularly as it would cost little to investigate. Two thousand five hundred men serving aboard three cruisers were asked to provide details from which Rahe could allot marks, add them up (a man whose wife had left him because he had been given a jail sentence would receive 65 + 63 = 128) and, on this basis, predict the likelihood of illness. Naturally the scale was not accurate for individuals, but when the men were divided into groups according to whether their marks were above-average, or below-average, the above-average group was found to have a hundred per cent higher sickness-rate than those in the below-average group.

In another test, this time with doctors, life episodes in the previous eighteen months were used to predict the likelihood of their falling ill within the next eight months. Of the one-third who had the highest rating on the scale, half were subsequently to report that they had been ill, as against only one in ten of the third with the lowest rating. At a symposium on 'Life Stress' sponsored by NATO, Rahe was also able to show a positive correlation between stressful episodes and heart attacks, the mortality-rate being significantly higher among those near the top of the stress rating scale.

Although Rahe's work provided valuable confirmation of the role of stress in heart disease, it did not hold out much prospect of finding new ways to prevent or treat heart attacks. In the same period, however, research of a very different kind was beginning to show how individuals, even if they could not avoid stressful events, might learn how to control reactions to them.

Generations of medical students had been taught that the body's autonomic nervous system is self-governing. Heartbeat, blood pressure, temperature and gastric secretions are all continually affected by events, physical and emotional, but the homeostatic mechanism ensures that they return to whatever is their norm. Just as no man by taking thought can add one cubit to his stature, so no man by taking thought can lower his pulse-rate or his blood pressure for long.

But was this dogma justified? In the 1960s Profesor Neal Miller of the Rockefeller University, New York, decided to find if rats could be trained by the standard behaviourist techniques of 'reinforcements' – positive, in the form of food pellets; negative, in the form of electric shocks – to control their temperature. So contrary was this to accepted beliefs that for years he could not even find assistants to work with him. Yet when the experiments were complete, and had been repeated by six other research teams, there could be no doubt; laboratory rats could learn to increase or decrease not just their temperature, 'but heart rate, blood pressure, intestinal contraction, peripheral vasomotor responses, amount of blood in the stomach wall and formulation of urine'.

Shortly before Miller published his results in 1969, Herbert Benson, Professor of Medicine at Harvard, had been approached by a group of followers of the Maharishi Mahesh Yogi, volunteering their services to demonstrate the degree of control over their bodies they were able to achieve by meditation. He had declined their offer. But after hearing about Miller's work, when they approached him again he accepted, and found that, like Miller's rats, people who had learned the technique could indeed exercise control over their autonomic nervous systems. If they could not do much in the way of lowering their blood pressure the reason, Benson realised, was that meditation had already brought their blood pressure down well below the level which would otherwise have been expected of them; further research at Harvard soon showed that people's blood-pressure levels could in fact be lowered by the practice of meditation. It was not immediately clear how the method worked, though a study of their brain rhythms on an electro-encephalograph during meditation showed changes reflecting a shift into an altered state of consciousness. In a state which could be described as negative concentration (or positive abstraction), the mind appeared to become capable of transmitting instructions which the autonomic nervous system would act upon.

## The Lobbies

So ingrained was the prejudice – as over the years it had become – against the idea that the mind could have some responsibility for heart disease, let alone that it could be used to prevent it, that the significance of these findings was not immediately recognised. But during the 1960s reports from other countries of trials which confirmed the Framingham results were leading to a greater willingness to realise that prevention of heart disease might be accomplished by a campaign to discourage smoking, to lower consumption of animal fats and cholesterol, and to persuade people with high blood pressure to undergo treatment. In 1970 the Inter-Society Commission for Heart Disease Resources, set up by the Nixon Administration to give advice on how to deal with the 'epidemic', felt justified in claiming that 'the relationship between the risk factors, particularly the major risk factors, is probably causal'. The need, therefore, was for 'a comprehensive and sustained public and professional nutrition education program' to effect the necessary changes in dietary habits, along with a campaign to emphasise the health hazards of smoking, and a ban on the advertising of tobacco in the mass media. There should also be 'a major national effort to detect and control hypertension'.

No comparable recommendations had ever been presented to control a disease. Quarantine to prevent the spread of plague, and limes to prevent scurvy among seamen, had been introduced by the authorities with little difficulty as soon as the need had been recognised. But to persuade the general public that such staples as bacon, butter and cheese could be a menace, and to stop them smoking (the report actually used the term 'elimination', not 'reduction') would be a formidable task.

There was no prospect whatsoever of the Administration backing the enterprise, because Nixon was preparing to fight his campaign for re-election. To propose measures designed to reduce drastically the consumption of dairy produce and tobacco would not merely offend those of his supporters who believed that the citizen should be left to look after his own health in his own way without government nannying; it would also swing the farm and tobacco lobbies against him. Such measures as were required to protect the health of the community, the Administration decided, should be left to the medical profession to recommend.

The cardiologists were not well placed to perform that function, even had they wanted to. They did not, as a rule, see patients until after the symptoms of heart disease had manifested themselves, when it was often too late to wean them from cigarettes or junk food. It was left to the epidemiologists to take up the challenge. In the early 1970s a massive experiment was launched in Chicago under the generalship of Professor Jeremiah Stamler: the 'Multiple Risk Factor Intervention Trial' was designed to find men who were at risk because of the number of cigarettes they smoked, the amount of animal fat they consumed, and the level of their blood pressure, and to persuade some of them to stop smoking, alter their diet, and lower their blood pressure, to find out if they lived longer than those who retained their old habits. A trial of this kind, however, takes years to complete. In the meantime, the cardiologists were able to carry on as before, treating cases of heart disease with surgery or drugs.

The drugs were of two main types, designed either to reduce the level of cholesterol in the blood or to lower blood pressure. The first type got off to an unfortunate start with Merrell's MER 29, very successful until it was realised that it produced adverse reactions, among them baldness and cataracts, but the manufacture of drugs to lower blood pressure soon began to prove extremely profitable.

## Hypertension

It had long been realised that high blood pressure was associated with a number of diseases, but as it displayed no symptoms, often leaving people unaware of its presence, it was not commonly regarded as an illness needing treatment in its own right. Eventually, however, the respected Sir Clifford Allbutt managed to convince his colleagues in the early years of the present century that they ought to take 'hyperpiesia', as he called it, seriously. The name did not survive; the idea did. It became standard practice for a doctor to take his patient's blood pressure, and to prescribe some medicine if it were above normal.

This did not go uncriticised. 'It is a mistake, and one made not unfrequently, to consider the high blood pressure as if it were a disease,' Sir James Mackenzie warned in 1925 in his *Diseases of the Heart*; 'that it may be a physiological process for the benefit of the organism is seldom considered'. Luckily, Mackenzie observed, the efforts which had been made to find ways to lower blood pressure artificially were 'usually of little effect'. Several drugs were marketed between the wars for that purpose, none of which proved a success.

The Framingham findings gave the pharmaceutical industry a fresh incentive. Tranquillisers were experimented with, and diuretics, and for a time they gained enthusiastic reports. But they failed to check the rising death-rate from heart attacks, and they produced some ugly side-effects. When in 1962 William Evans reiterated his criticism of anti-coagulants, he extended it to include the drugs then being introduced to lower blood pressure. In his time, he recalled, he had known fifty-eight remedies soundly recommended for the treatment of hypertension.'The earlier ones, though failing to do good, did no harm; but latterly the more potent drugs have produced uncomfortable and often distressing side-effects' – conjunctivitis and muscle pain, along with 'skin eruptions, swelling of joints, lupus erythematosus, agitation, depressive psychosis, suppression of urine, dissecting aneurism, and paralyticileus'. The discontinuation of such drugs, Evans urged, was overdue, because 'they have no effect on the *causes* of hypertension'.

Again, Evans's warning went unheeded. Cardiologists continued to hope that the fifty-ninth remedy, soundly – more often raucously – recommended by the manufacturers, would work safely and well. And early in the 1970s the saviour emerged: the 'beta-blockers' which, by inactivating hormones, reduced pain. Originally marketed as a remedy for angina, they were soon widely prescribed also to lower blood pressure and to stabilise heartbeat; they even, it was claimed, helped clear away some of the detritus from clogged-up arteries. Tests on ski-jumpers and racing-car drivers, too, showed that they did not impair performance. By the early 1970s they had come to be regarded almost as the male equivalent of 'the Pill' – the 'sweet oblivious antidote', Malcolm Carruthers noted in *The Western Way of Death*, which could clear away 'that perilous stuff, which weighs upon the heart'.

This climate, Carruthers warned, might change if, after the honeymoon period, side-effects began to come to light. Although in Britain clinical trials of the first of the beta-blockers, practolol, appeared to show that it was safe, even before Carruthers' book was in the shops his warning was seen to have been justified. A note had to be sent to doctors in 1974 to warn them that some patients treated with the drug, marketed by ICI as Eraldin, had suffered from corneal scarring, damaging their sight. The replies from doctors showed not only that such damage was much more widespread than had been realised but also that treatment with Eraldin was linked with cases of deafness, peritonitis and pleurisy. By the time the decision was taken to withdraw it from the market, eighteen fatalities had been attributed to it, along with more than six hundred cases of serious side-effects: skin disorders – patchy areas of the body developing a scaly layer; lupus erythematosus, and tear glands so weakened that patients had to keep their eyes artificially moistened. Some twenty patients had gone blind.

By this time other beta-blockers had been marketed, without such serious consequences. Doctors allowed themselves to be persuaded that ICI had simply been unlucky – as in a sense they were: the safety testing which their drug received had been more rigorous than the regulations required, and the delay in appreciating the seriousness of the side-effects was chiefly due to the inadequacy of the reporting procedures in Britain (the United States had been spared Eraldin, thanks to the Food and Drug Authority's caution). Hypertensive patients were commonly switched to one of the other beta-blockers. Yet it was by no means certain that these were performing their main function – to prevent the development of heart disease. Some trials indicated that people who took drugs to reduce blood pressure were less likely to suffer from strokes or heart attacks, but the evidence was often conflicting.

Typical of the inconsistencies was the announcement that a controlled trial in Sweden had shown that drugs to lower blood pressure seemed to prevent, or at least postpone, the onset of heart attacks in patients – a finding apparently confirmed by further trials in Prague and Budapest. But when the figures were subjected to more careful scrutiny, it was realised that, although deaths from heart attacks had indeed been reduced, deaths from other causes had increased, so that life expectation remained no higher among the treated groups than among the controls.

Yet periodically campaigns for the introduction of mass screening for hypertension continued to surface, in spite of uncertainty whether the treatment likely to be offered would be effective in reducing the mortality from heart attacks, and of the certainty of unwelcome consequences. 'We do not know whether the rigorous treatment of early symptomatic hypertension prolongs life or not,' Sir Henry Miller warned; 'what we do know from our experience of insurance examinations is that its detection can cause disabling anxiety.' A few years later an experiment confirmed his view: absenteeism among workers, it revealed, doubled among those who were told they had high blood pressure. Citing this finding, Professor Thomas McKeown pointed out in 1978 that not merely had incorrect diagnosis been common, but also 'some who are correctly diagnosed do not follow the prescribed treatment; in some who follow the treatment, control of pressure is not achieved; and some are treated unnecessarily'.

At that time it was still assumed that the beta-blockers were safe. A writer in *World Medicine* even claimed that they could turn out to be a bigger discovery than penicillin because, among other things, 'they lack the side-effects of the other drugs'. Yet in 1978, only six months later, Peter Nixon, consultant cardiologist at the Charing Cross Hospital, lamented in a letter in the *Lancet* that so much of a heart specialist's time now had to be devoted to treating iatrogenic disorders, which in his experience had been 'enormously expanded by the beta-blockers'. Unfortunately the side-effects were often mistaken for symptoms of the patient's illness, and 'all too often the doctor was so sure of his drug's virtues that he closed his ears to the patient's heretical reports'. In other cases, where the doctor realised that the symptoms were the result of his treatment, he was reluctant to stop it for fear of the possible effects on the patient, because by this time it was coming to be realised that patients taken off beta-blockers could suffer from withdrawal symptoms.

The safety of the beta-blockers, other than Eraldin, had been taken for granted for so long that Nixon's warning attracted little attention. But a few months later the *British Medical Journal* included a paper describing blindness after treatment for hypertension, and in a worried editorial cited a number of other cases of serious side-effects from the same cause. And just as the warning note about Eraldin had jogged doctors' memories about side-effects they had either not reported or had not attributed to the drug, so now a succession of letters followed, describing similarly unhappy and sometimes appalling experiences.

There was no shortage of drugs for hypertension, nor of doctors ready to prescribe them in spite of the mounting evidence that they dealt with the problem unsatisfactorily – notably a report in 1979 in *Science*, lending confirmation to Sir James Mackenzie's view that high blood pressure may be a physiological process for the benefit of the organism. Barry Dworkin and colleagues at the Rockefeller University had found that the function of certain molecules, 'baro-receptors', in the heart and the blood vessels appears to be to regulate blood pressure to meet the requirements of stress, suggesting that raised blood pressure can be an adaptation to stressful circumstances, designed to maintain homeostasis.

Yet it is also a warning signal that the body is being kept in a potentially dangerous state of tension; the tendency has therefore been for the supporters of drug treatment to cite trials which show a reduction of both blood pressure and heart disease as justification for continuing to use drugs. But such results need to be treated with caution. In a five-year randomised controlled trial undertaken in the 1970s in Bethesda, Maryland, involving nearly 11,000 people with hypertension, those who were given 'stepped care' – careful supervision, free treatment, even free transportation to appointments – achieved lower blood-pressure levels and a lower mortality rate than the controls who had merely had standard care. Inevitably the results were hailed as a vindication of drug treatment. But as the programme's organisers admitted in a hand-out, a different interpretation can be put on them. The lower death-rate in the 'stepped care' group could be attributed, at least in part, to the fact that the people in the group had received attention in the community of a kind never previously provided in the United States, or anywhere else. Further research, the report concluded, 'is required to test this possibility'.

## Coronary Care

By the 1970s setbacks in connection with the treatment of hypertension were of less concern to cardiologists than before. They had
more important matters on their hands, matters of life and death. In
the 1950s coronary care units had been introduced, to which patients
who had suffered a heart attack or a stroke could be brought by
ambulance, and wired up to an array of gadgets which would give
warning of any change in their condition, a dropping pulse-rate or
erratic heart beat, enabling prompt remedial measures to be taken.
Often they were shown to visitors as the hospital's proudest achievement, saving lives which without them would surely have been lost.

Gradually, however, it came to be recognised how small a contribution coronary care units could make to the survival rate following
heart attacks. For a start, they could only save the lives of those
patients who reached them in time; the results of a survey conducted
in Edinburgh, published in 1972, showed that almost half the deaths
from heart attacks occurred within an hour of their onset, and a
further twenty per cent of patients died before they could be brought
to a hospital. The following year a survey by the American Heart
Association confirmed that the position in the United States was much
the same. Even if it were conceded that the units could save lives,
Jeremiah Stamler commented, 'the overall net effect on mortality is
too small percentage-wise to be detectable in the mortality statistics'.

The cardiologists none the less claimed that units saved the lives of
the minority of patients who could be brought to them in time. Was
even this true? New drugs had to be rigorously tested before they
came on the market; no such tests had been applied to the treatment
the units provided. People who died in them, it was believed, would
have died anyway, whereas those who lived usually gave the credit to
the care they had received. But there was no way of testing this
assumption so far as individual patients were concerned.

A way did exist, however, roughly to gauge their effectiveness. As
there were not sufficient coronary care facilities in Britain to take in all
heart-attack cases, and as sometimes it was deemed wiser to leave a
patient in bed at home rather than move him to hospital, it was
possible to compare the results of home and hospital treatments
without incurring the suspicion that some patients were being deliberately sacrificed by being deprived of the benefits of hospital coronary
care. In the late 1960s a comparison was made of the mortality figures
between two such groups of patients, victims of severe heart attacks,
so far as possible matched for age, severity of symptoms and so on, at

four centres in the south-west of England. When H. G. Mather and his team published their report in the *British Medical Journal* in 1971 it revealed that whether patients had been taken to coronary care units or remained at home made no appreciable difference. For those who did not have complications necessitating hospital treatment, their conclusion was, 'home care is ethically justified, and the need for general admission to hospital should be reconsidered'.

By this time, coronary care units were also coming under attack for the unwelcome and sometimes prolonged discomfort inflicted on the patient; as John S. Bradshaw, a GP who was later to write books indicting medical science on this and other counts, complained in the *British Medical Journal*, 'We rush him, bells a-clanging and lights a-flashing', to a coronary care unit, where, 'thanks to the stress of it all, he is quite likely to suffer a psychiatric disorder'. Psychiatrists, Bradshaw unkindly added, could then begin to study the patient, if he survived the heart attack, 'which he'd be just about as likely to if he'd stayed at home'. Heart patients, in other words, were being subjected 'to variants of the very factors that we ourselves believe help *cause* the disease'.

This evidence made no impression on those who worked in the units. According to the epidemiologist Professor Archibald Cochrane, when the results of the Mather survey showed that patients treated at home did a little better than patients treated in coronary units, some joker transposed the figures, and showed them to a cardiologist, who denounced the trial as unethical: it had condemned people to die at home who might otherwise have lived. 'When, however, he was shown the table the correct way round, he could not be persuaded to declare coronary care units unethical.'

The cardiologists' assumption that heart-attack patients ought to be brought to a hospital for coronary care, if possible, rather than treated at home, survived even the results of further trials which underlined the Mather findings. One was a follow-up by Mather's team, dealing with an extended series of patients; their report in 1976 showed that out of 450 patients randomly allocated and matched into two groups, twelve per cent of those who had been treated at home had died in the month after their heart attack, compared to fourteen per cent of those who had been treated in hospital. After eleven months, the mortality figures were twenty per cent for those home-treated, twenty-seven per cent for those treated in hospital, thereby confirming, the investigators claimed, that for many people, particularly the over-60s and those without complications, 'home care is a proper form of treatment'. The authors of a similar survey undertaken on Tees-side came to a similar conclusion. It was not easy, they admitted, to make precise comparisons, but 'under present circumstances, for those who survive to come under care, home care is as good if not better than hospital treatment'.

A few months later, a comparison of the effects of treatment in a coronary care unit and in an ordinary medical ward – made possible by the fact that there were not enough beds available in the unit to accommodate all those sent to hospital – showed that there was no significant difference in mortality between them. But as always the cardiologists had the last word. Only they could tell whether a patient who had survived a heart attack would, or would not, need coronary care. If patients who had been allowed to remain at home were to die, the GPs could be blamed for not having realised that there were complications. Far from heeding the Mather findings, cardiologists continued to give the same impression about the need for coronary care as they had earlier done about the need for anti-coagulant therapy: that not to bring patients who had suffered a heart attack to hospital almost constituted professional negligence.

By 1978, so dissatisfied had Peter Nixon become with coronary care that he circulated a memorandum in Charing Cross Hospital inviting discussion on the subject. He cited several critical commentaries, from a reference to the low survival rates of patients with myocardial infarction treated 'amidst frightening technological paraphernalia', in the report of the first interdisciplinary workshop on Psychosocial Factors and Health held in Stockholm in 1976, to a survey in the *Lancet*, concluding that 'despite continuing claims for the life-saving value of hospital and pre-hospital coronary care, and despite very considerable investment of financial and human resources in their provision, community mortality from myocardial infarction has not changed'. The coronary care unit in Charing Cross Hospital had been one of the first in Britain, and one of the most highly regarded, but from his experience there, and from the evidence, Nixon had felt compelled to change his mind about its value, and to recommend that it should be closed.

## By-pass Surgery

During the 1970s, coronary care units gradually came to be over-shadowed by intensive care units, where, after the initial setback over heart transplants, the surgeons were enjoying an unexpected but very welcome bonanza.

Since early in the century a variety of surgical operations had been experimented with to treat angina, enthusiastic reports about their benefits being invariably followed by disillusionment and eventual discontinuance because of the high mortality rate. The first successful by-pass transplant, with the help of a vein grafted on to the artery, was carried out in 1967; inevitably the achievement was overshadowed by Barnard's heart transplant the same year. Once mastered, however, the operation proved relatively simple, and the fact that veins could be taken from the patient's own body meant that there was no graft-rejection problem. Soon, reports came in of patients who had suffered agonies from angina getting up and about again, taking exercise and enjoying life. Surely, it was argued, as their coronary blood-flow was restored, the risk of a heart attack must also be reduced? The cardiac surgeons made the most of the opportunity. In 1971, 20,000 by-pass operations were performed in the United States; by 1973 the number had risen to 38,000.

To equip and run intensive and coronary care units was extremely expensive; the manufacturers of the required gadgetry seized their opportunity, competing energetically for sales. Cardiologists were easily persuaded that their units would be incomplete without the latest invention; that they could be criticised, and perhaps sued, for not using it; that they would be made to look foolish when they found that colleagues (and rivals) in nearby hospitals had had it installed; that it was their duty to their patients – and so on. As cardiologists wielded great influence, and as their units brought prestige to a hospital, the sale would often go through. But there was no way of telling how effective the gadget would be, other than the promises in the promotional hand-outs and the company representatives' sales-talk. 'With literally hundreds of companies competing for a share of the market for such devices as electro-cardiographs, defibrillators, and patient monitors,' the Ehrenreich's report on behalf of the New York Health Policy Advisory Center warned in 1970, the average hospital administrator or the average physician is in no position to determine whether a particular feature of one model which adds several hundred dollars to the cost is really important, or whether it is merely the medical electronics equivalent of a chromium tail fin.'

Besides, the expense remained of little concern to American administrators, because 'in the final analysis the hospitals don't pay the bill, anyhow.' The cost had to be met by patients, either directly or through insurance.

Were these units really in the best interests of patients? In 1971 Edith Heideman, Chief Nurse of the Henry Ford Hospital in Detroit, recalled how the first intensive-care unit had been set up twenty years before to provide special attention for patients recovering from serious operations, in particular open-heart surgery. In the course of the intervening two decades, she lamented, the concept had been utterly subverted. The centre of attention was no longer the patient, but the gauges monitoring his blood pressure, heart-beat, fluid balance: 'banks of instruments that click, blink or bleep with (or without) the slightest provocation'. Patients who needed further attention, she found, were now afraid to return. 'I do not say that this is "unfortunate". I state flatly that it is criminal.'

In Britain, too, the new intensive-care units had begun to arouse concern. The aim of the medical profession, the London psychiatrist Eliot Slater argued in an article 'Health Service or Sickness Service' in the *British Medical Journal* in 1971, should be to restore and maintain health, and, failing that, to relieve, or at least alleviate, suffering. The aim should not be the preservation of life at all costs, for if the first two aims were fulfilled, that could be left to look after itself. 'Per se, it is not part of a doctor's ordinary duties.' This was being forgotten; instead, Slater feared, there was likely to be a further expansion of units for intensive care, haemodialysis and organ transplants because they 'claim very high prestige, and are the pride of their mother hospitals'.

In 1972 another critic, R. S. Blacher of the Mount Sinai School of Medicine, New York, drew attention to a side-effect of open-heart surgery which the surgeons had not allowed for: out of twelve patients referred to him following operations, eight had 'suffered a major psychiatric upheaval, and yet had managed to hide this from their medical attendants'. To confess to neurosis, in such circumstances, would have seemed base ingratitude; it was easier for patients to accept the assurance that they were doing fine – which, from the point of view of a surgeon primarily interested in their physical survival, they might be. C. D. Aring, a member of the editorial board of the *Journal of the American Medical Association*, admitted in the *Journal* in 1974 that a brief experience in an intensive-care unit had led him to believe that 'one should not want to be among its clientele unless profoundly unconscious'.

By this time it had also become clear that heart surgery was expanding 'explosively', as the *New England Journal of Medicine* complained, with 'little attention to efficacy, need or cost'. Patients were being induced to have operations, according to J. W. Kirklin of the University of Alabama, by techniques of persuasion 'that pass the bounds of scientific medicine'. There was no check on the expansion, nor was there likely to be in the foreseeable future because, as Bruce Dunkman and colleagues at the Veterans' Administration Hospital in Pennsylvania University pointed out in a survey in 1974, there were about 200,000 angina cases every year in the United States, and so there was nothing to prevent around 150,000 by-pass operations being undertaken annually. The implications were alarming: 'uncertainties abound, and there have been a sufficient number of disturbing experiences to warrant careful, critical appraisal and to caution that by-pass grafting should not be done in all patients with angina pectoris for whom the operation is technically feasible as an acceptable operative risk.' Where surgery was decided on, too, it should be done only by an experienced team.

Dunkman might be giving good advice, but who was to ensure that it was heeded? Surgical teams tend to think that they are skilled and experienced – or soon will be, with practice. By 1976 the number of operations had risen to over fifty thousand, making it, according to the *Chicago Tribune*, 'the fastest growing operation in the country'. The expense, too, was becoming formidable and was certain to increase. When in 1975 it was proposed that a nation-wide screening programme should be introduced to identify all members of the public who might benefit from the operation, H. H. Hiatt of the Harvard School of Public Health worked out the cost of the programme – around one hundred billion dollars, or almost as much as the entire resources then devoted to health care in the United States.

Signs appeared, too, that, having found the by-pass operation relatively simple and extremely lucrative, surgeons were beginning to use it indiscriminately. One investigation revealed that in the case of nearly half the patients referred for by-pass surgery, no attempt had earlier been made to find whether they would respond to any of the new anti-anginal drugs; yet in none of these cases had the surgeon recommended that surgery be deferred until after drug treatment had been tried. In 1977 the dangers were exposed by T. A. Preston, a cardiologist and associate professor of medicine at the University of Washington, Seattle. Preston did not dispute that by-pass surgery could relieve angina. It was not enough, however, to show that the operation worked; the question ought to be, how often was it

21

necessary? No attempt had been made to evaluate it by properly controlled trials designed to discover whether it was significantly more effective than alternative forms of treatment. Although patients were often assured that the operation was essential, 'no scientific study has substantiated the purported increased survival with surgery, and several studies have shown there is no evidence for the claim'. If this were made clear to patients, how many would agree to surgery? As things stood, patients often were not told the pros and cons of an operation in detail, the excuse being that the knowledge 'might undermine confidence'. The Food and Drug Administration had not the power, and the medical profession had not the will, to intervene. The overabundance of surgeons, the dependence of most cardiac surgeons on coronary artery surgery for most of their business, the organisation of medical care delivery and fee payment, and the absence of economic restraint on the consumer 'are all powerful forces to make it highly likely that coronary artery surgery is performed more frequently in the United States than it would be under a different economic system,' Preston feared. The conclusion was inescapable: 'financial remuneration enters the decision-making process', and the annual cost, as a result, had reached the billion dollars mark.

The medical profession, Preston concluded, must put its house in order; it must insist on properly controlled trials of surgical procedures, and find some way to reduce the financial incentive to perform operations. As it happened, a controlled trial had been set up by the Veterans' Administration, designed to compare the survival-rate of patients who had been given by-pass surgery and those given conventional drug treatment. Its report that year showed no significant differences between the two. Yet during the year 1977, it was estimated, 70,000 by-pass operations would probably be performed. If resources for national health care were limited, Eugene Braunwald of the Harvard Medical School argued in an article, 'Coronary Artery Surgery at the Cross-roads', surely there must be better ways of spending that money? An even more insidious problem, Braunwald warned, 'is that what might be considered an "industry" is being built around this operation', designed to create the facilities for by-pass surgery. This 'rapidly growing enterprise', he feared, was developing a momentum of its own; as time passed it would be 'progressively more difficult and costly to curtail it materially, if the results of carefully designed studies of its efficacy prove this step to be necessary'. Hiatt agreed. 'Contemporary medical practice permits individual doctors to implement a new surgical treatment,' he complained, 'without the constraints to which they are subject when they contemplate, for example, the use of a drug.' Like Preston, he felt that the time had come for some constraints to be introduced.

But no machinery existed to introduce them, and, as before, the cardiologists could reply that, even if the operations had not given entirely satisfactory results in the past, experience and practice were putting things right. A surgical team at the Hammersmith Hospital in London went further, claiming that the operation not merely provided dramatic relief of symptoms but also, because it enabled the patient to return to gainful employment, enabled the British taxpayer to recoup the cost 'by elimination of sickness benefit, increased productivity, and reduction in cost of medicines'. But the fundamental weakness in such papers remained; they ordinarily emanated from the team performing the operations, often with little or no attempt to provide controls.

Where trials were conducted independently, the results tended to be much less encouraging; Glenda Barnes and colleagues of the Division of Preventive Medicine at the University of Alabama found 'no improvement in return to work or hours worked after surgery'. And even where the results appeared to favour surgery rather than medication, care had to be taken to distinguish between real benefit and placebo effect, as Peter Perduzzi and Herbert N. Hultgren of Palo Alto emphasised in the journal *Circulation*, following a large-scale randomised test comparing drug treatment and surgical treatment. That surgical operations, as well as drugs, could engender placebo effect had been demonstrated earlier by Henry Beecher; Perduzzi and Hultgren had found it to be 'a common phenomenon after any type of coronary surgery', leading to 'a tendency to minimise symptoms and limitations in responding to the follow-up questionnaire'. One reason, Peter Nixon suggested in a letter to *Circulation*, was that coronary surgery 'creates such large, painful and expensive decision-making' that patients feel bound to justify their decision by making the operation 'work for them'. A 'very important point', Perduzzi and Hultgren agreed in their reply.

## Diet – Or Stress?

If the results of orthodox medical care and treatment were so unsatisfactory, why was there not more of a demand from the public and its elected representatives for a switch of attention away from hospitals, coronary care units and by-pass surgery, towards measures designed to introduce and implement policies derived from the Framingham findings, and research into the effects of stress?

In the United States the public had begun to get the Framingham message. Between the mid-sixties and the mid-seventies, consumption of eggs, butter and milk declined, eggs by twelve per cent, milk and cream by nearly twenty per cent, butter by over thirty per cent. In the same period the rise in mortality from heart attacks was first halted, then reversed, so that by 1975 mortality was about a fifth lower than it had been ten years before. As people were also smoking less, the benefit could not be attributed simply to the change in diet, but at least it lent credence to the epidemiological findings.

These were also being confirmed by trials in other countries. One, in particular, produced a striking result. Finland had the highest mortality rate from heart attacks of any country in the world, and the Finns had set up an experiment to find whether they could reduce it by persuading citizens to switch from saturated (mainly animal) fats to 'poly-unsaturates' by using soft margarine in place of butter, and vegetable oil instead of lard, a more acceptable option than having to forego fats altogether. While eight hundred citizens remained on their normal diet, high in saturated fats, eight hundred others switched to a diet low in saturated fats but high in poly-unsaturates. After six years, the roles of the two groups were reversed. When the performances were compared at the end of the twelve-year period, it was found that 'on the saturated fat diet twice as many people died from coronary heart disease. When the diets were reversed, so were the mortality rates.'

The quotation was in a 1973 promotional hand-out from Van den Berghs and Jurgens, reporting the results. Their enthusiasm was understandable; they marketed a 'soft' poly-unsaturated margarine. So strong was the evidence accumulating in favour of the beneficial influence of poly-unsaturates that even the British, who had held out against acceptance of the Framingham findings, were converted. A committee set up by the Department of Health, reporting in 1974, accepted that the incidence of heart disease 'correlates positively with the proportion of food energy derived from fat', and although its members could not bring themselves to agree that saturated fats should be replaced by poly-unsaturates, this was unanimously recommended two years later in the report of a joint working-party from the Royal College of Physicians and the British Cardiac Society.

The report proved too much for the dairy industry. Critical comments by bodies such as the Royal College of Physicians were not in themselves a source of much commercial concern, as the experience of the tobacco companies had already shown, but the idea of rivals using them to promote their claims, and thereby to win more space on supermarket shelves, was a different matter. The farm lobby had already gone into action in the United States; in Europe, it now set up a 'Front', the European Organisation for the Control of Circulatory Diseases (a title which could be made even more high-sounding by the use of the initials EOCCD, which suggested a link with the European Economic Community). There was no shortage of cardiologists, some of them eminent, to attend the Organisation's conferences and to express a variety of objections to the canonisation of poly-unsaturates and the condemnation of animal fats – objections which found their way into the advertisements of the Butter Information Council.

On one issue, the dairy lobby had a good case. The 1970 report of the Inter-Society Commission on heart disease had asserted that there was a firm relationship between the level of cholesterol in the blood and the risk of heart disease, but further research, some of it conducted at Framingham, had shown that this had to be qualified. Cholesterol, it turned out, was not so simple a substance as had been thought. Some of its components were a threat to health, and when found in the blood constituted a risk factor, but one of them actually appeared to provide some protection *against* heart attacks. In addition, it had become clear that the blood cholesterol level was not, as had been assumed, necessarily correlated with the consumption of animal fats and cholesterol-filled food, such as yolk of egg.

When headlines began to appear on the lines of CHOLESTEROL IS NOT THE HEART ATTACK VILLAIN, the reaction of the public lay between amusement and confusion, while cardiologists who had been sceptical of the Framingham findings made the most of them. 'A generation of research on the diet-heart question has ended in disarray,' George V. Mann wrote in the *New England Journal of Medicine* in 1977, a sentiment echoed in Britain by two powerful figures in the medical establishment, Professor J. P. Shillingford and Sir John McMichael. The dairy industry's spokesmen were able to turn the tables on soft margarine. Cholesterol and animal fats in general, they claimed, had been unjustly pilloried. There was no evidence that switching to poly-unsaturates would prevent, mitigate or cure heart disease, the Butter Information Council insisted in its evidence to an all-party House of Commons committee in 1977. The possible long-term effects, too, were not yet known. For a time, the story was assiduously circulated that tests on animals had linked the consumption of poly-unsaturates with liability to cancer. Animal fats, it implied, so far from being a health hazard, might actually be providing protection.

This was the more confusing as the Framingham findings had had the advantage of being relatively easy, for those who felt inclined, to act upon – except, of course, for heavy smokers, who had to experience the difficulty of giving up cigarettes. Eating rather less saturated fat and cholesterol was hardly traumatic. As the Royal College's 1976 report pointed out, people were not being expected to give up meat, butter, cream and eggs altogether, but simply to reduce their intake, which could be done almost painlessly by switching where possible to poly-unsaturates (A. A. Milne's king had a justifiable grievance when he was offered marmalade instead of butter, but if soft margarine had been insinuated as the layer between his bread and his jam, he probably would not have noticed – still less if his 'french fries' had been cooked in corn oil rather than in lard).

The dairy lobby's intervention had sown the seed of doubt, however, and governments, with the farm vote in mind, were relieved to be able to exploit it. Although the House of Commons' committee the following year rejected the Butter Council's submission, and recommended a campaign 'to encourage people to moderate their fat intake, or switch to poly-unsaturates', a few weeks later the Minister for Agriculture, John Silkin, went to Brussels to support unblushingly a proposal to reduce the price of butter in order to encourage higher consumption, his objective being to reduce the dimensions of the 'butter mountain', an irritation to British taxpayers, who could not understand why continental farmers were being subsidised to produce surplus food.

Similarly, a scheme which the Swedish government had launched to persuade the public to eat less animal fat, which for a time looked like succeeding, gradually fizzled out – doubtless, the *New Scientist* observed, because 'while one government department was spending money on health and nutrition education, another was providing handsome subsidies to protect Swedish farmers by increasing people's consumption of beef, butter, cheese and pork'. Government action in other countries followed a similar course, leaving the public under the impression that the Framingham findings need no longer be taken seriously.

Evidence continued to appear, however, indicating that the initial inference drawn from Framingham – that if people stopped smoking, reduced animal-fat consumption and took steps to reduce the blood pressure, they would run less risk of heart attacks – was justified. During the 1970s the Stanford Heart Disease Programme, with the help of the local media, set out to discover the effects of an intensive publicity campaign to this end on the population of two Californian communities, Watsonville and Gilroy, with a third, Tracy, as the control. The results were encouraging; at the end of the trial the inhabitants of Watsonville and Gilroy had a significantly better record than those of Tracy. Nevertheless, the Framingham findings remained suspect; in particular, their emphasis on the danger of animal fat. How could members of well-off families in the old days have consumed those massive quantities of meat, butter and cream without coming to harm? Why, even Henry James – not ordinarily thought of as a gourmand – describing the butter he was given for lunch at Bourg-en-Bresse on his tour of France as 'poetry', had remarked that he 'ate a pound or two of it'.

The answer, it has gradually come to be realised, is that a high cholesterol level in the blood and a high saturated-fat consumption are indeed risk factors; trials in many countries have shown that people with either or both are more prone to heart attacks. But the two are not directly linked; the consumption of a large quantity of butter or eggs does not necessarily increase the cholesterol level in the blood. What, then, is responsible for this increased level, when it occurs?

For a time, the chief suspect in the United States was sedentary living: over-frequent recourse to automobiles and elevators. Our ancestors, it was suggested, could eat their gargantuan meals because they led more energetic lives. This notion, however, did not fit in with the Framingham findings, which appeared to show that lack of exercise was only a minor risk factor. Still, the idea of the beneficial effects of exercise had quickly caught on; jogging became a national pastime or chore, and it appeared to be lent justification by the report, which had appeared in the *Lancet* in 1966, of a trial conducted in Britain by Professor J. N. Morris and colleagues. London bus drivers, they had found, had higher blood pressure and higher blood cholesterol levels than bus conductors; they also had twice as many heart attacks. Surely this must be because London buses are double-deckers, so that conductors are compelled to climb up and down the stairs scores of times each day?

Seven years later the team reported the results of an investigation they had carried out among over 16,000 civil servants, all office workers, who had recorded the amount of exercise they had taken. 'Habitual vigorous exercise during leisure time reduced the incidence of coronary heart disease among male sedentary workers,' the investigators found. Even gentler activities, such as gardening, were sufficient to provide a measure of protection. Two American doctors, members of the American Joggers' Association, wrote to the *Lancet* to lend support to Morris's findings. A fifty-four-year-old male patient, they claimed, whose coronary arteries had been found to have narrowed by ninety-nine per cent, ninety-five per cent and eighty per cent, had nevertheless been capable with training of running forty-two kilometres in four hours and fifty-two minutes.

The implications were startling. Perhaps fatty degeneration of the arteries should not be regarded as so sinister, after all. Given the stimulus of exercise, the body's homeostatic mechanism could learn to compensate for it. Disconcertingly, though, the Framingham team still offered the theory little support. They did, indeed, indict obesity as a risk factor, and one of the team, William B. Kannel, agreed that it was promoted by 'a combination of indolence, sedentary living and over-eating'. But the evidence in favour of exercise as a protection remained weak. Might there not be some other element involved? Bus drivers, for example, had the continual strain of driving through the traffic-laden and pedestrian-ridden streets of London, while the conductors had only the occasional vagaries of passengers to worry about. Civil servants who took exercise, too, might be of a different personality-type from those who did not; or the exercise might be having an indirect influence by making them healthier, and giving them more zest for life. Either way, might it not be a combination of the physiological and the psychological which was providing protection?

## Type A – Type B

Finding ways to quantify the psychological component, if it existed, in order to be able to convince doubters by providing consistent results, remained a problem. In spite of the accumulating evidence of the role of stress in connection with heart disease, it was still brushed aside, as a survey by David Jenkins in the *New England Journal of Medicine* showed in 1971. The researchers, Jenkins recalled, had encountered great difficulties. They had been a mixed bunch, some of them unfamiliar with the behavioural sciences, most of them unfamiliar with epidemiology, and all of them plagued by the problem of how to sort out the many variables and imponderables. They had also been faced with scientific conservatism. Until the mid-1960s their results had been shrugged off as being spurious, or at best 'interesting, but not substantiated'. Nevertheless, a succession of well-designed trials had identified certain risk factors: migration, anxiety (especially when suppressed), life-dissatis-faction, environmental stresses and a 'coronary-prone behaviour pattern'. The results had made little impression, but such factors should no longer be ignored, Jenkins argued, in epidemiological studies. 'The accumulated evidence places several of the psychosocial variables reviewed among the major risk factors to coronary disease.'

The 'coronary-prone behaviour pattern' to which Jenkins referred was no longer the version favoured earlier by Alexander, Dunbar and the supporters of the psychosomatic theory, though it followed a similar pattern. And Rahe's scale of stressful events had also been seen to be not entirely satisfactory for an obvious reason – the same event may cause different, sometimes diametrically opposed, reactions in different individuals. For Smith, the death of his spouse may be traumatic; for Jones, it can come as a blessed relief. And at the other end of the scale, to be detected in some minor violation of the law may deeply disturb somebody who has never erred before. A technique was needed to qualify the scores according to the reaction of the individual to the episode, and this, although theoretically feasible, would not have fitted in with the Holmes/Rahe objective, which was to provide *objective* evidence of the reality of the element of stress.

A possible alternative had been suggested at a symposium of the British Cardiac Society in 1957. Two cardiologists from the Edinburgh Royal Infirmary, M. F. Oliver and G. S. Boyd, had pointed out that, although there had been a seventy-fold increase in the mortality rate from heart attacks since the 1920s, hospital records did not show any increase in the degeneration of the arteries in that period. Was it not possible, they suggested, that the remarkable social and economic developments in the period had created stresses, particularly for those who 'have inherited an ambitious and conscientious personality'? Some confirmation was lent to this idea, they thought, by the fact that in Scotland the incidence of heart disease was 'greatest in executive, professional, business and intellectual occupations, where the fat con-sumption is high and there are heavy responsibilities demanding pro-longed and exacting mental strain'.

Here, then, lay an interesting field of study. There might be no objective way to divide the people in those occupations into two groups: one of the ambitious, conscientious type, the other of the more relaxed. But there was nothing to prevent the division being made subjectively, and a method had been evolved by two Californian cardiologists, Meyer Friedman and Ray H. Rosenman.

As they were to recall in 1974 in their book *Type A Behaviour and Your*

29

*Heart*, they had both practised for years along orthodox lines, concentrating upon such indicators as cholesterol and blood-pressure levels, but they had gradually been forced to accept that there must be some other pathogenic force at work. Why, for example, should men be more at risk than their wives? The stock answer was that there must be a hormonal difference; but why, in that case, did it not apply also to laboratory animals – or to humans in a few parts of the country where, for no known reason, men and women were equally at risk? The clue came from a woman they encountered. The trouble with Californian men, she suggested, was that they were so often under stress.

Their curiosity aroused, Friedman and Rosenman despatched a questionnaire to one hundred and fifty San Francisco businessmen, asking them whether they had observed certain characteristics in colleagues or friends who had had heart attacks, and in well over two-thirds of the replies, one of the characteristics they nominated was 'excessive competitive drive'. Probing further, Friedman and Rosenman built up a composite picture of the 'Type A' man, and found that it fitted their own patients. Almost invariably, they 'exhibited an habitual sense of time urgency and excessive competitive drive'. Often, because of it, they were also easily aroused to anger. Their patients, the writers realised, had endlessly displayed these traits; 'but we had been too busy or preoccupied with other matters to receive, much less comprehend, these "signals"'.

As a check on this theory, the blood-cholesterol levels of a group of accountants were recorded for a period of six months, from the beginning of a year. The levels, it was found, rose when the April tax deadline loomed, and fell after it had passed, although the accountants' diets and life-styles had not changed in the period. Delighted, Rosenman and Friedman presented the evidence to the next conference of the American Heart Association. It was greeted with 'absolute silence – no questions, no comments, no criticisms, just silence'.

It would be essential, they knew, to provide confirmatory evidence. They went to work again, along the – by now grudgingly sanctioned – epidemiological lines. They nominated eighty men in business and the professions in San Francisco who, on the reckoning of friends and colleagues, were Type A. As a control group, eighty men regarded as having no such sense of urgency, no such competitive drives or suppressed hostility, were classified as Type B. Although the habits and diets of both groups were similar, it was found that the Type As had had seven times more coronary heart disease than the Type Bs.

Could the method be used to predict heart attacks? With the

co-operation of banks, airlines and business firms in California, Friedman and Rosenman recruited three thousand five hundred healthy volunteers, and divided them into As and Bs. After a decade, two hundred and fifty of them had suffered from heart disease. There had been nothing in their habits to suggest that one group was more at risk than the other, but the casualty rate among the As was three times higher than that of the Bs, and not one of the Bs died of a heart attack.

Friedman and Rosenman's research had attracted little notice before their book appeared in 1974. Even then, the stock objections – that the authors had not presented conclusive proof for their case – could be raised. In the preface to the British edition, Sir Peter Medawar criticised this negative attitude; to think in terms of positive proof in such circumstances was to take a rather simple-minded view of the nature of the scientific process, 'for theories of this compass and degree of complexity are never "proved" outright, though sometimes they can be disproved'. He knew of no evidence, however, to unseat the theory, which to him had 'a rather frightening authenticity'. Nevertheless, the Department of Health's Committee on heart disease that year dismissed the subject in a footnote: 'In the opinion of the Panel there is not at present enough firm evidence to warrant discussion in this report of emotional stress as a risk factor.' And the Royal College of Physicians' Committee, two years later, though conceding that most doctors and many people believed stress to be a risk factor, insisted that it had not yet been demonstrated that any 'readily measurable (or modifiable) behavioural factor' was involved.

## Biofeedback

The discovery that Type A individuals were more at risk than Type Bs, even if it came to be accepted, would in itself offer only a limited degree of protection to those in Type A category. They might school themselves to avoid occasions of stress, but this would be of little help if their careers or their home lives kept them in stressful situations. A technique was required which would enable Type As to learn how to relax, and how to cope with stressful circumstances. Even before Neal Miller's discoveries about the ability of laboratory rats to influence their autonomic nervous systems, and Herbert Benson's about the value of meditation in lowering blood pressure, the possibility that people could learn, in effect, to shed their Type A personalities was being investigated by Elmer and Alyce Green of the Menninger Foundation in Texas.

31

Half a century before this, the power of auto-suggestion had been preached by the French chemist Emile Coué, and demonstrated by a German doctor, Johannes Schultz. Patients in a relaxed frame of mind, Schultz had found, could warm up their extremities – their finger tips – by as much as five degrees by auto-suggestion, and he had developed 'autogenic training' to encourage patients to use the same method to treat everyday disorders – coughs, colds and aches. It had attracted little notice within the medical profession, still wedded to the belief that such control was impossible. But among his disciples was Wolfgang Luthe of Montreal, and a book which Luthe wrote on the subject had attracted the Greens' interest. They carried out similar experiments with volunteers, and also with a yogi, Swami Rama, who offered to 'stop' his heart while connected up to an electro-cardiograph. What the machine registered would, had it been connected to a patient, have been described as a heart attack, but Swami Rama got up after the experiment as if nothing had happened, and went off to give a lecture.

Elmer Green had been trained as a physicist, and this gave him the idea of adapting the technique of 'biofeedback' which had been developed in France a century earlier but had been little used, except in the form of the 'lie-detector'. Instruments could be made which would transmit information about the autonomic nervous system, thereby providing the subject with a guide as to whether his technique of relaxation (whatever it might be: some individuals would find classical music soothing, others, irritating) was getting effective results.

It was not easy to provide this biofeedback in connection with blood pressure; the standard 'arm-cuff' procedure was too cumbersome and inconvenient, and for a time the Greens concentrated on other work. But in 1974 a medical journalist who had come to write about the Foundation, and who had experimented with biofeedback to control the temperature of her hands, decided to undertake an experiment on her own, and without telling either the Greens or her own doctor, she gave up the Valium which she had been taking for her hypertension, and instead tried meditation; in a week her blood pressure was within the normal limits. When she told the Greens what had happened they recommended her method to another patient who, though heavily dosed with anti-hypertensive drugs, still had a very high blood pressure and pulse-rate, as well as kidney trouble. By the end of a week her blood pressure had begun to fall, as had her formerly high pulse-rate. Soon, she needed drugs no longer, much to her cardiologist's surprise; he had thought she would never be able to dispense with the drugs she had been taking for sixteen years. At the same time, her kidney trouble vanished. More research along these lines would be needed, the Greens admitted in their book *Beyond Biofeedback* in 1977, and simpler ways to monitor pressure; but at least experience in this and other similar cases had been a help 'in determining which way to go'.

Researchers in other countries have confirmed the American findings. A paper by Chandra Patel and W. R. S. North in the *Lancet* in 1975 described a trial in which thirty-four patients at a London hospital were randomly divided into two groups, one of which took a course of yoga with biofeedback, with the help of a gadget monitoring their skin resistance (it showed relaxation by means of an audio signal) while the other was simply asked to try to relax; the difference was found to be 'highly significant'. It also proved significant in further tests on factory workers considered to be at particular risk of heart disease because of their blood pressure or blood cholesterol levels and their smoking habits. They were randomly allocated to two groups, one of which received eight weekly training sessions with biofeedback; the biofeedback group had a significantly greater fall in blood pressure and cholesterol levels, and its members were smoking less than the controls. Surveying the reports on the medical applications of meditation in 1978, B. Frankel of the Hahnemann Medical College, Philadelphia, found that, although biofeedback alone appeared to have only a short-term effect, used with relaxation methods such as yoga, transcendental meditation, and progressive muscle relaxation it had 'been associated with long-lasting changes in blood pressure'.

While this research was proceeding, more information had been produced about the psychosocial risk factors. Hans Thiel and his colleagues in the cardiovascular department at the University of Oklahoma found that of two groups with similar family backgrounds, blood pressure and blood fatty-acid levels, the group with the stress problems, ranging from divorce to insomnia, had a far higher incidence of heart attacks. In 1977 Professor James Lynch of the University of Maryland School of Medicine produced statistics showing the remarkable differences in the mortality-rate between white American males aged sixteen to forty-six according to whether they were married, single, widowed, or divorced; the figures per 100,000 for heart disease were respectively 176, 237, 275 and 362. His book contained none of the sentimentality implicit in its title, *The Broken Heart: the Medical Consequence of Loneliness.* On the contrary, it was packed with statistics and case histories to support the thesis that loss of human contact – of affection and love – is a risk factor, whether in the form of bereavement, as in Rahe's list, or through incarceration in the unfamiliar and daunting environment of a coronary care unit, enslaved to gadgetry and routine.

Perhaps the most valuable endorsement of the stress theory, however, came from the Framingham team, because nobody could suggest that they had been biased in its favour. Stress had not originally been included as one of the possible risk factors. On its later inclusion, resistance to it had remained: partly because the subjective element in any assessment of emotional states presented the team with problems; partly because they, too, had been indoctrinated with the belief in the organic theory of disease, and had no wish to jeopardise their prospects of obtaining full recognition by allowing that so suspect an interloper as stress could affect their calculations. As late as 1976 William Kannel, in his survey of the epidemiological lessons learned at Framingham, complained that the 'evaluation of the relation of "emotional stress" to coronary disease is hampered by varied criteria and concepts and imprecise methods of measuring the phenomenon'; in so far as it has been possible to measure it, in an analysis of life stresses and the personalities coping with them, 'little evidence of psychologic or social influences on the incidence of coronary disease was uncovered at Framingham.'

The team had therefore continued to concentrate upon the established suspects – smoking, diet and hypertension – along with the occasional newcomer, identified by the same epidemiological techniques: soft water (people who live in areas where the drinking-water is hard are less heart-attack-prone); salt intake (its level, it was found, tends to correlate with blood pressure), and lack of sufficient dietary fibre. But when the Type A/Type B theory was presented, it was realised that no attempt had been made to investigate the Framingham population for stress along those lines. An additional trial was slotted into the continuing research schedule, and when its results were presented in 1979 at an American Heart Association Conference, they showed that Type A males had well over twice the incidence of coronary heart disease of Type Bs, and that Type A females actually had four times the incidence of Type B females.

Why had the Framingham research failed to recognise the stress component before? Partly for the excuse which Kannel gave: stress had not been so easy to quantify as blood pressure and fat consumption. But the main reason, James Lynch suggested, might be that Framingham 'was really another Roseto all along, disguised under miles of computerised medical data'. Framingham was socially stable; the divorce- and crime-rates, for example, were low. It was consequently less representative than had been assumed.

Convincing though the psychosocial evidence had become, it was still rarely encountered in the establishment medical journals, or at conferences on heart disease. But adversity makes strange bedfellows; in the late 1970s its supporters at last began to obtain a hearing, thanks to an improbable sponsor, the dairy lobby. Among those who were invited to contribute papers at the conferences promoted by the European Organisation for the Control of Circulatory Diseases were Malcolm Carruthers of the Maudsley and Peter Nixon of Charing Cross Hospital, trying to persuade their colleagues of the need to take account of personality factors and stress in preventing and treating heart disease, and critical of the Framingham team for not having – at that stage – done so. The alliance was unlikely to be lasting, but at least it compelled a few eminent cardiologists to listen to the evidence about the importance of the psychosocial component which they had so long rejected.

## The Medical Model

From the evidence becoming available in the 1960s and 1970s there was a strong case for moving away from curative medicine to preventive psychosocial measures. In spite of some continuing uncertainties over the Framingham findings, they were reasonably consistent about the affluent countries of the West, suggesting that environment and life-style must play a general part in the processes by which heart disease had become a twentieth-century epidemic, with a coronary-prone personality-type as the predisposing factor for individuals, and with stress as a precipitant. Yet there was little indication, by 1980, that anything effective was being done or planned to utilise this information more effectively, and the reason was becoming clear.

First, there were powerful forces opposed to the kind of changes which would be required if the evidence implicating cigarettes and animal fats as risk factors in the coronary epidemic were to be not merely accepted, but also acted upon: governments, in particular. Whatever their political complexion, governments were showing themselves ever more proficient at confusing the issues. Following the publication of a pamphlet by the British Department of Health in 1979, recommending a general reduction in the intake of animal fats, the Ministry of Agriculture's Food Standards Committee issued a recommendation that food manufacturers ought not to be obliged to put the fat content of their products on the labels.

In 1980 the Americans went one better. A report presented to the Carter Administration by the Food and Nutrition Board of the National Academy of Sciences dismissed the case for reducing the quantity of animal fat and cholesterol in the diet as unproven, inviting people not to fuss any longer about replacing saturates with polyunsaturates or other such fads. This was not particularly surprising in itself; it was merely echoing what individual cardiologists such as Mann and Shillingford had been saying for years. But it sounded authoritative in that it came from a body set up to provide the Administration with expert, disinterested advice on, among other things, health care.

Expert it might have been; disinterested it was not, as investigative journalists soon found. A group of firms involved in the food-processing industry had met the costs of preparing the report, and the report itself had been drafted by two men who earned a substantial income from acting as consultants to the American Egg Board and the California Dairy Council. 'A dubious guide,' was the *New York Times* verdict on the report; the *Washington Post* thought it had 'soiled the reputation of the Board and of the Academy'.

Although organisations representing sections of the medical profession have been putting out pleas for more attention to be paid to preventive measures, they also have done little to shift the emphasis away from curative medicine. Again, the reason is obvious: the profession is run by specialists whose interest lies mainly, often exclusively, in the treatment of people who have already had the disease with which their specialty deals. Often they appear neither to know nor care about research that indicates the possibilities of prevention. When a questionnaire was circulated in 1976 to physicians in the United States, asking them to list what they considered to be the most important advances in connection with diseases of the heart and lung, the answers revealed that neither the Framingham nor the Type A/Type B findings had made any impression; the replies cited new surgical procedures and new forms of drug treatment.

How inadequately prepared cardiologists have been to deal with the psychosocial component of heart disease can also be gauged from the textbooks of the late 1970s. They sometimes mentioned the Framingham findings, but rarely devoted any space to them or considered their implications, and when stress or personality types were referred to at all, which was seldom, it was usually only to emphasise that they were not proven risk factors. As for prevention through relaxation and biofeedback, to judge by the textbooks it could scarcely have been said to exist.

In 1978, for example, a new treatise appeared: *Management of Essential Hypertension*, by F. Gilbert McMahon. Professor McMahon's credentials for such a survey were impeccable: in addition to his university post he was Medical Director of the New Orleans Public Health Programme and President-elect of the American Society for Clinical Pharmacology and Therapeutics. Of the fifteen chapters in the book, fourteen were devoted to the management of hypertension by drugs, and the fifteenth, on diet, concerned itself with the advisability of a reduced salt intake, and (though of this he was doubtful) of weight reduction. Similarly the *Yearbook of Cardiology* for 1978, designed to keep doctors and students abreast of new developments, conspicuously failed to keep them abreast of developments in the understanding of stress or how to deal with it.

With the exception of *Circulation*, the specialist journals – and there were several: the American and British heart journals; the American *Journal of Cardiology*, *Blood* and others – might almost have put the psychosocial element under an interdict, so rarely did it feature in their columns. When a glossy newcomer, *Hypertension*, joined them in 1979, it might have been expected to give some attention to the work being done on lowering blood pressure by psychological methods; yet of close to a hundred research papers included in its first year of publication, none dealt with that aspect of the subject.

Although the need for more attention to be paid to preventive measures is frequently urged in editorials in medical journals, the only form in which it has featured at all prominently in clinical practice has been screening. Yet screening has proved far from reliable. The electrocardiograph, in particular, introduced in the 1950s, has been a disappointment, partly because of problems of interpretation: when fourteen American cardiologists were asked to examine a set of tracings, their selection of those which revealed evidence of diminution of the blood supply varied from five per cent to over fifty per cent of the tracings, partly because heart attacks do not necessarily come at the end of a long-drawn-out disease process which can be mapped. Screening may give no warning; obituaries of the popular young British actor Richard Beckinsale reported that he had been screened twice in the twelve months before his death. Peter Nixon has argued that the introduction of the electrocardiograph may even have increased the mortality rate. Whereas doctors half a century ago advised a patient who was worried about his heart to take things easy, they now reassure him if his ECG shows no positive indications. All too often, Nixon claims, he has heard a patient after a heart attack say, 'I was sure I needed to look after myself, but I just had to carry on when the doctor said the ECG was normal.'

The chief defect of screening has been that, in conformity with medical preconceptions, it has rarely allowed for the effect of personality configuration of the Type A/Type B kind, and it can hardly be expected to predict either the likelihood of stressful occasions or the reaction of individuals to them when they occur. Business firms that have arranged for their executives to be screened would ordinarily also hope that the procedure would be comprehensive. But in this case if it were to indicate the Type As at risk, they would in all probability be the very people whom the company would least wish to spare – the go-ahead, go-getting individuals. As a GP wrote recently in *World Medicine*, the way to help prevent heart disease 'is to look at the work-loads and life-styles imposed by the companies to see if something needs to be done in that area, rather than taking the easy way out by forking out a few pounds occasionally for yearly check-ups'.

Cardiologists frequently defend themselves from the charge that they do not pay enough attention to preventive measures other than screening, by arguing that not enough is yet known about the natural history of the disease. 'There is a tendency to canonise prevention,' Professor Meihler of Utrecht told the members of the EOCCD conference in Bonn in 1978. 'This is all right if prevention can be effected like in polio. But as long as the cause of our present-day epidemic coronary heart disease has not been identified, the medical profession should continue to treat its patients and should aim for the truth, that is basic research according to established rules.'

Sticking to the 'established rules' has ensured that the great bulk of the resources available for research have continued to flow into hospitals and laboratories, with only a token fraction doled out for research into the psychosocial component.

Theoretically, the state-sponsored and charity-supported agencies could have ensured that a growing share of the funds available for research would be channelled into prevention. Invariably, though, such bodies are dominated by cardiologists, either directly on the fund-distributing committees, or indirectly as their advisers. What can happen, as a result, is illustrated by the story of the British Heart Foundation, a charity founded in the 1960s.

To achieve the respectability required to secure charitable status – and to impress the public, the better to attract support on flag days and at jumble sales – such foundations have felt that they needed the patronage of eminent specialists. Predictably when – ten years later – the Foundation launched a campaign to increase its income for the first time to more than a million pounds, the brochure set out the eight categories of research on which its efforts were being concentrated. The primary task was to try to find what leads to arteries clogging up. Second on the list was improved care of heart-failure patients, with the help of drugs; third, control of hypertension, also with drugs; fourth, heart surgery; fifth, machines designed to restart hearts which have stopped beating; sixth, pacemakers to keep hearts beating in time; seventh, beta-blockers, and eighth, coronary care units.

Research into how arteries clog up could include diet among its possibilities, but in practice it has been almost exclusively devoted to investigations into the biochemical processes involved, and into drugs to counteract them. As for stress, of the eighty-odd grants distributed by the Foundation in 1978 only one was for research into its contribution to heart disease, and one for research into biofeedback, along with two for research into the problems of psychosocial care after (and not infrequently as a consequence of) hospital treatment.

The bulk of the research conducted with the Foundation's funds has remained related to the cardiologists' preconceptions, in particular hospital care. The boast of the University of Newcastle-upon-Tyne cardiac department, for example, in its report for 1978, was that it had been 'a year of rapid expansion in the Department', the form the expansion took being the extension of facilities to allow the admission of even more cardiac surgical patients. 'Since then an intensive programme of research has been embarked upon, particularly in relation to the coronary care unit and the progressive coronary care unit.' Already, the report claimed, one important result had been achieved: methods formerly in use to monitor patients' progress in coronary care units had been found to be faulty.

The irony appears to have escaped the writer of the report; if substantiated, the finding would discredit many of the results used in the past to justify the units. And, by a further irony, doubt has since been thrown on the usefulness of part of the Newcastle unit's own work – the assessment of the merits of new techniques to treat arrhythmia (irregular heart-beat). It has long been taken for granted that arrhythmias need to be treated, and endless types of drugs have been tried out. Patients have even been issued with portable recorders, so that they can hasten back for more treatment whenever irregularity recurs, and the pacemakers which have been manufactured, marketed and introduced to ensure regularity have been hailed as one of the great modern medical advances. It recently occurred to doctors at the Nottingham City Hospital to check whether there is, in fact, any link between abnormal heart rhythms and mortality risk. A trial was undertaken of 260 patients who had suspected heart disease, or had had a heart attack. Some were treated with beta-blockers; others were put on placebos. When the results were analysed, it was found that there was no significant difference in the prospects of patients who had, or did not have, abnormal rhythms, or between those who were on beta-blockers and those who were on placebos. The survival rate was the same.

Periods of irregular heart beat, in other words, 'do not constitute an independent risk factor', a finding which 'raises grave doubts about the value of studying arrhythmias to assess drugs intended to reduce mortality'. It also, the Nottingham team might have added, raises further questions about the validity and the usefulness of much of the research into arrhythmias which has in the past been conducted in coronary care units where it has been endlessly monitored, demonstrated to students, and treated. 'In these days,' Peter Nixon has lamented, 'a physician has to fight hard to keep his patients out of the sort of coronary care unit which breeds "wonderful experiences of

arrhythmias" for its staff, and incubates sudden death for inmates.'
Yet if past experience is a guide, arrhythmias will continue to be
monitored, demonstrated and treated, simply because they are so
convenient for research purposes.

Recently biochemical work in the molecular field has been absorb-
ing an ever-increasing proportion of research funds, insulating
research still further from the psychosocial component of heart
disease, in spite of the insistence of those researchers who have
recognised that the importance of stress is such that it must be taken
into consideration. Over twenty years have passed since Oliver and
Boyd argued that by disturbing the body's endocrine balance,
emotional stress must influence cholesterol metabolism. In 1962, John
E. Peterson and his colleagues in California showed that changes in
cholesterol levels in the blood in experimental stress conditions were,
in their term, 'remarkable' – and rapid. At the EOCCD Conference
in London in 1979 Malcolm Carruthers described research into the
ways in which auto-suggestion effects biochemical changes in the
blood. But reports of this kind have been ignored.

The lack of interest shown by biochemists in such evidence was
illustrated at another gathering in london later in 1979: the seventh
International Congress on Thrombosis and Homeostasis – research
into why and how the blood clots or stagnates. Well over a thousand
papers were presented, almost all of them dealing with refinements in
biochemical lore, under such titles as 'Purification of staphylocagulase
by a bovine prothrombin-sepharose 4B column and its physico-
chemical properties' or 'Differentiation of Platelet membrane associated factor V activity and membrane catalytic surface activity'. Not a
single paper dealt with the possible effects of stress on the blood: not
one.

*'Water under the bridge'*

One of the cherished illusions common to all professions, medical,
legal or commercial, is that whatever past failings may have been, they
are being put right, and can consequently be dismissed as 'water under
the bridge'. In medicine's case, the illusion is ministered to by the
constant stream of new diagnostic gadgets, new surgical techniques,
and new drugs. So far from past mistakes being regarded as an
indication of some weakness in the system, they can consequently be
held up for inspection as proof of the way the profession learns from
its misadventures.

That the profession has in fact been on a treadmill, rather than on an escalator, is particularly obvious in relation to treatment and research in connection with heart attacks. Cardiologists are continually tempted to revert to earlier methods; to revive some disused, and even discredited, idea and try it out again on patients. Thus recently there has been a move to restore anti-coagulant therapy to respectability, on the premise that, as a writer has claimed in the *Lancet*, it may have been 'bad trials, therapeutic greed and emotive opposition' that gave anti-coagulants their dubious reputations; and perhaps denied their benefit to millions. A few weeks later the *Lancet* itself, admitting that in connection with heart attacks 'the therapeutic scene is barren', argued that 'a new approach is necessary'. But the new approach turned out to be a reversion to the days when the emphasis of research was on the detritus in the arteries – the 'platelets' which block them up; 'support is gathering again for the old idea that platelet deposition is important'. And so the cycle continues, keeping the laboratories in business, and giving the excuse to continue to ignore the evidence for the psychosocial component. A report published in 1981, for example, giving the joint recommendations of the International Society and Federation of Cardiology Scientific Councils on Atherosclerosis, Epidemiology and Prevention and Rehabilitation in connection with secondary prevention in survivors of heart attacks, deals with the role of exercise, smoking and diet, as well as drugs – but does not even mention the role of stress or personality type. Nor are cardiologists the only offenders: the 1981 report of the committee of the Royal College of General Practitioners working party on the prevention of arterial disease has the same omission. Yet researchers in the psychosomatic tradition, or those exploring along the lines Selye pioneered, are continuing to demonstrate the importance of stress in the precipitation of heart attacks. Ward Cassells of the Harvard Medical School, for example, has shown from an extensive trial that there is a massive increase in the risk of a fatal coronary in the months following retirement. And though retirement or redundancy may be unavoidable, the Type A can at least learn how to control his stress and his blood pressure, so as to be able to cope with such crises.

When confronted with this evidence a cardiologist can reasonably argue that persuading people to smoke less, eat less saturated fat, and go to meditation classes is not his business. His job is to treat patients who have not taken the necessary precautions, and there are likely to be plenty of them. Agreed; but what is more difficult to put across to him is that, as his specialty is at present constituted, it is not merely appropriating funds which ought to be diverted to prevention; it is misusing them by providing treatments which are unnecessary and may be dangerous, as well as being inordinately expensive.

Automatically to treat hypertension with drugs, in view of their record, is absurd, the more so when investigations have shown that, in the *Lancet*'s words, 'up to half of patients do not take their drugs regularly', and 'of those that do a large proportion report side-effects'. It is not as if there is no alternative; 'there is now evidence from randomised controlled trials that a variety of techniques of meditation and relaxation lead to a fall in blood pressure in the longer term', the *Lancet* concedes, adding that it seems likely 'that reduction of blood pressure by dietary change and relaxation will have a beneficial effect on mortality'. Yet the great majority of patients with hypertension are still being prescribed drugs.

Surveys critical of coronary by-pass surgery for angina have also gone unheeded. 'We cannot go on indefinitely trying to cope with heart disease by open-heart surgery,' Lewis Thomas has pleaded, 'carried out at formidable expense after the disease has run its destructive course.' But the number of such operations has continued to mount; by 1980 over 100,000 were performed annually in the United States. Again, it is not just that a more determined campaign for preventive measures could render such operations unnecessary; they are not as a rule necessary even when the angina has been contracted. Some people keep their angina for years, then aggravate it through stress 'and crash into infarction and sudden death almost regardless of the appearances of the coronary arteries', Peter Nixon has warned in the *American Heart Journal*; others 'generate angina, get over their troubles, and recover'. The essential treatment, he believes, should consist of helping them to surmount their problems. The operation may by-pass some of the debris and damage, 'but how can it teach them to survive? It is surprising how uncommonly surgical treatment is sought when a strong and humane attempt has been made to meet the basic needs.'

This could also apply to some of the patients who qualify for heart transplants. How many of them could have avoided the need for a new heart, if a strong and humane attempt had been made to discover and relieve their stresses earlier? For that matter, how many of those who survive for any length of time do so because they *have* relieved their stresses? Asked what he intended to do when he left hospital in 1979 after the first of the new run of transplants in Britain, the patient sagely replied that he would be 'getting out of the rat-race'. Was it being in the rat-race which had damaged his heart? Did leaving it enable him to enjoy life in a way he had not done before – and live on?

With heart transplants, in any case, the main ground for criticism is simply that the expense of maintaining the units required is so disproportionate to the results so far obtained. Rebuking one of the trustees of the National Heart Research Fund for boasting that the success of the operation would enable heart transplants to become 'commonplace', Peter Draper of the Guy's Hospital Unit for the Study of Health Policy has recently reminded those who control such funds that not merely can heart surgery give no answer to the main problems of heart disease, but also the publicity for the few who survive diverts attention from the need to find ways to reduce the great number who die from heart disease in Britain – around 400 of them every day.

Coronary care units also continue to operate, and to proliferate, in spite of their failure to reduce that mortality. Recently fresh attempts have been made to justify their existence, notably in a report in the *British Medical Journal* putting the case for mobile coronary care – fleets of ambulances manned by doctors or trained paramedical staff. Trials of the system in Belfast, and later in other cities, have suggested that the fact that it enables the appropriate resuscitatory measures to be taken on the way to hospital cuts down the numbers not merely of patients who succumb before they reach the hospital's coronary care unit, but also of those who die in the units, presumably because the time-lag before the resuscitation begins is shorter. The authors of the paper – K. M. Rawles and A. C. F. Kenmure of the Aberdeen Royal Infirmary – maintain that this makes the debate between home care or hospital care irrelevant. As in Britain 'a substantial majority of patients with myocardial infarction are admitted to hospital for social or medical reasons,' this must be the starting point 'of any endeavour to see whether these patients can be brought under coronary care at an earlier stage to try to reduce the formidable pre-hospital mortality rate'.

The authors assume, in other words, that because four out of five heart-attack patients have been taken to hospital in the past, this is right and proper and should continue. In fact, their evidence can be given a very different interpretation. Granted that further research continues to confirm the value of immediate coronary care following heart attacks, and that sufficient funds are made available for mobile units to spread, the resuscitation will ordinarily have to be done by paramedicals, as it is inconceivable there will be enough doctors to go round in all the ambulances. But if the paramedicals can perform the task adequately, as apparently they do, why should they necessarily take the patients to hospital? Might not the reduction in mortality, thanks to the prompt resuscitation, prove just as valuable for patients who remain at home?

A greater contribution that could be made to the reduction of mortality, in all likelihood, would be to introduce mobile coronary care in the form it has been tried out in Brighton, where thousands of people have been instructed in what to do when a friend or neighbour or somebody on the bus has a heart attack. But such self-help projects have been rare; the medical profession has mistrusted them. As a recent paper in the *British Medical Journal* has shown, the information available to the public on how to cope with heart attacks and heart disease in general has been lamentably inadequate.

The greatest need, however, is for better dissemination of advice on how to reduce the risk of contracting heart disease: how to make use of the Type A/Type B findings, and to take the appropriate measures to avoid or control stress; how to react to indicators of possible trouble ahead – hypertension, breathlessness, palpitations, angina – not by a helpless surrender to a lifetime of beta-blockers, or whatever fashionable replacement follows when they are eventually discredited, but by flexible courses such as those which have been introduced for heart patients at the Charing Cross Hospital, involving relaxation, exercise and diet: courses designed to fit not the preconceptions of some guru but the requirements of individuals, related to their heredity, constitution, home environment, jobs and life-style.

# 2

# Cancer

Cancer is not a disease peculiar to our civilisation – it has afflicted almost all communities in all eras; but it is second only to heart disease as the most lethal of the illnesses from which our civilisation suffers. In some respects it is more sinister than heart disease: it kills more young people, and at any age, it kills by what appears to be a remorseless and often painful process. The fact that the time between diagnosis and death may vary from weeks to years has tended only to add to cancer's ill-repute, much as a judicial death sentence is harder to bear if the condemned man does not know the date of his execution. Given the choice between a cure for either cancer or for heart disease, most of us would surely vote for the cancer cure.

Although recent research has provided a mass of information about how tumours develop, it has done relatively little to explain why they should take their varied forms; why some should develop to a certain stage, and then stop growing; why, sometimes, they should actually 'regress' (in the case of warts, sometimes astonishingly quickly), and why some tumours become malignant, with metastases (secondary growths) developing in other parts of the body. Although certain hazards – the effects of radiation, for example, and of carcinogenic substances absorbed into the lungs or intestines – have been detected, research has done little to find effective ways to prevent the commoner types of cancer. The emphasis has consequently been on discovering cancerous growths at as early a stage as possible and treating them; by surgery, to remove the growth; by irradiation, to cauterise the growth; by drugs, to control the growth.

Herbs or drugs to combat tumours, and surgical operations to remove them, have been used in all civilisations, but not until the 1890s was a way found which appeared to offer patients better survival prospects: radium treatment. Irradiation, it was found, though it harmed healthy cells, could be used to destroy cancer cells. And although the hopes aroused were not fulfilled, they were revived in the 1940s by refinements in surgical and irradiation techniques, coupled with the introduction of experimental cytotoxic drugs, designed to single out cancer cells for destruction while leaving healthy cells alone. For the next twenty years optimism prevailed. Cancer, surely, was being slowly but systematically conquered.

Occasionally a voice would be heard warning that the progress claimed might not, strictly speaking, be related to the treatment which patients were receiving. In 1958 a correspondent suggested in the *British Medical Journal* that the improvement in the mortality rate following surgery should be credited to improved surgical techniques and the reduced risk of post-operative infection, thanks to antibiotics, which meant that more patients survived their operations. What were claimed as cures, too, might simply be remissions which ought properly to be attributed to the vagaries of the natural history of the disease. 'There are many modes of behaviour in a malignant tumour,' Sir Gordon Gordon-Taylor mused in one of his last lectures, also in 1958, following a lifetime of experience with cancer patients. 'It may proceed relentlessly to its ending, it may run a hurricane course, it may linger on for many years and may not even be the final cause of the death of the patient.' This being the case, J. Kenworthy Ogden of Petersburg, Va. wrote in the *British Medical Journal*, 'I question the wisdom and truthfulness, in the present state of our knowledge, of instilling in the mind of the general public that sometimes cancer, especially early cancer, is a curable disease'; there was 'absolutely no proof', he insisted, to back up that belief.

Proof, in the form of statistics purporting to show how surgery and irradiation were curing patients, could be spurious, as Hardin Jones, the tough-minded professor of medical physics at the University of California, Berkeley, bluntly told his colleagues in 1969. Patients whose cancers were considered inoperable were being used by surgeons as the controls in 'trials', thereby giving the misleading impression that those patients who were being treated with surgery and irradiation were benefiting. Correcting the statistics to allow for this bias, Jones calculated that the life-expectancy of untreated cases of cancer appeared actually to be greater than that of treated cases.

The first intimation to the public that all was not going smoothly came the following year, when President Nixon launched his 'War on Cancer' campaign, one of the public-relations exercises designed to help him to victory in the forthcoming Presidential elections. He took care not to antagonise the medical profession by suggesting that anything was wrong with the policies which had been adopted; only the funds to help researchers supply the still missing answers were lacking. The government-backed National Cancer Institute was even provided with a 'hot line' which could be used to talk direct to the President on budgetary matters, enabling it to by-pass the National Institutes of Health, which ordinarily acted as the medical research organisations' go-between with the Administration (though this was in fact a public relations gimmick; Congress was insisting upon providing more money for cancer research than the Administration felt able to dispense). The National Cancer Institute's bulletins began to present glowing progress reports. 'The five-year survival rate for cancer patients in the 1930s was about one in five,' the Institute's Director, Frank J. Rauscher, recalled in 1974. 'Today, the figure is one in three.'

Rauscher's version was promptly challenged by Dan Greenberg in the bulletin he was editing in Washington, *Science and Government Report*. The communiqués issued by the leaders of Nixon's 'War on Cancer' campaign, he complained, resembled too closely for comfort those of General Westmoreland on the progress of the war in Vietnam. He felt it necessary, therefore, to report 'a fundamental but rarely discussed finding, namely, that after 25 years and several billion dollars expended on research for cures, survival rates for the most common types of cancer – those accounting for some 80 per cent of all cases – are virtually unchanged'. Although some improvement was noticeable among the less common types, the overall figures had changed little.

Rauscher's figures were not incorrect, but to Greenberg they involved 'statistical sleight-of-hand'. Survival rates had improved, but virtually all the improvement had been achieved before 1955. 'It wasn't that more patients were surviving *cancer*; rather, they were surviving cancer *operations* that previously killed them.' A patient in the mid-1970s, therefore, 'supposedly the beneficiary of two decades of ever-expanding cancer research, has approximately the same chance of survival as a patient whose case was diagnosed before any of that research took place'.

Greenberg's article attracted some respectful notice: the *New England Journal of Medicine* published his further onslaught on the cancer establishment, and the editor of the *New Scientist*, Bernard Dixon, noted that the damning statistics came from the National Cancer Institute's own files. Dixon had himself come across cancer researchers who privately had expressed similar views to Greenberg's, but in medicine as in war, he had realised, 'dissent is tantamount to treason and dishonour'. So it proved. Greenberg's evidence could not be contradicted, but it could be, and was, brushed aside. 'Continuing improvement in survival took place during the 1960s and is continuing into the 1970s for a substantial segment of cancer,' the Institute blandly insisted in a reply to its critics. 'Prognosis for more than half of all patients with cancer is better now than it was ten years ago', and the upward trend was 'real and consequential'.

If an upward trend really existed, it should soon have been apparent in the statistics. Examining the Institute's 1977 collection, Greenberg was able to show that, even if they were open to some conflicting interpretations, 'they strongly indicate that the last twenty-five years – a period in which research and treatment expenditures have soared – have not produced any significant over-all changes'. Again, survival times had improved in certain types of cancer, but they were among the least common. His attack on the interpretation of the statistics went unheard; the Institute continued to ignore its own data, and to maintain that the research it funded was paying dividends – as did the cancer fund-raising agencies in Britain. So the myth that cancer was being gradually but inexorably conquered was maintained.

## Lung Cancer

The site most commonly attacked by cancer is the lung. In Britain, where the mortality rate from lung cancer is the highest in the world, it kills nearly 40,000 men annually – forty per cent of all the male cancer patients. For women the rate, though lower, is second only to that of cancer of the breast, and the indications are that it will soon head their mortality statistics, too. And although in other countries the figures have been a little less menacing, lung cancer is everywhere recognised as the most lethal of the common forms of the disease, because it has defied all attempts at treatment. As a small minority of patients survive, and a tiny minority actually recover from, lung cancer, claims have periodically been made on behalf of certain surgical techniques, or some cytotoxic drug, but there is general agreement that, by the time it is diagnosed, no type of treatment is likely to do more than prolong survival for a few weeks.

That lung cancer was becoming increasingly common was realised soon after the First World War, but as Thomas McKeown – a medical student in the 1930s – has recalled, 'There was little discussion of aetiology or of the possibility that the disease might be due to influences which could be modified or removed.' As with heart disease, in other words, there was no inclination to introduce epidemiological surveys, to see if they would come up with any illuminating findings. But when the alarming rise in mortality became clear – from fifteen deaths per million of the British population in 1918, it was to rise to over 900 per million in the course of the next half century – the suspicion was sometimes voiced that an environmental carcinogen might be responsible; there were two obvious suspects, exhaust fumes from internal combustion engines, and tobacco smoke. Shortly after the Second World War two members of the Medical Research Council, Richard Doll and Austin Bradford Hill, conducted an investigation at twenty London hospitals, questioning six hundred lung-cancer patients about their smoking habits, and using as controls patients who had cancers of other kinds, or did not have cancer. Almost all the lung-cancer patients, Doll and Hill reported in 1950, were cigarette-smokers, a far higher proportion than among the controls. A second report, four years later, confirmed and amplified the findings. Not merely were people who smoked at much greater risk of contracting lung cancer than non-smokers; there was also a significant correlation between mortality from lung cancer and the number of cigarettes smoked.

Doll and Hill realised that they would need to try to set up a prospective trial rather than rely, as they had initially done, on retrospective evidence. They would also need to use greater numbers, if their work was to carry conviction. Casting around for a way to obtain a larger sample without incurring great expense, they hit upon the idea of sending out a questionnaire to the 60,000 doctors in Britain, asking them to provide details of their smoking habits. Two-thirds replied – an unusually high response rate, enough to provide the investigators with the evidence they needed. For the next five years, whenever the death of a patient who was a doctor was reported as being from lung cancer, Doll and Hill wrote for confirmation to the doctor who had signed the death certificate, and if necessary to the hospital where the patient had been treated. By this means they were able to compare the mortality rates of smokers and non-smokers, and also of heavy and light smokers. Their 1956 report further amplified their earlier findings. There was 'a marked and steady increase in the death rate from lung cancer as the amount smoked increases'. Only one doctor-patient who had not smoked had died of it. For those who smoked, the risk was proportionate to the amount; medium smokers were nearly twice as likely to die of lung cancer as light smokers, and heavy smokers were nearly twice as likely to die as medium smokers. These proportions, too, were consistent at any age over thirty-five. Perhaps most important of all was another finding: doctors who had given up smoking appeared to have significantly improved their prospects of escaping the consequences.

By this time research along similar lines by E. C. Hammond and D. Horn in the United States was producing similar results. Here, then, was the opportunity for the medical profession to put its weight behind a campaign for the prevention of lung cancer, waged with the help of the simplest of all possible prescriptions: 'Stop smoking cigarettes, and your chances of contracting lung cancer will fall to near zero.'

But there were difficulties. One was the consequence of the profession's mistrust of epidemiological evidence, until backed by laboratory findings. What, critics demanded to know, was the actual *cause* of lung cancer? Was there a carcinogen in the tobacco, or in the smoke? Was tar, or nicotine, or some other constituent the culprit? Research began with a view to finding the answer to questions such as whether filter tips provided protection, and until all the issues were settled it was deemed unfair to convict cigarettes, much as it is often considered unfair to condemn somebody for murder on the strength simply of circumstantial evidence, however damning.

Another more serious problem was presented by the leading statistician of the era, Sir Ronald Fisher. The great majority of cigarette smokers, he pointed out, did not get lung cancer. It was therefore absurd to maintain that smoking was the cause. Might there not be some genetic factor, predisposing people both to smoking and to lung cancer? The following year Hans Eysenck, Professor of Psychology at the University of London, was able to lend some confirmation to Fisher's hypothesis by presenting the results of tests which showed a significant relationship between extroversion, as measured on a personality scale, and proneness to lung cancer, suggesting the possibility that the life-styles of extroverts might be responsible both for their smoking habits and for lowering their resistance.

Eysenck's intervention had the curious effect of encouraging the medical establishment to accept the statistical evidence, and stop worrying about the lack of an identifiable cause. Advice from a psychologist was unwelcome. A committee set up by the Royal College of Physicians did not hesitate to assert, when it reported in 1962, that cigarette smoking was 'the cause' of lung cancer. Two years later, the US Surgeon-General's Advisory Committee took the same line. And since that time it has been generally, even if not universally, agreed within the medical profession that whether or not the link between smoking and cancer is causal, the case against cigarettes (pipes and cigars emerged relatively unscathed from the trials), linked as they also are with mortality from bronchitis and heart disease, is so strong that society would be better to dispense with them, if only to be on the safe side.

The Royal College and the Surgeon-General's Committees were saying, in effect, that 'if stopping cigarette smoking is going to save tens of thousands of lives annually, it is worth doing even at the cost of some restrictions on the liberties of the subject'. But what form should the restriction take? The lesson of what had happened in the United States between the wars had shown the futility, and indeed the danger, of trying to eliminate any form of socially-established drug-taking by simple prohibition. The College's report accordingly suggested gradual reform, beginning with restrictions on the sale of cigarettes to children, on advertising, and on smoking in public places; higher duties on tobacco, and warning notices on cigarette packets.

At the time these seemed quite tough proposals, and they alarmed both the tobacco manufacturers and the Government, dependent for revenue from the duties. Soon, however, an easier alternative was found. Legislation was not required, it was announced, because the tobacco companies had agreed to accept a system of 'voluntary' control. For the rest of the decade, and throughout the 1970s,

successive governments and representatives of the industry got together periodically to ensure that neither the companies' profits nor
the Chancellor of the Exchequer's revenue should be jeopardised by
the introduction of restrictions on smoking of a kind which might be
effective.

Certainly, they agreed, children should not be allowed to buy
cigarettes. But what tobacconist could refuse a child claiming to be
getting them for dad? As for smoking in public places, such as cinemas,
that was surely a matter for the owners or managers. A Labour
Minister of Health, Kenneth Robinson, managed to secure a ban on
cigarette TV commercials, but its only appreciable effect was to
improve the finances of newspapers and magazines. As for the health
warnings put on cigarette packets, they soon became notoriously
'invisible' to buyers.

Realising what was happening, the Royal College of Physicians
Committee returned to the attack in a second report in 1971,
demanding tougher measures. Cigarette smoking, it warned, had been
shown to be as important a cause of death as the great plagues.
'Action to protect the public against the damage done to so many of
them by cigarette smoking would have more effect upon the public
health than anything else that could now be done in the whole field of
preventive medicine.' But the fact that the committee had to reiterate
its demands in the third report, six years later, was the measure of its
failure to make any real impact.

In 1977, however, the hopes of the anti-smoking campaigners – by
this time represented by a pressure group, Action on Smoking and
Health (ASH) – rose when a report on preventive medicine was
published by the House of Commons All-party Expenditure Committee. Among other measures it called for a ban on all advertising of
tobacco products; the removal of cigarette-vending machines from
places where they could be used by children, and an assurance that the
price of a packet of cigarettes should always rise in real terms, to keep
pace with inflation. The recommendations, ASH's director claimed,
constituted 'perhaps the most important political development on
smoking in more than a decade'. But by this time the tobacco
companies had been shrewd enough to begin to diversify their
promotion. If they carried on with aggressive promotional campaigns
through direct advertising they might rouse public opinion, forcing the
Government to abandon the system of 'voluntary' agreement. So they
pretended that they were co-operating with the Government by
reducing direct promotion, while starting to concentrate more of their
resources on indirect promotion, such as the sponsoring of sporting

and cultural events. They hardly bothered to maintain the polite fiction that their sponsorship was solely for the good of the pastime. In 1979 a Rugby League football game, sponsored by John Player, was actually called off when it was learned there would be no TV coverage because of a technicians' strike.

Sponsorship had the additional advantage of particularly appealing to the young. Older members of the public were getting the Doll/Hill message, with the help of anti-smoking campaigns backed by the Government-sponsored Health Education Council and by ASH; during the 1970s fewer older people smoked. But this mattered little to the manufacturers so long as more young people could be hooked. Although, as part of their agreement with the Government, the tobacco companies had promised not to encourage smoking by the young, they now proceeded to step up their advertising in cinemas – largely patronised by the young. They used magazines read mainly by the young to launch new advertising campaigns. And when the Advertising Standards Authority insisted that their advertising must not be designed to appeal directly to the young, they switched to advertisements designed to appeal indirectly, with open-air vistas evoking healthy living in the wide-open spaces, in the hope of exploiting the association of ideas.

In the winter of 1979–80, the 'voluntary' agreement came up for re-negotiation, and one of the negotiators on behalf of the Department of Health was a junior minister, Sir George Young. In opposition he had urged tougher curbs on smoking; he had just made a moving speech on the subject at the Fourth World Conference on Smoking and Health in Stockholm, concluding with the hope that by the end of the century smoking would be 'a habit indulged in by consenting adults in private'. Would he be allowed to be as good as his words, now that he was in office? The forces ranged against him were reviewed in a *Guardian* survey of the evidence against tobacco at the close of the 1970s. 'How does a drug which kills 50,000 people a year,' it asked, 'escape from the controls which are imposed on even the mildest cough medicine?' It went on to provide the explanation in the form of a line-up of the ministries which would be out to thwart any attempt by the Department of Health to make the controls more effective, a list amplified a few days later in the *Observer*.

The Department of Trade would be opposed to any move to cut down the production of cigarettes, because the tobacco industry had a profitable export business to 150 countries. The Ministry of Overseas Development had recently provided substantial grants to three Commonwealth countries to help their tobacco-growers. The Department of Industry had just given £30m in cash grants to cigarette manufacturers to build new factories in regions of high unemployment, a move naturally welcomed by the Department of Employment, which would also be concerned about the fate of the 36,000 retail outlets. The Ministries for Sport and for the Arts could hardly wish to have the substantial subsidies provided by the tobacco industry withdrawn. Most important of all, the Treasury would not care to lose the £2,300m a year from the tobacco duties.

The shadow-boxing lasted for a year before, in November 1980, the Conservative Social Services Secretary, Patrick Jenkin, revealed the terms of the latest 'voluntary' agreement. The concessions which had been wrung out of the industry were humiliatingly trivial: TV commercials for cigars with the same name as cigarettes were to be withdrawn; spending cuts on poster advertising were agreed, and changes of wording were to be made in the health-warnings on packets. But what had come to be the vital issue, sponsorship, was left out of account. A letter in the *Guardian* from a Scottish Health Educational Group, appearing the same day as the minister's report of his deal with the tobacco companies, reminded him just what sponsorship was achieving for them. For a sum roughly the equivalent of a thirty-second TV commercial, one cigarette company had had its brand vigorously promoted on BBC television for over twenty hours, simply by sponsoring the world snooker championship.

The only semblance of a victory which the Minister could claim was that the agreement would run for only two years, not, as the industry had demanded, four. But nothing in the past record of Conservative governments – or Labour governments either – suggested that they would be much tougher the next time round.

Filling in the background to the 1979 Stockholm conference on smoking and health, Janet Watts of the *Observer* had in effect forecast what was later to happen – the eating of fine conference-room words – and why. In 1966, she recalled, the Conservative Health Minister Iain Macleod had frankly admitted that smokers contributed over £1,000m a year to the Exchequer 'and no one knows better than the Government that they simply cannot afford to lose so much'. By 1979 that sum had doubled, and the Government was feeling the pinch both of recession, which made it reluctant to lose *any* revenue, and of inflation, which made it reluctant to put up the cost-of-living index by increasing the tobacco tax. Sir George Young, she noted, had for years been one of the staunchest anti-smoking campaigners, but he had also told her 'in government we have to make progress by consent, without upsetting too many people'. When in 1980 the

Government released details of its capitulation to the industry, a Gallup poll had just shown that two out of three people in Britain favoured an outright ban on cigarette advertising. It would not, then, have upset too many people. But it would have upset the tobacco barons, the Chancellor, and several other Ministers. In spite of the humiliation, Young chose not to resign.

In the United States, attempts to curb cigarette smoking have met with equally determined and, if necessary, ruthless opposition, as President Carter's Health Secretary, Joseph Califano, found to his cost, after launching his crusade against smoking in 1978. The *Sunday Times* correspondent in Washington, Henry Brandon, happened to be with a White House aide when a telephone call came through which 'appeared to test his patience'. The caller, it transpired, was Califano; the aide's patience was tested because his job was to keep State governors happy, and eight of them had just rung him, expressing their bitter resentment at Califano's views. The nation's six hundred thousand tobacco growers, the aide explained to Brandon, had received seventy-five million dollars-worth of grants and loans from the Government the previous year; the governors had to be reassured with the pledge that whatever the Secretary of Health might say, the Secretary of Agriculture would not permit any reduction in tobacco subsidies. It came as no surprise when Califano was among those sacked in the Presidential purge the following year.

### The Implications

That conventional treatment brings no appreciable benefit in the great majority of lung-cancer cases is not now seriously disputed. It has been confirmed, in fact, in an investigation sponsored by the US National Cancer Institute. Thirty thousand volunteers were divided into two groups: the members of one were subjected to careful and regular screening with X-rays and sputum tests, three times a year, while the members of the other group were left to their own devices, though regularly reminded of the desirability of at least an annual check-up. 'There is at present no significant difference,' an interim report disclosed in 1978, 'in total lung cancer death in either of the two groups.'

The commonest kind of lung cancer, John Cairns asserts in his *Cancer: Science and Society*, 'is somewhat inaccessible to surgery, spreads rapidly, and usually causes death within a few months of diagnosis'. Any gain in survival-time from improved conventional treatment, too, will have to be set off against the unwelcome side-effects that are 'their all too familiar accompaniment'. As things stand, the only immediate hope of reducing lung cancer's mortality rate lies in preventing the spread of addiction to smoking (the evidence about whether the addiction is to nicotine or to the smoking habit or both is confused and contradictory). Admittedly the evidence against smoking remains statistical. Such carcinogenic properties as have been found in tobacco cannot in themselves account for the disease. In an analysis of the evidence, however, the epidemiologist, C. J. Roberts, has shown why absence of knowledge about the cause or causes of lung cancer ought not to be allowed, if an association has been established, to prevent us from proceeding as if the cause *were* established.

There are eight criteria, he suggests, which provide a powerful presumption of a causal relationship. What is the relative risk in those exposed? Has the association been repeatedly observed in different places and at different times by different observers? Is the association limited to a particular disease? How confident can we be that the suspected cause antedated the observed effect? Is there good evidence of increasing risk with increasing doses? Is the suggestion of causality biologically plausible? Does the suggestion of causality conflict with other known facts about the history and etiology of the disease? And what is the effect of intervention? If these questions are asked about cigarette smoking and lung cancer, the association can be seen to be sufficiently consistent to justify the conclusion, Roberts feels, 'that cigarette smoking is indeed causally related to lung cancer'.

Even if it is conceded that tobacco or tobacco smoke are not in themselves the cause, the evidence that cigarette smoking is a risk factor is strong enough to justify a much more forceful campaign for more decisive measures to curb it, particularly among the young. The record of the medical profession in this campaign, however, does not inspire confidence in its ability to rouse and marshal public opinion for a concerted onslaught upon the drug-peddling alliance of government and industry. For a start, it lacks the machinery to implement policies, even when agreed; although, in Britain, the General Medical Council could in theory take action, in practice it has not cared to give a lead in such matters. The profession's spokesmen, therefore, tend to be the Royal Colleges, but they do not speak with one voice.

Surgeons do not care to have their impotence in connection with lung cancer emphasised as one of the reasons for a campaign against smoking. They do not like to admit it even to themselves; and it would be cruel, they argue, to patients with lung cancer to admit that there is so little hope. Some of them boast that they never tell a patient of their diagnosis, even if he wants to know. Cancer surgeons consequently cannot be expected whole-heartedly to support, let alone to spear-head, a campaign to make the public more aware of the grisly reality which John Betjeman pictured in his 'Devonshire Street, W.1':

> No hope. And the iron nob of this palisade
> So cold to the touch, is luckier now than he.
> 'Oh merciless hurrying Londoners! Why was I made
> For the long and the painful deathbed coming to me?'

The Royal College of Physicians, too, can do no more than exhort doctors to use what influence they have with their patients – as it did in 1972 when it reminded them that they had 'a unique opportunity for preventing common, dangerous and disabling diseases (heart disease and bronchitis, as well as lung cancer) by persuading their patients to give up cigarette smoking'. But this left it up to individual doctors, and although a higher proportion of doctors than of the rest of the community gave up smoking, photographs taken at medical conferences continued for a while to show smoke-wreathed rooms, and patients continued to see prescriptions written out by nicotine-stained fingers. No positive step was therefore taken by the profession to launch an effective anti-smoking campaign of its own.

Although the profession can claim that it should not be held responsible for the sins of governments and industry, evidence has emerged recently which suggests that it could have acted much more decisively within its own frontiers, and at the same time helped to bring more effective public pressure to bear. In the summer of 1979 the *British Medical Journal* carried a paper describing the results of a campaign which a few general practitioners had waged against cigarette smoking among their patients in London, giving them advice and leaflets setting out the evidence, and instituting follow-ups to find out how they were faring in their attempts to break the habit. Judging by the results, the doctors claimed, a nationwide campaign conducted along similar lines could reduce the number of smokers by as many as half a million people a year. The estimate might be optimistic, but the doctors had shown that the profession could have played a more direct part in preventing lung cancer had it been capable of organising such a campaign on a national level.

## Breast Cancer

The difficulties faced by the medical profession in exercising effective control over the specialties which compose it, have been even more clearly demonstrated by the course of events in connection with cancer of the breast, the most destructive form the disease has taken among women: it is diagnosed in about 90,000 women in the United States every year.

Late in the nineteenth century the practice began of cutting out not just the tumour, but the entire breast, including the lymph nodes – the glands which regulate lymph flow. The theory behind mastectomy was plausible: if, like a garden weed, the cancer could be taken out by the roots it would be less likely to spring up again, particularly if irradiation was employed as an additional safeguard, to destroy any lurking cancerous cells. The disfiguring operation was made easier to justify by the fact that patients were most commonly past menopause. The Victorian assumption was that, by then, they would no longer need to nurse children, or even to present a sexually attractive appearance to their husbands. Soon, mastectomies became standard, and although in 1937 the *British Medical Journal* printed an article claiming satisfactory results for a more conservative operation, combining excision of the tumour with irradiation, the need for mastectomies was rarely challenged until the 1950s, when concern began to be voiced that there was no experimental proof of their effectiveness.

In the *Annals of Surgery* in 1963 Hugh Auchinloss of Columbia University asserted that the operation had been persevered with only because it was sanctioned by tradition, training, and 'personal prejudice tinged with emotion': it accomplished nothing, he argued, that a more conservative operation 'would not do as well'. At a meeting that summer of the Canadian Medical Association, George Crile of Cleveland suggested that by removing the lymph nodes, mastectomies might actually be reducing the patient's survival prospects, by interfering with her natural resistance. Surveying the evidence, E. F. Lewison of the Johns Hopkins Medical School had to admit that he could nowhere find any justification for them. 'Breast cancer has a long and perilous history,' Lewison concluded, 'a dark and dire present, and thus far, unfortunately, a flourishing future.' No reliable trials had compared mastectomy with other forms of treatment, yet its limitations had been exposed by the unchanging incidence of breast cancer, the mortality from it, and the survival rate, over the years. 'In recording our surgical triumphs,' he asked, 'are we merely measuring the natural history of this malignancy?' The most impressive feature of the evidence was 'the striking similarity and surprising uniformity of long-term end results, despite the widely differing therapeutic techniques as reported from this country or abroad'. What was needed, he urged, was a large-scale randomised trial to compare the results of different methods, to find which, if any, really did improve the survival rate.

Setting up such a trial, however, presented a problem. It could no longer be a matter of giving one group of patients mastectomy while the matched group simply had their tumours excised. A variety of mastectomies was in use: simple, extended simple, modified radical, radical, extended radical, and super-radical. The more radical – in effect, the more extensive and disfiguring – the operation, the more its practitioners tended to insist that their patients' survival prospects must not be jeopardised by exposing them to less radical surgery, and all but a tiny minority were consequently opposed to trials of 'lumpectomy' – simple removal of the tumour. Still, a couple of trials had begun to compare simple mastectomy with radical mastectomy. After ten years, the one held in Copenhagen revealed no significant difference in the patients' survival rates. The one in Cambridge also showed no significant difference in survival, but as healing was delayed in the radical mastectomy group, the report recommended the adoption of the simpler operation.

The reaction of some orthodox cancer specialists was not just to reject this evidence, but to denounce Crile and those who shared his opinions. They were the medical equivalent of Lysenko, one critic sourly claimed in the *Journal of the American Medical Association*; 'a very small, but highly vocal, segment of the profession' who had been 'vigorously condemning generally-accepted and time-tested radical procedures'. Generally-accepted and time-tested they were, but the test of time was in fact continuing to show that radical surgery was futile. 'Despite improved surgical techniques, advanced methods in radiotherapies, and widepread use of chemotherapies,' Thomas Dao of the Roswell Park Memorial Institute, Buffalo, wrote in 1975, 'breast cancer mortality has not changed in the last 75 years.' The same year a survey of the statistics led W. P. D. Logan of the World Health Organisation to assert in the WHO *Chronicle* that not merely had there been no decline; breast cancer mortality might actually have increased.

## Mammography

By this time, however, cancer surgeons had found a new rationalisation for their work. For some years past women had been urged to palpate their breasts periodically, and to go to their doctor the moment they found a lump. But many women did not take this precaution, and those who did could not notice the growth until it was well developed. With the help of regular X-ray examinations, it was now claimed, tumours might be detected in their formative stage, before they developed metastases elsewhere, and trials carried out by Sam Shapiro and colleagues in New York showed that tumours could indeed be detected anything up to eighteen months earlier.

There was no proof, Shapiro warned, that earlier detection improved the survival-rate, and if young women had annual screenings – as they would need to do, to keep ahead of detection by palpation – they ran the risk that the cumulative effect of the X-rays might *cause* cancer. Caution suggested that, for a while at least, only women over the age of fifty should present themselves for routine screening. The American National Cancer Society, however, was in no mood for caution. Here it saw its chance to exploit the publicity. A campaign began for mass screening which, by the 1970s, sometimes approached hysteria. Young women, it implied, were still being condemned to death by the thousand for lack of X-ray screening facilities, and with the help of roused public opinion, the Society was able to stampede the government-backed National Cancer Institute into supporting a mass screening trial of women between the ages of thirty-five and sixty. Fifty million dollars, most of it provided by taxpayers, was spent on setting up the required screening centres around the country, to which nearly three hundred thousand women came for their first screening.

As has so often been the case, it was the *New England Journal of Medicine* which in 1975 sounded a warning, to doctors, by publishing Dan Greenberg's 'Progress in cancer research; don't say it isn't so'. The Society, Greenberg complained, had been asserting that breast cancer was 'one of the most curable of the major diseases in this country', in spite of the fact that all the statistics showed that the mortality rate had not changed over the past seventy years. 'The vast and ill-conceived undertaking that was created by the National Cancer Act of 1971,' he feared, had 'merely spawned a monolithic bureaucracy that with a heavily supported P.R. apparatus is simply misleading the American public'. The Society ignored him; bulletins continued to appear claiming that the results of its programme were encouraging. 'The news, so far,' the National Cancer Institute's director Frank Rauscher assured a Senate Health Committee in 1976, 'is very good indeed.' But by this time the Institute's advisory teams were becoming aware that the results were, in fact, so discouraging that there could be little justification for continuing to submit young women to the additional risk they might run from annual exposure to X-rays. The Institute exercised its governmental authority: women under fifty, it instructed the Society, should not remain part of the screening programme unless they were regarded as at high risk.

The Society took the decision with bad grace. 'It thrives on arousing hopes, fears and donations,' Greenberg commented. Having 'bowled over doubters when the age question was raised', it was not prepared to lose face by giving up so easily, and it managed to find an ingenious way to circumvent the Institute's instructions. 'High risk' was held to include such criteria as large breasts, one of the ruses which enabled the Society to hold well over two-thirds of the under-fifties already in the scheme, and it embarked on a public-relations campaign in the media, including *Reader's Digest*, to justify such screening. A past president of the Society actually used the argument that even if a cancer risk from overdoses of radiation existed, by the time the women contracted cancer there was 'an excellent chance that science will have learned to control the disease'.

Meanwhile the Shapiro trials continued, and a further report, published in 1977, confirmed the earlier findings. Although screening appeared to offer some hope for women over fifty, it offered none for women under fifty. The report also showed that one of the chief arguments in favour of mammography, its reliability, was fallacious: nearly half the breast cancers detected by other means, such as palpation, had been missed by radiographers. A smaller but by no means negligible proportion of women, too, had had 'false-positive' X-ray diagnoses; on subsequent examination they were found not to have cancer. The Society was now given the more precise instruction that women under fifty should no longer be asked to volunteer for screening, unless they had already had cancer, or came from a family with a marked cancer history.

The British were lucky, on this occasion; the Department of Health's caution saved them from rushing into mass screening for breast cancer. When the campaign for screening began in Britain, it adopted the traditional device of a committee of enquiry under Professor Thomas McKeown, the most unlikely man to be swayed by hysteria – also present, though less violent, in Britain. Largely on the strength of the Shapiro findings, the committee came down in 1970 against the introduction of mass screening, and although there were angry mutterings, the decision received support the following year in a series of articles in the *Lancet*. One of these made the practical point that, even if it had been shown that mass screening made a valuable contribution to the control of breast cancer, which it had not, the provision of the manpower and equipment required would be a crippling financial burden.

Nevertheless, as recently as 1978 the 'British Breast Group' of cancer specialists expressed the hope that the obstacles to more generally available screening would soon be removed, reaffirming, without providing any evidence for their conviction, that 'early diagnosis of breast cancer is important, and that it improves the survival rate'. Since this, the British United Provident Association has also claimed that screening is saving lives, but its figures are un-impressive: out of nearly fifty thousand screened, only about two hundred cases were diagnosed; taking into consideration the fact that they were presumably diagnosed sooner than women who had not been screened, the survival rate has hardly improved sufficiently to offset the cost and the possible risks from screening. 'The evidence that earlier diagnosis improves survival is still not convincing,' Lester Barr and Michael Bailey of the Royal Marsden Hospital, Sutton, have claimed in the *British Medical Journal*. 'It seems likely that dissemin-ation of disease beyond the breast may occur before the appearance of the first symptom, let alone diagnosis.'

Early diagnosis is of value, they suggest, only in that it may reduce the amount of radical surgery. Controlled trials have continued to show that radical surgery is unnecessary: following trials carried out in Italy, Umberto Varonesi, head of the Italian Cancer Institute, has con-firmed that there is no difference in the survival rates of women who have been operated upon, whether they have had radical or con-servative surgery – news which has prompted the *New Scientist* to express the hope that women suffering from breast cancer will 'no longer have to be disfigured by having their entire breast removed'. Past experience offers little to justify such optimism. When the BBC *Man Alive* programme filmed a version of radical mastectomy, an eminent surgeon who appeared on a follow-up programme asserted that it was 'an operation which is virtually never performed nowadays; indeed in my surgical lifetime it has never been performed in Britain'; because it was an operation which 'causes quite dreadful deformity', for the BBC to show it had been 'positively dishonest'. Investigation disclosed that the surgeon was misinformed; the operation had continued to be performed.

One of the saddest features in connection with radical mastectomy has been that surgeons have so often been unable to face telling patients what is about to happen to them. 'I *thought* a mastectomy was having a breast removed,' a correspondent complained in the *Sunday Times*, following an article on the subject. '*Nothing* prepared me for the shock of the devastation of chest and armpit and the permanently damaged arm.' Nor had she been prepared 'for the successive annihilating waves of disgust and depression which make life more or less intolerable. The rate of survival may look good in the statistics, but statistics don't count the cost.'

It is hard, then, to escape the conclusion that the public has been systematically deceived about the benefits of mastectomy. As Auchinloss lamented twenty years ago, cancer surgeons work by faith rather than by science, faith sanctioned by tradition and training, and supported by emotional prejudice. Naturally they do not care to admit that so disfiguring an operation is and always has been unnecessary. Equally understandably, those women who have had their breasts cut off, and who live longer than the average survival time between diagnosis and death, tend to ascribe their good fortune to the fact that they were sensible enough to seek an early diagnosis and to have their cancer removed, root as well as branch, before it had a chance to spread. So the myth has been sustained.

It must be described as myth because, as Klim McPherson and Maurice S. Fox explain in their chapter on the subject in John P. Bunker's salutary survey, *Costs, risks and Benefits of Surgery*, 'The requirement of continuation of "accepted practice" discourages the simplest kind of investigation that would permit distinction between fact and belief on the issue of the benefit provided by surgery.' It is not possible to assert dogmatically that surgical intervention is futile, from the point of view of extending survival, but 'the clinical evidence that has accumulated demonstrates persuasively that radical mastectomy offers no greater benefit to the patient than does simple mastectomy'; and there is no proof that limited surgery, 'lumpectomy', would not be just as efficacious. And if doubt exists about the value of any kind of surgery, 'then the desirability of screening to detect presumed "early" cases must be re-examined'. Again, the natural history of the early stages of breast cancer is obscure; the claim that early detection and removal prolong survival ignores the possibility that in such early stages tumours may be slow to develop, or even, like warts, develop quickly, but also disappear quickly.

At last there are signs that the myth cannot be sustained for much longer. In 1980 the feuds which had been simmering for some years between the supporters of surgery, radiotherapy and chemotherapy respectively came out into the open in medical journals, sometimes violently. A British surgeon, R. T. Marcus, complained in the *British Medical Journal* that general surgeons like himself were being given to understand they were not fit to treat breast cancer; he rounded savagely on surgery's critics by recommending that when in doubt what to tell a patient who had cancer, they should simply say 'I know you are dying; but we are still arguing about which poison to give you'. And in the same issue, a radiotherapist warned that maintenance chemotherapy may be 'fraught with major unknown dangers of inducing further occurrence of malignancy'.

The doubts whether mastectomy of any kind is necessary have since increased. More and more surgeons are beginning to question its value, the *BMJ* has admitted; and the *Journal of the American Medical Association* has devoted a long editorial – by a coincidence, in the same week as the *BMJ*'s – to the campaign which has been building up in the United states for 'breast-saving surgery'. The *BMJ* proposes a 'tightly controlled randomised study' to settle the issue; but doubt has since been cast on the idea by Sir Reginald Murley, a former President of the Royal College of Surgeons, and by Sir Geoffrey Keynes – in such trials, he fears, the control is 'too often a form of self-deception, the supposed control being upset by too many uncontrollable variants of the conditions under investigation'.

It was Keynes who, as a young man, had carried out the research and written the paper which the *BMJ* had published in 1937, questioning the value of mastectomy. His views, he recalls sadly, 'were clearly unpalatable to most surgeons. They turned their heads the other way, preferring to follow a surgical dogma, however irrational it might be shown to be.' The writer of a letter to the editor of *World Medicine* had earlier made a telling prediction: 'I suspect that a few years from now our record in the treatment of breast cancer to date will be one that we will be ashamed of – that is, if we have the sensitivity to know how much suffering we caused this tragic group of patients'.

## Cerival Cancer

Why have cancer specialists been so reluctant to admit that conventional methods of treatment have failed? Particularly as in the next most common forms of cancer, those of the digestive tract, the record is little more impressive?

The chief reason is that the specialist's fading hopes have periodically been revived by improved screening techniques, which have enabled the surgeon, the radiologist, and the physician to tell themselves that they will at last be able to catch the cancer before it has time to spread. But screening by taking 'smears' has proved an unreliable ally, as has been shown in connection with the campaign to eradicate – as for a time it was hoped it would do – cancer of the cervix. The incidence of carcinoma of the neck of the womb is comparatively low, accounting only for between two and five per cent of all female cancers. But claims for the value of early detection, through screening and prompt treatment, have not merely given the impression that countless lives have been saved: they have also been used to boost the importance of screening in general.

It had long been known that some women have cervical cancer *in situ*, cancerous cells showing no disposition to spread. At some point, however, they could become 'invasive'; doctors presumed that if women were screened and cancer *in situ* dealt with wherever it was found, if necessary by a hysterectomy, they would have a better chance to escape invasive cancer later. This belief appeared to be justified when the results of a screening programme in British Columbia showed that, among women who had been screened, so that those with cancer *in situ* could be detected and treated, there had been a reduction in the incidence of detected invasive cancer from 28.4 cases per 100,000 in 1955 to 19.7 in 1960. 'We believe that a population screening programme,' the researchers claimed, 'is capable of virtually eliminating invasive carcinoma of the cervix.'

When the report was published in 1962 a campaign began to build up, first in North America and then in Europe, for the introduction of mass screening. In Britain it was led by Malcolm Donaldson, Director of the Cancer Department at St Bartholomew's Hospital, and a tireless protagonist of early detection and treatment. (He dedicated his book *The Cancer Riddle* to 'thousands of patients in the past who have died owing to Fear and Ignorance of the Disease, which has prevented them from seeking medical advice at a time when, in many cases, the disease would have been curable'.) In a letter in the *British Medical Journal* in 1965 he claimed that 'the battle against uterine cancer has been won'. Pressure both from within and outside the medical profession was put on the Labour Health Minister, Kenneth Robinson, to complete the victory by introducing free screening on the NHS for all women, and in 1966 Robinson announced that a nation-wide service was to be introduced, aiming to make screening facilities available for thirteen million British women.

Expensive though it would certainly be, the scheme was held to be justified by the number of lives it would save. Or would it? A pathologist in a Swansea hospital, David Ashley, pointed out a flaw in the interpretation of the British Columbia evidence. It was not certain, he argued, that the fall in the death-rate was related to the screening; the rate had been falling in Britain, too. In any case, what had not been taken sufficiently into consideration was the possibility that the cancers *in situ* found and treated as a consequence of screening might never have developed into invasive cancer.

In earlier studies the assumption had tended to be that cervical cancer developed in a straightforward fashion, like a seed growing into a plant. When it had been found that some cancers *in situ* remained that way for years, it was argued that, like some seeds, they might have a long latent or dormant period before becoming invasive. But suppose they never did become invasive? The proportion that remained non-invasive was unknown, but it might be substantial. Women with this type of cancer, who had had it detected by screening and then treated, might have lived out their allotted life span without this treatment, with its attendant risks and side-effects, and also without suffering from the uneasiness that the diagnosis of cancer induces, arising from the fear that treatment may not prevent recurrence.

Ashley's article attracted little notice, as it appeared in the worthy but obscure *Journal of Obstetrics and Gynaecology of the British Commonwealth*. But other critics took up the issue. O. A. Husain, Consultant Pathologist to the London Screening Centre, pointed out that if such a high proportion of the women who had been screened and treated in British Columbia had been saved from death due to cervical cancer, it was a little difficult to explain why the overall mortality rate there from cervical cancer had remained unchanged. And following an investigation sponsored by the Nuffield Provincial Hospitals Trust, E. G. Knox of Birmingham University recommended that little purpose would be served by going ahead with the screening plan until the natural history of the disease was better understood.

These criticisms attracted some attention in the newspapers. But as ministries do not care to admit that they have allowed themselves to be taken for an expensive ride, the pretence had to be maintained that the service would eventually be shown to be saving lives. Evidence has yet to be provided to justify this hope. Meanwhile the rate of diagnostic error from the tests on the cervical 'smears' – in particular 'false positives' indicating cancer where it is later found that none exists – has been disturbingly high, and thousands of women have had hysterectomies without there being any proof that the operation was necessary, because there is still no way of knowing whether a cancer discovered *in situ* would later have become invasive.

On this there is a curious form of double-think among specialists. 'It is axiomatic that cancer *in situ* when established is irreversible,' Roger Cotton, Professor of Diagnostic Oncology at the University of Nottingham, has claimed, 'but moderate and mild dysplastic changes in the cervical epithelium may revert spontaneously to normal.' In other words, dogma has it that the later tumour cannot go into reverse, but the earlier one sometimes does. Cotton then cites an investigation to check up on a hundred women whose cervical smears had been positive, but who for various reasons had not been treated; of the sixty who agreed to a fresh examination – on average, five years after the first – there was no sign of cancer in nineteen, and in twenty the cancer was still *in situ*.

The time-span of the development of invasive cancer, according to Cotton, 'varies enormously, from being extremely short to forty or more years'. For some women, as John Cairns has pointed out in his *Cancer: Science and Society*, this in effect means that screening would be of no benefit because they would not live to suffer from invasive cancer, and for others it would be of no benefit because 'fully invasive cancers emerge after little or no preliminary warning'. The only satisfactory way, therefore, to find whether screening works would be to compare a group of women who have been regularly and efficiently screened with an unscreened group, matched for age and, so far as possible, any other relevant characteristics. But this has proved difficult, because 'once a programme has been launched and has captured the public's imagination, it becomes no longer practicable or even politic to set up an experiment with proper controls', since there is an outcry that the control group, unscreened, will be in effect condemned to death. As a result there is still no evidence that it makes any statistical difference whether women are screened or not.

Yet to point this out has continued to be regarded as heretical; when Professor Archibald Cochrane did so he was denounced in the media. 'One very distinguished colleague wrote (rather irrelevantly) accusing me of "causing misery to thousands by telling lay people that there was no cure for carcinoma of the cervix",,' Cochrane has recalled. 'I wrote and asked him what his evidence was that carcinoma of the cervix could be cured, but he did not answer.'

Nothing since has conclusively demonstrated that screening for cervical cancer is effective, let alone cost-effective, but in the absence of findings from controlled trials there has been 'just enough in the jigsaw of information to make withdrawal of screening unethical', as the *British Medical Journal* has put it, while remaining 'insufficient for unassailable recommendations'. Epidemiologists are less cautious. The risk of dying from cervical cancer is in any case so small, in Cairns's view, that for many women it 'will probably seem to be too slight to warrant the expense and inconvenience of continued check-ups'. C. J. Roberts agrees; as there is no proof either that screening for cancer *in situ* reduces mortality from invasive cancer among those screened, or that the treatment of invasive cancer, when it is found, is effective, he doubts whether the disease satisfies the criteria of suitability for screening.

Perhaps the last word on the subject can be left to a consultant pathologist, A. R. Kittermaster, writing in *World Medicine*. He felt diffident, he explained, about giving advice on screening for a disease which, as a man, he could not contract. When he considered a roughly equivalent disease which he might get, such as cancer of the prostate, he would certainly be willing to have the equivalent test if he had suspicious symptoms; 'but if anyone – and particularly a female – suggested that young men should start having regular smears to diagnose and treat pre-malignant lesions, twenty years before the average age for invasive cancer, I should be highly suspicious of the whole affair'. Certainly he would want proof that treatment in such circumstances had a dramatic effect on the death-rate; and if he knew (as he did for cervical lesions) that having a smear carried an unavoidable risk of an incorrect diagnosis, 'then I would tell whoever was advocating the smear to go jump in the lake and poke their nose – or rather, finger – somewhere else'.

## Side-effects

Statistics compiled to assess the value of screening, and of the various forms of treatment which may be used following diagnosis, ordinarily show only the change, if there is one, in the duration of life between diagnosis and death. They give no indication of differences in the quality of life in that period because there is no way in which they can be measured, except subjectively by the patient. Yet simple prolongation of life ought not to be boasted about as a clinical achievement if a few additional months are bought only at the price of severe pain and disability, or mental and emotional distress.

*Radiotherapy*

In 1937 Percy Furnivall, Consulting Surgeon to the London Hospital and one of the leading clinicians of his time, discovered that he had cancer of the tongue. It came as no surprise to him when irradiation was prescribed; he knew that it was the stock form of treatment. A year later he described its consequences in the *British Medical Journal*, saying how deeply he regretted having undergone it. A lithe six-footer, he had always been a keen sportsman, and at the age of seventy, when the cancer had been diagnosed, he had still enjoyed his round of golf. Now, his weight had fallen to eight stone and he suffered from ulcers and neuritis. 'I can only walk about two hundred yards, and am a bent and feeble old man,' he wrote. 'I would not wish my worst enemy the prolonged hell I have been through.' Soon afterwards he wrote again to say that letters had been pouring in to him from other sufferers. A few weeks later the *British Medical Journal* printed his obituary.

At that time, and for some years to come, no thought had been given to submitting radiotherapy to controlled trials. Some cancer surgeons had their doubts, but only the most eminent dared to express them. 'I have not yet had the nerve *not* to use X-ray therapy,' Sir Arthur Porritt confessed in 1965. 'Perhaps if I live long enough I may one day.' There was so much belief in radiotherapy, he lamented, yet so little knowledge.

More knowledge, however, was to be obtained from a controlled trial which had just begun in Manchester, where seven hundred patients were treated by radical mastectomy followed by radiotherapy, while a matched group had radical mastectomy without radiotherapy. In 1967, after ten years had elapsed, no difference was found in the survival-rates of the two groups. A similar trial was then undertaken on an international scale, with over two thousand patients; this time, to compare the results of conservative mastectomy with and without radiotherapy. After five years there was again no difference in the survival-rates of the two groups.

The second trial afforded a clue. The only difference noted was a reduction of *local* recurrence at the original site of the cancer, following radiotherapy. Evidently radiotherapy was fulfilling its function at the point of contact, but making no contribution to halting the spread of the disease. Yet if it were not prolonging survival it was not merely futile, it was also condemning some patients to the misery which Furnivall had suffered.

In 1977, an article, 'I have breast cancer', appeared in *World Medicine* telling a similar story. When 'Frances Farrell' – the pseudonym of a nurse who was also the wife of a doctor – heard the diagnosis, she 'never doubted that the traditional treatment was not only inevitable, but that questioning its worth would be fruitless'; she consequently accepted radical mastectomy with radiotherapy. She felt very sick, with a burning sensation, but this, she was assured, was not the result of the irradiation. The treatment failed; she had to have further surgery, and by the time she described her experience in her article, she knew that it too had failed.

To what purpose? All that the radical mastectomy had done was disfigure her; 'amputation of the breast', she felt, would be 'the more honest term to use to women when suggesting the treatment'. She had also been seriously incapacitated. 'I *should* be grateful that I found the lump when it was barely palpable,' she explained, 'but I'm not. A year later I'm full of remorse after voluntarily forfeiting over a year in imposed ill-health.' The radiologist had done 'what I think is inestimable damage to my good, healthy organs, on a purely hypothetical basis, in order to get an extension of time at the expense of the quality of life'.

The letters which *World Medicine* received about the article were revealing. Some critics suggested that 'Frances Farrell' had simply been hysterical. But after her death a few months later Barbara Evans, consultant editor of the journal, rebutted the charge. She had gone to see 'Frances Farrell', and 'in twenty years of medical journalism I have never interviewed a woman whose intellect and character made so deep an impression on me'. Other critics sought to dispute the claim that radiotherapy does nothing to prolong survival, but none produced any evidence. One radiotherapist frankly admitted that 'of course, survival statistics are not improved by radiotherapy

71

after surgery'. Its justification, he claimed, lay in its ability to reduce the recurrence rate at the site of the operation; 'that is one of its triumphs'. In any case, 'late morbidity', as he euphemistically described the side-effects, was 'acceptable in the vast majority of patients'.

Would it be acceptable *to* the vast majority of patients? Like 'Frances Farrell', they have not been given the choice; not, at least, in a way which would have enabled them to make the decision whether or not they wish to have radiotherapy, given the lack of evidence that it prolongs survival. Some correspondents suggested that, on the contrary, irradiation might actually reduce survival-time. 'The harm done to the thymus by radiation lowers the cellular immunity which is part of the body's natural defence against cancer,' June Marchant, a lecturer in the biology of cancer who had herself had a radical mastectomy, pointed out. 'Any decrease in local occurrence is cancelled out by the increased tendency of metastases to grow at distant sites.'

*Chemotherapy*

In her article June Marchant disclosed that the dying 'Frances Farrell' had also been given drug treatment. Its effects had been hideous. 'Her despairing husband told me that after her cytotoxic cocktail she developed pituitary malfunction and diabetes insipidus, and lay in a stupor.'

Treatment with cytotoxic drugs is a comparative newcomer. As late as 1967 Sir Stanford Cade, a London consultant in both surgery and radiology, dismissed chemotherapy as the treatment of last resort for cancer; it had 'never cured patients'. Had Sir Stanford – two correspondents from a chemotherapy unit asked, in a letter to the *British Medical Journal* – ever actually tried chemotherapy for *early* cancer? As the cancer mortality rate was still rising, it should surely be worth trying. 'But the long-repeated exercises in surgery and radiation which have hitherto shown little reward are still being pursued', in spite of the fact that trials with drugs had shown encouraging results.

Since then, new drugs or combinations of drugs have endlessly been claimed as having encouraging results – 'breakthroughs', as they are commonly described in the media. But as Mary Costanza warned in an article on the subject in the *New England Journal of Medicine* in 1975, there is good reason to temper optimism with scepticism. The new drugs may be effective against tumours, but at the expense of upsetting the body's immunity from other disorders, and some drugs appear actually to promote tumour growth.

In the case of cancer, there has been no question of trying out drugs alone to compare their results with the accepted forms of treatment. Patients, the argument runs, must not be put at risk by depriving them of the benefit of mastectomy or irradiation. So drugs have been used primarily as back-ups – as 'adjuvant chemotherapy', in the current jargon, and it has not been easy to assess their precise effects. This has not deterred researchers from making enthusiastic claims. In 1979 the *New England Journal of Medicine* carried a paper on chemotherapy for cancer of the bronchus, asserting that its natural history had been impressively modified. 'The protean clinical manifestations can often be completely ameliorated for variable periods,' the authors claimed, enabling the patient 'to obtain effective palliation and prolongation of life'.

Examining the article's small print, the *Lancet* pointed out that the natural history of the disease appeared to be modified for only one patient in ten, and even this advantage was bought at a heavy price. Four out of every five patients who were given the drugs had adverse reactions: nausea, vomiting, mouth ulcers, loss of hair. These side-effects had been dismissed as 'favourable trade-offs for the symptoms and signs of cancer', but, as the *Lancet* pointed out, it had yet to be proved that the substitution of one set of symptoms and signs for the other made any difference to the survival-rate in the majority of patients, because no controlled trial had been held.

The results of such a trial in Britain have since been reported. Overall survival of patients with primary breast cancer, according to the findings, has not improved in the past ten years 'despite increasing use of multiple-drug chemotherapy. Furthermore there has been no improvement in survival from first metastases, and survival may even have been shortened in some patients given chemotherapy.' What some of these patients have had to suffer has been described in a 'consensus statement', put out by a high-powered committee of the US National Institutes of Health in 1980. Adverse reactions to chemotherapy, it warns, can be remote as well as acute. Among the acute symptoms it lists are bone-marrow suppression, nausea, vomiting, loss of appetite, weakness, mouth ulcers and hair loss: among the remote effects, organ damage, sterility and secondary cancers. The assessment of adjuvant chemotherapy, therefore, 'must balance efficacy against toxicity. The basic measure of therapeutic benefit is therapeutic survival with an acceptable quality of life.'

Having made this pronouncement, however, the committee has to admit that no such balance can be struck, because individual patients put a different value on survival. Doctors concerned in trials tend to dismiss side-effects with soothing phrases, such as 'well-tolerated', or even to ignore them altogether. In 1976 Gianni Bonnadonna of the Italian Cancer Institute in Milan published a paper in the *New England Journal of Medicine* claiming success for adjuvant chemo-therapy following radical mastectomy. The procedure was criticised on the ground that the massive doses involved produced very serious adverse reactions, and the suggestion was made that the dosage should be reduced. In a further paper in 1981 Bonnadonna was able to show that, in retrospect, the trials demonstrated that the duration of survival was related to the size of the dose. Should these findings be found to apply to chemotherapy for cancer in general, the outlook would indeed by gloomy, because they would suggest that the price for survival, in terms of adverse reaction, is likely to remain high.

Cancer victims have usually not realised what they will suffer to gain a few more months of life. Often they have been given no inkling of what they will have to go through. And the fact that combinations of drugs are now in favour is going to mean that more patients are going to be called upon to 'volunteer' for trials, to assess the merits of different combinations, with no guarantee that they will be fully and impartially briefed.

## Deception and Self-deception

It is difficult, in the light of the evidence, to find any justification for continuing with the current methods of cancer treatment. Little suggests, let alone proves, that they have made any significant difference to the survival-rate of patients diagnosed as having any of the commoner forms of cancer. All that Cairns can claim for surgery, for example, is that in most forms the removal of the primary tumour makes the patient feel better, and it may save patients who would die from, say, intestinal obstruction, were the tumour not removed. There is no convincing evidence that, otherwise, surgery lengthens survival time. Irradiation can be effective against single tumours, but there is nothing to show that it can stem the spread of cancer by metastasis. Chemotherapy with cytotoxic drugs has had too brief an existence for its effects to be confidently assessed, but as yet it has had no perceptible influence on the prognosis for the common cancers. 'Viewed overall,' Cairns concludes, 'non-surgical methods have not had a major impact on cancer mortality.'

Nor is the outlook any more encouraging for people who do not have cancer, or at least are not aware that they have it. Their interest is actuarial, Cairns remarks: what they really want to know is whether their chances of *not* dying of cancer have improved. Again, the answer is in the negative: 'there has been no recent major advance.' Statistically the chances are much the same as they were twenty years ago. Such progress as has been made is in the control of relatively uncommon forms of the disease, including leukemia, and these, the Cambridge epidemiologist Richard Peto has contended, form so distinct a group that it would have been wiser not to classify them as cancer in the first place.

The enthusiasm for early detection of tumours, in order that treatment may begin sooner, is consequently hard to justify. Yet it has persisted. Levitt and Guralnick argue that 'the old saying that a stitch in time saves nine can be applied to cancer; if the cancer is detected early enough it can be destroyed before it travels to nine other sites, or even more'. But neither they nor any other supporters of early detection have been able to produce convincing statistical evidence that screening has been instrumental in saving lives.

Admittedly figures have often been presented which appear to show that early detection improves survival prospects, but as J. E. Enstrom and D. F. Austin pointed out in 1977 in a *Science* article on interpreting cancer statistics, one of the necessary consequences of the use of methods which promote the earlier detection of tumours is that survival-rates need to be adjusted. If, for example, cancers which have an average four-year survival-rate after diagnosis are detected on average a year earlier, then an increase to a five-year average in the survival-rate after diagnosis, though it may sound impressive, simply means there has been no improvement in the effectiveness of the treatment. When such adjustment is made, they claimed, the rates appear to have remained roughly constant.

The best-documented exposure of the weaknesses of conventional therapies that has recently appeared is *Cancer: Myths and Realities of Cause and Cure*, by two professors of anatomy, M. L. Kothari and L. A. Mehta. Orthodox medicine's assumptions about cancer, they argue, are based on a myth, 'including such "facts" as that cancer is *caused* by an agent (and hence can be prevented by ridding humanity of that agent) and that it can be diagnosed at a stage when a pre-emptive strike at it would assure a cure'. Cancer cannot be prevented or treated, they claim; so diagnosis cannot affect the ultimate issue. Although reviews of the book by cancer specialists were generally critical, they were also respectful. As the authors backed their contentions with over three hundred source references, most of them from medical books and journals of impeccable orthodoxy, it was not easy to dismiss them as cranks. The then deputy editor of *World Medicine*, though he found the book puzzling, conceded that 'an intellectually respectable case can be made for suggesting that the abandonment of all (well, nearly all) our surgery, radiotherapy and drugs would make precious little difference to our mortality rates'.

It is difficult to dispute Illich's thesis that we, the public, have been the victims of what amounts to a massive confidence trick played on us by the medical establishment. 'Establishment' is the operative term. It is not the medical profession, as such, that bears the responsibility, so much as the way in which the profession is structured, leaving control over the prevention and treatment of cancer to the specialist's near-monopoly, operating within the profession's own near-monopoly. Where the causes of a disease remain unknown, immunisation impracticable, and treatment ineffective, he is naturally at a loss. As he cannot just stop treating patients, he does what his ancestors did when they bled, purged, cupped and blistered, clinging to the hope that sometimes what they did might work. As he is periodically given fresh ground for hope with new procedures, or new combinations of procedures, and as a small proportion of his patients survive to be exhibited on the credit side of the clinical balance sheet, he is not forced simply to fold his hands and bow out, except in the cases where cancer is far advanced, and then he can claim that detection has been delayed too long.

Yet the specialist cannot always delude himself that conventional treatment works. He is constantly tempted to lie to doomed patients, either by reassuring them, if they know they have cancer, that there is a good chance of the treatment providing a cure; or, if they do not know, by telling them they have some less sinister disorder. Inevitably this has bred mistrust, particularly as friends and relations, told about the deception but brought into the conspiracy of silence, are naturally going to be more worried if ever they have reason to suspect that they themselves have cancer. So cancer has come to be widely regarded as a juggernaut of a disease, proceeding inexorably and relentlessly to the sufferer's destruction.

Cancer specialists, like cardiologists, have been able to insulate themselves because their peers in the profession observe the convention that members of one specialty do not criticise another – not, at least, in public. Occasionally there have been rumblings of discontent, particularly about the way in which cancer specialists have deluded the public into accepting the urgency of whatever treatment they recommend. 'There must be few, if any, surgeons who do not put patients with known or suspected cancer into the urgent category,' James Angell, a consultant urologist at a Middlesex hospital, has complained recently in *World Medicine*'s 'Questionable Dogma' series. Which operations, he asks, are the most consistently successful? Those which are *not* urgent. 'And which are the *least* successful operations? Need I answer?' The idea that cancer is the most urgent of diseases to treat, Angell argues, is so ingrained that he cannot ever remember being without it; yet it is 'so hard to justify by the exercise of reason that it just has to be dogma'. But *World Medicine* is unusual. For the most part the medical journals obey the convention which, for many years, Fleet Street also obeyed: dog does not eat dog. As a result it has been possible to lull the profession as a whole into assuming that the campaign for the conquest of cancer is proceeding satisfactorily.

Such outright criticism as there has been has come from lay sources. A disturbing exposure of the profession's self-deceptions has appeared in, of all places, *Penthouse* magazine. In 'The Great Cancer Fraud' consumer-reporters Gary Null and Robert Houston lead off with the bleak statistic that, in spite of all the claims for advances and breakthroughs, in the preceding decade the proportion of people in the United States dying of cancer actually rose from one in six to one in five. Nor could this be attributed to increased life expectation, leaving more people cancer-prone, as it was in fact a little lower in the 1970s than it had been in the 1960s.

Null and Houston put part of the blame on the media for slavishly swallowing the line put out by the medical establishment – the American Medical Association, the drug industry, and the cancer fund-raising bodies. In order to demolish counter-attractions offered by the purveyors of alternative forms of cancer therapy, the media have not merely lent support to the establishment in its violent and often unscrupulous campaigns against them; they have also permitted a protracted cover-up of the failure of orthodox methods. And what makes the cover-up even more disturbing, indeed horrifying, is that the need to pretend that conventional methods give good results has perpetuated forms of treatment which are cruel as well as useless: directly, as in the case of mastectomy; indirectly, as in the case of the side-effects of radiotherapy and cytotoxic drugs. Even if it were eventually to be demonstrated that early detection and treatment along conventional lines can prolong survival by a few weeks – and on balance, it cannot be for much longer than that, or the improvement would already be reflected in the mortality statistics – it is questionable whether this should be counted as time gained.

There is also the cost: billions upon billions, spent by patients, by their relatives and by the taxpayer. 'Conventional medicine is costly,' Levitt and Guralnick point out; 'a cancer patient can expect to spend between $20,000 and $100,000 for a full course of proven treatments.' If they *were* proven, individuals or their families could feel the expenditure is justified, but to use that term in this context is extraordinary.

The cancer specialists have continued to justify themselves by pretending that they are winning the campaign. A massive industry has been built up and sustained on the hopes, and the funds, raised on the strength of successive impending breakthroughs. And the flow of propaganda designed to persuade the public that the war on cancer is being won has continued unabated. Vincent Devita, appointed by President Carter to head the National Cancer Institute, claimed in 1980 that to call the Nixon programme a failure was 'quite wrong'; and he unleashed a string of statistics of the all-too-familiar kind, consistently misleading since not derived from properly controlled trials.

*Cancer Research*

Such confidence has no justification. Cancer research has a record of conspicuous failure even sadder than research in cardiology. This is partly because so much effort has been put into the exploration of what is now coming to be accepted as a blind alley: the search for a cancer virus, or viruses. Hopes have periodically been raised by 'breakthroughs', as when Albert Sabin, who had earlier introduced the vaccine against polio, claimed he had found a link between human cancer and the herpes virus. But nobody else could reproduce his findings, not even Sabin himself, as he had later to admit.

The virologists' stranglehold (as their critics think of it) on research has been seriously challenged only by the immunologists. 'I am convinced,' Paul Ehrlich had written in 1909, 'that during development and growth malignant cells arise extremely frequently, but that in the majority of people they remain latent due to the protective action of the host.' Immunity was not the result of the body's action against germs, but was 'determined purely by cellular factors', weakening, Ehrlich thought, in older people. Not until nearly half a century later did Sir Macfarlane Burnet, winner of a Nobel prize for his work in immunology, formally challenge the medical profession, on immunology's behalf, to face the need for a fundamental re-direction of research. 'The understanding and control of cancer,' he asserted, 'is the most urgent problem of medicine today.' It would not be understood or controlled so long as the whole bias of research was reductionist, concentrating on the behaviour of cancer cells themselves, rather than on finding out what went wrong with the body's auto-immune system, allowing or encouraging the cells' misbehaviour.

At the time, Burnet's plea made little impact; the virologists were too well entrenched. But the cracking of the genetic code by Francis Crick and James Watson meant that the idea of cancer as the consequence of a breakdown of auto-immunity, genetically pro-grammed, had to be taken seriously. The immunologists went to war, with Watson deriding the reductionist cancer research of the time as 'scientifically bankrupt, therapeutically wasteful and ineffective', and Burnet claiming that an unbiased survey of virology's results up to the 1970s would show them to be 'a major disappointment'. Every pathologist, he thought, and every academically-minded physician must be aware that 'a steadily growing number of sub-acute and chronic diseases are being spoken of as auto-immune', and he was in no doubt that cancer would be shown to be one of them. In 1974 Graham Currie of the Chester Beatty Research Institute went further;

there was already abundant evidence, he claimed, for 'an important role of specific immunological reaction in the natural history of tumours'.

How far was this simply another manifestation of the way in which researchers' wishes are fathers to their hopes? A survey that year, in the *New England Journal of Medicine* of the results achieved by the immunologists showed that they, too, had been disappointing. And by this time the environmentalists were beginning to make themselves heard. The design of the medical model, they argued, had been at fault: cancer is most commonly caused by carcinogenic substances in the air, or in food and drink.

*Environmentalism*

The environmentalists' John the Baptist was Perceval Pott, the British surgeon who two centuries before had noted that the 'climbing boys' employed by chimney sweeps were particularly susceptible to cancer of the scrotum. Periodically since that time cancer links had been discovered with substances used in industrial processes, and the effects of radiation had come to be better understood. In the 1950s the statistical link between cigarette smoking and lung cancer was established, and by the 1970s there was growing concern about carcinogens in manufacturing processes, in household goods, and in food preservatives. Tests on laboratory animals revealed that a great many substances in common use, from cyclamates to saccharin, could produce tumours, and epidemiological studies began to suggest that the western world's unbalanced diet might be a risk factor in cancer, as well as in heart disease.

By 1977 the idea that cancer might be primarily environmental in its origins had begun to attract more attention, particularly in the USA, largely because of a growing realisation that the Nixon campaign, designed as it had been for political ends, had failed to ask the right questions about how the funds collected could best be spent. There had been a shake-up, too, at the top: Rauscher, who had been the campaign's commander-in-chief, had left the National Cancer Institute to become vice-president of the charitably-funded American Cancer Society; he was succeeded by Arthur Upton, a New York pathologist who had already opposed some of the promotional enterprises of his predecessor. 'We are in the midst of a revolution in the way the scientific community identifies carcinogens,' the Director of the US National Institute for Environmental Health Sciences told an international conference of cancer researchers in Lyons that autumn. As with heart disease, the revolution was largely the consequence of the results of epidemiological studies. Estimates of the extent to which these carcinogens could be blamed for the incidence of the disease varied, but there was general agreement at the conference, organised by the International Agency for Research on Cancer, that they could be held responsible for the majority of cases.

Even if this were accepted, though, a long delay would ensue before the responsibility could be sorted out between the carcinogens. The delay between exposure and symptoms – sometimes up to forty years – 'often makes it scientifically impossible', the US Occupational Health and Safety Administration had warned, 'to identify carcinogens in the atmosphere', or, for that matter, in the diet. And difficult though it was going to be to identify individual carcinogens, it would be even harder to detect them if, say, two substances not in themselves carcinogenic could become so in combination. Nor would it be possible to hold prospective, as distinct from retrospective, trials on human subjects without running into ethical problems; and opinion was divided over the extent to which trials with laboratory animals (apart from any ethical objections to them, too) could give results which would be valid for man.

The claims of the environmentalists have consequently posed little threat to established forms of research or treatment. They may even have had some responsibility for a rapprochement between the virologists, the molecular biologists and the immunologists, who have a common interest in keeping their research empires going, and if possible expanding.

'I have a feeling,' George McGovern told the directors of the National Institute of Health and the National Cancer Institute, in 1978, when they were giving evidence to a senate committee, 'that we are losing the war on cancer because of mistaken priorities and mis-allocation of funds.' McGovern's chief concern was that the managers of the research funds had poured them into laboratories, while declining to support projects designed to discover carcinogenic substances in the atmosphere or in the national diet. By this time, he pointed out, there was serious public concern about saccharin and food preservatives; 'but we have a National Cancer Institute which spends only *one per cent* of its budget on the diet-cancer relationship, when approximately one half of all cancers may be diet-related'. The Director of the National Cancer Institute hastened to reassure him: the funds for research in that field were to be increased – to *two per cent* of the total. He could hardly have given a clearer indication of the way in which research funds in the United States have been swallowed up by the cancer specialists and the scientists under their wing, leaving the crumbs to the investigators of possible environmental and psychosocial risk factors.

The British people have been no better served. Surveying the projects funded by the Cancer Research Campaign and the Imperial Cancer Research Fund, the *British Medical Journal* has commented that prevention plays a minute part in their activities; less than two per cent. 'Should not the public have more say,' the editorial concluded, 'on how the money is to be spent?' But how is the public to be given the opportunity? Like the Heart Foundation, the major cancer charities are largely controlled by specialists. Naturally they favour projects which help them in their hospital work, providing them with better-equipped operating theatres, improved radiotherapy machines, more powerful drugs. 'The generals in the war on cancer come from the ranks of surgery, biochemistry, radiology and virology,' Dan Greenberg pointed out in his 1974 *Science and Government Report.* 'Their training and inclination is to carry on with what they have been doing ever since they began their careers.'

What some charities have been doing is empire-building. By the late 1970s the American Cancer Society had assets of over $200m, and an income of around $150m. Of this income, fifty-six per cent went on administration (some of the executives pulling in up to $75,000 a year); and less than thirty per cent on research, two-thirds of it supporting institutions with which the Society's directors are affiliated. The Society's overriding concern, after fund raising, is to avoid being accused of lending support to any research of which the medical establishment disapproves – a policy which has led the Society's science editor to resign, after twenty-five years' service, from exasperation at the way it resolutely 'closes the door on innovative ideas'.

Since they have attracted influential people as patrons, the fundraising organisations have been able to escape serious investigation. When Edward Heath became Prime Minister in 1970 he decided to hold an inquiry into cancer research, but he entrusted it to a man who had long been the scientific establishment's go-between with the state, Lord Zuckerman. Zuckerman's report, published in 1972, was anodyne. Conventional research, he had to admit, had failed to produce results, but this was nobody's fault. The cash was there, the facilities were available, the scientists were hard at work; the problem was simply a shortage of fresh ideas.

In reality there were plenty of fresh ideas in search of sponsors, but they had been systematically blocked, often unseen, by the cancer charities. A typical example was a project designed to explore the evolutionary aspects of cell proliferation. In the 1950s a London surgeon, Douglas Lang Stevenson, began to investigate the possibility that cancer is a throwback, in evolutionary terms, to the process by which a lizard which has lost its tail grows a new one. Could it be, he wondered, that the shock of the loss of the tail is the trigger which sets off the growth of its replacement? And if so, might not the susceptibility of humans to cancer represent a misguided throw back to the earlier evolutionary device?

This tied in with the results of experiments conducted half a century before by the Danish researcher Johannes Fibiger. Fibiger noticed that some tumours in rats contained a parasite, and by careful experiments he ascertained that the two were linked, a discovery for which he was eventually awarded a Nobel prize. But as Bernard Dixon has shown, in a defence of his findings, Fibiger's work was misunderstood. He did not claim that the parasite caused the cancer; it was the irritation which the parasite caused that was responsible. And this idea was soon to be confirmed by the research which showed that, although coal tar was not in itself carcinogenic, tumours could be induced if it were rubbed into laboratory animals' ears.

Stevenson surmised that certain traumatic episodes might, for humans, be the equivalent of the irritation – or of the shock which prompted lizards to renew their tails. What was needed, he argued, was research which would relate this to the observations of so many eminent authorities, from Astley Cooper to Heneage Ogilvie, to find whether such a link could be established, and to use the better understanding of the cancer process which it would provide. If he had put up a proposal for an investigation of the effects of shock on tumour development in laboratory animals he would have had no difficulty in securing funds, but because he wanted to investigate the effects of stress on humans, often in unquantifiable forms, he stood no chance. An official of one of the cancer charities who was sent copies of his papers, some already published in medical journals, declined even to submit them for formal consideration, on the ground that Stevenson's work was unscientific, and although Stevenson was awarded the Lawson Tait Memorial Prize, given for work of outstanding significance conducted without the use of living animals, the main cancer charities took no interest.

That Zuckerman had found no fresh ideas was consequently not surprising. His report referred to research into possible environmental causes of cancer, such as pollution, only in passing; psychosocial research did not even rate a mention, and he was able blandly to conclude that, even if additional resources were made available, these could not be effectively spent. As a result, cancer research has remained confined largely to wards and laboratories.

Even on that level, according to a report in 1979 by Helen Tate, a statistician working for the Medical Research Council, it has been incompetently managed. There have been too many projects on too small a scale for their results to be trustworthy; too much unnecessary duplication; too great a concentration on the rarer forms of cancer. No clearing-house has been established to collect and sort out the accumulating information. 'Miss Tate and her colleagues,' in the *Lancet*'s view, 'have exposed a situation which can only be called a disgrace.'

The *Lancet*'s own prescription, though, were it to be followed – multi-centre co-operative trials in an attempt to get results by 'testing different combinations of drugs and radiotherapy' – could produce even worse consequences. They would be extremely expensive, and they would also be open-ended, because of the limitless number of permutations. As if realising its error, the *Lancet* back-tracked two weeks later. Given virtually unlimited funds to spend on cancer, an editorial speculated, *first* thoughts might suggest the setting up of multi-disciplinary units and specialist centres, with research facilities. But 'funds spent on these', it had to admit, 'are unlikely to lead to any fundamentally new insight into cancer problems'. More attention should instead be paid to research into environmental factors and stress.

That the *Lancet* should have presented these two opposing views editorially is the measure of the existing confusion. So long as the destination of research funds, whether provided by the taxpayer or through charities, is settled by the cancer specialists, there is no prospect of any substantial switch of resources to prevention away from the ward and the laboratory. Where it is pointed out that recent research had done nothing for patients suffering from the commoner forms of cancer, the reply will continue to be that it will eventually pay off (molecular processes are being 'magnificently elucidated', as Victor Richards has put it in *The Wayward Cell: Cancer*. 'No quick or glamorous cure for cancer has emerged from this brilliant work, but the foundation on which eventual solutions will be built has been immeasurably broadened').

Tests with laboratory animals will continue, in spite of the growing realisation that, although they may occasionally throw up clues of the kind which Fibiger followed up, they are rarely in themselves of help in understanding human cancer. 'It has to be said, painful though this may be,' Paul Strickland of the London Radium Institute admitted in 1977, 'that conclusions derived from experimental systems under laboratory conditions and using animal tumours are almost totally irrelevant to our understanding of human breast cancer.' They have shown no more relevance, he might have added, to any of the other common forms of cancer. Although the last two decades have seen a great expansion in the exploration of the molecular biology of tumour viruses in animals, Professor W. H. Jarrett of the Glasgow Veterinary School has pointed out in *Nature*, encouraging 'the development of new concepts and the unravelling of previously unsuspected cellular mechanisms' and enabling techniques to be devised to control cancer in the laboratory and the farmyard, none of them has been found to be relevant to the problems posed by the common human cancers.

Investigators who have seen colleagues win Nobel prizes by laboratory research, however, cannot be expected to accept that their work with animals, though it may contribute to advancing the frontiers of knowledge, may be without relevance to the problems raised by the disease in man. They will continue to research on the same lines as long as they are allowed to. The reply from the Imperial Cancer Research Fund to the *British Medical Journal*'s criticisms has made it clear that no change of policy is contemplated; it has simply echoed Zuckerman's belief that there are not enough relevant worth-while projects outside the conventional range. It even asks, innocently, 'How does one predict which area is relevant?' To guess which areas will continue to be considered 'relevant' by the Imperial Cancer Research Fund presents no difficulty; its management will continue to fund only the projects which the cancer specialists recommend.

There will, of course, be occasional grudging concessions to public opinion, as there have been with regard to research into environmental carcinogens. Here, the cancer charities have evolved an ingenious let-out. They now concede that the cause of cancer may sometimes be environmental, and support a handful of projects in this field. But they argue that as so many carcinogenic substances have now been identified, satisfactory prevention will hardly be practicable, and this provides them with the excuse not to switch more of their funds to such research.

In one sense this can be justified. Cairns makes the point that with the exception of lung cancer, all the commoner forms of cancer have been known since before the present century, and 'in the United States there has been little change in the incidence and death rate from cancer as a whole in the last thirty years, during which time the annual production of pesticides, synthetic rubber and plastics (three of the products most commonly indicted for carcinogenicity) has risen more than 100-fold'. Cairns does not dispute that such products may in the future be shown to cause cancer, but he does not think that they should be made scapegoats today.

This, however, simply reinforces the idea that carcinogens are not necessarily carcinogenic in themselves, and that cancer follows as a consequence of some as yet undiscovered interaction of the carcinogen with its host, just as it requires irritation as well as parasites or coal tar to induce tumours in laboratory animals. What, then, is the missing ingredient?

There is one obviously important clue. Cancer is not in fact a juggernaut, proceeding relentlessly to destroy the victim. Some cancers have a lower survival-rate than others, but none has a hundred per cent fatality rate. In other words, some forces must be at work within certain individuals which afford them a measure of protection. One possibility is that, as in heart disease, predisposition plays a part. To some extent it would be genetic, but it could also be influenced by psychosocial factors, much as somebody who is genetically heart-attack-prone is more likely to succumb if he is a 'Type A', and if he is put under severe stress. What, then, is the evidence for psychosocial factors in cancer?

## Cancer and Personality

The idea that cancer is brought on by worry and grief dates back to classical times, and it has often been confirmed by observation. Among the commonest causes of breast cancer, Sir Astley Cooper, the leading London surgeon of his time, remarked in 1845, are grief and anxiety. 'Much has been written on the influence of mental misery, sudden reverses of fortune, and habitual gloominess of temper on the deposition of carcinomatous matter,' W. H. Walshe wrote in his treatise on cancer the following year. 'If systematic writers can be credited, these constitute the most powerful form of the disease.' It had never been demonstrated, Walshe admitted, that mental disquiet was the cause, but that the two were often found together was undeniable. 'I have myself met with cases in which the connection appeared so clear that I decided questioning its reality would have seemed a struggle against reason.'

In his lectures to students at the Royal College of Surgeons a few years later, James Paget, although admitting that he was talking of a general impression for which he could not provide factual evidence, emphasised the significance of mental distress in connection with cancer. 'I do not at all suppose that it could of itself generate a cancerous condition of the blood, or that a joyous temper and prosperity are a safeguard against cancer; but the cases are so frequent in which deep anxiety, deferred hope and disappointment are quickly followed by the growth or increase of cancer that we can hardly doubt that mental depression is a weighty addition to the other influences that favour the development of the cancerous constitution.'

And in 1885 the American surgeon Willard Parker expressed the view that there were 'the strongest physiological reasons for believing that great mental depression, particularly grief, induces a predisposition to such a disease as cancer, or becomes an exciting cause under circumstances where the predisposition has already been acquired'.

By that time, however, it was considered heretical to attribute organic disease to emotional disturbance. The most that was allowed was that 'nerves' might be involved. As late as 1925 the *British Medical Journal* accepted that nervous influence must indirectly be regarded as of great importance in the production of cancer. But the belief was growing that cancer must have a single causal agent, probably a virus, and although doctors continued to observe that patients who had 'the will to live' might survive longer than those who 'turned their faces to the wall', this was not considered to be of much significance for the purposes of research into the origins of the disease. Even those doctors who preached the psychosomatic theory – Georg Groddeck, Wilhelm Reich, Flanders Dunbar – applied it to cancer more cautiously than to other disorders, and the first major textbook of the subject, Weiss and English's *Psychosomatic Medicine*, referred only to the emotional problems of patients after they had been diagnosed as having cancer.

From time to time, however, signs of dissatisfaction with the prevailing orthodoxy were apparent. In 1957 Sir Heneage Ogilvie, Consulting Surgeon at Guy's Hospital and editor of the *Practitioner*, put forward the startling proposition that medical science should cease to look for the answer to the question 'Why do so many of us get cancer after the age of 48?' and concentrate on the real problem: 'We all have cancer at 48. What is the force that keeps it in check in the great majority of us?' From his own observation, Ogilvie had come to a conclusion which he presented in the form of an aphorism – though, as Paget had done, he admitted he had no factual evidence to back it. 'The happy man never gets cancer.' In his experience the instances where the onset of cancer 'followed almost immediately on some disaster, a bereavement, the break-up of a relationship, a financial crisis, or an accident, are so numerous that they suggest that some controlling force that has hitherto kept this outbreak in check has been removed' – an echo of 'Dr Thomas', musing about cancer in W. H. Auden's 'Miss Gee':

> Nobody knows what the cause is
> Though some pretend they do.
> Its like some hidden assassin
> Waiting to strike at you.
>
> Childless women get it
> And men when they retire.
> It's as if there had to be some outlet
> For their foiled creative fire.

Isolated attempts were being made to test this hypothesis. In 1952 some disciples of Franz Alexander in Chicago reported that, in a study of forty cases of breast cancer, among the major psychosocial characteristics were sexual repression and an inability to express and discharge pent-up feelings of hostility. And from the records of personality tests on people who had subsequently died of cancer, a New York doctor, Lawrence LeShan, and a research psychologist, Richard Worthington, reported three years later that they had found 'startling similarities in their personality configurations and in their life histories'. Four features constantly recurred: the loss of an important relationship prior to the development of the tumour; the inability to express emotions success- fully; unresolved tensions concerning a parental figure; and sexual dis- turbances.

The next step was to check these retrospective findings with living cancer patients, and the Ayer Foundation agreed to provide the neces- sary funds. But no hospital or research centre in New York would allow LeShan to talk to cancer patients, even with their consent. He had to find individual patients on his own, a laborious task, and for the next fourteen years he used whatever opportunity arose to take case-histories of their lives and life-styles. These confirmed the earlier findings – in particular, that the onset of cancer frequently occurred following the loss of some important emotional relationship. There also, he found, appeared to be some connection between the personality-types of cancer patients and the duration of their survival between the cancer diagnosis and death.

Surprisingly, in 1959 LeShan's paper was accepted for publication by the *Journal of the National Cancer Institute*, which had shown no inclina- tion to include such heresies before; perhaps because 1959 was a time of self-doubt in medical circles, when for the first time for many years the physician's and the surgeon's methods came under worried scrutiny, notably in Dubos's *Mirage of Health*. That year, in his presidential address to the American Cancer Society, Eugene Pendergrass echoed Ogilvie's opinion. Pendergrass had seen how cancer patients might remain well for years following treatment; 'then an emotional stress, such as the death of a son in World War II, the infidelity of a daughter-in- law or the burden of long unemployment seem to have been precipitat- ing factors in the reactivation of their disease which then resulted in death.' There was solid evidence that the course of disease in general was affected by emotional stress: in the search for ways of controlling tumour growth, therefore, it was his hope 'that we can widen the quest to include the distinct possibility that within one's mind is a power capable of exerting forces which can either enhance or inhibit the progress of this disease'.

But how could research provide evidence of a personality component in cancer, of a kind which would be accepted as scientific? Sir Julian Huxley had pointed the way: if there were a genetic basis for psychosomatic differences, he had written in his *Biological Aspects of Cancer* (1958), a psychosomatic component was predictable. It was left to the behaviourist Professor Hans Eysenck to follow up the clue, his research establishing the existence of a difference in proneness to cancer between extroverts and introverts.

## Kissen and the Psychological Factor

Another researcher was exploring the territory by a different route: the Glasgow physician David Kissen, who ran the only unit in Britain specifically designated to undertake psychosomatic research. His interest in the subject had been aroused during research into the possible relationship of emotional stress to the onset of TB, in the course of which he had investigated the effects of smoking, not simply because it could be an alternative explanation, but also because he thought that smoking might prove to be part of 'the emotional configuration of the tuberculous', as he put it. In a trial with two groups, one consisting of TB patients who had suffered a relapse, the other of TB patients who had not, Kissen found there was no difference in their smoking habits. But with the help of a questionnaire Kissen confirmed LeShan's findings: there were significantly more cigarette smokers among those in the fifteen-to-twenty-four age group who had had emotionally stressful experiences before the onset of their TB, and TB patients in general who reported such stressful experiences smoked appreciably more than those who had none to report. The link, in other words, was not just between smoking and relapse, but between smoking coupled with an emotional stress factor and relapse.

Might this not also be true of lung cancer cases? Kissen provided patients attending chest clinics in three hospitals with a questionnaire, to be filled in before diagnosis. They were asked, among other things, for information about earlier illnesses, particularly in childhood; about recent emotional problems of a kind which had occasioned stress, and about how they handled such problems. After they had been diagnosed they were divided into two groups: 161 patients with lung cancer; 174 controls. The patients with lung cancer, Kissen found, had had more childhood illnesses, and a significantly higher proportion of them 'admitted to a conscious tendency to conceal or bottle up emotional difficulties'. Summing up the results of his research in 1964, Kissen suggested that, if the view were accepted that lung cancer has a number of risk factors, including both exposure to cigarette smoke and a particular personality type, 'it would appear that *the poorer the outlet for emotional discharge, the less the exposure to cigarette smoke required to induce lung cancer*'.

Kissen went on to ask if ways could be found to apply the knowledge gained from his research to help people to avoid lung cancer? People with cancer-prone personalities, he suggested, should be helped to break the smoking habit, and to be on the safe side they might contemplate moving from town to country, to reduce the impact of urban carcinogens. But it would also be a valuable exercise if a study could be made of cancer patients in general who had been treated for the disease, to see whether any form of psychological after-care improved the chances of survival – care which, he pointed out, could in any case be valuable, by helping patients to handle the emotional problems which arose as a result of the diagnosis and the treatment.

Up to this point Kissen's and LeShan's research had attracted little attention in the leading medical journals, and when, in 1963, the New York Academy of Sciences sponsored a conference on 'unusual forms and aspects of cancer', the psychosomatic aspect was not among the subjects listed for discussion. Kissen wrote to the Executive Director of the Academy, Eunice Thomas Miner, suggesting that the omission had been unfortunate because the opportunity had been missed 'to draw the attention of scientists and clinicians to this important but much neglected area'. Surprisingly, he did not receive the usual rebuff or polite evasions; Miner tactfully replied that the subject was sufficiently important in its own right to merit a separate conference, which was duly held. In 1965 the publication of the proceedings in the Academy's *Annals*, and of Eysenck's meticulously-documented *Smoking, Health and Personality*, made it difficult for the medical establishment to ignore the issue any longer.

Eysenck did not deny that there might be a carcinogenic element in cigarette smoking, but he provided a mass of evidence to show just how flimsy the grounds had been for jumping to the conclusion that the connection must be causal. If it were, why should nine heavy smokers out of ten survive into old age without contracting lung cancer? 'Cigarette smoking is neither a necessary nor a sufficient cause of lung cancer,' he concluded. He was not even certain that it was a contributory cause; on his reading of the evidence, the more likely culprit was atmospheric pollution.

Eysenck's case was not welcomed by the medical establishment; still less was the implication that the missing link might be psychological. Yet the evidence could not lightly be dismissed. The National Institute of Mental Health gave a grant to George L. Engel, Professor of Medicine and Psychiatry at Rochester University in New York, to study the relationship of emotional stresses to the onset of cancer and other illness, and newspapers began to publish articles on the subject. 'Could the mind be a cause of cancer?' the medical correspondent of *The Times* inquired; scientists might still scoff at the idea, 'but the wise clinician is studying it with sympathy and interest'. Even the *Lancet* unbent sufficiently to take a respectful look at Kissen's findings, concluding that, although it might be premature to accept them, it was important that the investigation should continue: 'in our state of ignorance about the origins of cancer we cannot afford to disregard them.'

Unluckily, Kissen himself could not continue his research. Although he contributed papers to the New York meeting, he was not well enough to attend, and his death in 1968 at the age of fifty-two removed a man whose 'precision of methodology and objectivity', as the *Medical Officer* had described it a few months earlier, had won the respect even of those who felt uneasy about his excursions into little-explored psychosomatic territory. Kissen had done his best to make clear that, when he used the term psychosomatic, he used it with precision. Psychosomatic, he always insisted, implied an *interaction* of the psychological and the physical; it did not mean that the psychological *caused* the physical for which 'psychogenic' was the correct term. The two co-existed, having varying degrees of importance in different types of illness and in different individuals. Kissen wanted to emphasise this, he explained in his paper to the New York conference, 'because it has been my experience in discussions of psychosomatic topics with some physicians, and even with some psychiatrists, to find hostility to the psychosomatic approach in the mistaken belief that the absence of, or minimal references to, somatic factors imply a denigration of somatic factors in favour of the psychological. It is important that such misconceptions should be cleared up.'

But they were not cleared up – again, largely because the structure of the medical profession made such clarification difficult. Cancer specialists had been taught that the mind and the emotions played no part in the process by which cancer began, or spread, a view they continued to teach their students. They rarely saw evidence in their specialist journals which might upset their preconceptions, and where such evidence was referred to, as in the *Lancet*, it was invariably accompanied by a warning about the need for further research. With few exceptions, such as Ogilvie and Pendergrass, cancer specialists tended to be temperamentally immune to ideas of the kind which Kissen's work prompted. They might still be prepared to accept the possibility that the 'will to live' could delay the inevitable termination, but they could not see what they, as specialists, could do, other than give reassurance (whatever that might mean) to help prolong the survival period. And even if they were prepared to accept the possibility that a cancer-prone personality existed, they could claim that the concern rested not with them but with the psychiatrists. Soon after Kissen's death, his unit ceased to function as a separate entity.

His findings, however, have since been confirmed. In 1975 H. S. Greer, a psychiatrist at King's College Hospital in London, reported

that, using the Kissen technique of giving personality tests before
diagnosis to women with breast tumours, and then dividing them into
two groups according to whether the tumours were found to be malignant or benign, he had found that two-thirds of the cancer patients had
described themselves as controlling their emotions, some to an extreme
extent – 'never, or not more than once or twice in adult lives, have they
openly shown anger'; whereas only a third of the control group were in
this category. Yet so little attention did such work receive that when, in
1976, a symposium was held in New York on ways by which cancer might
be prevented, papers on research projects along similar lines were a
novelty – this being the reaction to the paper from Claus and Marjorie
Bahnson of Jefferson Medical College, Pennsylvania. At the earlier
New York conference they had described 'repeated findings that cancer
patients tend to deny and repress conflictual impulses and emotions, to a
higher degree than do other people'; now, they reported that they had
been able correctly to identify which patients had, and which did not
have, cancer, in eighty per cent of cases, simply by examining the
answers the group had given to a questionnaire about their life experiences and emotional problems.

If epidemiological research had revealed that, say, two out of three of
a group of cancer patients had had a lifetime preference for tea at
breakfast, while two-thirds of the controls had always drunk coffee,
work would have immediately begun to isolate the carcinogen in tea-
leaves. Research into cancer-prone personalities offered no such prospects, and the prejudice remained against psychosomatic research as
such – as Theodore Miller noted in his James Ewing Lecture to the
Society of Surgical Oncology in New York in 1977. When he had
mentioned to his wife that he proposed to talk about psycho-
physiological aspects of cancer, Miller – Professor of Surgery at
Cornell – told his audience, her reaction had been to warn him that he
'had better not go around saying that cancer is a psychosomatic disease',
and he was well aware that 'trying to convince the members of this
society that cancer has a psychosomatic basis would be like trying to
convert a bunch of lions to a life of vegetarianism'. Nevertheless he had
found a couple of hundred references in the medical literature to the
relationship of personality and the emotions to tumour growth, and
because he had himself realised that only patients who were optimistic
about their prospects benefited from surgery, he would no longer operate on any patient 'who expresses the fear that he would not survive
the operation'. He had also found that recurrence of cancer often
followed a year or so after some emotional crisis. The influence of the
psyche on cancer might not yet be scientifically proved, he admitted, and

93

he was careful to point out that the influence was not necessarily exercised by some abstract ghost-in-the-machine creating the cancer: the psychosomatic effects could be connected with hormonal activity. However it might operate, 'we have enough evidence to warrant further investigation and application, both in the laboratory and in the clinic'.

As Miller had realised, what was remarkable about the evidence for a cancer-prone personality type was its consistency, whether its source was a life-time of observation or epidemiological research. Summing it up in 1977 Kenneth Pelletier, Director of the Psychosomatic Medicine Center at Gladman Memorial Hospital in Berkeley, California, listed the most common emotional risk factors: a severe disturbance in childhood, leading to a sense of loss and insecurity, and a subsequent disposition to bottle up feelings – particularly of hostility. In middle life, such people might achieve healthy relationships, fall in love, and enjoy a stable marriage; often they are regarded by their friends 'as exceptionally fine, thoughtful, gentle, uncomplaining people'. But when their stability is again threatened, by marital or work problems, the death of a spouse or retirement, the old self-doubt returns. 'With a high degree of predictability, such individuals are found to succumb to cancer within six months to a year.'

Impressive though Pelletier's documentation was, it had no more effect on the medical profession than had Kissen's pioneering work, and the only attention *that* had received in any of the leading medical journals, Greer lamented in a paper in *Psychological Medicine* in 1979, had been the single *Lancet* editorial thirteen years earlier. His comment at least goaded the *Lancet* to go over the ground again in another editorial, but this time with a difference.

The research in the 1960s had been primarily designed to discover what connection, if any, there might be between personality types, stress-inducing occasions, and cancer. In the 1970s the emphasis had shifted to finding ways to apply the knowledge gained in order to exploit it for prevention and treatment: in particular, seeking to stimulate the imagination along the lines Schultz had pioneered with his form of biofeedback half a century earlier. The 'Simonton husband and wife team', the editorial explained, were trying to stimulate their patients' imaginations, training them 'to picture their tumours being overcome by the body's defences'. A few years earlier, such a notion would have been referred to only to excite derision, but the discoveries in connection with biofeedback, and the subsequent revelations about the influence of the emotions on hormonal and biochemical processes had bred caution.

## Visualisation Therapy

From his experience with cancer patients, and his study of the papers dealing with psychosomatic research, Carl Simonton – radiotherapist at Fort Worth – had similarly come to the conclusion that the most important single factor in the precipitation of cancer was the loss of a significant object – a loved one, a job, even a fantasy. It was not so much the loss itself as the individual's response to it – dictated, to some extent, by the personality of the individual, particularly 'a tendency to resent (that is, a tendency not to forgive), a tendency towards self-pity, and a marked inability to form and maintain meaningful relationships'. Simonton had originally discovered this from his own experience; he had had cancer at the age of seventeen, and had come to realise how closely his personality at the time fitted the pattern which he later found in his patients. So he began to supplement his radiotherapy with a form of treatment he adapted from the techniques of meditation and biofeedback, in ways designed to mobilise resistance to the disease by enlisting the imagination.

The patient would be encouraged to relax; 'then, I have him mentally picture his cancer – picturing it the way it seems to him – and the way he views the treatment: how he sees the body and the body-cells operating against the malignancy, and so on'. A gardener might visualise the cancer cells as slugs or greenfly; a mother, as nits in her children's hair. 'The cancer would be a snake, a wolverine, or some vicious animal,' one of Simonton's patients recalled; 'the cure, white husky dogs by the millions' – a way of visualising the battle between the good and evil cells. The snake would shrink, and finally disappear, 'then the white army of dogs would lick up the residue and clean my abdominal cavity until it was spotless'. Alternatively, the cancer cells could be seen – as they might be by a priest – as souls to be saved, cleansed from sin.

The Simonton method enabled a check to be made on whether visualisation therapy was effective. The system Simonton and his wife Stephanie adopted at the Center was to obtain estimates from five members of the staff of the attitudes of individual patients to their treatment. In a run of 152 consecutive cases, a good response to treatment turned out to be related to positive attitudes; the twenty cases where the clinical response was rated as most satisfactory were all in this positive category, and none of the patients responded badly. The response, too, was good even in cases which, by normal standards, had a poor prognosis. The patient's attitude seemed to be 'at least as important as severity of disease in determining the outcome'.

Other doctors who have tried visualisation therapy – using a variety

of aids to obtain the preliminary relaxation, including autogenic training – have reported similar findings, and, small though the numbers
involved in such trials have been, the consistency of the results lends
confirmation to the idea that the imagination can be harnessed to secure
remission of symptoms, improving the survival-rate. And it could turn
out also to be responsible for some cases of regression, in which cancer
not merely ceases to spread, but retreats, and sometimes disappears
altogether.

In their *Beyond Biofeedback*, Elmer and Alyce Green describe an
example from their own experience. A patient with bladder cancer
which had spread through his body, rendering it futile to operate, turned
out to be a good hypnotic subject, and was given hypnotherapy to
control his pain. One of his doctors decided to try an experiment to find
whether by visualising his brain as a kind of control room and switching
off the appropriate tap, he could influence the course of the disease. Not
merely did he succeed in stopping the blood-flow to the bladder; he also
reported that he could 'see' the tumour contracting, and his health
improved so remarkably that he was able to leave the hospital, returning
only for periodic examinations. Unluckily in the course of one of them
his bladder wall was accidently ruptured, and he died as a result. But an
autopsy showed that the bladder cancer was indeed of the size to which,
he had claimed, he had managed to shrink it, and the metastases around
the rest of his body had disappeared.

### 'Spontaneous Regression'

Cases of this nature, where a cancer which has been diagnosed (sometimes disclosed by surgery) and pronounced inoperable has subsequently not merely ceased to develop, but has even diminished in size or
disappeared, were reported occasionally around the turn of the century.
The reports were sufficiently rare, however, for the belief to grow that
diagnostic error was the simplest explanation: tumours might cease to
grow, for a time, but they could not actually diminish in size. This
attitude was in part a reaction against stories of miracle cancer cures
wrought by healers or peddlers of cures; it was cruel, the argument ran,
to arouse hopes that could not be fulfilled. Nevertheless reports of
regressions continued to appear from time to time, and in 1956 T. C.
Everson and W. H. Cole, investigating some six hundred of them, found
that, although in most cases the evidence was not sufficiently well
documented for a verdict to be reached, in a few of them it was hard to
doubt that regression had occurred.

Possibly endocrine influences were at work, they surmised, or fever; or perhaps surgery had removed the carcinogenic agent. They were careful not to hint at the possibility of psychosocial forces being involved. Their paper was entitled 'Spontaneous Regression of Cancer', and this threw a lifeline to the specialists; henceforth if a patient produced evidence of regression following a visit to a healer – or to one of the establishments which offered special diet or therapy, frowned on by the medical establishment even when doctors were in charge – it could be attributed to coincidence.

Medical scientists, however, remained uneasy: 'spontaneous' was too obvious a let-out. The immunologists had their answer: if tumours represent a breakdown of the body's auto-immune mechanism, regression must mean that it has started to work again. But this only shifted the question back: what switches it on again? They still resisted the idea that the mind might be involved; Sir Macfarlane Burnet included 'psychosocial trauma' along with viruses and industrial pollution among the environmental factors which he did *not* believe caused cancer. His supporters have tended to follow his lead. 'The cause of most cancers in man,' Philip Burch, Professor of Medical Physics at the University of Leeds, has asserted (much to the irritation of those of his colleagues who continue to cling to the assumption that tobacco and/or tobacco smoke are carcinogenic) 'is to be found, not so much in a hostile and inadequately controlled environment, but rather in the intrinsic properties of the biological constitution.'

Suppose, though, that one of the intrinsic properties of the biological constitution is to interact with the hostile and inadequately controlled environment. If so, the imagination may be the intermediary, or catalyst, for the interaction of the genetic endowment with the environmental forces, whatever they may be. It could, for example, lead to unconscious hara kiri, with cancer as the weapon – a possibility that has had to be taken more seriously since the results of a long-term prospective study undertaken from Johns Hopkins Medical School have revealed that the personality configuration of students who contract cancer late in their lives is strikingly similar to that of students who later in their lives commit suicide. But it could also promote recovery, switching the body's auto-immune mechanism on again; this, after all, is what appears to happen in the case of warts.

The issue was not squarely faced within the medical profession until the publication, early in 1980, of a collection of research papers, *Mind and Cancer Prognosis*, edited by Basil Stoll, consultant physician at St Thomas's Hospital. In his preface, Stoll claims for the book that it examines 'the emotional impact of a diagnosis of cancer upon the patient, his methods of coping with the mental stress, and the goals which have been suggested for psychological supportive treatment' – an examination to which cancer specialists can hardly object, except those who flatly refuse to let their patients know they have the disease. But Stoll goes on to say that the book also has an interrogative aspect: to examine the evidence 'for the widespread, but unproven, belief that the attitude of mind of the patient with advanced cancer may, in some cases, accelerate or delay the onset of death'.

Between them, the eighteen contributors to the book – most of them American doctors or scientists, half of them psychiatrists – present evidence from a variety of sources, experimental and anecdotal, supporting the thesis that cancer is, in fact, a product of the breakdown of the body's immunological mechanism; that the trigger can be stress, emotional as well as physiological, and that the human imagination can be employed in various ways to hold up or reverse the process by which cancers ordinarily grow and spread. Stoll and his contributors are at pains not to offend susceptibilities by dogmatic assertions about the role of the mind, and the importance of the role of the hormones is generally emphasised. Still, as George Curtis, Professor of Psychiatry at the University of Michigan, points out, 'awareness has dawned that most, if not all, endocrine systems are responsive to the psychological stimuli'. For immunologists to try to continue to behave as if psychological stimuli are irrelevant is simply unscientific.

In his paper on restraint of growth and spontaneous regression Stoll claims that, although only about twenty cases of spontaneous regression have been reported annually, the accumulating evidence suggests that the incidence is probably 'many hundred times as large', and if a breakdown in auto-immunity is responsible for cancer, 'psychological triggering factors may be involved in some cases, because both immunological and endocrinological changes can be triggered off by cerebral cortical activity'. In view of the fact that 'faith, religiosity and very powerful belief appear to be common factors in many of the patients reported to show spontaneous regression of cancer', and that, in some cases, emotionally uplifting incidents precede remission's onset, 'is it possible,' he asks, 'that mental or emotional factors may be involved in some of the so called "inexplicable" cases of spontaneous regression?'

Cautiously, Stoll does no more than put the question. But on the book's evidence it is at least clear that, as he argues, the notion of 'spontaneous' regression ought to be abandoned. The Australian psychiatrist Ainslie Meares has suggested 'atavistic regression' as an alternative. In certain altered states of consciousness, Meares believes, the mind is liberated to perform its proper controlling function; in a sense it backs down in order to permit the natural homeostasis of the body to take over and set things to rights – if it is not too late. Accordingly his meditation technique is less directed than the Simontons', and more akin to that of the yogi. In a report on over seventy patients, most of whom came to him after they had found that the disease was in an advanced or terminal form, he has described how the great majority of those who were able to come to twenty meditation sessions reported a reduction of pain, some being able to stop taking pain-killing drugs. They also said that their morale was much improved. Around ten per cent of the patients far outlived their specialists' prognosis; and in a further ten per cent there had been a regression of their tumours 'in the absence of any organic treatment which could account for it'.

## Healing

That the mind is capable of exerting such an influence over tumours should not occasion surprise. It has been demonstrated in controlled trials that warts can be got rid of by suggestion in a few days, as well as being a matter of common knowledge in country districts where 'wart-charming' lingers. There have been some well-authenticated cases, too, of some deep psychological or spiritual experience precipitating the regression of cancer. One of them has recently been accepted as miraculous by the Vatican, which is not given, these times, to taking such a decision lightly. In 1965 John Fagan of Easterhouse, Glasgow, was operated on for stomach pains and 'a huge carcinoma' was discovered, with metastases. A further operation the following year showed the cancer was spreading; his wife was instructed in how to provide terminal care, and on 4 March 1967, when the emaciated patient weighed only five stone, his wife was warned that his death was imminent, and he told her that he was ready to die.

Two days later, the doctor visited the Fagan household expecting to sign the death certificate, only to find the patient, who had not taken food for seven weeks, alive, hungry and obviously very much better. A medallion of the Blessed John Ogilvie, a Jesuit executed in 1615 for his faith, and beatified three hundred years later, had been given to Mrs Fagan by the local parish priest and his assistant to pin on her husband's jacket, and they had prayed for him. 'My god,' the doctor was to recall saying, 'It's a miracle' – but he added, 'I didn't mean it! I didn't think, because I don't believe in miracles, but I can't explain this cure.' Whatever the explanation, a gastro-enterologist appointed by the Vatican to investigate the case five years later reported that there was no trace of cancer, and ten years after Fagan had been given up, he was still to all appearances healthy.

Fagan claimed that he had been no more than 'a wishy-washy' Catholic before his cure; Francis Chichester was a man of no religious faith. In *The Lonely Sea and the Sky* Chichester described how in 1957, following a lung X-ray, he was exhibited to a group of medical students by one of the leading surgeons in Britain as 'a typical case of lung carcinoma', and, following a biopsy which confirmed the diagnosis, he was told that one lung would have to be removed. His wife Sheila persuaded him to refuse the operation, took him from the hospital to a nature-cure clinic, and eventually back to their home; she then organised a group to pray for him. In 1960, at the age of fifty-eight, Chichester won the first solo sailing race across the Atlantic.

Although his experience convinced Chichester of the power of prayer, at the time of his recovery 'faith' can hardly have been a decisive factor. Most healers believe that there is a healing force – divine, spiritual, psychic or para-magnetic – which can be directed at a patient; 'distant healing', they assume, can work without the recipient's knowledge. The leading British healer in recent years, Harry Edwards, repeatedly offered to co-operate in a controlled trial, in which the effects of absent healing would be monitored by having two matched groups of cancer patients, one of which would be prayed for, while the other would provide the control group. Edwards was not sure that the healing force could be directed 'blind' in this way, at patients whose identities neither he nor the hospital staff would know (because which group was which would be disclosed only after the test period had finished), but he thought the experiment worth trying, if only in order to prove that he was not averse to his method being tested in ways acceptable to medical science. The idea, however, was not acceptable to the doctors he approached. Either the healing force did not exist, he was repeatedly told, in which case such a trial would be pointless, or it did exist, in which case any doctor involved in it could be struck off the Medical Register for allowing his patients to be treated by a medically-unqualified practitioner.

A similar 'double bind' blocked Edwards's efforts to prove retrospectively that cancer patients had been healed, by comparing the diagnostic reports showing that they had terminal cancer, and the later reports showing that the cancer was no longer there. (In order to prove that they really had had cancer, X-ray photographs and biopsy findings were required. But patients whose cancers had been found in this way ordinarily had been given some form of treatment, and it could be claimed that this must have been responsible for the healing. In one instance the patient's doctor claimed that by a remarkable piece of good luck, the entire cancer must have been removed when the 'smear' was taken for the biopsy.) Where there had been no treatment, there had rarely been indisputable evidence of the cancer, and in the few cases where it was available, 'coincidence' – spontaneous regression – could be invoked.

The removal of the ban on doctors enlisting the help of medically unqualified practitioners left the way open, in the late 1970s, to carry out the kind of trials Edwards had been hoping for, and preliminary results raised his hopes; out of a total of 337 patients who co-operated, only 17, or five per cent, died in the first months of the trial, though in that period the number of deaths predicted by diagnosis was seventy. But Edwards died before the venture was fully established, and it had to be abandoned.

## 'Illness as Metaphor'

Although there is now more willingness to admit the possibility of a psychosomatic component in cancer, if the past is a guide the chances of treatment along the Simontons' lines being accepted as a front-line technique alongside surgery, irradiation and drugs, let alone of displacing any of them, must be considered poor. In this case, it is not only the specialists who are reluctant to accept that the imagination needs to be involved in the prevention and treatment of the disease; it is also the patients. To attribute a heart attack to an over-dynamic personality is one thing; it is much less easy to admit, as Simonton felt bound to do, that cancer may be related to self-pity and an inability to maintain meaningful relationships. And this feeling is accentuated because of cancer's ugly mystique, described by Susan Sontag in her *Illness as Metaphor*.

Sontag's declared aim in the book is to banish the fantasies which have attached themselves to certain illnesses. Cancer, she urges, should be regarded and treated as a disease like any other, purged of the sinister connotations which make it 'not just a lethal disease, but a shameful one'. But she then goes on to reject the psychosomatic interpretation because, she complains, it makes the patient culpable: 'widely-believed psychological theories of disease assign to the luckless ill the ultimate responsibility both for falling ill and for getting well.' Most people who fall ill, certainly, like to think of themselves as unlucky, the victims of mischance. Any suggestion that their illness may be related to an inability to give loose rein to their emotions or, worse, to enjoy happy relationships is unpalatable. But this is not the same as suggesting that

101

they are blameworthy. As David Black puts it, describing the Simontons' theory, 'It is crucial for patients to understand that this new approach to medicine is not a court before which they will be condemned.' A woman with breast cancer has not made herself sick, 'but her sickness is an expression of something more than the activity of a virus, and the problem she faces is to find a less physically compromising way to express her blocked needs or, better yet, to change the situation in which those needs became blocked in the first place'.

Few patients, however, want to accept the responsibility for making such reappraisals. Treatment, they have been conditioned to assume, is for the doctor to prescribe. In any case, often they are not told they have cancer. Not merely do most specialists avoid dealing with their patients' emotional problems; most of them feel justified in lying. In *The Cancer Reference Book* Levitt and Guralnick claim that according to various studies, '77 to 87 per cent of doctors favoured avoiding the truth.' The practical consequences, they point out, can be unfortunate, as when a patient does not put his affairs in order because he has no idea that he is soon going to die. But it also deprives patients of the possibility of trying alternative therapies which, even when they do not appreciably increase the survival time, could at least help to make their last weeks more serene.

'I've never told a patient he or she had cancer,' a writer claimed in *World Medicine* in 1977, 'and I never will. I don't care tuppence about their affairs.' He was answered a few months later by Phyllis Shaw, senior research psychiatrist at an Oxford hospital. At the time she read the article, she had just been told she had bowel cancer, with metastases in the liver. She went home, prepared for the problems with which as a psychiatrist she was already familiar. 'I was, however, unprepared for the amazing experiences which were to follow, and I can only describe as spiritual, although I am not a member of any church.' The outcome had been banishment of fear and sadness, a closer, more loving relationship with family and friends. Considering this, she asked, 'What right has any mere human being to deprive another of the opportunity to work through the sort of experience that I have had?' And when she died, not long afterwards, a friend wrote to confirm that she could not have preserved her dignity, in view of the ravages of her illness, 'had she not at all times been kept fully aware of her condition'.

# Prospects

For a doctor not to disclose to patients that they have cancer is hard to justify; not to tell them if they want to know the truth is surely inexcusable. The fact that secrecy is so often maintained, however, is itself a symptom of the structural disorder from which the medical profession suffers. In a sense, the development of specialisation is itself cancerous, leading as it does to a proliferation of what are largely self-governing cells.

In theory, there has been nothing to prevent a cancer specialist from telling patients that, in view of the manifest failure of conventional methods, they would be well advised to refuse surgery, irradiation and drugs, and try some alternative therapy which at least will do them no harm. In practice, specialisation has blocked any such development. Eminent consultants who have recognised the importance of the emotions in connection with cancer have not had the training to supplant or supplement orthodox treatment with, say, psychotherapy, and a consultant who referred cancer patients to a psychiatrist or a clinical psychologist would be regarded by his colleages as mad himself.

Few cancer specialists have even been aware of the findings of pioneers such as LeShan, Kissen, Meares and the Simontons, rarely referred to in the leading medical journals, even more rarely in specialist journals. Textbooks on the subject have either dismissed them in a paragraph or two or ignored them altogether. Levitt and Guralnick's *Cancer Reference Book*, though in other respects it lives up to its sub-title's claim that it gives 'direct and clear' answers to the questions which people ask about cancer (for the most part very sensible answers), devotes only two of its two hundred and fifty pages to possible psychological links, in the section 'unproven methods of treatment'; the reader is left unaware of the results of recent research in this field. And Cairns's *Cancer: Science and Society*, though it provides an admirable survey of other aspects of cancer, does not even mention a psychosomatic component.

Research, too, has come to be identified with randomised controlled trials, and forms of treatment which depend for their effectiveness on subjective reactions of patients to their doctor or psychotherapist or the members of their group cannot easily be subjected to controls. This applies even to tests of the drugs which periodically win a following as cancer 'cures', the most recent being Laetrile, a substance manufactured from apricot kernels, which has been a source of violent controversy over the past decade. If the influence of the imagination on the body's chemistry is accepted, it is difficult to reject the hypothesis that the

103

imagination may also affect the performance of certain drugs – not just in a general way, through placebo effect, but through specific inter- actions, perhaps even of the kind the ancients believed in, when they prescribed incantations to accompany their herbal remedies.

This remains speculative; what cannot now be disputed is that the imagination may exert an influence on all forms of treatment, and consequently ought to be considered in all research. The leading medi- cal journals have not been entirely unaware of this need in the past. If the malignancy of a tumour is related to factors of host resistance, the *British Medical Journal* observed editorially in 1965, 'it might be fruitful to spend more time studying the metabolic, immunological and psy- chological responses of the patient'. But medical journals have no say in the distribution of research funds, and those who control them still show little enthusiasm for investigations of the psychosocial element, in spite of the fact that the few research projects which have managed to attract sufficient funds to finance controlled trials have continued to provide confirmatory evidence.

The results of a prospective multi-disciplinary trial conducted by Greer and colleagues at King's College Hospital, published in the *Lancet* in 1979, have shown that 'recurrence-free survival was signifi- cantly more common among patients who had initially reacted to cancer by denial, or who had a fighting spirit, than among patients who had responded with stoic acceptance or feelings of helplessness and hope- lessness'. Patrick Dattore and colleagues from Kansas University have described how they made personality assessments of 200 patients, and later compared the 75 who had developed cancer with the 125 who had not; a significantly larger number of patients in the cancer group, it transpired, had been identified in their personality assessments as people who repressed their emotional conflicts even to the point of being unaware of them. Researchers from the Department of Psychiatry at the University of Pennsylvania, too, have found that by giving patients a questionnaire to fill in concerning their problems in childhood and adolescence, in jobs and in marriages, a much more accurate prediction can be made of which of them will contract lung cancer than from their smoking habits alone.

The need now is for more flexible, multi-disciplinary research projects of a kind which abandon the attempt to find a cause, in favour of the search for possible psychosocial risk factors. A recent survey in the *British Medical Journal*, for example, has shown that although mortality from lung cancer among doctors who give up smoking has declined, the net gain when mortality from other causes, such as accidents, poison- ings, cirrhosis of the liver, and suicide, is taken into account is much less impressive. For some people, the inference is, smoking cigarettes can be a solvent of stress; in the unlikely event of the habit being banned they might need their drug on prescription. Medical scientists will not find it easy to accept the significance of such variables in interpreting the statistics, but to individuals they may be all-important – one man's stress-reducer may be another man's poison.

As the director of the US National Cancer Institute, Vincent T. Devita, has recently admitted, however, the entire research system 'tends to exclude people on the fringe who have ideas that are radical departures'. The Institute 'ought to pay a lot more attention to them'. But, caught up as it is in the system, it cannot.

# 3

# Mental Illness

Easily the most prevalent of all the diseases of civilisation are those loosely categorised as 'mental'. In the West, a third or more of all patients in hospitals have been admitted for psychiatric treatment, and if the mentally handicapped are included, the proportion rises to nearly a half. In addition, uncounted numbers of people are being treated by their doctors for milder psychotic and neurotic symptoms, or for disorders that have a stress component such as insomnia or alcoholism. Mental illness, too, still carries with it the remnants of a stigma, which makes it the more feared.

The story of Senator Thomas Eagleton's enforced withdrawal as George McGovern's running-mate in the 1972 Presidential elections, after it was disclosed that he had undergone ECT for depression, is only the most notorious of many similar instances on both sides of the Atlantic. In 1978 the Prudential Assurance Company sacked a man who had worked for them for eleven months, and had given satisfaction, because they found that he had received voluntary treatment in a mental hospital five years earlier. When his case was taken up by the National Association for Mental Health, the company spokesman explained that the employee had failed to disclose his medical history, but in any case, 'you must bear in mind that we expect the man from the Pru to be acceptable in people's homes' (so acceptable had this man been to his colleagues that they actually held a one-day protest strike). In another case a clerk who had been working in a borough unemployment office was refused a contract with the Civil Service Commission because as a student, many years before, he had received treatment in a mental hospital. This in itself, the National Association were told when they took up his case, was enough to settle the issue.

Anyone's natural reaction on reading such accounts, if he has ambitions to succeed in politics, the Civil Service or big business, would be to avoid psychiatric treatment at all costs. In view of the current state of psychiatry, too, this would be wise. For a start, treatment can be something of a lottery, as psychiatrists are divided into factions. 'Some

methods emphasise psychopharmacology, some behaviour modification, others epidemiological methods, social psychiatry or psychotherapy, while others prefer an eclecticism which tries to combine promising
features in each approach,' Professor John Cohen and John Clark of the
University of Manchester explain in their agreeably detached guidebook
to the subject, *Medicine, Mind and Man.* 'There are the Freudian,
Kleinian and Jungian schools, and there are peripheral and marginal
groups that are sceptical of the traditions cultivated in academic departments, and even highly critical elements hostile to psychiatry as an
authentic medical discipline.' (They might have added that – as the best
known of the hostile critics, Thomas Szasz, has observed – the supporters of different schools often behave more like members of religious
cults than scientists. They denounce each other publicly, and sometimes
rancorously.)

The prevailing confusion was neatly illustrated by Arthur Koestler in
a paper delivered at a World Psychiatric Symposium in 1969. As the
only outsider invited – presumably 'to represent that infernal nuisance
in the psychiatrist's life, the patient' – he had found himself on another
plane of reality from the psychiatrists. They talked as if their diagnostic
terminology was meaningful, yet it was manifest that the same symptoms meant something quite different to different groups, as Morton
Kramer had just demonstrated in his paper 'A Cross-national Study of
Diagnosis'. A patient of any age admitted to a mental hospital in Britain
with a particular set of symptoms would run a ten times higher chance of
being diagnosed as a manic-depressive, Kramer had shown, than somebody with identical symptoms in the United States. In Koestler's age-
group, the over-sixties, the disproportion was even more marked, as
with the same symptoms, manic-depression was diagnosed twenty times
more in Britain than in the US. 'On the other hand, if I were to go off my
head in America, I would stand a ten-times higher chance of being
classified as a case of cerebral arterio-sclerosis than in England; and a
thirty-three per cent higher chance of being classified as a schizo.'

These findings, Koestler pointed out, had subsequently been confirmed and amplified in other studies. In one, conducted on behalf of the
US Department of Health, a third of the American psychiatrists concerned, on the basis of a patient's elaborate case-history, diagnosed
schizophrenia. When the same case-history was presented to British
psychiatrists, none diagnosed schizophrenia. Nor were the differences
of opinion accountable for in simple national terms. The American
psychiatrists were themselves evenly split three ways: schizophrenia,
neurosis, and 'personality disorders' (a rag-bag category invented to
incorporate cases where nothing more specific can be offered). In

another experiment in which thirty-five experienced American psychiatrists were invited to diagnose a case, fourteen plumped for neurosis, twenty-one for psychosis. A patient's fate depended, Koestler concluded, not on his symptoms but 'on the psychiatric school, the ethnic background, and apparently even the age group to which the diagnostician belongs'.

The larger lunacy that orthodox psychiatry has promoted in the guise of scientific diagnosis was further exposed in 1972 in an experiment undertaken by David L. Rosenhan, a psychologist at Stanford University. He and seven friends – two psychologists, a graduate student, a pediatrician, a psychiatrist, a painter and a housewife – presented themselves individually at twelve different mental hospitals, some public, some private, in different States, some on the east coast, some on the west. None of them had had any psychiatric problems, and they agreed to claim only that they occasionally 'heard voices' saying words which sounded like 'empty', 'hollow', or 'thud'. Otherwise, when questioned they were to stick to the simple truth and throughout behave as they would normally do (allowing for some understandable nervousness at the outset, for fear of being detected in their deception). All were admitted to hospital, seven as schizophrenics, one as a manic depressive. They did whatever they were told, except that they only pretended to take the drugs prescribed for them (over two thousand, in all, between the eight of them, including some of the most powerful, such as Thorazine). Once admitted, they had agreed, their objective would be to secure release as soon as possible by showing that they were sane.

Often their fellow patients quickly realised that there was nothing the matter with them, and guessed that they might be engaged upon research, but neither psychiatrists nor hospital staffers had any suspicions. Whatever they did could be, and often was, taken down and used in evidence of their disorder. Their note-taking, for example (they had agreed to take notes openly), in the case-records of three of them was entered as 'patient engages in writing behavior'. And the time spent in the hospitals before they were released as 'in remission' ranged from seven days to fifty-two.

Rosenhan then played a similar trick, but in reverse, telling the authorities at a mental hospital that he proposed to plant another pseudo-patient on them to see whether they could detect him. Of around two hundred admissions in the agreed period, forty-one were confidently identified as the pseudo-patient by one or other member of the hospital staff, twenty-three of them by one psychiatrist. In fact no such pseudo-patient existed. A diagnostic process which leads to such errors, Rosenhan commented, 'cannot be a very reliable one'. There was no question, he emphasised, of the doctors and nurses being callous or irresponsible; the system itself was at fault. Entering a mental hospital, patients cannot know (and the doctor who refers them to the hospital is often hardly better informed) what to expect; yet once admitted, they have little choice but to accept whatever diagnosis and treament are prescribed.

## Retrospect

That mentally-ill patients should receive treatment of any kind is a comparatively recent development. Towards the end of the sixteenth century insanity began gradually to be regarded as a disease rather than as possession by demons, but little could be done for the insane; they were 'put away' in lunatic asylums, commonly remaining in them until death. Individual psychiatrists would periodically introduce a greater measure of freedom, and offer what would now be described as psychotherapy, but this was exceptional. It was not until the 1920s that, following the discovery of the value of insulin in treating diabetic patients, experiments suggested that it could also be used successfully in treating schizophrenia, and shortly afterwards surgeons began to report impressive results from operations designed to remove part of the frontal lobe of the brain. In 1938 an Italian psychiatrist, recalling the tradition that epileptics rarely contract schizophrenia, surmised that an induced epileptic-type fit might benefit schizophrenics – the technique he tried, sending an electric shock through the brain, starting the fashion for electro-convulsive therapy. This trio – coma introduced by insulin or other drugs, brain surgery, and ECT – was to remain the staple psychiatric treatment in mental hospitals until the 1950s.

Although each of these methods was hailed on its introduction as a great advance, their track record proved distinctly uneven, as W. H. Trethowan, Professor of Psychiatry at Birmingham University, has recently recalled. Insulin coma was still in vogue when he first took up psychiatry in the late 1940s, but eventually trials revealed that it 'had no specific effect on schizophrenia other than that due to the enhanced attention which the patients undergoing coma therapy received'. Its successor, 'continuous narcosis', kept patients in a barbiturate-influenced sleep for twenty or more hours a day for weeks on end. This, too, was eventually recognised to be useless, and occasionally produced alarming side-effects. He also cites a number of other experimental therapies which have had to be abandoned or greatly modified.

Trethowan's critical survey is gentle compared to the onslaught on psychiatry, past and present, in *Mind Control* by Peter Schrag – an American journalist, teacher, author, and a past winner of the National Endowment Creative Writing Fellowship. Schrag's main concern is to show how the powers wielded by psychiatrists can be, and have been, used to control and even to punish patients, rather than to treat them, and, worse, how this has been exploited by organisations such as the CIA. But he also provides a great deal of well-documented and damning evidence to show how flimsy are the grounds for accepting that orthodox psychiatric treatment of *any* kind is on balance effective.

## Electro-convulsive Therapy

From the start, electro-convulsive therapy aroused controversy. Nobody could produce a convincing explanation of how it worked, other than the vague 'controlled fit' assumption. Attempts since to provide an explanation in neurochemical terms (ECT 'stimulates brain noradrenaline') have not been enthusiastically received. The main line of defence remains that clinical experience has demonstrated its value, and this has been maintained by some psychiatrists who are far from being slavish adherents either of orthodoxy or of prevailing therapeutic fashions.

In ordinary circumstances ECT would have been tested by controlled trials, but psychiatrists claimed that the control group, who would receive only dummy shocks, would be deprived of a valuable form of therapy, which would be unfair and unethical. When Sylvia A. Riddell, a clinical psychologist at a south-London hospital, surveyed the available reports about the efficiency of ECT she could find only two tests in which controls had been used. Neither of these indicated that the recipients of ECT had fared any better than those who had received only simulated shocks. After twenty years of such research, she commented, in her paper on the subject in *Archives of General Psychiatry* in 1963, there was still no agreement 'as to the mode of action, therapeutic aim, and conditions for optimum therapeutic efficacy. In terms of scientific knowledge,' she concluded, 'the position is very little different now from that in 1937.' In 1976, surveying what had been published in the meantime, Geoff Watts felt it not unreasonable to suggest that her comments were 'just as applicable today'.

In the interim, the contention of those sceptics who argued that any benefit which patients received from ECT must mainly be due to placebo-effect had received a striking testimonial in an article published in

*World Medicine.* The writer described how a new ECT machine had been introduced in a mental hospital, and used with apparent success on patients for two years before it was found that it was not working – never had worked, in fact, since its installation. For obvious reasons, the writer did not care to divulge his own name, and when, three years later, the editor of *World Medicine* wrote to him saying that as the story had obtained very wide currency on both sides of the Atlantic, he might like to identify himself and the hospital so that the circumstances could be properly investigated, he replied that the Medical Defence Union had advised him that to do so would be 'most unwise'. Anybody using the story as evidence against ECT, therefore, the editor pointed out, must 'accept that it has the status only of an unconfirmed, uninvestigated anecdote'. Nevertheless the fact that he had accepted it and, presumably, trusted the writer's word for it, constitutes some evidence for its authenticity. Understandably, towards the end of the 1970s growing public disquiet aroused by this and other stories led to a campaign against ECT, using evidence of the kind Schrag was to present in his *Mind Control* and supported by a strange mixture of allies ranging from the film *One Flew over the Cuckoo's Nest* to the Church of Scientology.

The most damaging criticism of all was the evidence collected from a variety of sources by Leonard Roy Frank and published in his *History of Shock Treatment*, showing that whatever beneficial effects may eventually be credited to ECT in general, its results in individual cases have all too often been so destructive that a high overall success-rate would be needed to justify them. By the late 1970s opposition to ECT had reached the point where it was impossible to resist the pressure for properly controlled trials, and when the initial results were given to a conference on 'ECT after Forty Years' in Leicester, the *British Medical Journal* felt that the doubts which had been raised about the efficacy of ECT 'seem to have been resolved'. The *Lancet*, however, found the results confusing. Certainly they were far from being as conclusive as the *BMJ* believed, and in subsequent trials, although the patients who have had ECT have done better than the controls, the results are not as yet sufficiently consistent to provide an unassailable case in its favour.

Recently, too, the adequacy of the controls used in the trials, and indeed in ECT in general, has been called in to question by Professor Douglas Gordon of the City University in London. Gordon is not a critic of ECT as such; he believes its benefits to be indisputable. But he has been disturbed to find that no attempt is usually made to relate the 'dose' to the thickness and density of the patient's skull, in spite of the variations; even in the same skull, 'the bone on one side may be more than ten times as resistant as that on the other'. For the results of trials to be

111

really meaningful, in other words, skull soundings would need to be taken, and the necessary allowances made.

Even if trials conducted with all due care were to show that ECT can be effective, a problem would still remain: how to select suitable cases for treatment? ECT's backers always emphasise that this is essential. Again and again, when the effectiveness and safety of ECT are extolled, the qualification is appended, 'in properly-selected cases'. But how are patients to know if their case has been properly selected? Their psychiatrist may have years of experience and a good intuitive sense to guide him, but he may be engaged in a controlled trial, which will result in some patients being allocated at random to be treated and the rest to be the controls.

*Leucotomy*

The story of the use of brain surgery in the treatment of psychoses has yet to be comprehensively told. The available evidence, summarised by Schrag, is an appalling indictment of the medical profession for its failure to exercise control over what was, and to a great extent still is, vivisection, with psychotics as the guinea-pigs.

Its peak period came just after the Second World War when, Schrag recalls, 'it was used for everything from schizophrenia to voyeurism, delinquency to drug addiction'. Fifty thousand operations were undertaken in the United States alone, four thousand of them by one surgeon. 'Lobotomies', as they were called, were carried out by a variety of experimental techniques designed to sever the frontal lobes of the brain, the most notorious being the 'ice-pick' version. While a medical student held the patient's head, the neuro-surgeon inserted the instrument like an ice-pick, and tapped at it with a hammer, wiggling it the while. Eventually it became apparent that lobotomies, on balance, were doing patients more harm than good, but they were not abandoned. It was simply explained that a more effective and safer operation, leucotomy, had been devised (it was in fact a modified lobotomy). Since then even more sophisticated techniques have been introduced, such as the insertion of electrodes into the brain.

That the early form of brain surgery for mental illness was destructive is not now in dispute: the expression 'lobotomised' still occasionally surfaces colloquially to express a zombie-like condition. And although the newer techniques are claimed to be more effective and safe, as Schrag points out 'there are no systematic studies to verify that claim' in the United States. In Britain the only systematic study of any kind was published in the *British Medical Journal* in 1978, its chief aim being to discover how extensively the operation was performed (the numbers had dropped in 1976, following adverse publicity, from around 150 to 120, but past experience suggested that they would rise again once the fuss died down).

When in 1981 the BBC put on a television programme on the subject, *Surgery of the Last Resort*, only one psychosurgeon could be found to defend his practice, and the defence proved to be disturbing, because he had to admit that he had seen very few of his patients after they had been discharged from hospital. When asked whether he believed that informed consent had always been given, he replied that as patients could not fully understand the issues, the problem of consent was 'more apparent than real'; and he objected to the idea of independent assessment.

A few days later another neurosurgeon explained the difference, as he saw it, between medical consent and legal consent. Legal consent might be possible to obtain from some patients, he told a *Guardian* reporter 'but you have to ask if they would thank you for the operation afterwards'. It was also important, he added, 'to consider that you might be guilty of negligence if you failed to act because you didn't have the full consent'. As it happened, this admission coincided with an announcement from the Royal College of Psychiatrists that it was advising its members to obtain a second opinion, from an independent psychiatrist, before recommending a patient for psychosurgery. This could only be a recommendation, as a Royal College has neither the will nor the power to instruct its members in their duties. That would be held to interfere with the right of the doctor to prescribe whatever treatment he believes in, even where the treatment has no justification from clinical trials.

All that can be said with confidence about the reported results of psychosurgery for mental illness is that, having been largely derived from the teams who perform them, they are untrustworthy and sometimes positively misleading. In one case which Schrag cites, a woman who had had two operations refused to have another, and committed suicide: this result was claimed as 'gratifying' because it showed she must have been 'functioning'. Another report on a nine-year-old boy noted that, though formerly destructive and sadistic, he had 'displayed marked improvement in behaviour and memory' following the operation. In fact, the boy's capacity to memorise had been destroyed, his I.Q. test scores sinking from 115 to 60.

## Psychoactive Drugs

Of all the methods used to treat mental illness, drugs have had the most success, tranquillisers in particular. They arrived by a roundabout course, through experiments to find whether an extract from rauwolfia, 'the snake root', could be used in the treatment of high blood pressure; when it was noticed that the drug calmed patients down without making them sleepy, psychiatrists began to use it instead of sedatives. With the introduction of meprobamate, marketed as Miltown or Equanil, the tranquillisers fanned out from mental hospitals into the community, where they have enjoyed burgeoning sales ever since.

The emergence of tranquillisers, along with amphetamines – 'pep pills' – and, later, anti-depressants, helped to transform many mental hospitals. Previously psychiatrists and nurses had 'functioned as guardians and custodians in a hellish environment where despair prevailed, and surcease by death offered the only lasting respite for their suffering charges', as Frank J. Ayd, Jr., publisher of the *International Drug Therapy Newsletter*, has recalled. 'Since the chemotherapeutic revolution, the transformation in mental hospitals defies description. Visit one today, you will be impressed by the serenity you observe and feel.' Still more heartening, tens of thousands of patients who, before, could never have left hospital have been able to do so, to return to their families and their jobs. In the community, too, people who previously could not have coped with their life-stresses have been able to tide themselves over difficult times, avoiding hospitalisation with the help of the drugs their doctors prescribe.

This is the picture as it has commonly been presented for public consumption. The reality is less heart-warming. True, tranquillisers and anti-depressants did usher in a great change in mental hospitals, but they were not solely responsible. Similar results had been achieved before in the few hospitals where the psychiatrist in charge had the courage to introduce the 'open door' system, removing restraints and leaving wards unlocked, as at Warlingham Park in south London.

The tranquillisers helped, by enabling the system to be extended to other hospitals where the psychiatrists in charge had been nervous about the 'open door'. The chief effect of the drugs, it has often sardonically been suggested, has been on the psychiatrists and nurses who hand them out. At last they can relax, and deal with the inmates as patients, rather than as prisoners. The hospital awakening has also revealed the extent to which inmates had suffered not from the symptoms of their mental illness but simply from their incarceration, from 'the institutional neurosis', as Russell Barton called it in his book on the subject, in which he showed that a great deal of what had been attributed to schizo-phrenia – for example, catatonia, the state in which many patients sat for hours like statues – was really the mental equivalent of bedsores.

The tranquillisers' lack of responsibility for any improvement in the condition of patients was to be strikingly illustrated by the results of trials held in a London hospital, and published in the *British Medical Journal* in 1957. Outpatients were treated for tension with six different pills, including a barbiturate, a placebo, and meprobamate, each taken over a period of a fortnight. The patients reported on them without knowing which pill was which. The barbiturate was easily the most effective; none of the others, including meprobamate, was rated higher than the placebo. A survey the following year of nearly a hundred such trials showed no reason to believe that patients with anxiety fared on balance any better on meprobamate than on placebos; it was ten times more expensive than barbiturates, and, even at that early stage, reports were coming in of allergic reactions to it, and a risk of addiction.

Privately, many doctors now admit to having been the victims of 'Sorcerer's Apprentice Disease'. The tranquillisers work so successfully in keeping their patients satisfied that the temptation to prescribe them has been irresistible, and it has mattered little whether it is the drug or the placebo effect, so long as it works. Unluckily patients, becoming habituated, have become demanding; a doctor who refuses their de-mands would lose them to one of his more pliable colleagues. Even before the close of the 1960s the Bishop of Chester was complaining that patients had come to regard their doctors 'as a kind of grocer who will deal out to them the pills which they think they need'. By the mid-1970s 200,000,000 tranquillisers, anti-depressants and sedatives were being prescribed annually in the United States alone; yet even this figure was surpassed in Britain, in proportion to the population, as the National Health Service provides psychoactive drugs free (apart from the government-levied tax on each prescription). Britain as a result led the world in their consumption. By the mid-1970s only one tranquilliser prescription in eight was for a recognised psychiatric disorder.

Other psychoactive drugs are unquestionably more potent than a placebo, but this does not necessarily ensure their effectiveness in treating mental illness. The results of trials of anti-depressants, and indeed of all drugs used in the treatment of serious psychosis, have been endlessly confusing and contradictory. Some reports have claimed that chlorpromazine is the most effective drug so far discovered for the treatment of schizophrenia, yet in a trial conducted in California by Maurice Rappaport, when eighty patients diagnosed as acute schizo-phrenics were assigned at random to the drug or a placebo, not merely

115

did those on the placebo do better while under treatment, but also after release far fewer of them had to return to hospital with relapses in a three-year follow-up period.

The excuse most commonly offered for their widespread use is that, even if psychoactive drugs are overrated and over-prescribed, they are helping to keep people out of mental hospitals by enabling them 'to function better through periods of potentially disabling anxiety', as the booklet issued to celebrate the jubilee of the Association of the British Pharmaceutical Industry has put it. But do they, on balance, function better? Following a carefully-mounted trial, in a London mental hospital, to find how patients taken off drugs fared in comparison to those remaining under drug treatment, Henry Rollin observed that 'the same pessimistic prognosis obtains whether these chronic psychotics are treated with psychotropic drugs over prolonged periods of time or not'. 'The majority of those who live in the community,' George Crane, Director of Research at the Spring Grove State Hospital, Baltimore, commented in *Science* in 1973, 'continue to be unproductive, and are often a burden to their families.'

## General Practice

Sufferers from psychiatric illness who are returned to the community, or whose symptoms are not sufficiently marked to justify admittance to a mental hospital, have been poorly served by general practitioners. This is not the GPs' fault; until very recently they have not been trained, while medical students, to deal with psychotic or neurotic patients. 'The teaching of psychiatry in most medical schools still consists of a series of six, sometimes more, lectures together with demonstrations of the more florid psychoses,' Philip Hopkins, a London GP, wrote in the *Postgraduate Medical Journal* in 1960. 'Normal psychology is seldom taught, while the subject of psychodynamics is rarely mentioned.' As a result, the newly qualified GP who found himself confronted with patients suffering from psychiatric disorders – if he recognised them; and often he would not, because he had only seen them in their institutional neurosis form – would have no option but to refer them to a psychiatrist. And although more attention is now being paid to the subject in medical schools, psychiatry is still notoriously the poorest of poor relations.

Those doctors who have specialised in psychiatry, too, have often remained ignorant of the nature of mental illness in the community, because of their institutional ties. A doctor working in a mental hospital, especially if it happens to be one of the many vast institutions hidden away behind high walls, is unlikely to have the time to see patients in their home environment, even if he would like to; so he is in no position to assess the strains put upon patients when they are discharged home.

The need for psychiatrists to take psychosocial factors into consideration has recently been demonstrated by the results of a research project conducted by George Brown, a professor of sociology in London University, and his colleague Tirril Harris. In their *Social Origins of Depression* they describe how they interviewed over 600 women, some depressives, some randomly chosen as controls, in a London borough. Given that the sample was representative, the findings indicate that, in the great majority of cases, depression's onset is related to life events, such as a bereavement or loss of a job. Depression occurs, however, only when there are what the authors call 'vulnerability factors': lack of a close relationship with husband or lover; loss of a mother in early childhood; the presence of three or more children living at home; and unemployment – not, Harris suggests, for a job's intrinsic interest, but for its social contacts.

If, as the *British Medical Journal* has recently agreed, 'the role of life events in precipitating relapse in schizophrenia is now firmly established', the psychiatrist cannot expect to be able to judge whether patients ought to be admitted to or discharged from hospital unless he knows about their home circumstances; but few psychiatrists have regarded this as part of their function. The kind of mistakes which occur as a result were described recently by a psychiatrist in an article in *World Medicine*, on a conference he had attended held to discuss the case of a forty-seven-year-old woman with no previous history of disorder who claimed to be suffering from persecution by her neighbours. The diagnosis ranged 'from depression, depression with paranoid features, paraphrenia, paranoid schizophrenia, to menopausal syndromes', several speakers 'trotting out that reliable old warhorse, schizo-affective state'. The recommended treatments 'ranged from anti-depressants, single and combined, to tranquillisers and on to ECT'. Ordinarily, social workers contribute little at these conferences. 'They will speak only after the great white chiefs have spoken, or else when spoken to.' But on this occasion one of them, 'bearded and be-jeaned; he appeared to be going on 19', happened to know the patient. He also knew, and described, her neighbours: an alcoholic husband and wife who kept four dogs and six cats. They were forever fighting; and the wife had just been

117

admitted to a mental hospital. 'Where now were all the flowers of argument that a few minutes previously had been used to prove one point, then another, then to disprove both?' the psychiatrist mused. 'Their protagonists tried frantically to gather their evidence for a rearguard action, but before any could set up a face-saving manoeuvre the conference room had to be vacated.'

## Side-effects

Surveying the evidence in *The End of Medicine*, Rick J. Carlson noted that the difficulty is, 'given the current state of the art, to determine who needs treatment and who does not'; yet treatment has continued to be 'dished out every day under the banner of science'. The diagnostic labelling is not merely often grossly inaccurate; it 'can be viciously destructive as well' – a view which Schrag's evidence has since amply confirmed. 'As long as the psychiatrist's basic technique was talk (or incarceration), the labels were simply the familiar trinkets of mystification – the scientizing of the classic stigma of madness,' he observes; 'but once they become indications for supposedly specific drugs, including many highly powerful drugs, they assume a new significance.' And, inevitably, they spell danger for patients, as any form of treatment designed for specific disorders is likely to be if the diagnostic criteria are faulty.

The reports of trials of psychoactive drugs ordinarily concentrate upon their effects: information about their side-effects is harder to come by. It was not until the late 1960s that Michael Shepherd, Professor of Epidemiological Psychiatry in London University, discovered with the help of sampling techniques how much more serious were side-effects than had been admitted. Wherever it has become mandatory on manufacturers to list known side-effects in their promotion, the contents tend to be disturbing; chlorpromazine, for example – one of the most extensively used of all the psychoactive drugs, has been known to cause 'drowsiness, fainting, dizziness and, occasionally, a shock-like condition, pseudo-Parkinsonism, motor restlessness, persistent tardive dyskinesia, psychotic symptoms, catatonic-like states, convulsive seizures, hyperglycemia, hypoglycemia, dry-mouth, nasal congestion, constipation'. Some side-effects – rashes, impaired salivation, and even reduced sexual drive – are so common that the patient is often told not to think of them as the result of the particular drug, but as a concomitant of chemotherapy.

Side-effects can turn out to be irreversible, continuing even after the course of drug treatment has ended. One of the more disturbing developments of recent years has been the increase in cases of what has been called 'persistent tardive dyskinesia', first described by the American psychiatrist George Crane in 1973 as a nervous disorder in which the tongue and the lips develop uncontrollable sucking motions, 'pursing, rolling and incessant champing in synergy with rhythmic contractions of the jaw'.

This syndrome had not been known before the introduction of the phenothiazines, and Crane had no doubt that it was associated with them. Its onset, he warned, was not related to the size of the dose; it often appeared only after medication had been suspended ('tardive' meaning 'delayed'), and there was no known treatment for it. 'Persistent' in other words, could mean irreversible. In spite of this warning the prescribing of phenothiazines continues unchecked, and persistent tardive dyskinesia has become a major problem, particularly in the United States. According to George Gardos of the Boston State Hospital, psychiatrists' reaction to it has 'shifted from curiosity and mild concern to panic'.

A further cause for concern has been the periodic discovery, years after a new drug has been introduced, that it has side-effects which have not attracted attention earlier. When anti-depressants were first marketed it was claimed that they could interrupt the manic-depressive cycle, blocking the swing from gloom to exhilaration. They could: but a study set up by the National Institute of Mental Health later showed that, although individual swings were less intense, the time interval between them became shorter. Another development which has been causing growing concern is the frequency of what have come to be called 'paradoxical' reactions – a further instance of the ingenuity now being displayed in the invention of euphemisms. Tranquillisers which work satisfactorily in normal conditions may simply exacerbate hostility or anger under provocation: they may calm a harassed mother for a time, but when her children start playing up, something snaps, and she batters them. The manufacturers of Valium admit that some people react to it with 'acute hyperexcited states, anxiety, hallucinations, insomnia, rage and sleep disturbances', and the results of tests at Harvard Medical School suggested that individuals on a tranquilliser show more hostility, in a staged group conflict, than did the controls.

Other side-effects that have recently been traced to tranquillisers include accidents. In a survey of drugs associated with road accidents Sir Richard Doll and colleagues at the Regius Professor's department at Oxford examined the medical records of three hundred drivers who had been brought to hospital with injuries sustained in road accidents: the proportion of those who had been taking tranquillisers was higher than in the control group, and although the numbers were too small for the trial to be regarded as more than a pilot study, they sufficed to indicate that patients given tranquillisers 'should at least be warned that they are at special risk'.

Confirmation of the risk had been provided coincidentally only the day before Doll's report was published in the *British Medical Journal*. A new tranquilliser was launched with the claim that laboratory tests, and tests in cars fitted with dual controls, had proved that driving ability was unimpaired – intimation that some, at least, of the established tranquillisers had been causing such impairment. Even the belief that the tranquillisers are not addictive has had to be abandoned. As early as 1965 the American Medical Association's Committee on Alcohol and Addiction warned that the way in which doctors were acceding to patient's demands for psychoactive drugs was leading to developing states of tolerance: 'they have a barbiturate-like action that can produce both psychological and physical dependence.' But such warnings have had no appreciable effect; as the prescriptions for tranquillisers and other psychoactive drugs have continued to increase, cases of addiction cause increasing concern.

Of all the unwelcome consequences produced by developing forms of psychiatric treatment over the past fifty years, the ugliest has been the way in which they have been used to control patients, or punish them for recalcitrance – ECT being prescribed for a patient who refuses a drug, for example, or vice-versa. That this happens has often been denied, but as Schrag shows, some psychiatrists have let their colleagues down by actually boasting about it – notably one who, believing it was good for patients to work in the hospital grounds, persuaded them to do so by threatening them with three ECTs a week if they refused. Gradually, he reported, the number of patients 'volunteering' (his term) for garden work increased. He did not know whether this was due to the beneficial effects of the ECT or their fear of it, but 'in either case our objective of motivating them to work was achieved'.

In Britain, allegations in a TV documentary that ECT had been used to control inmates' behaviour in Broadmoor were at first indignantly denied; but, although not proved, investigation convinced the *Lancet* that 'the cuckoo's nest may not be as empty as we supposed'. The extent to which brain surgery, ECT and drugs are used for control and punishment cannot even be guessed at; patients can rarely be certain whether the psychiatrist has punishment in mind when he prescribes, and he may not be aware of his motives himself – any more than the Victorian headmaster who said, with relish, 'this is going to hurt me more than it hurts you.' Some behaviourists actually believe that 'deliberate painful applications' may be a necessary part of the treatment. This, according to Schrag, is the view of a director of the Riverside, California, mental health services, who has claimed that 'the concept of punishment is largely a semantic philosophical problem which may be avoided in practice by substituting new phrases such as "aversive conditioning".

## The Myth and the Realities

What has gone wrong, to leave psychiatry in so chaotic a condition? The most trenchant analysis in recent years has been Thomas Szasz's *The Myth of Mental Illness*. In his preface Szasz, a professor of psychiatry at the State University of New York, described how, after he had established himself as a psychiatrist, he became increasingly aware of 'the vague, capricious and generally unsatisfactory character of the widely used concept of mental illness and its corollaries, diagnosis, prognosis and treatment': the only clear definition of mentally-ill people, he came to the conclusion, is that they are people who go to a psychiatrist. They should stop going to a psychiatrist, he advised. Whatever may be the matter with them, they are not *ill*.

It was this provocative assertion – that the psychoses and neuroses ought not to be regarded or treated as illnesses in the same sense as, say, rheumatism or measles – that attracted most attention on both sides of the Atlantic. But the book also contained some penetrating criticism of psychiatry on its own terms. Psychiatry has gone astray, Szasz argued, because psychiatrists have accepted the medical model, a model constructed at a time when it was assumed 'that the detection of physico-chemical disorders in the bodily machinery is the proper task facing the investigating physician'.

The model had defined social as well as clinical status within the profession; psychology and psychoanalysis, having no solid foundation in physiology, could be 'given only second-class citizenship'. Their practitioners' ambition had consequently been to show that they deserved to be up-graded, most easily achieved by keeping theory and practice rigorously mechanistic. Even Freud did his utmost, for as long as he could, to keep his theories within the recognised physiological framework. But the break eventually had to come, and when it did, orthodox psychiatry remained organically-orientated, with the psychologically-orientated Freudians, Jungians and others left as outsiders. Only in the United States did psychoanalysis acquire a measure of uneasy recognition as a medical specialty.

The psychiatrists' hope that, by keeping within neurological guidelines, they would begin, as Szasz put it, to 'share in the social status inherent in the role of the physicians' could not be fulfilled. From the start, they found it hard to keep mental illness in the organic category, as the symptoms were so often and so obviously related to life stresses. They settled for a compromise: the belief that psychoses are probably caused by an organic brain disease, neuroses by psychosocial disturbance. But this distinction has neither logical nor empirical foundation. 'To regard "minor" upheavals in living as problems in human relations,' Szasz pointed out, 'and more "major" upheavals as due to brain disease, seems to be a rather simple example of wishful thinking.'

Still, as he had to admit, the idea did possess a kind of common-sense appeal, and it served to maintain some common ground between psychiatry and neurology. It also ensured that the bulk of the research effort in mental illness would be concentrated on the search for neurological rather than psychosocial causes. And historically, it could be claimed, this made sense. It had long been known that certain plants and fungi contain hallucinogens, and that alcohol in sufficient quantities can precipitate delusions; toxicity of a similar kind might be triggered by some neurochemical fault within the brain – a view which had received reinforcement when it was found that the symptoms of tertiary syphilis stemmed from earlier infection with a spirochete.

The discovery of a genetic risk factor in schizophrenia added to the likelihood that its cause was not psychogenic. Franz Kallman of the New York Psychiatric Institute showed that there was a close correlation between the chance of developing schizophrenia and the closeness of blood relationship to a schizophrenic; in short, that insanity did 'run in families', as had long been assumed. This might, admittedly, have been accounted for by the fact that the presence of a schizophrenic in the family, particularly as a parent, could be expected to have a disturbing effect within the family circle. But Kallman's research disposed of this idea. An identical twin, he had found, was five times more likely to contract schizophrenia than a non-identical twin. If psychological disturbance were the cause, there was no reason for this difference.

At the same time, reports were appearing of the encouraging results apparently being achieved by neurological research. The most spectacular of them made headlines in the early 1960s: the Yale psychologist Jose Delgado claimed to show how a bull could be stopped in mid-charge at a matador by means of a radio-controlled electrode planted in its brain. The media revelled in the story, the assumption being that science had found a way to convert angry bulls into creatures as placid as Disney's Ferdinand. If animals, why not humans? Delgado went on to try to show that through electrical stimulation of the brain people, too, could be made more placid; other experimenters began to use it to treat patients.

Gradually, disillusionment set in. Whatever Delgado's electrode did for bulls, it could not do for humans, and a reappraisal of his work revealed the reason. Closer examination of the film showed that the charging bull was stopped 'because so long as the stimulation was on, it was forced to turn around in the same direction continuously'. There was no evidence, S. Elliot Valenstein of the University of Michigan Medical School explained, 'to prove that aggressivity had been modified'.

The greatest concentration of research effort, however, was along neurochemical paths. Here, too, there were frequent reports of encouraging results. Yet by the close of the 1950s Seymour Kety, head of the National Institute of Medical Health's Laboratory of Clinical Science in Bethesda, Maryland, and dedicated to demonstrating the neurochemical basis of schizophrenia, felt compelled to admit in the course of what the *British Medical Journal* described as a 'masterly and authoritative review' that, so far as he could judge, nothing had been accomplished by way of establishing biological causes: 'the signposts pointing the way to their discovery are at present quite blurred out; to me, at least, illegible.'

Recalling Kety's verdict four years later, a *BMJ* editorial noted that from 1956 to 1961 no fewer than seventeen hundred articles had been published describing research into the somatic aspects of schizophrenia, 'the bulk of it biochemical'. Most were based on the discovery, or presumed discovery, that certain chemicals are more likely to be found in schizophrenics than in other people, such as 'a very labile factor in fractions of human globulin'; 'the presence of "taraxein", an allegedly toxic euglobulin'; an 'increase in the urine of indoles not attributed to exogenous factors', and the presence of hyperaminochromia in the urine, 'said to contain in excess certain chromogenic substances, including degradation products of trytophan metabolism and compounds related to indolic derivatives of adrenaline'. Yet none of these ideas had been proved. 'The arguments that can be brought forward in favour of intense biochemical inquiry into the pathology of schizophrenia are very strong,' the editorial concluded, but 'not much success has yet been achieved'. This might come as a surprise, in view of innumerable reports which had appeared of significant findings, 'but the history of research is so strewn with unconfirmed observations and unwarranted inferences that scepticism ceases to need apology, and becomes an obligation'.

Nothing has happened in the meantime to require any apology for that scepticism, as an admirably balanced survey of our knowledge about schizophrenia, issued by the Office of Health Economics, has recently shown. Its problems remain unsolved; in spite of years of painstaking research no biochemical culprit has been found, and there is a dearth of reliable information both about the short-term effectiveness of the treatments in use, and about the long-term value of the medical and social services employed.

Neurologists and orthodox psychiatrists have nonetheless remained unshaken in their beliefs, hopelessly hooked on the organic theory of the psychoses; even some of the most intelligent, such as the neurologist Sir Henry Miller, who before he was appointed Vice-Chancellor of the University of Newcstle (and later, whenever he was given half a chance) constituted himself as the psychiatrists' scourge.

Miller was a big man, physically and mentally, admired and loved by all except the not inconsiderable number of fools whom he failed to suffer gladly, and about whom he would express himself pungently in committee, in print, or in company. His only recorded complimentary reference to psychiatry was when he described it as 'neurology at its highest level', but before his audience recovered from the surprise at hearing such a eulogy from so unexpected a source, he went on to explain that this merely meant that the unfortunate psychiatrists were practising 'neurology without physical signs'. When neurologists had finally understood all the neurochemical processes involved in mental illness, Miller implied, the psychiatrist's diagnostic function would disappear, and his services as a therapist would no longer be required except to help patients over emotional trauma resulting from their illnesses.

Miller gave a lucid exposition of the neurological case at a lecture in Edinburgh in 1966, when he bluntly claimed that endogenous depression – the kind which 'usually comes out of the blue without any evident cause' (as distinct from the exogenous variety, which can be related to an outside cause such as a bereavement) – is 'a pathophysiological disturbance of "organic", or more accurately "physiogenic", origin'. As such, he insisted, 'it was as near to a clinical entity as almost any disease in internal medicine', its claim to that status being 'at least as good as that of acute appendicitis – another banal disease of which the cause still escapes us'. In typical cases its diagnosis should be no more difficult. The precise cause, he assumed, would soon be found. Already, in fact, 'most exciting clues' to the possible physical basis of the disorder were being unravelled by research into noradrenaline, the transmitter substance of the peripheral sympathetic nervous system.

These most exciting clues have been endlessly followed up since then, without yielding any convincing explanation for endogenous depression, and Miller's insistence that it is easy to diagnose has been exposed as wishful thinking by Morton Kramer and others in the diagnostic trials which Koestler used on the basis of his criticism of psychiatry. One reason for the failure of research to trace its origins has been the almost fanatical resistance of Miller and most other senior neurologists, along with many psychiatrists, to the idea that endogenous depression may not be organic or physiogenic, but, like the exogenous kind, the product of psychosocial stresses. Miller was prepared to concede that the symptoms displayed might reflect a variety of personality differences, including the individual's psychological make-up, but he was adamant that psychological factors played no part in the causing of the symptoms.

In explaining why, however, Miller revealed that he had not understood what the advocates of the psychosomatic approach had actually argued. Endogenous depression, he claimed, 'strikes often and most dramatically in an unexpected way at the stable, energetic, extroverted middle-aged "success"', not at 'the feckless, inadequate patient' – as, he clearly assumed, the psychosomatic school had taught. On the contrary, their picture of the depression-prone personality was very close to his own – closer to it, in fact, than that of most neurologists.

That Miller, in other respects so shrewd in his judgments, should have had this blind spot is the measure of the dominance which the organic or physiogenic theory of disease had obtained over his generation of doctors. He could not see that, even if a relationship were to be established between mood and cerebral noradrenaline, psychosocial disturbances might still be responsible for the chemical changes. Yet as Szasz pointed out, the assumption that, if neurological changes are found to occur, the mental disorder must be organic, is misguided. Szasz thought it reasonable to accept that if, say, an Englishman decides to study French, 'certain chemical (or other) changes will occur in his brain as he learns the language'. But it would still be a mistake to infer, Szasz insisted, even if such changes could be demonstrated, 'that the most significant scientific statements concerning this learning process are expressed in the language of physics. This, however, is what the organicist claims.'

Jung had much the same idea. There must, he felt, be some chemical changes related to schizophrenia, triggered by 'toxine X', as he called it – a notion which was followed up in 1957 by Ian Stevenson, who was soon to become Professor of Psychiatry at the University of Virginia. An 'either/or' attitude had developed, Stevenson observed; either the psychoses are organic/physiogenic, or they are functional/psychogenic.

In his view, the believers in neither one nor the other idea had a monopoly of the truth, 'and only those are completely wrong who think they are completely right'. There could be no doubt, he agreed, that heredity strongly influences the predisposition to schizophrenia, that the disorder is accompanied by important physiological and biochemical changes, and that it may be ameliorated, if not cured, by physical forms of treatment. But the physiogenic theory needed to be broadened to take account of the facts that schizoprenics usually showed some impairment in their relations with other people long before the onset of the disorder; that the onset was commonly precipitated by psychological stress, and that psychotherapy had had some measure of success in treatment. A plausible hypothesis, Stevenson felt, was that stress released into the bloodstream some metabolic substance resembling mescaline or LSD. Such a substance could then interfere with the action of the brain, disrupting perceptions and thought in the manner found in schizophrenia, and although nobody had identified any such substance, he thought that someone eventually would. He warned, however, that the biochemical mechanism might not lie 'in the abnormal release of an abnormal substance, but in an abnormal susceptibility of the cells of the brain to disruption by such a substance'. Even if ways could be found to reduce or prevent the chemical changes accompanying the stress, they would not remove the stress; it would still be necessary to deal with that – or, rather, with 'the attitudes which have made events stressful for the patient'. Consequently there should be no claim for a cure until the patient has learned to modify those attitudes, and thus to master the stressful situations. 'The patient must go out the way he came in, otherwise events will force him back.'

Four years later Humphry Osmond described research he had been undertaking, which appeared to confirm Jung's and Stevenson's expectation. In the 1950s a colleague of his in the psychiatric department at St George's Hospital in London had drawn his attention to the resemblance of the chemical formula of the mind-bending drug mescalin to that of adrenalin. Might not this mean, Osmond wondered, 'that adrenalin, the hormone believed to be poured out from the suprarenal glands when we are frightened, active or alert, might by some accident of body chemistry turn into a chemical which would have the same effect on the brain as mescalin does?' Later, Osmond began to work in Canada with Abram Hoffer, and they found that a derivative of adrenalin, adrenochrome, could produce the symptoms of schizophrenia in normal people. But he felt that the toxic substance – Jung's 'toxine X' or, as Osmond and his colleague called it, after Mescaline, 'M-substance' – ought not to be regarded simply as a villain, to be arrested and liquidated. Schizophrenics, research has shown, can tolerate doses of histamine that would kill normal people. They suffer less from allergies; they are less likely to become arthritic; they are less susceptible, in fact, to a number of physical disorders. 'Perhaps this great illness is so widespread throughout mankind,' Osmond surmised, 'because it is brought about by a mechanism which is usually beneficial, but in certain people works too well and protects at too great a price.'

## The Double Bind

This echoes Sir James Mackenzie's theory about high blood pressure, that it may be 'a physiological mechanism for the benefit of the organism'. Could schizophrenia perhaps represent an earlier release mechanism, designed to enable the individual to escape from some intolerable emotional situation? Ian Stevenson recalled that some of the early psychoanalysts had surmised that a certain type of malicious and inept mother might be responsible for giving her child the disorder. 'There was even popular for a time an epithet, "schizophrenogenic mother",' he recalled – though he thought it 'said more about the unkindness of psychologists and psychiatrists to mothers, than about the hostility of these mothers to their children'. As it happened, however, a more sophisticated version of this theory had just been offered by Gregory Bateson and colleagues of the Veterans' Administration Hospital in Palo Alto.

The 'double bind' hypothesis links schizophrenia to situations in which the individuals, children or adolescents, find themselves where, no matter what they do, they 'can't win' – the kind of situation expressed in the 'Heads-I-win, tails-you-lose' tag, and it was to be introduced to a wider public in the writings of Ronald Laing. A child, Laing explained, may be subjected to 'mystification' by the contradictory demands of convention and feeling. Thus he may instinctively realise that his mother resents him, and he may resent her, but neither of them can express their resentment, because such is the force of conditioning that neither of them is conscious of it. Mothers *love* their children! Children *love* their mothers! To think anything different is inconceivable. So an elaborate pattern of deceit can arise, to preserve the self-deception, ranging from the mother saying, 'You must be tired, darling, go to bed,' when what she really means is, 'Get out of my hair,' to accusations and punishments 'for his own good', designed simply to gratify sadistic parental impulses. In such circumstances some children rebel; most accept, and collude; but a few crack under the strain.

127

Laing went to work with a colleague from the Tavistock Institute, A. Esterson, to test the validity of his double-bind theory by applying it to forty-two patients aged from fifteen to thirty-five, diagnosed as schizophrenic, in mental hospitals in the London area. Their form of psychotherapy consisted of 'a systematic clarification and undoing of patterns of communication that we can take to be "schizogenic" within the family', along with 'a similar clarification and undoing of such patterns of communication between patients, and between staff and patients', making sure at the same time that there was continuity of personnel working with the family both during and after the patients' stay in hospital. All patients were discharged within a year of admission, their average time in hospital being three months, and only seven had to be readmitted within another year. There were no comparable British figures for the results of conventional forms of treatment, but the seventeen per cent readmitted was lower than comparable figures for the United States, and seventy per cent of those who had not been readmitted were 'sufficiently well adjusted socially to be able to earn their living'.

Were 'mystification' and the double bind, then, the solution to the riddle? Among those whom Laing and Esterson thanked for their assistance in the project was G. M. Carstairs, Professor of Psychological Medicine at the University of Edinburgh, who, in a letter to the *British Medical Journal*, while complimenting them for their courtesy, pointed out that they had not thought fit to avail themselves of his major criticism of their findings. Following trials in which he had been involved in Edinburgh, the proportion of previously hospitalised schizophrenics who had relapsed by the end of the year had been only eighteen per cent – remarkably close to the Laing/Esterson figure. The Edinburgh patients had not had the benefit of the de-mystification procedure, but had simply had 'a greater frequency of contact with doctors and other psychiatric personnel in the follow-up period' than was usually provided. 'I suggest, therefore,' Carstairs concluded, 'that our studies both indicated the non-specific response on the part of schizophrenic patients, to an increased amount of personal attention.'

Carstairs' comment, though, was not so much a repudiation of Laing – who had himself stressed that there was no form of treatment of proven value except 'sustained careful interpersonal relations and tranquillisation' – as a warning that a great deal more research would be required if the double-bind, mystification hypothesis were to be thoroughly tested. And by this time, orthodox psychiatric opinion was hardening against Laing. The young took him up as a cult figure, but he was far from popular among parents, for obvious reasons. When they

brought their child along to a psychiatrist and he diagnosed schizophrenia, they were not going to thank him if he explained that they were
responsible for the child's condition.

Perceptive though Laing could be about family relationships, therefore, his work aroused deep resentment. When a 'breakthrough' was
announced in 1977 – the alleged discovery of a neurochemical cause of
schizophrenia – a writer in the *New Scientist*, Elaine Morgan, observed
that, if the expectations were fulfilled and it became a medically con-
trollable disorder, 'the relatives of sufferers will doubtless be too full of
relief and gratitude to point out that in many cases apologies are in order
for the smear campaign they have undergone in recent decades'. All that
Laing's theory achieved within the medical profession was to increase
doctors' mistrust of psychiatry, and that of orthodox psychiatrists of
psychogenic speculation. The running has since been made by a few
other existentialists (Laing thought of himself as one); by clinical
psychologists caught up in the growth movement – its adherents offering a range of therapies, some derived from eastern mysticism, some
from encounter-group practices, aiming to enable individuals to establish their identities and thereby avoid mental illness; also, occasionally,
by individuals in the medical profession who are not themselves
psychiatrists or neurologists, but who feel that neuropsychiatry is falling
down on the job.

The endocrinologist Professor Ivor Mills of Cambridge University,
for example, has presented a variant of the stress theory. His interest
was initially aroused when, as a young doctor, he became irritated by the
fact that so many hospital beds were occupied by attempted suicides,
most of them in the fifteen-to-twenty-four age group. Whereas among
animals overcrowding intensified stress, with humans, he speculated,
the factor is competitiveness, not necessarily with other humans, but in
order to achieve standards – social, intellectual, financial. If so, the
movement towards a more egalitarian society would actually increase
the strain; the greater the equality of opportunity the less the excuse for
failure. And this in turn could increase the incidence of nervous disorders, such as depression.

Mills is not hostile to conventional methods of treatment, counselling
or psychotherapy. On the contrary, he continues to have faith in the
anti-depressants, even to the point of light-heartedly advocating that
they should be put into the water supply. But this, he emphasises, is
simply because such drugs can lift a depression sufficiently to enable the
patient to begin to cope rationally with his problems; 'the problems
don't go away, but it is the secondary aspects of stress behaviour that
cause all the trouble', breaking up a marriage or the relationship

between parent and child. To Mills the label 'endogenous', implying that the cause is a disorder of the metabolism, is simply mumbo-jumbo. Some people have a biochemical make-up which leaves them with a low base-line resistance to stress, but the evidence has convinced him that, by and large, 'depression is always linked to the pattern of life-disturbing events'. To call a depression 'endogenous', therefore, is simply conceit on the part of the doctor, 'because he can't see or appreciate the outside event, or combination of circumstances, which has triggered it off'.

Such opinions remain unconventional. The 'either/or' syndrome still holds, and research in neurochemistry continues to expand, assisted by the discovery of the neurotransmitters, the chemical messengers of the brain. Fortunately for the researchers' prospects, they are so numerous, with such complex interactions that to keep pace with the results has become a full-time occupation; at the American Society for Neurosciences annual meeting in 1979 no fewer than three thousand contributions were presented. They merely demonstrated that, as of old, the experts are finding out more and more about less and less.

If, as the *BMJ* had claimed six years earlier, scepticism had become an obligation, it is even more obligatory today. Yet the same old enthusiastic accounts of triumphs continue to find space. 'Now there has been a breakthrough', Elaine Morgan claimed in the *New Scientist* article in which she castigated Laing; the kind of breakthrough that occurred when it was found that general paralysis of the insane, 'which had been widely blamed on social stress, was caused by the syphilitic spirochete'. This 'breakthrough' was the supposed discovery that schizophrenia is caused by 'a specific defect in part of the brain's limbic system', in a neurotransmitter substance, gamma aminobutyric acid. 'The moral for anyone in charge of allotting funds for research in psychiatric problems is surely crystal clear,' Morgan concluded. 'The psychotherapists mean well, but experience consistently shows it is the "organic" approach which delivers the goods.' Needless to say, this particular version of the goods has proved to be no more of a breakthrough than its predecessors.

Even those authorities who realise that to think in such simplistic terms is foolish, nevertheless cling to the hope that the organic approach is basically the right one. The issue whether schizophrenia is organic or psychogenic is in David Horrobin's experience the most bitterly contested in all psychiatry, and its resolution 'will have far-reaching consequences not only on science and medicine, but in politics, philosophy and literature as well'. Unlike some of the supporters of the organic/physiogenic cause, he admits that there may be interactions; 'disturbance of psychological origin may have physical consequences and disturbances of biochemical origin may be exacerbated by psychological stresses'. Yet he goes on to say, 'There is nevertheless a feeling that one sort of disturbance will prove to be primary.' His belief is that we are now very close to demonstrating that schizophrenia is caused by a defect in the synthesis of a biochemical called 'Prostaglandin E1', and he takes for granted that if a chemical agent is then found capable of compensating for the defect, and restoring schizophrenics to health, it will prove that stress is not the cause of the disease.

This reluctance to face the evidence that mental illness, though its symptoms can be induced by toxic substances and may be the result of neurochemical changes related to stress, may nevertheless often be a stress disorder, goes some way to account for the low esteem in which orthodox psychiatry is still held in the medical profession. When a psychiatrist expresses the belief that mental illness is physiogenic, this simply encourages neurologists to share Miller's assumption that, when all is made clear by research, psychiatry will wither away, leaving neurology in full possession. Yet far from recognising this, psychiatrists have been attempting to find an even firmer mechanistic grounding. As George Engel, Professor of Psychiatry and Medicine at the University of Rochester, New York, observed at a recent conference on psychiatric education, 'Many psychiatrists seemed to be saying to medicine, "Please take us back and we will never again deviate from the medical model!"' – the reason for their worry being, as one of them put it, that 'psychiatry has become a hodge-podge of unscientific opinion, assorted philosophies and "schools-of-thought", mixed metaphors, role diffusion, propaganda and politicking.'

Engel did not dispute this criticism, but he doubted whether a return to the bosom of the medical profession was the remedy; the problem, he felt, was that the medical model is inadequate for psychiatry. The trial of the 'Yorkshire Ripper' has been a melancholy confirmation of this thesis; junior counsel for the prosecution was able to make the evidence of the psychiatrists who appeared for the defence look so ridiculous that the judge had to intervene to remind the court that it was not they who were on trial. Of course there are psychiatrists who follow the reasonable courses set out in such works as Anthony Storr's *The Art of Psychotherapy*, accepting no single model, and trying to draw from whatever source, Freudian or behaviourist, will most benefit the patient. But there are not many of this species. The patient can think himself lucky if he is referred to one of them.

# 4

# Iatrogenic Disorders

If nominations were called for to select *the* disease of our civilisation, the one with the most familiar symptoms in our time, though in the past it was assumed to be of so little account that it did not acquire a name, it would be the one which has come to be called iatrogenic: illness caused by medical treatment.

The term came into use in medical circles in the 1950s, but it was not until the publication of Illich's *Medical Nemesis* that the public began to realise that it referred to something more than isolated unfortunate episodes, such as the thalidomide disaster. The disabling impact of professional control over medicine, Illich claimed in his introduction, had reached epidemic proportions. '*Iatrogenesis*, the name for this new epidemic, comes from *iatros*, the Greek word for physician, and *genesis*, meaning origin.' It was of three main kinds: clinical, 'when pain, sickness and death result from medical care'; social, 'when health policies reinforce an industrial organisation that generates ill-health'; and cultural and symbolic, 'when medically-sponsored behaviour and delusions restrict the vital autonomy of people by undermining their competence'.

Iatrogenesis is as old as medicine. The Hippocratic writings acknowledged its existence by including the injunction to physicians, 'At least, do no harm.' There are innumerable historical accounts of the destructive effects of bleedings and purgings, and of surgery undertaken without precautions to prevent infection. Immunisation procedures, too, have had some lethal consequences, as in the case of Koch's tuberculin. But iatrogenic symptoms did not become a built-in clinical fixture until less than fifty years ago, when it was found that patients treated with the sulpha drugs suffered from a predictable incidence of adverse reactions, ranging from mild malaise to death.

The Americans were the first to experience the consequences, and fortunately for them, they took some heed of the warning. In 1937 more than a hundred people died after taking a preparation of a sulpha drug which proved highly toxic; as a consequence, the Food and Drug Au-

132

thority was set up, with power to insist that new drugs must be adequately tested before manufacturers could receive a licence to market them. The FDA soon found, though, that it could not restrict the sale of a drug simply because it caused some adverse reactions. With the introduction of penicillin and the antibiotics, side-effects became an everyday occurrence. Some were drug-related, in that it became possible to warn patients that they might expect to have a rash or a dry mouth while taking the treatment. Others were 'idiosyncratic', the reaction being specific to the patient. Occasionally they proved fatal, but this, it could be argued, was the necessary price for the spectacular benefits from the wonder-drug era.

The initial intimation that the price might become excessive came after cortisone had been introduced in 1949, for the treatment of rheumatic disorders. It proved extremely effective, enabling formerly bed-ridden patients to resume normal lives. But the principle upon which it was based – simulating hormones which the patients' bodies were not producing – meant that, in most cases, the dose had to be kept up, in some cases increased, if the benefit was to be maintained. And this often upset the body's homeostasis, leading to a breakdown of resistance to streptococcal and staphylococcal infections. Some patients, too, grew grossly obese on cortisone; others developed diabetes; men went bald and women grew beards, and there were cases of drug-induced manic depression.

The first survey to show how widespread and alarming adverse reactions had become was L. Meyler's *Side-effects of Drugs*, which appeared in 1952, but the drug companies had their answer ready. New types of drug, or variations on old types, were by this time being marketed as 'free from side-effects'. The new corticosteroids, developed from cortisone, shed the 'cortico' as soon as the paternity ceased to throw lustre on them; marketed simply as steroids, they were claimed to be free from cortisone's risk. But when these claims were investigated by the Senate Committee which sat under Estes Kefauver, its report in 1961 revealed that there had in fact been side-effects, which had been played down, or even covered up, in drug companies' promotion.

## Chloromycetin

The most disturbing of the report's case-histories concerned chloramphenicol, an antibiotic marketed as Chloromycetin by Parke Davis. The drug had been promoted for its 'broad spectrum' capabilities against many common infections, but very soon it had been discovered that one of its side-effects could be aplastic anemia, a disorder in which the bone marrow ceases to nourish the blood supply, with serious and sometimes fatal consequences. As a result the FDA had withdrawn its licence. But as the drug had been found to be highly effective against typhoid and one or two rarer infections, the manufacturers had been allowed to put it back on the market, provided that it was accompanied by warnings of its dangers if used indiscriminately.

Parke Davis had complied with the FDA's commands in their advertisements in the medical journals. In their direct mail to doctors, however, the Kefauver committee found, it had watered down the warnings, and the company's representatives, visiting doctors, had been briefed to explain that Chloromycetin had not merely been 'officially cleared' but had also been given an 'unqualified sanction'. They had even been told to memorise, and repeat verbatim, that intensive investigation by the FDA, 'carried on with the assistance of a special committee of eminent specialists appointed by the National Research Council, resulted in unqualified sanction of continued use of Chloromycetin for all conditions in which it has previously been used'.

The fact that Chloromycetin had been out of favour for a while now worked to its advantage. Doctors who had been having trouble with the side-effects of other antibiotics, or finding that bacteria were resistant to them, began again to prescribe Chloromycetin, so that by the time the Kefauver committee was collecting its evidence, it had the biggest sale of any antibiotic. And although the way in which the company had deliberately and successfully set out to mislead the medical profession was clearly brought out in the report, the exposure was to make no perceptible difference; in 1963 a survey revealed that more people were dying from the drug's side-effects than were being saved from death in the rare conditions for which it was recommended.

In Britain, where promotion was less restricted, the *British Medical Journal* warned its readers about the dangers of Chloromycetin, and pointed out that its use was not justified except for those rare conditions for which it was indicated. Yet soon after the publication of its warning editorial, and of the Kefauver report, a full-page advertisement in the journal recommended Chloromycetin for respiratory infections, bacterial and viral pneumonia, whooping cough, gastro-intestinal infections, urinary infections, and many more.

*Thalidomide*

The publication of the Kefauver findings would have made little difference had it not been for the thalidomide affair. How small an impression they had made can be gauged from the fact that, although at the time the report appeared there had just been some worrying accounts of the side-effects of thalidomide, linking it to peripheral neuropathy – numbness or weakness of the limbs and extremities – the manufacturers continued not merely to promote their product as a sleep-inducer, but to emphasise its safety as one of the main selling-points, and the medical journals continued to accept their advertisements. Even when a paper appeared in the *British Medical Journal* in 1961 by two doctors from the Middlesex Hospital, describing thirteen cases in which the symptoms 'resembled neuropathy associated with malignant disease', and seemed to be irreversible – they had continued after medication with the drug had ceased – an advertisement was published in the same issue claiming that it was both highly effective 'and outstandingly safe'. The *British Medical Journal*'s reaction to the ensuing letters of protest was to allow the company to 'make the position clear' in a two-page spread admitting that there had been side-effects, but reiterating the company's claims for the safety of the drug. By a wry coincidence, it was in this same week that the report appeared that was to indict thalidomide for teratogenicity – damage to foetuses in the womb, and it was only then that the manufacturers, the Distillers Company, withdrew it.

Yet little publicity was given to the withdrawal. The excuse for the silence was that pregnant women who had taken the drug might be unduly alarmed, but inevitably, as a result, some women who had it in their medicine cupboards, and had found it effective against insomnia, continued to take it. In Canada, it was not withdrawn for three months after its teratogenic properties had been unmasked. Only the United States were spared the full effects, because Dr Frances Kelsey of the FDA had noted a letter in the *British Medical Journal* drawing attention to the peripheral neuritis risk. Knowing that it was sometimes an indicator of serious trouble for patients, she had held up the licence which an American company was calling for – an action for which she was roundly abused – smeared, even, by the implication that she must have some discreditable motive.

The thalidomide scandal enabled Kefauver to push a Drugs Bill through Congress in 1962, in spite of dogged opposition by some leading Republicans, backed by the industry's Washington lobby. In Britain it led to the setting up of the Committee on the Safety of Drugs, with power to regulate the testing of drugs before they were marketed. But any

135

expectation that the reforms would lead to a substantial reduction in the incidence of iatrogenic disorders was to be dispelled by the publication in 1965 of Morton Mintz's *The Therapeutic Nightmare*, revised and updated two years later as *By Prescription Only*, revealing in detail some of the continuing slippery manoeuvrings of the drug companies, and the pusillanimity of the medical profession in its dealings with them. And, not surprisingly, there have since been several ugly episodes.

## Clioquinol

The worst example is the story of clioquinol, manufactured by Ciba-Geigy and sold all over the world under many different labels, Enterovioform and Mexaform being the best known, primarily to thwart that bane of tourists, 'Mexican' or 'Gyppy' tummy.

The drug was particularly popular in Japan until, in 1970, the suspicion arose that it might be responsible for 'SMON' – subacute myelooptic neuropathy – which took the form of stomach pains and loss of sensation at the extremities, sometimes leading to incontinence, paralysis and blindness. Yet not until 1976 did the company concede that the drug might be the cause of the disease. By this time a court hearing had disclosed that the number of people who had contracted SMON had reached five figures, nearly a thousand of them having died or, unable to bear the agony, committed suicide. Delivering its verdict in 1978, the Tokyo court emphasised that the cause – not 'A cause' – of SMON was clioquinol, and that when the defendants had begun to manufacture it, 'they were already guilty of not having taken the necessary steps to avoid possible disastrous results'.

But why, if the results in Japan had been so disastrous, had tourists elsewhere not suffered a similar fate? In the United States the explanation was obvious: the FDA had not licensed the drug. In Britain, however, it had been lavishly promoted; estimates put the number of travellers and tourists taking it at a quarter of a million. The explanation was in fact simple: the recommended dosage in Britain was far lower than in Japan – so low, in fact, that the *British Medical Journal* had dismissed the drug as nothing more than a placebo, and when Andrew Herxheimer, the editor of the consumer-oriented *Drug and Therapeutics Bulletin*, was asked for his opinion on trials which, according to the company, had demonstrated the drug's effectiveness, he replied that the evidence was so insubstantial that it was 'difficult to see how its continued use can be justified'.

## Steroids

In all common disorders treated by drugs, some patients have suffered unwelcome consequences; the evidence suggests that, if the effects of drug treatment were more systematically monitored, many more would come to light. In the early 1960s, for example, an extensive long-term trial was mounted in the United States, the University Group Diabetic Program, to test three types of treatment in common use for diabetes. Some patients received insulin in fixed doses; some had insulin in doses varied by the doctor; some were given the biggest-selling diabetes drug, tolbutamide; and some a placebo. Later, another group received phenformin. By 1969 the mortality rate of patients on tolbutamide was so much higher than the rest that the decision was taken to withdraw it from the trial, and to issue a warning about it. Later, phenformin also had to be withdrawn – the first drug to be formally banned by the Federal Secretary of Health. When the mortality rates of the groups taking insulin were compared with those of the control group on the placebo, it was found that there was no difference. Neither was there any difference in effectiveness; management by diet alone had worked just as well.

The history of the steroids has been even more lamentable. When they came on the market the manufacturers claimed that they were safer as well as more effective than cortisone in the treatment of rheumatic disorders. As early as 1957 Richard A. Kern warned the College of Physicians in Philadelphia that this was untrue. 'The abuse of steroid therapy is widespread,' he asserted, 'and its consequences are serious.' It led to atrophy of the body's own hormone-manufacturing system, so that patients could not be taken off the drugs, and this had led to 'a dreary succession of disasters in patients', leaving them 'in essence, man-made cases of Addison's Disease. But whereas naturally-occurring Addison's Disease is a great rarity, there are thousands of cases of iatrogenic Addison's Disease today.'

Four years later the Kefauver Committee report confirmed that the side-effects of the steroids were indeed appalling. Yet new ones were being marketed, described as safe. In particular Merck's Decadron had been lavishly promoted as more effective and safer than its predecessors, with such slogans as 'No worrisome side-effects attributable to Decadron have occurred as yet'. Not merely was this untrue, the report observed; the company knew it to be, yet had continued to use it. With its help Merck had captured over a quarter of the extremely lucrative steroid market.

It continued to be lucrative. Prescriptions for steroids mounted, partly because of energetic promotion, partly because so many patients became dependent upon them. Their effects, Michael Kelly of the Melbourne Institute of Rheumatology realised when he investigated them, were horrifying. Worried by the high death-rate of arthritis patients treated with cortisone, he had greeted the earliest steroid, prednisone, with relief. 'My critical faculties were dimmed for two years,' he was to recall. Eventually, however, he found that the death-rate of patients on prednisone was also alarmingly high, and a search through medical journals from other parts of the world convinced him that steroids were even more of a threat than he had realised. In 1964 a paper appeared in the *Lancet* describing a trial being held in London to provide more information about the side-effects of long-term treatment with steroids, so that they could be used 'rationally and safely' in the future. Although the information revealed just how ugly the side-effects could be, Kelly pointed out in a letter to the *Lancet* that it did not give the whole story. In 1961 more than two hundred people had been involved in the trial; the number had since fallen to less than a hundred. What had happened to the others? 'We have not been told,' Kelly complained, 'how many are still alive.' Ominously, the information was not forthcoming.

Kelly continued his inquiries, and came across evidence that the damage from steroid treatment was even more extensive than he had feared. In a paper 'What are the Collagen Diseases?' the following year, he recalled that the term had been introduced in 1942 as a name for a rare disorder of the white fibres of bone, cartilage or connective tissue; later it had been extended to cover a variety of unexplained symptoms in the muscles, the arteries, and the skin. By the time Kelly became interested, over five hundred papers had been published on the subject, describing a great variety of similar symptoms for which no cause had been found. Could there be a common denominator? Kelly realised that almost all the patients had been treated for rheumatoid arthritis with cortisone or one of its steroid derivatives. Before 1949 the collagen diseases, as originally defined, had been rare and slow to progress. After 1949, when cortisone had been introduced, they had become much more common, and progressed more rapidly, often to a fatal outcome. 'The majority of patients alleged to have collagen disease,' Kelly feared, 'are rheumatoid patients suffering from steroid toxic effects.' Steroids 'are drugs of addiction for doctor and patient, used irrationally for a host of previously non-fatal diseases', he concluded. 'These diseases now have considerable death rates.'

By 1964 the side-effects of steroid treatment for arthritis had become so notorious that they were being edged out of this market by the newer 'anti-inflammatory' type of drug. To the relief of the steroid manufacturers, however, they were now being used in the treatment of several other disorders; they were proving particularly effective against many forms of skin trouble, clearing them up in a few days, sometimes overnight. Soon steroid creams were being energetically promoted and widely prescribed for skin diseases.

For a while, adverse reactions seemed minimal; as late as 1973 the writer of an Office of Health Economics' survey would claim that 'remarkably little evidence has accumulated of adverse side-effects.' But gradually it came to be realised that if steroid treatment were prolonged, or used by people with certain types of sensitive skin, it could cause rosacea – a reddening, roughening of the face. Steroid creams could even begin to eat away the skin. In Britain by 1977 there were some 20,000 victims a year of steroid-induced rosacea – not a new form of the disorder, according to Andrew Warin of the Institute of Dermatology, but an uglier one: 'doctors never used to see this type of severe rosacea before these potent preparations came into use.' Yet the potent preparations continued to be prescribed, and only one manufacturing company, Schering, enclosed a warning leaflet in the package. Even this was often removed by the chemist, the usual excuse being, as a spokesman for ICI, one of the other manufacturers, explained, that 'it is up to the doctor what to tell the patient'.

The Committee on Safety of Drugs did not intervene, and when an article by Christine Orton appeared in the *Guardian*, in 1975, describing her unfortunate experiences with her child's infantile eczema, she was deluged with letters from other parents who had had the same trouble. The point on which there was most agreement, she found, was that doctors' methods of treatment had been a disaster. 'If one message comes loud and clear, it is to throw away the steroids and cortisone creams.' This had been a shattering revelation to her, as they had been prescribed for her son from the start, and although she had heard 'dark rumours' of the damage they could do, she had declined to credit them. Yet here was the evidence that the rumours had been correct. They were supplemented by a letter from a doctor which the *Guardian* published, spelling out the severity of adverse reactions to some steroids: not just local scarring of the skin, when they were applied for any length of time, but also absorption into the system, resulting in 'a very very long list of changes in many organs of the body'.

Ironically, the doctor's aim was reassurance. Such adverse reactions, he claimed, were 'usually reversible'. In other words, sometimes they were *not* reversible; the facial scarring could be lasting, perhaps permanent. Yet when Christine Orton had suggested to her specialist that, in

139

view of the evidence, it might be sensible to try gentler remedies sanctioned by folklore, he had dismissed them as cranky, and prescribed another steroid. Two years later the chairman of the National Eczema Society, set up following the revelations in the *Guardian*, complained that, of the eleven firms engaged in the manufacture of steroid creams, only two issued any warning to patients about possible adverse reactions, and children, even babies, were still being prescribed the creams, 'often by repeat prescription, over the telephone'.

Steroids used in the treatment of skin diseases, the *Lancet* had to warn that autumn, 'are double-edged weapons that are widely misused'; in spite of ten years of such warnings, the problem had reached the stage when 'at every clinic, the dermatologist is likely to see at least one patient with a complication of steroids'. To judge by those which the *Lancet* listed, 'complication' was putting it mildly.

As symptom-removers, the record of steroids is unsurpassed. Consequently they have been hailed, again and again, as the drug of their choice by doctors who have tried them out in some new role. Yet invariably their record has been disillusioning. A recent *British Medical Journal* article has provided a typical example, in a survey of Crohn's disease. The introduction of steroid treatment had 'promised easy control of the disease', but eventually retrospective studies showed that the steroids 'often gave only short-term benefits, and might be harmful'. No type of drug has given more impressive results in the short term; none, in the long term, has done such widespread damage.


## Cimetidine

During the 1970s it became increasingly difficult for the pharmaceutical industry to produce new drugs which could be described as breakthroughs, but one which appeared to fulfil this aim was cimetidine, marketed in 1976 for the treatment of stomach ulcers. The drug, it was claimed, controlled most of the acids which irritate the digestive tract, enabling people to eat what they liked without suffering ulceration, and sparing them from surgery. Such was its success in its publicised capacity as 'the executive's friend' that the British version, Tagamet, won a Queen's Award in 1978 for technological achievement.

This was all the more gratifying to the industry in that stomach ulcers had frequently been claimed as psychosomatic, a claim borne out by an unusual piece of research by two New York doctors, Stewart Wolf and Harold G. Wolff, and described in their *Human Gastric Function* in 1947. Their human subject was Tom, a janitor at the hospital in which they worked, who as a child had sneaked into the family kitchen to take a gulp of clam chowder, and so scalded his throat that for the rest of his life he had to take his nourishment through a tube direct into his stomach. It occurred to Wolf and Wolff that here was their opportunity to follow up research which had been done over a century earlier when a Canadian doctor, William Beaumont, was treating a trapper who had been accidentally shot in the stomach. Although Beaumont had been primarily interested in physiology, he had observed that on one occasion, when the trapper had been angry, the food passing through his stomach had been yellow with bile. Wolf and Wolff decided to see what would happen if they gave Tom an unpleasant surprise, such as pretending they had heard he had been fired. They found that his digestive tract went pale – much as people's faces do in shock. The lining dried out, so that when abrasive food particles passed along it they could cause bleeding.

There could hardly have been a clearer illustration of the mechanics of psychosomatic processes, confirming as it did that stomach ulcers were 'visceral neuroses', as John Ryle, Regius Professor of Physics at Cambridge, had described them in 1934, in an attempt to persuade his colleagues to accept that nervous disorders could result in organic lesions. 'Of all the major diseases,' Guirdham claimed in *A Theory of Disease* in 1957, duodenal ulcer was the one 'in which the connection between emotional conflict and a physical lesion is most clearly revealed to us'; it could be regarded as 'the psychosomatic disease *par excellence*'. The fact that cimetidine cleared up stomach ulcers so effectively suggested that whether or not there was a psychosocial component really hardly mattered; here was a safe and simple cure.

Hardly had cimetidine been approved by the FDA for sale in the United States, however, when the *New England Journal of Medicine* reported the unwelcome fact that stomach ulcers frequently recurred as soon as treatment with the drug was suspended – a verdict echoed in the *Lancet* the following year. The healing of ulcers might be very rapid, its editorial observed, but seventy-to-ninety per cent of cases suffered a relapse within a few weeks, or at most months – a fact which a consultant surgeon, writing in *World Medicine*, viewed with sardonic satisfaction; the flow of patients to his operating theatre, he forecast, would soon be starting up again after the interlude.

The recurrence of ulcers when the treatment with cimetidine was stopped need not have disturbed the makers. The drug might then establish itself – George Teeling-Smith, Director of the Office of Health Economics, observed in 1980 in a monograph on the benefits and risks of pharmaceutical innovation – 'as a prolonged and perhaps lifelong therapy'; this would have made it very profitable, if his expectation – 'it seems likely that it will provide a safe alternative to surgery' – had been fulfilled. But shortly before his commentary appeared, a group of surgeons in the Manchester Royal Infirmary claimed there was evidence to suggest that treatment with cimetidine could not merely mask the development of gastric cancer: it might actually cause it; and a few months later Peter Reed, a consultant at the Royal Postgraduate Medical School, Hammersmith, reported that tests he had undertaken with more than three hundred people, although they did not prove that cimetidine was carcinogenic, had provided worrying evidence that it might be – evidence sufficient, a member of the Committee on Safety of Medicines admitted, for the Committee to have refused to license the drug, had they known about it at the time.

## Valium

Commenting on the case against cimetidine, Dennis Parke, Professor of Biochemistry at the University of Surrey and also a member of the Committee, remarked to the *Sunday Times* that if it were correct, 'it would cast doubt on the whole basis on which we determine drug safety'. But the whole basis was soon to be further threatened when another drug was indicted, a drug far more widely prescribed through the West than either cimetidine or clofibrate.

In the course of some work on muscle cells, David Horrobin and his colleagues in the Clinical Research Institute in Montreal found that diazepam, although not carcinogenic, appeared to promote cancer, and trials with rats established that it speeded up the growth of breast tumours. Diazepam is better known by its trade name of Valium, and it has been widely prescribed for women with breast cancer. The National Cancer Institute of Canada declined to support further research, but two years later a report from Basil Stoll of St Thomas's Hospital in London showed that women taking tranquillisers tended to have tumours which spread more rapidly than those in women who were not, at the time cancer was diagnosed. Horrobin and his colleagues wrote to the *Lancet* to suggest that, in view of their earlier discovery, the issue 'merits urgent investigation'. Diazepam, they pointed out, had been screened to ensure it was not a carcinogen, but it had not been screened to find whether it might be a carcinogen-promoter.

The response of the Canadian National Cancer Institute's spokesman, however, when the evidence was brought to his attention, was that Horrobin's investigation was 'not worth doing', and the director of the Montreal Clinical Research Institute insisted that Horrobin must resign.

When the manufacturers of Valium, the Swiss firm of Hoffman LaRoche, asked a consultant toxicologist to the industry, Dr Francis Roe, for an opinion, he was ill-advised to fall back on what Colin Tudge of the *New Scientist* criticised in his account of the affair as 'an attempt at character assassination'. Roe dismissed Horrobin as 'a brilliant student' whose career had 'somehow disintegrated'; examining Horrobin's career, Tudge found that, on the contrary, it has been 'of the kind that is known as "glittering"'. And whether or not diazepam turns out to be one of them, the existence of cancer promoters, since confirmed by other researchers, is itself a warning that, in future, this possibility will need to be taken into consideration in all trials of drugs.

The lessons from these, and from many other drugs, is that side-effects remain a built-in hazard, and that controlled trials provide a far from effective protection against them. It is certainly true, as the pharmaceutical industry's spokesmen are careful to point out, that the fault often lies less with the drug itself than with mis-prescribing and over-prescribing; but so long as the medical profession refuses even to contemplate imposing stricter limitations on the prescribing of danger-ous drugs, this is inevitable. To argue, as defenders of a dangerous drug so often do, that it will entail no risk if correctly prescribed, is the equivalent of rejecting fresh road safety regulations on the pretext that those which are in existence are sufficient if drivers will only take due care. Nor can the industry escape responsibility. Too often it has been as a consequence of its skilful promotional campaigns that drugs *are* mis-prescribed and over-prescribed.

## Incidence

How serious is the problem presented by adverse reactions to drugs, in general? Ordinarily when a new type of disease begins to cause concern, its incidence is carefully studied and documented. But in 1970 Owen Wade, Professor of Therapeutics and Pharmacology in the Queen's University, Belfast, and a member of the Medicines Commission, had to admit in his *Adverse Reactions to Drugs* 'that the burden of drug-induced disease in the community is not known'. One of the profession's chief tasks in the 1970s, he argued, would be to assess it: 'The need more and more is to be able to balance the benefits that are derived from treatment with a drug against any ill-effects it may cause.' Yet by the close of the 1970s hardly any progress had been made along the lines he had proposed.

A few surveys have been reported. In 1975 Nelson S. Irey of the Armed Forces Institute of Pathology in Washington, examining the evidence, found that estimates of the frequency of adverse reactions to drugs in hospitals ranged from fifteen per cent to forty per cent. In Britain, according to *Adverse Drug Reaction Bulletin*, the figure is between ten per cent and eighteen per cent, a discrepancy possibly accounted for by the fact that fewer powerful drugs are employed. The incidence of side-effects in patients treated out of hospitals is, for obvious reasons, more difficult to estimate, but investigation of a sample of over eight hundred patients in a general practice in Britain has shown that over forty per cent had either 'certainly' or 'probably' suffered an adverse reaction to a drug they had been prescribed. But these statistics convey little, as there is no accepted way of estimating the proportion of reactions which are hardly noticeable, such as a mild skin rash, and those which can be unbearable, driving the victims to desperation. And as Franz Inglefinger, editor of the *New England Journal of Medicine*, pointed out, even if the available statistics were accurate, which obviously they were not, they have little meaning, because the need is for figures for the incidence of *unnecessary* adverse reactions – unnecessary because alternative treatment is available – and no way has been found to collect them.

Estimates of the number of fatalities from drugs have been even more tentative. In American hospitals between 5,000 and 11,500 deaths, Irey thought, were primarily attributable to adverse drug reactions. In Britain the Registrar General's figure is close on 3,000 deaths a year from 'therapeutic misadventure'. Statistics drawn from post mortems are notoriously unreliable, however, and ordinarily they indicate only the immediate cause. For example, a verdict of 'aplastic anemia' would be given rather than 'anemia as a consequence of the ill-advised administration of chloramphenicol', even if that could be established. Whether symptoms are recognised as drug reactions depends on the diagnostic acumen of the doctor; where there is a long gap between the administration of the drug and the reaction, he cannot be expected to make the diagnosis with any certainty, particularly since he himself may not have prescribed the drug.

## Indirect Reactions

Some side-effects are sufficiently often related to a particular drug for their incidence to be roughly predictable, and attributable to the drug's pharmacological action. They can be primary, as in the pain from iodine on a cut, or secondary, as in the onset of an infection owing to the disruption of the body's homeostasis by a steroid. Also common, however, are hypersensitivity reactions, caused by individuals being (or becoming) allergic to a drug. Some drugs appear to accumulate within the body, leading to eventual breakdown. In addition, other adverse reactions attributable to drug treatment need to be weighed in the scale against its advantages.

Chief among these reactions, and the cause of justifiable concern, is the spread of addiction to medical drugs, first encountered in the eighteenth century in connection with opium, and later described by de Quincey in his *Confessions of an English Opium Eater*. Ironically, when heroin was introduced a century ago it was welcomed because it was believed not to be addictive, unlike opium or its derivative morphine. Only since the last war, however, has addiction to medical drugs become a serious social evil: first with amphetamines, then with barbiturates; most recently with tranquillisers. Every year the number of people who cannot do without their 'uppers' or their 'downers' (or both) is on the increase.

Consumption of psychoactive drugs also increases the risk of accidents, as Sir Richard Doll pointed out in connection with the tranquillisers, and as John Harvard, Secretary of the British Medical Association, has recently emphasised. All too often, he fears, people do not realise that the drug which has been prescribed for them contains ingredients liable to affect driving skills for hours after it has been taken. Barbiturates 'slow down reaction times, reduce perception'; anti-anxiety drugs 'depress the emotional responses concerned with self-preservation'; anti-depressants 'may cause fatigue; blurred vision has also been reported'. Even cold cures often contain drugs which can affect drivers.

'The risk is increased,' Harvard complains 'by the manufacturers' failure, in many cases, to include a warning on the label.'

## Resistant Strains

Also iatrogenic, although at one remove, are the consequences of over-prescribing and mis-prescribing antibiotics which encourage the development of resistant strains of micro-organism. The most notorious example concerns typhoid, against which chloramphenicol proved remarkably effective. Owing to the success with which its makers marketed it for other infections, resistant strains were soon being reported from all over the world. Thousands of patients have since succumbed to typhoid in Mexico as the result – according to Professor E. S. Anderson, Director of the Enteric Reference Laboratory at Colindale in London – 'of the long-term indiscriminate use of chloramphenicol and other antibiotics'.

The situation can only be remedied, Anderson warns, 'by more rational antibiotic usage'. But who is going to ensure that antibiotic usage becomes more rational? If in the United States and Europe doctors have ignored the earlier warnings, there is no reason to suppose they will be influenced by reports of typhoid deaths in Mexico. Nothing effective has been done to check prescribing, and fresh reports of resistant strains of other bacteria have been coming in, including a penicillin-resistant gonococcus which has suddenly emerged in cities scattered all over the world, leaving the disturbing impression that it cannot have been the result of some single random mutation, gradually being spread by intercourse.

With the increasing use of antibiotics in animal-feeding stuffs, in spite of regulations against the practice, the day is rapidly approaching – an international symposium held in Limburg in 1978 was told – when antibiotics will be remembered only as a once valuable, but 'temporary and historical' form of treatment. That year two more 'supergerms', as they were christened, were uncovered: a penicillin-resistant pneumococcus (which meant, as the *New England Journal of Medicine* glumly observed, that penicillin could no longer be automatically prescribed on diagnosis of pneumonia, as it had been for years), and a strain of salmonella, so often linked with food poisoning, which had become resistant to many antibiotics. The National Center for Disease Control in Atlanta has since announced yet another sinister development: the vibrio responsible for the 'El Tor' variety of cholera, one of the commonest, has become resistant to tetracycline, the drug usually used to treat it, and to a number of other antibiotics. More recently there have been several other reports of drug-resistant strains.

## Surgery

When a new drug is produced, clinical trials have to be conducted before it is passed for general use. No such monitoring is applied to new surgical operations, nor are trials periodically carried out to test whether they are necessary and, if so, whether they could be made safer. As a result many pointless types of operation have been introduced and used for years on unsuspecting patients, few of whom have dared to question the surgeon's verdict.

The most notorious example of such an operation, performed on hundreds of thousands of patients before it was finally discredited, was for the removal of 'foci of infection' from the gut or the jaw. The London psychiatrist William Sargant has recalled that during his training at St Mary's Hospital in London, one of the students' jobs was to try to explain to puzzled patients why all their teeth should have to be extracted, while those of the enormously successful surgeon, Sir William Wilcox, filthy though they were, remained in place. Focal sepsis operations 'made large fortunes for several members of the staff, and staff members were even elected because of their work in it, and stayed on working in it for years after it was discredited'.

The next fashionable operation was for 'slipped disc', for lumbago – lower-back pain. Introduced during the Second World War, a paper in the *Lancet* claimed that 'nearly all recurrent attacks of backache, and many cases of chronic backache, are due to disc lesions' – to the displacement of one of the spine's shock absorbers. Disc surgery, the authors asserted, was free from risk, and would provide a cure in nearly every case. By 1949 a standard orthopedic text-book was describing the operation as the only form of treatment which held out any real prospect of a cure for lumbago, one of the commonest forms of everyday incapacitating illness; it was later to be estimated that two out of every three cases of backache serious enough to require specialist attention were operated upon. As late as 1959, the *American Journal of Surgery* contained a paper describing results varying from good to excellent following surgery in nearly a thousand cases over a twenty-year period. Yet by that time, the operation was beginning to fall out of favour. By the mid-1970s it had come to be regarded as a treatment of last resort, to be tried only if all other methods had failed, and where there was a risk of serious complications if the cause of the pain were not found.

What had happened to discredit the disc operation? It is unlikely that this will ever be known, for a curious reason. Whereas the stages by which an operation becomes fashionable are usually well documented, with numerous papers describing the growing success-rate, papers describing the growing awareness of attendant problems are rarely published, partly because they might be latched on to by the press and television, but chiefly because they are rarely submitted for publication – or, indeed, even written. There is, however, one almost infallible indicator of trouble in store: papers defending a surgical technique but insisting that its success depends upon the correct selection of patients. Inevitably this means that there has been an unwelcome proportion of failures. But it would require heroic self-sacrifice on the part of a surgeon to document these, quite apart from the risk of his patients hearing about his confession. As a result, the full story of the decline and fall of the reputation of such operations as those for focal sepsis and slipped disc is likely to remain untold.

'That any sane nation, having observed that you could provide for the supply of bread by giving bakers a pecuniary interest in baking for you, should go on to give a surgeon a pecuniary interest in cutting off your leg, is enough to make one despair of political humanity,' Bernard Shaw observed in the Preface to *The Doctors' Dilemma*. 'But that is precisely what we have done. And the more appalling the mutilation, the more the mutilator is paid.' Not only that, Shaw went on to point out. We also make the surgeon the judge of whether the operation is necessary, making it certain that 'we shall be dismembered unnecessarily in all directions by surgeons who believe the operations to be necessary solely because they want to perform them'.

The fact that in Britain most operations are performed without financial benefit to the surgeon makes it possible to estimate how far Shaw's criticism was justified, by comparing surgery in Britain and the United States. In 1970 John P. Bunker of Stanford University made this comparison, and presented the findings in the *New England Journal of Medicine*. The United States, he had found, had twice as many surgeons in proportion to the population, who on average each performed twice as many operations. This did not necessarily prove that half the operations in the United States were unnecessary, he admitted, but it did suggest that far too many doctors were surgeons; 'so we have the paradox of a country that provides "luxury" surgery for the well-to-do but cannot provide basic medical care for the indigent'.

Tonsillectomy is generally agreed to be the operation most often performed unnecessarily. Hiatt has put the proportion of unnecessary tonsillectomies at ninety per cent. Frederick North, Professor of

Pediatrics at the University of Pittsburg, thinks it is even higher. One damaging piece of evidence about its misuse is that more tonsils are removed in August than in any other month. 'There are a number of reasons why this occurs,' Rick Carlson observed, 'but a principal one is that the physicians need to keep busy.'

The most commonly performed single operation in the United States is the hysterectomy. Within the profession, these operations are also widely held, except by the surgeons who perform them, to be rarely necessary. The proportion which *are* necessary cannot be established, because surgeons have not allowed the introduction of any system of audit. Until this is introduced, it will not be possible to assess the full extent of iatrogenic suffering from unnecessary – and in the case of cancer, disfiguring – surgery; but on the available evidence, US surgeons stand indicted of behaving as Shaw claimed.

# 5

# Infectious Diseases

Civilisation used to be continually threatened by devastating pesti-
lences – the bubonic plague, the sweating sickness, smallpox, cholera
and many more. They swept into Europe, and later America, usually
from the East. Carried by rats or lice or people, they were transmitted
from country to country in spite of efforts to stop them by such early
experiments in preventive medicine as quarantine. Nobody knew what
caused them. For centuries the prevailing view was that they must be
the instruments of God's wrath. Then for a time it was believed they
were carried by miasmas: noxious emanations, invisible but pervasive
(Dickens's description of 'Eden', which Martin Chuzzlewit and Mark
Tapley found, graphically conveys the popular conception). In the
middle of the nineteenth century, however, medical science came up
with the answer. Pasteur, Koch and their disciples showed how infections are carried from place to place, and person to person, by germs
invisible to the human eye except under a microscope. And although the
germ theory was contested for a time, it soon had to be accepted that
each infection has its specific pathogen, germ or virus. This in turn
enabled bacteriologists to provide immunity with the help of vaccines
or, failing that, to find a 'magic bullet', as Ehrlich called it: a drug specific
to the disease, capable of routing the bacteria responsible.

This, at least, was the scenario presented between the wars, notably
by Paul de Kruif in his *Microbe Hunters* and later best-selling works,
which helped to establish bacteriologists among the folk-heroes of our
time. Some of them, de Kruif had to admit, had been self-seekers,
downright unscrupulous in their experiments with people. Still, they had
done humanity so great a service that their peccadilloes could be
forgiven.

Enthusiastic though de Kruif had been, events were soon to suggest
that he had underestimated the contribution of his heroes. The discovery and marketing of sulpha drugs in the late 1930s, followed by penicillin and antibiotics, provided a means for treating infections far more
efficiently than even Ehrlich had dreamed. These magic bullets did not

have to be directed at a single target; in their 'broad spectrum' capacity they could be used as the equivalent of machine-gun fire, mowing down pathogens of many kinds. With the discovery of vaccines to immunise children against polio, diphtheria and other childhood diseases, a new era dawned. It even seemed reasonable to hope that before long disease, as distinct from accidents, need no longer be feared in civilisation, especially as the mortality statistics, showing improvements in life expectation each year, continued to justify the prevailing optimism.

The way in which infectious diseases have been brought under control, and some of them all but banished, is still generally regarded as modern medicine's great triumph. True, viruses have remained obstinately resistant to antibiotics and other drugs, and it has not been possible to repeat the immunising success achieved with polio. Nevertheless, the belief remains that the discovery of methods to deal with viruses can be only a matter of time. In any case, the basic premise remains well established: that, as the early bacteriologists proved, infectious diseases are caused and spread by pathogens, and that the way to deal with them is either to provide protection through immunisation, or, where that is not possible, to treat the diseases they cause with powerful drugs. It is as simple as that . . .

It is not, however, quite so simple, as an examination of three infectious diseases, tuberculosis, influenza (including colds), and urogenital disorders serves to show.

## Tuberculosis

As recently as thirty years ago, respiratory tuberculosis was still commonly regarded as *the* disease of civilisation. Epidemics of cholera, smallpox and typhoid came and went: TB remained ever present, a lurking threat. It sometimes struck, too, at young children or adolescents from well-to-do families, where fear precluded its mention in polite conversation. When it was talked about, the tones were hushed. 'Everybody,' Kafka wrote shortly before he died of it in 1924, 'drops into a shy, evasive, glassy-eyed manner of speech.'

Although TB is no longer so greatly feared, something of its old menace remains. Along with cancer, it forms the staple of Susan Sontag's *Illness as Metaphor*. Her contention is that the metaphorical construction put upon 'consumption', as it used to be called – that it literally 'consumed' people ('TB is disintegration, febrilisation, dematerialisation') – hindered recognition that it is simply an infection, like any other, with a single 'simple physical cause', susceptible to 'one program of treatment'.

This is still a widely accepted view, as is the belief that, until a century ago, consumption was not merely common, but usually lethal owing to ignorance of its cause and consequently the lack of any effective remedy. But when in 1882 Robert Koch discovered the tubercle bacillus, the mystery was solved. For a while, admittedly, he had difficulty in convincing the medical profession. Doctors had been trying to wean the public from the prevailing superstition, as they thought it, that consumption was infectious. (In the preface to *The Doctors' Dilemma*, Bernard Shaw was to recall that he could remember the time when doctors no more dreamt of its being infectious 'than they now dream of sea-sickness being infectious'.) Their attempts to educate the public not to shy away from consumptives, who were often refused accommodation (when they died, their belongings were often put on a bonfire), naturally made unwelcome Koch's claim that the bacilli were transmitted in sputum. But by perseverance in his researches and by systematic demonstrations, first with laboratory animals and then with humans, he succeeded in winning acceptance for his tubercular theory, and the disease henceforth took that name. Koch's discovery, too, made it possible to provide a vaccine, with which children could be immunised. Although for many years no drug could be found to treat the disease successfully, surgery could be used to collapse or remove diseased lungs, and in less severe cases patients were sent to sanatoria of the kind which Thomas Mann described in *The Magic Mountain*, where careful nursing, the mountain air and proper nourishment enabled many of them to recover. Gradually mortality fell until, after the Second World War, a combination of immunising programmes, mass X-ray screening, and the new chemotherapy at long last brought it down to its present very low level.

The reality is less creditable. That Koch discovered the bacillus associated with the disease is one of the few incontrovertible features of the story. But his 'tuberculin', which he introduced in 1880, proved a disaster. He was hailed as a deliverer when the news was announced – as the *Lancet* succinctly put it, 'glad tidings of great joy'. Conan Doyle, on his way to fame with Sherlock Holmes, showed less enthusiasm. Following a visit to Koch's Berlin headquarters, he warned that, as the remedy was designed to act not on the bacilli but on the tissues in which they proliferated, it would not get to the root of the evil. 'It continually removes the traces of the enemy, but it still leaves him deep in the invaded country.' Worse, in some cases it stirred up tubercular activity where it had lain dormant. Soon it was found that Doyle had been right, and tuberculin had to be abandoned.

Doyle, however, noted that, because the action of tuberculin was decisive for diagnostic purposes, 'this alone is a very important addition to the art of medicine'. So in a sense it was; henceforth TB could be diagnosed in its early stages with confidence. But in the absence of any effective method of treatment, this came to be regarded chiefly as a form of reassurance for people who did *not* have TB, and although mountain sanatoria for those who could afford it could sometimes provide an agreeable retreat from life's cares, many patients had to go to squalid old fever hospitals where, because TB was still taken to be infectious, they would ordinarily receive visits only rarely, and then only from their nearest and dearest.

The discovery of the new vaccine, the bacillus Calmette-Guérin – BCG – although it raised hopes that TB could be eventually eliminated, also met with a disastrous setback. In 1926 two hundred and forty-nine babies were given, in error, a powerful injection of virulent bacilli, instead of the attenuated BCG; over seventy of them died. Partly as a consequence, mass immunisation did not really get under way until after the Second World War, at the same time as the introduction of mass screening, to try to detect people with the disease before its symptoms became apparent, so that they could be isolated and given treatment before they became a danger to the community. The results of the combined operation had not been evaluated, however, before streptomycin, followed by other drugs, began to render the programme redundant.

Still, the assumption prevailed that BCG immunisation had worked well. Just how well could not be estimated with any certainty, however, because where it had been introduced there had usually been strenuous and effective opposition to controlled trials, in case the children in the control groups died as a result of not receiving BCG's protection. Where trials had taken place, the results had not been encouraging, but some excuse had always been found for ignoring them, such as that the numbers of children involved were too small, or the trial protocol insufficiently rigorous. Suspicion arose, however, when a survey by the World Health Organisation showed, among other things, that the country with the lowest respiratory TB rate in Europe, Holland, had never introduced a national immunisation programme. Eventually it was decided to hold a large-scale controlled trial of BCG in India, which was carefully conceived and meticulously carried out. The results, published in 1979, revealed that the protection given by BCG was 'zero'. As the *Lancet* mildly commented, 'The history of immunisation is a story of setback, controversy and surprise.'

The value of mass X-ray screening in the British campaign had also been grossly exaggerated. It proved far from reliable. In 1959 Henry Garland, Professor of Radiology at Stanford University, estimated that one out of ten patients diagnosed from X-rays as having TB did not in fact have it; in evaluating X-ray photographs 'one experienced physician is apt to disagree with another in about one third of cases'. (He would also, Garland sardonically added, contradict his own earlier diagnosis in about one case in five, when shown the pictures over again.) Those who really had the lesions would not necessarily have developed TB: the available evidence suggested that the proportion would have been small. The cost of the screening, too, coupled with the cost of keeping those detected by it in isolation until the symptoms did or did not appear, would soon have proved prohibitive, had not the introduction of the new anti-TB drugs after the Second World War rendered such expenditure unnecessary.

The drug's effectiveness has not been in dispute: only the use which the drug companies have made of it in their propaganda. As Dubos argued, and Thomas McKeown has since confirmed, there is no evidence that medical science can claim any credit for the steady decline in the mortality rate before the 1950s, by which time it had sunk to 50 per 100,000 from 500 per 100,000 deaths in 1845. The new drugs merely delivered the *coup de grâce* to a bacillus that was already facing defeat. And this raises the question: Why? Dubos insisted that there has been no falling-off in the pathogenic powers of the bacillus: tests on animals show no sign of change. 'But if the bacillus has not changed,' he pointed out, 'its human host certainly has.' The cause of TB, in other words, needs to be looked for in the condition of the people who contract it.

TB has been chiefly associated with poverty, insufficient nourishment, and squalid living conditions, a historical link which prompted the British Department of Health's Advisory Panel on medical aspects of nutrition to cite TB alongside heart disease as an example of the need to think in terms of risk factors rather than of a single physical cause. Its 1974 report nevertheless insisted that the bacillus is the *primary* cause, because 'the disease does not occur in the absence of the organism'. Yet this really only makes the bacillus the disease's identity tag. There is no proof, as yet, that the bacillus is harmful to man except when it finds a suitable host. It could be that not poverty as such, but deprivation, mental and emotional as well as physical, is the chief risk factor.

Epidemiological surveys have shown that, where there are pockets of TB in well-to-do countries, they usually occur among immigrant groups. In most parts of the United States, the TB mortality rate fell steadily during the nineteenth century, but it rose for a time in the 1860s in New York, Boston and Philadelphia. The most plausible explanation is that this resulted from the mass immigration of the Irish, uprooted from their homes across the Atlantic, and meeting a far from friendly welcome. It has been found that individuals, too, who are rootless, moving often from home to home, job to job, are statistically more TB-prone.

Until the present century it was widely believed by doctors, as well as old wives, that consumption – at least when contracted by adolescents and young men and women of well-to-do families – was related to emotional deprivation, the kind of unfulfilled and unfulfillable yearning that consumed Keats. 'I have very often observed that a consumption of the lungs,' Richard Morton wrote in his 1688 treatise on the subject, 'has had its origins in long and grievous passions of the mind.' A century later Leopold Auenbrugger, the Austrian doctor who introduced percussion as a way of diagnosing chest disorders, presented the same idea, attributing consumption to 'affections of the mind, particularly ungratified desires, the principal of which is nostalgia'. René Laennec, the inventor of the stethoscope (designed more to spare women's blushes than as a hearing aid) agreed. More surprisingly, so did Sir William Osler a century later, when such an opinion had become unfashionable. To predict the outcome of pulmonary tuberculosis, he claimed, 'it is just as important to know what is in a man's head as what is in his chest'.

Between the wars such views were dismissed as outmoded and un-scientific, but with the emergence of psychosomatic medicine, research began again, on a small scale, to explore this territory. TB bacilli, Flanders Dunbar observed, were everywhere. What was needed was an explanation 'why one person never gives the germs a chance, and

155

another seems to provide a virtual broth culture in which they thrive', and she cited a number of cases in which the broth seemed to have been provided by an emotional crisis. The Duboses were more cautious: it would have to be left for the future 'to unravel the subtle mechanism by which the psyche and the soma influence each other'. And at that period, few of the Duboses' contemporaries thought the subtle mechanism important enough to merit investigation. But in Glasgow in 1951 David Kissen embarked on a trial designed 'to ascertain, by investigations using controls and subjecting the results to statistical analysis, the part played by emotional factors in the onset or recrudescence of pulmonary tuberculosis', the first investigation of its kind (his work with cancer came later). His aim was to try to bring the emotions within the compass of scientific respectability by subjecting them to the same tests, so far as practicable, as drugs. For this he needed controls – a matched group of people who were not suffering from the disease, and a sufficient number of patients for the results to be presented in percentages in a form which would satisfy the statisticians.

At first sight this seemed an impossible demand. How could an unrequited need for affection be diagnosed with any certainty, in order that it might be slotted into statistics? Kissen elected to sound out patients not about their feelings, but about their life-stories. Patients coming to a local hospital for chest disorders were asked to fill in a questionnaire giving, among other things, such information as whether they had recently suffered a bereavement, a divorce, an unhappy love affair, or other likely causes of worry or despair. Since the questionnaires were filled in before the patients had been tested or diagnosed, a control group provided itself automatically from those patients who were later found not to have TB. The results were striking. Of the 267 patients participating in the test, one third were found to have TB, and sixty-five per cent of these had suffered from some episode of a kind likely to cause severe emotional stress, compared to only twenty-six per cent of those who did not have TB. In the severe emotional-stress group, over ninety per cent of the episodes were in the category 'break or serious threat of break in a romance, engagement, or marriage'.

In a second investigation Kissen used a similar method to find if emotional factors bore any relationship to relapses, following a period when the disease had been quiescent for a year or more. Again, the control group was ready-made: the patients who had not relapsed. Although the numbers were smaller, the findings were even more striking. Of the patients who had relapsed, over seventy-five per cent had preceding emotional-stress factors; of those who had not, less than twelve per cent.

Kissen's third investigation was more complex. He knew that some psychosomatic researchers, among them Eric Wittkower of McGill University, had been investigating the personality structures of TB patients, and Wittkower had claimed that they appeared to share an inordinate need for affection. This was a subjective assessment, impossible to make wholly objective, but Kissen felt that it was worth following up with a questionnaire designed to be as objective as possible. As in the initial investigations, patients were interviewed before they had been tested or diagnosed. They were asked questions about their childhood, previous illnesses, their parents' attitudes, their feelings about their families and friends. From their answers it was possible to make a tentative assessment whether their need for affection might be considered normal or inordinate (the interviewers found that 'in telling the story, particularly concerning life situations or relationships with parents, the intimacy of the subject to the patient, as shown by the facial expression and the mode of telling, made a strong impact', but this was not something which could be statistically expressed).

Following diagnosis, the patients who were found not to have TB provided the control group. The results confirmed Kissen's earlier findings: emotional factors, in particular a 'break in a love link', occurred in a significantly higher proportion of TB patients than of the control group. They also showed that the outstanding personality trait common to the TB cases was an inordinate need for affection, the figure being no less than one hundred per cent, compared with only sixteen per cent in the controls. Deprivation of affection in childhood also occurred far more often in the TB cass: sixty per cent, compared with sixteen per cent.

Kissen presented these findings in 1958 in his *Emotional Factors in Pulmonary Tuberculosis*, along with a survey of historical attitudes to TB, and assessments of the work of other researchers; in a section on psychosocial aspects he was able to show how closely his results tied in with those of the epidemiologists. It was known, for example, that in wartime TB mortality rose; the stock explanation had been that people's resistance must have been lowered by physical privations. But in that case, the great depression of the early 1930s could have been expected to cause a similar upturn in the death-rate. It had not. During the depression, Kissen pointed out, there had been material insecurity, 'but there was no particular threat to personal or family relationships'. In the war years, by contrast, 'the threat to personal and family relationships was as great as could be', with numerous broken love links.

In the Second World War, too, the TB deaths in the Channel Island of Jersey soared at the time of the German invasion, despite an initial lack

157

of any malnutrition and dropped again as soon as the Occupation ended, although the island did not recover material prosperity for some years. The Duboses had noted that the heaviest incidence of TB in Indian communities had been in the reservations, 'after they lost the freedom of their favorite hunting grounds' – a deprivation that could be regarded as a form of broken love link. The epidemiological evidence in general, Kissen felt, tied in with Wittkower's findings: 'The typical life situation involving the break or threatened break in a love link predisposes to tuberculosis in those who have the susceptible personality trait.'

Finally, Kissen considered the therapeutic implications of his and earlier psychosomatic findings. If a break in a love link was a risk factor in TB, clearly the policy of sending patients whenever possible to sanatoria would have to be reconsidered. As it happened, reports had been appearing of comparisons between the results of home and sanatorium treatment: none had shown that the sanatoria provided any significant benefit. It would be sensible, he suggested, to consider each case from the psychological viewpoint. In the case of young children, particularly, the trauma of separation ought to be avoided except in cases where, say, disharmony between the parents could be held responsible for the child's condition. The potential benefits of psychotherapy would also need to be considered, though he was well aware that the medical profession showed little enthusiasm for it, and psychologists and psychiatrists disagreed on the form it should take.

Meticulous though Kissen's research had been, it stood no chance of acceptance unless similar projects were mounted in other centres, and gave similar results. But by 1958, when his *Emotional Factors in Pulmonary Tuberculosis* was published, the incidence of TB was falling, the more rapidly because cases which would formerly have been hopeless could be successfully treated with the new drugs. The part which emotional stress played in precipitating TB became of historical interest only; there seemed no point in setting up further trials. Yet even if Kissen's findings came too late to be of much practical benefit, they remain valuable as a contribution to a better understanding of the mechanics of infection. They demonstrated, as convincingly as any small-scale epidemiological study could hope to do, the need to take into account risk factors other than the infecting agent, germ or virus, even when the culprits are at first sight as improbable as broken love links.

## Colds and Flu

'We have put space-probes on Mars, and men on the moon, but' – and so familiar is the cliché that it hardly needs to be completed – 'we have yet to find a cure for the common cold.' Or, for that matter, for influenza. It has not been for want of trying. Yet it rarely occurs to those who ruefully use this excuse for their snuffles that a possible reason is researchers' failure to ask the right questions. They have tended to assume that the symptoms are caused by invading viruses, ordinarily spread by the coughs and sneezes of people already infected. Familiar as we all are with the way that colds and flu pick off members of a family or an office staff over a period of a few days, this sounds no more than good common sense. Yet there is evidence that the obvious explanation is not the right one.

There is little point in trying to distinguish between colds and flu in this context. Whether a patient has a cold or flu can be ascertained in the laboratory, but in the great majority of cases the decision whether a patient's symptoms should be attributed to the one or to the other is made by rule of thumb. Although the rule varies from household to household, the general assumption is that the symptoms – sore throat, aches, shivering, running nose, and general malaise – qualify as flu only if they are severe, particularly if there is a temperature of over 100°F. If there happens to be a flu epidemic, however, the symptoms of what would ordinarily be regarded as a cold may achieve promotion.

This, in turn, has encouraged the belief that whereas a cold is no more than an inconvenience, flu is a *real* illness, justifying a few days off work. As specimens of mucus are not as a rule submitted for laboratory identification, the diagnosis is usually made by the patients themselves, or their families. The doctor is expected, if he is consulted at all, to fall in with it, unless he elects to pronounce some more serious verdict. To try to separate the incidence of the two is consequently unrewarding.

If the outcome is fatal, flu almost invariably gets the blame. About fifteen thousand people are recorded as dying of it each year in Britain, a third of them otherwise healthy and under sixty-five (these statistics, however, are misleading, because they include deaths arising from complications accompanying or following an attack of flu). In major epidemics the toll rises, yet except in the still notorious epidemic at the end of the First World War it has never been sinister. It is chiefly a source of concern because of man-hours lost in industry; though here, too, it can cover a multitude of syndromes, including protracted hangovers and days at the races as well as any disorder which a doctor cannot diagnose, but feels is not sufficiently serious to worry about. The term 'flu' has consequently become 'probably the most abused and most meaningless term in the whole sphere of medicine', the Medical Correspondent of *The Times* complained in 1969, little more than a synonym for a severe cold, because it is 'considered a more respectable excuse for a few days off work.'

For all practical purposes, he added, 'the treatment of the two conditions is the same'. It has remained the same to this day. Hundreds of preparations are on the market: temperature-reducers, pain-killers, decongestants. Multi-purpose block-buster drugs have been dreamed up to perform all these functions. Sometimes they even promise mutually exclusive effects, such as assisting expectoration but suppressing coughs: a recent survey by medical experts for the British consumer magazine *Which?* has warned against drug combinations of any kind, adding that 'no "remedy" can affect the course of a cold – it won't clear up any quicker, whatever treatment you use'. The best that modern medicine can do is to make the symptoms more bearable.

When a 'rhinovirus' was first discovered, and assumed to be the cause of colds, hopes were immediately raised that colds could eventually be dealt with by immunisation, but there were to be endless setbacks. The initial blow was the revelation that more than one virus was involved. Even then, it was believed that some form of prevention would soon be available; in 1962 the director of the US Institute of Infectious Diseases unwisely boasted that effective immunisation against the common cold would be available within five years. By the end of the five years many more rhinoviruses had been discovered; in 1972 it was calculated that eighty-nine 'clearly different' types had been identified, and it was not long before even the experts lost count.

A number of different strains of flu virus were also found, but not so many, and the hope lingered that for each of them – they often were labelled, according to their country of presumed origin, 'Hong Kong', or 'New Guinea' flu – a vaccine could be prepared, so that the authorities could open an immunisation campaign the moment that a particular strain was identified, anticipating the arrival of the epidemic. An opportunity to assess the value of the system on a national scale presented itself in 1976 when a flu virus was detected at Fort Dix, New Jersey, resembling the 1918 variety which had spread with such terrifying rapidity, killing an estimated twenty million people in different parts of the world. As it had been no respecter of purses, proving if anything more lethal to the well-off, the feeling was that there was no time to lose. President Ford was persuaded that here was his chance to save the lives of hundreds of thousands of American citizens with the help of a nation-wide immunisation programme, 'An ideal way', as the Center of

Disease Control's director put it, 'to celebrate the nation's 200th birthday.' That it might also do something to rescue the Republican Party from the discredit into which it had fallen over Watergate, and to improve Ford's re-election prospects, can hardly have escaped his advisers' notice. If it had, it was quickly brought to their attention by angry Democrats, unwilling to oppose the plan and unable to outbid it (except Senator Kennedy, who took the opportunity to call for an extension of the programme to include several other diseases to 'give our children a legacy to remember us by'). The required authorisation was rushed through without difficulty, and the planned biggest-ever enterprise of its kind was launched.

One influential critic, however, was cynical from the start. If the flu was so dangerous, the *New York Times* wanted to know, why had it not spread? Only a single case had occurred at Fort Dix. It had been identified, too, only as 'very similar' to the 1918 strain. 'The President's medical advisers seem to have panicked,' the *Times* decided, 'and talked him into a decision based on the worst assumptions about the still poorly-known virus, and the best assumptions about the vaccine.' The pharmaceutical industry, which could have been expected to leap at the opportunity offered by the President, shared some of the *Times*'s doubts. Firms declined to co-operate unless and until they were guaranteed indemnity against loss. This turned out to have been a sensible precaution. A few of the early recipients of the vaccine developed paralysis, and the campaign fizzled out in a welter of actions for damages, the claims totalling over two billion dollars, for everything from death to stained clothes. The epidemic never materialised.

The Fort Dix episode was the most spectacular flop in the efforts to provide the public with protection against flu, but it was far from being the only one. Occasionally vaccines appeared to provide some protection, but the failure rate remained too high to encourage the public to accept immunisation on any substantial scale. With flu as with colds, it has become clear that the hope of finding an effective way to control the viruses is illusory. They are simply too adaptable.

Their behaviour – as Marguerite Pereira, director of the World Health Organisation's influenza section, has explained – is even more devious than had been realised. Not merely are they able to mutate into new and different strains; they can do so in two ways, by 'shift' and 'drift'. In a 'shift', the virus 'changes itself so completely that everyone becomes susceptible' – even people who have just gone down with flu. A 'drift' is more subtle: it is as if the virus manages 'to change its coat in such a way that it is no longer recognised by the sentries'. With 'shift', in other words, the virus changes its character: with 'drift' it remains the same, but adopts a disguise. Either way, it can make a mockery of immunisation. Recent research suggests that flu viruses may be engaged in even craftier tricks. Not merely do they form new strains; they occasionally re-combine, with even more disconcerting consequences.

In its survey at the close of the 1970s, the *British Medical Journal* ruefully conceded that immunisation as a policy has failed. 'Few viruses have been studied so intensively as influenza's, and its structure and replication are fast being explained in terms of their detailed chemistry,' an editorial observed. 'Yet paradoxically we have no satisfactory vaccine, no effective chemotherapy, and apparently little in the way of preventive hygiene to stop an epidemic in its tracks.' Not only has the concept of the flu virus had to be modified with the successive discoveries of the different strains, of 'drift' and of 'shift', but also to these were now being added sub-types, allowing for 160 (at the latest count) possible combinations. 'The prevailing mood,' the editorial concluded, 'is qualified pessimism.'

## 'Cognitive Dissonance'

Have researchers, then, been on the wrong track, working as they have on the assumption that colds and flu are caused by the viruses associated with them, which are transmitted from person to person?

After the Second World War a Common Cold Research Unit was set up in Britain by the Medical Research Council; it began by investigating the stock explanations, such as the hazards of sitting around in damp clothes in a draught. The first director of the unit, Sir Christopher Andrewes, described the results in his book *The Common Cold*. Volunteers were asked to take hot baths, and then to stand around in damp bathing costumes in a cool corridor for half an hour, 'or as long as they could stand it'. Later they were allowed to dress, but had to continue to wear damp socks. The procedure caused much discomfort, but it did not cause colds.

Still more surprisingly, although colds could be induced by inoculating volunteers with rhinoviruses, it proved very difficult to induce the symptoms simply by exposing the volunteers to close contact with others who had been inoculated, or who had developed colds. Colds, as Andrewes put it, turned out to be 'by no means a very infectious kind of disease' – a verdict which has been confirmed by other trials.

If they are not infectious, in that sense, why should people catch them, and why should they appear to be transmitted from person to person?

Until recently any idea that there might be a psychosomatic component would have been ridiculed, but since the publication of results of a recent investigation at the Common Cold Unit, it has been harder to resist acknowledging the possibility.

The experiment was designed and carried out by psychologists Richard Totman and Sylvia E. Reed of Nuffield College, Oxford, and J. W. Craig of the Common Cold Unit, its aim being to find if 'cognitive dissonance' has an effect on symptoms – or on what people feel about the symptoms – of the common cold. The theory, originally advanced some twenty years earlier, is that individuals who find themselves holding, or required to hold, two cognitions, or assumptions, which are inconsistent with each other experience uneasiness of the kind that some of Galileo's contemporaries, for example, felt when confronted with his evidence. The presence of such dissonance, the theory holds, gives rise to pressure to reduce it by self-justification – ranging, in the case of Galileo's contemporaries, from refusal to accept the evidence of their own eyes, to refusal to look through his telescope. At an everyday level, cognitive dissonance occurs whenever we have to choose between two courses of action; to tend to employ rationalisations to justify our choice. People who agree to try some unorthodox or painful form of treatment, for example, tend to claim that it has done them good (and often actually to *feel* it has done them good), even if no positive benefit can be observed.

Forty-eight volunteers took part in the cognitive dissonance experiment. All were injected with two rhinoviruses which, they were told, would give them moderate colds. Half of them were then offered a choice: would they like to try an anti-viral drug at the same time? They were warned that, if they agreed, at the end of the trial a tube would be stuck down their throats so that their stomach juices might be sampled. The experimenters' assumption was that, if the cognitive dissonance theory was correct, all those making the choice, irrespective of which alternative they selected, 'would justify their decisions by "attenuating" the experienced severity of their colds'. As the 'anti-viral drug' was in fact a placebo it would be possible to compare their symptoms with those of the control group, who had not been given the choice, since all forty-eight would in fact have received the same dose of the two rhinoviruses.

What happened was 'an effect exactly opposite to that predicted'. The symptoms of those volunteers who had been offered the choice, whether or not they had accepted the bogus 'anti-viral drug' (and the non-existent 'intubation') were *more* severe than those of the controls. A possible explanation, the experimenters suggested, was that simply being asked to make the choice had induced anxiety, and this was responsible for the symptoms' greater severity. Whatever the reason, the report concluded, it was clear that 'the symptoms of the common cold were significantly modified by the psychological manipulations involved' – a verdict echoed and supplemented by Bernard Dixon: 'Whatever the truth, it is clear that the simplistic picture of infection still taught in medical schools up and down the land requires modification'; the implications, he thought, 'could shake the foundations of microbiology'. And although at first glance the findings might appear to bear little relevance to the wider issue of how to control colds or flu, the report of a different kind of experiment under way at the time showed that they might determine whether or not to launch an immunisation campaign.

When in 1969 a flu epidemic disrupted postal and telecommunication services in Britain, the Post Office decided to conduct a large-scale test, with the government defraying the cost of the vaccine. Immunisation was offered to all of its 400,000 employees, and a controlled trial was set up, 'pairing' offices, one of each pair acting as control, and not receiving the 'shots', to see what difference, if any, immunisation would make. In those offices where immunisation was offered, four out of ten workers accepted, and although the proportion dwindled to a quarter in the course of the experiment, it was high enough to offer a reasonable assessment of any differences in sickness rates. The flu epidemic that winter was not serious, but the number of cases reported in the Post Office was sufficient to show that the sickness rate was lower among immunised workers. Although the reduction was small, around four per cent, it was statistically significant, leading the chief medical officer to the Post Office to conclude that, although immunisation would not prevent epidemics, it could 'provide a small degree of protection against the disruption they can cause, as well as producing a small but worthwhile reduction in overall sickness absence rates in the winter months'.

A further examination of the figures, however, revealed that the vaccine itself could not be given the credit for the reduction. In offices where it had been offered there had been a reduction of the sickness-rate among those who had *not* accepted it, as well as those who had. 'What seems inescapable from this meticulously-designed investigation,' Dixon commented, reviewing the evidence, 'is that some folk employed by the Post Office gained solely from an awareness that their employer had resolved upon measures designed to safeguard their health.' Vaccination, the report concluded, might be justified in terms of cost benefit, 'but it is uncertain to what degree this depends upon psychological factors such as placebo effect'.

With placebo effect beginning to acquire a measure of clinical respectability, it proved possible to take the study a stage further at the Common Cold Unit, where Totman had now reported the results of a research project which has thrown fresh light on the ways by which colds are resisted. From its earlier work the Unit had arrived at an estimate that two out of three colds are aborted before they break out into the familiar symptoms, and research had concentrated on investigating the role of antibodies as the protective force. Totman and his team measured the antibody levels of fifty-two volunteers, and also estimated their stress levels. They were then given rhinoviruses through nasal drops, kept in isolation from each other, and any resultant colds were checked for severity – objectively, with nasal washes, as well as subjectively. Stress levels, it was found, were a better predictor of the severity of the colds than antibody levels.

If, as the *New Scientist* claimed in its report of the experiment, it shows that 'psychological factors play a large part in deciding whether or not we can stop cold viruses multiplying', Dixon's comment on the implications of the earlier cognitive dissonance findings, that they could shake microbiology's foundations, is even more applicable to these later results. Admittedly some of the psychological factors are bound to be of a kind which are unavoidable: redundancy, say, or bereavement. The results of the experiment, however, have also justified Selye's insistence that it is not the occasions of stress but the reactions to them which decide the outcome. The severity of the symptoms of a cold, too, Totman suggests, may be related to the extent to which the individual who has caught it feels sorry for himself.

The microbiologist, though, ordinarily concerns himself only with his own narrow sector. He is rarely equipped either by training or temperament to find out how far antibody levels simply reflect stress or cognitive dissonance. The reaction of the scientific establishment to the evidence has been to intensify the quest for new vaccines. Part of the effort has gone into trying to improve those already in existence, either by inserting additives designed to stimulate antibodies, and to increase the length of time for which the vaccine, if it happens to be right for the epidemic, will remain effective (peanut oil, it has been claimed, is one such ally), or by improving the purity of the vaccine, to enable it to be strengthened without the risk of more unwelcome reactions.

## Uro-genital Tract Infections

Until the 1950s the ways in which infections of the urethra and vagina arise and are transmitted appeared to present few problems. The only two serious disorders in this category were syphilis and gonorrhea. The infecting organisms, spirochetes and gonococci, had been identified; the means of transmission, sexual intercourse, had been established, and along with a few much rarer conditions they had accordingly been classified as venereal disease. In theory, admittedly, they might be transmitted by other means, but in practice, it was assumed, intercourse must have been responsible. In the lecture which was given on the subject to men and women called up for the forces during the Second World War they were warned that although catching VD was not a punishable offence, concealing it was, and it would be useless for offenders to claim in extenuation that they had not had sexual intercourse, because such excuses as 'I must have picked it up off a lavatory seat' would not be accepted. The only complication was that men occasionally suffered from symptoms which, although they closely resembled those of gonorrhea, could not be traced to gonococci; this form of disorder came to be known as non-gonococcal, or non-specific, urethritis. Women, too, sometimes had infections such as 'thrush' which were not categorised as venereal. Uncertainty remained about the cause; it might be poor hygiene. But soon, it was assumed, bacteriology would come up with the explanation.

With the appearance of penicillin and antibiotics, syphilis and gonorrhea became less of a menace, but at the same time the incidence of NSU, as non-specific urethritis came for convenience to be called, began to increase, for which no satisfactory explanation could be found. Vaginal infections were also being more commonly reported, but some of the organisms related to them, and thought to cause them, had been tracked down. Thrush was ascribed to the fungus (or yeast) Candida, and another infection, trichomonas, was traced to protozoa. Inevitably it came to be accepted that the greater sexual freedom of the permissive society must be responsible; that, like those of VD, the organisms involved were transmitted from partner to partner. There were even venereologists who wanted to re-classify NSU, vaginal thrush and 'trich' as VD. Others, uneasy in the knowledge of the attached stigma, preferred STD – sexually transmitted disease.

However they are described, three things have become clear. They are extremely common. In Britain (where the statistical evidence is more comprehensive than in the United States) it has been estimated that they account for six in every hundred GP consultations, and this of course excludes people who for one reason or another prefer to by-pass their GP. The diseases are responsible for a great deal of discomfort – too mild a term, in many cases, where the symptoms can mean days of real suffering. And so far, no satisfactory way has been found to prevent them.

Reassurance is endlessly ladled out. Anybody who catches a sexually-transmitted infection today, the writer of a GPs' guide to the subject in the medical magazine *MIMS* recently boasted, 'stands an excellent chance of a complete cure'. This is not the view of Rosalinde Hurley and John de Louvois of the London Institute of Obstetrics. Almost all the known facts about vaginal thrush – easily the most common infection – are 'enumerative and descriptive', they point out; 'little is known of the factors affecting the pathogenesis, recrudescence or recurrence'. As for claims for the effectiveness of treatment, 'reported cure rates of 95 per cent or more are comforting to the practitioner, but tend to derogate the sufferings of those countless uncured or partially cured women, who are seen as a class of medical failures'. All in all, a *British Medical Journal* editorial has recently admitted, 'a real advance in the control of recurrent Candida infection has yet to come'.

Advance in the control of cystitis, where the inflammation is in the bladder and its outlet, has also yet to come. 'Of all the conditions coming under the broad heading "urological",' Peter Evans remarks in his book on the subject, 'cystitis is one of the most problematic' – for two reasons. The symptoms may arise without any sign of infection; or the infection may be present without the symptoms. 'The founding of lay organisations that seek a better deal for sufferers illustrates our basic shortcomings,' Professor A. W. Asscher of the Welsh National School of Medicine has admitted in the *British Medical Journal*. Among the reasons are 'our inability to eradicate the source of urinary pathogens; the existence of a large reservoir of covert infection in the healthy population; the frequency of recurrent infection after treatment; and the most taxing problem of all, the occurrence of symptoms similar to urinary tract infections in the absence of infection'.

In spite of this evidence, the accepted (and taught) version of urogenital infections is that each is caused by its specific pathogen, and that they are transmitted either through sexual intercourse or, in the case of cystitis, poor hygiene. Such infections, the *MIMS* writer claimed, 'must come from somewhere'. But to think of a pathogen as the cause of a disorder when it can swarm in the body without arousing any symptoms, and when the symptoms can occur without its being present, is absurd, and for some years immunologists have been arguing that the infections really represent an allergic-type reaction. This would not mean that they cannot be transmitted. Obviously they can be passed from man to woman, and vice-versa, during intercourse. But ordinarily a male would not harbour female organisms for long. Where 'trich' is found in male urethra, Neville Rosedale, a consultant venereologist at the West Middlesex Hospital, has explained, it has been sexually transmitted, but 'the converse does not follow, and I have believed for many years that trichomonal vaginitis is most often not acquired as a sexually transmitted disease'.

Rosedale bases his belief on what he admits is 'dangerous ground, i.e. clinical experience'. Again and again girls come to clinics with an infection after their first intercourse, sometimes with a boy for whom it has also been initiatory. At the other end of the scale, trich is a not uncommon finding in a woman who resumes sexual intercourse, after having had none for several years, with a man who claims to have had no other sexual contact and in whom no sign of trich can be detected. The stock explanation is that it cannot easily be found in the male. 'I have another theory; perhaps it was not there in the first place.'

It is impossible in individual cases to be certain that the man has not been harbouring trich. But Rosedale has one piece of evidence in favour of this theory; his cure-rates for women over the years, in cases where the male partner has not been investigated or treated, are almost identical with the cure-rates claimed in other clinics where the male has been investigated and, as a rule, treated with the same drug as the woman, whether trich has been found or not. This contrasts with, say, gonorrhea, where the reinfection-rate when the partner is *not* treated is high. There is consequently no need, Rosedale argues, for the male partner to be treated in trich cases – or, he also claims, in cases of thrush.

This evidence can be explained if vaginal infections are commonly an allergic-type reaction. It would also explain the frequency of recurrent reinfection after treatment to which Asscher refers in his *British Medical Journal* article. But how to account for symptoms appearing in the absence of infection? A *BMJ* editorial, discussing the implications of a controlled trial designed to test whether a new drug would prove to be a prophylactic against thrush, noted that, although the group receiving the drug had fewer symptoms than those on the placebo, 'there was no difference between the two in the frequency with which Candida alone was isolated'. After the trial had ended, too, some patients who were free from fungi had a recurrence of their symptoms: 'In other words, there was a complete dissociation of symptoms and Candida infection.'

Why, in that case, did the editorial claim that 'Candida infection is, of course, the commonest cause of vaginitis'? How can it reasonably be described as the *cause* of the symptoms, if they can occur irrespective of whether the organism is present? There are other reasons for rejecting straight cause-and-effect. As A. T. Schofield, a consultant venereologist in Newcastle, argues in his book *Sexually Transmitted Diseases*, to think in such terms is to go in the face of the evidence. The immunologist J. L. Turk, too, has flatly asserted that Candida 'is not a pathogenic organism under normal conditions', only so when the body's natural immunity is weakened. And if this is so, the real cause of the symptoms is whatever disrupted the body's homeostatic mechanism.

One suspect, as usual, is stress: in particular, the effect of the emergence of the permissive society. Annually for the past twenty years and more, hundreds of thousands of people who have been brought up in the belief that sexual promiscuity (or even sexual intercourse before marriage) is wicked, have been pitchforked in their adolescence into communities where such views are ridiculed. The stresses occasioned by the subsequent breaking of taboos must in the aggregate be formidable. If sexual embarrassment can trigger a blush, we can hardly rule out the possibility that it can also trigger irritation in the urethral tract. And just as blushes appear on the face – as if they were a deliberate punishment, because only on the face is the blush such a give-away – may not the same process select the site for urethritis?

The reaction may be even more complex, as a young doctor working in a Dublin hospital shortly after the Second World War discovered soon after he qualified. Appointed to look after the hospital's VD clinic for out-patients, he was shocked to find that no attempt had been made to diagnose the disorders presented there, except by visual inspection and routine questioning. The Wasserman test for syphilis had been available for over forty years, but it had not been used. Anxious to forward his career by preparing a research paper, he decided to conduct a survey of the incidence of the different types of VD in the city, and he realised it would stand no chance of acceptance unless he could certify that the cases which he was describing had been properly diagnosed. Accordingly he introduced the Wasserman test as routine.

He was not surprised to find syphilis in some cases where it had not been suspected. What astonished him was that in others, where syphilitic-looking chancres had appeared following intercourse with prostitutes known to be infected, the Wasserman reaction was negative (the Wasserman reaction was unlikely to be incorrect: it tended to produce many false positives, but only rarely a false negative). The doctor knew about 'hysterical VD', which was common in Catholic Dublin. Worried husbands who had been unfaithful used to often come to the clinic with 'the itch', and he was able to reassure them that it was

169

not venereal. But that hysterical mimicry could produce actual chancres staggered him. Over the years, he realised, hundreds of patients must have been subjected unnecessarily to the unpleasant and painful forms of treatment then in use, as well as to the resentment of their wives and the contempt of their friends if their plight became known. Had he written a letter about his findings it might have found its way into a medical journal – particularly if it were flippant. But a serious research paper, he realised, would stand no chance of acceptance, except perhaps by one of the psychiatric periodicals, and as psychiatry was not his specialty, the paper remained unpublished.

The implication of such findings is not that the symptoms of uro-genital disorders are purely psychogenic; it is simply that, as factors other than micro-organisms are involved, they must be allowed for. In so far as an allergic-type reaction may be responsible, too, the proliferation of bacteria or fungi may be more an effect than a cause. Yet this is not generally appreciated; and even if neither the treatments nor the stigma are today so disturbing as they were thirty years ago, partnerships can still be threatened, and sometimes even broken, by the anger aroused when what is thought to be a sexually-transmitted disease is contracted.

A recent lay contribution to *World Medicine* gives an idea of the confusion, and worse, which has been created by the way in which some venereologists have been clinging to their belief in sexual transmission, while others have rejected it. When the writer, a magazine editor, was diagnosed as having trich, she was asked by the female doctor to get her boy friend to come to the clinic for treatment. He came, but saw a different – male – doctor who told him after tests that there was nothing the matter with him, and that no treatment would be required. The woman doctor was furious when she heard. 'Take these pills and tell him to take them,' she advised, 'otherwise you'll get the trichomonas back again.'

Patients tend to admire the consultant who has no doubts. They want the comforting reassurance that the cause of their symptoms has been traced, and that a remedy is available. The consultant, for his (or her) part, is in any case often disposed to present clinical opinions dogmatically. When, as here, there are two mutually contradictory theories, it can be the cause of confusion – and worse: suspicion, resentment, agony of mind.

## The Terrain

If respiratory TB, colds, flu, and urogenital disorders are at all representative of the infectious diseases, the accepted assumptions about infections are clearly untrustworthy. Why then, has this not been recognised? It has been, however, and by some of the shrewdest, as well as some of the quirkiest, minds at work in medical science – among them Pasteur, no less. At the time when Pasteur came up with his germ theory of disease, Claude Bernard was seeking to convince the medical profession of the importance of the body's homeostatic mechanism in the prevention of disease. To Bernard, pathogens were like the seeds described in the New Testament parable of the sower: some falling by the wayside, some on stony ground, some among thorns, and only those falling on fertile ground taking root, and bringing forth fruit. Pathogens, Bernard argued, obeyed the same rules; they could flourish only where the host was accommodating. Pasteur agreed. On his deathbed, according to a friend who was with him, he reiterated that Bernard had been right: 'The germ *is* nothing; the terrain is everything.' Recognition that the terrain played a part, though, did not in itself relegate the germ to a walk-on role. It could still be regarded as the cause of the disease, even if some people might be able to resist its depredations better than others because of their sound constitutions, and good health. Yet no matter how healthy an individual might be, he surely could not survive a Borgia-dispensed glass of wine.

This assumption, too, could be shown to be fallacious, as it was by Max von Pettenkofer. Following the example of the social reformers in Britain in the Victorian era, such as Chadwick and Southwood Smith, Pettenkofer had claimed that he would be able to bring typhoid under control in Munich by ensuring that a supply of pure water from the nearby mountains flowed into the city, and that sewage was drained carefully out of it: the resultant dramatic fall in the incidence of the disease soon proved him correct. When Koch's bacillus was described as the cause of cholera, Pettenkofer offered to demonstrate that it was not. Obtaining from Koch a culture of the bacilli taken from a fatal case in Hamburg, Pettenkofer proceeded to swallow it. Although huge numbers of bacilli were retrieved from his stools, he suffered nothing more sinister than mild diarrhea. Fellow-workers who tried the same experiment – among them the Russian Elie Mechnikoff, later to win a Nobel prize for his work in immunology – also came to no harm.

It could still be argued, none the less, that they must somehow have acquired immunity. Nobody, surely, was going to suggest that the self-confidence with which Pettenkofer and the others drank their germ-ridden draughts had anything to do with their escape? But this was precisely what A. T. W. Simeons was to claim, on the strength of his observations of a cholera epidemic he had dealt with when he arrived in the tropics as a newly-qualified doctor in the 1930s.

As he was to recall in his *Man's Presumptuous Brain*, he could not help noticing 'the strange fact that the healthy adolescent, the busy mother and the wage-earning father are more often stricken than the very young children and the old and decrepit'. Why? It was hardly likely that the cholera 'vibrio' would single out the strong in preference to the weak. Something in the host's reaction must be responsible, and there was one useful clue. Koch had found that acid kills the vibrio. To make sure that Koch would not be able to accuse him of cheating, therefore, von Pettenkofer had actually taken a dose of bicarbonate of soda to neutralise his stomach acidity before he drank Koch's cholera culture. As the normal acid level in the human stomach ordinarily suffices to give protection against cholera, Simeons reasoned, some force must be at work to lower that level in breadwinners and busy mothers, since it was hardly conceivable that they were in the habit of consuming more antacids than grandparents and babies. There is one other known way by which the flow of acid is known to be checked: fear. It was those who are most afraid of death, Simeons realised, whom cholera was most likely to kill, while those too young to understand the danger, or too old to worry much about it, would survive. 'Fear might thus play an important role in the selection of victims; and in this sense it would not be incorrect to say that even in cholera psychosomatic mechanisms can be of importance.'

Simeons was careful to point out that this interpretation would only apply where a germ was taken into the stomach. Peace of mind would be no protection against a pathogen injected direct into the blood-stream by, say, a flea infected with bubonic plague. Nevertheless he had not merely re-emphasised the importance of the terrain in connection with epidemic diseases; he had also demonstrated that 'terrain' did not simply mean the sum of genetic and constitutional make-up allied to physical fitness.

In *Disease and the Social System*, published in 1942, Arthur Guirdham further challenged the germ theory in connection with the disease which at that time was taken to present the strongest evidence in its favour, diphtheria. Its mortality rate had been rising until in the 1890s an anti-toxin was introduced; thereafter it had fallen rapidly, though with occasional disturbing upturns. Why, Guirdham asked, did the bacteria lodge in some children's throats and not in others'? Why did people in whose throats it lodged sometimes die while others escaped even being

172

ill? 'Why do attenuated organisms cause diseases in some? Why do virulent strains fail to infect others?' The answer was usually 'compressed into the blessed shibboleth, "immunity"'. But this, Guirdham protested, simply shifted the issue a step back. It did not explain why certain individuals enjoyed the immunity; that, he felt, required exploration.

Immunologists seeking acceptance of the 'blessed shibboleth' were about to explore it, among them T. P. Magill of the New York College of Medicine, Brooklyn. 'We rejoice in our complete emancipation from the concept of evil spirits,' he told the American Association of Immunologists in his presidential address at their annual meeting in 1954. 'We boast proudly of our knowledge of infectious agents; and we are confident that emancipation and knowledge have enabled us to vanquish completely infectious disease.' What was the basis of this confidence? All that had in fact happened was that 'microbes' had been substituted for 'evil spirits'. It was still 'the unwanted and aggressive agent, be it evil spirit or microbe, that attacks the unaggressive host; and which, be it evil spirit or microbe, can be cast out or destroyed by the appropriate means'. Consequently people still found it hard to consider other possibilities: that the host might be the aggressor, 'taking undue advantage of the reasonably peaceful microbe', or that infection might be 'a matter of ecology'.

'The physician or the medicine man of each age has attributed the control and cure of disease during his own particular era to the therapeutic procedure then in vogue,' Magill warned in his conclusion. 'The possibility that infection is a biological phenomenon dealing chiefly, perhaps, with ecological relationship escaped the past, as it has escaped the present.' Even in the case of diphtheria, he felt, the value of the national immunisation campaigns ought not to be accepted uncritically. They had done no more than speed up the decline in mortality; other factors might be involved.

Five years later A. H. Gale, Director of Postgraduate Medical Studies at the University of Bristol, confirmed that there must be some other factor at work in diphtheria. In his *Epidemic Diseases* he was careful to insist that he did not wish to deny credit to British research, but he felt bound to draw attention to a puzzling feature which had received insufficient attention. Immunisation had been directed not at the bacillus, but at the toxin which the bacillus produces. The campaign, therefore, need not have had any effect on the bacillus. It might reasonably have been expected, in fact, 'that the number of healthy human carriers would increase, as the number of overt cases diminished', but this had not happened. There was evidence that the bacilli had declined step by step with the progress of the campaign, in spite of the fact that it was not

173

supposed to affect them. Why? Gale was unable to explain, but the discovery raised the possibility that the decline in diphtheria mortality might, as Miller had implied, have been largely coincidental with immunisation.

In the same year, 1959, the first full-scale, well-documented attack appeared on the dogma aspect of the germ theory: René Dubos's *Mirage of Health*. Scientific research had been extremely effective in the discovery of the agents of the infectious disease, he conceded, and the elucidation of some of their properties, 'but it has led by necessity to the neglect, and indeed has often delayed the recognition, of the main other factors that play a part in the causation of disease under the conditions prevailing in the natural world' – such as people's physical condition and the impact of their environment upon them. The tubercle bacillus was one example. 'It can be stated with great assurance that most of the persons present in the very room where Koch read his epoch-making paper in 1882 had at some time been infected.' Probably they still carried virulent infection in their bodies, as Koch himself did. The illusion that bacteria were the cause of diseases, Dubos explained, had been produced because Pasteur and Koch were working with laboratory animals, 'experimental artefacts'; without realising it, they had devised experimental conditions 'that lent themselves to an unequivocal illustration of their hypothesis – situations in which it was *sufficient* to bring the host and the parasite together to reproduce the disease'.

Pasteur's first paper on the germ theory, Dubos recalled, appeared in the same month as Darwin despatched the letter in which he first propounded his theory of evolution. By a historical accident, the two theories achieved recognition together, shaping medical attitudes; this had led to a kind of aggressive war against microbes, aimed at their elimination from the sick individual and from the community. Because epidemics of the major killer diseases had ceased to be a serious threat, the belief had grown that this campaign had been chiefly responsible, yet the evidence pointed to the fact that bacteriology had in fact contributed little to the reduction of either morbidity or mortality. The conquest of the infections was 'in large part the result of a campaign for pure food, pure water, and pure air, based not on a scientific doctrine but on philosophical faith', the work of reformers seeking to eradicate the social evils of the Industrial Revolution. These reformers had in fact been responsible for bringing under control some of the disease problems generated by ruthless industrialism; even the advent of the antibacterial drugs had represented 'no more than a ripple on the wave which has been wearing down the mortality caused by the infection in our communities'.

In the essay on germs in *The Lives of a Cell*, Lewis Thomas has since taken a similar line. 'Staphylococci live all over us,' he observes, yet 'when you count them up, and us, it is remarkable how little trouble we have.' Streptococci 'are among our closest intimates'; it is our reaction to them that gets us into trouble. From an evolutionary point of view the notion of micro-organisms causing infection is implausible, if it can lead to illness and death because 'the man who catches meningococcus is in considerably less danger for his life, even without chemotherapy, than meningococci with the bad luck to catch a man'.

These criticisms of the germ theory, and there have been many more, appear to have made no appreciable difference to the public's attitude, and very little to the bacteriologists'. But bacteriology no longer has the dominant role that it formerly enjoyed in relation to infections. Whether or not bacteria cause the diseases associated with them, and whether or not the social reformers should be given the credit for bringing them under control, has become an academic issue for historians of medicine to wrangle over; the bacteriologist has been upstaged by the virologist.

So long as viruses were thought simply to be germs so tiny that they could pass through filters designed to stop the germs' passage, bacteriology could incorporate them, but with the gradual recognition that they were not so much bacteria as 'little packets of nucleic acid', as they were sometimes described, virology was encouraged to branch out on its own. In 1961 it received the accolade of a cover story in *Time* magazine, and for the next few years a succession of headlines of the 'Drug Advance on the Brink' type forecast the marketing of a new vaccine or drug which would repeat the triumph of the anti-polio vaccines, dealing with viruses as the antibiotic had dealt with germs. Even after viruses had been given (up to a point) a separate identity, however, they were still regarded as behaving like germs – invaders which caused infections by damaging cells and proliferating within the human body. But the belief did not square with the facts. By 1967 a *Lancet* editorial was admitting that 'virulence is not synonymous with virus multiplication, for some viruses multiply well without producing any disease in the host; whereas others may form toxins which are damaging or even lethal when injected, without further multiplication of the virus'.

Viruses, Lewis Thomas noted, 'instead of being single-minded agents of disease and death, now begin to look more like mobile genes', perhaps a mechanism for keeping new genes in circulation; if so, 'the odd virus disease, on which we must focus so much of our attention in medicine, may be looked on as an accident'. This is naturally not something virologists have cared to emphasise, nor, as it happens, is it something the public have wished to hear. People have become accustomed to the idea that viruses behave like particularly sinister germs, arriving on the breath, or by contact ('I can't kiss you, darling, I've a terrible cold'), or by lurking in inadequately frozen food. So a curious concordat has been arrived at, for the benefit of both doctor and patient. Confronted with a disorder he cannot immediately diagnose, the doctor tells his patients 'you have a virus', secure in the knowledge that most of them will be happy with his diagnosis and with his prescription, even though it is no more than a palliative (or, all too often, an antibiotic, though research has shown antibiotics to be useless against virus disorders).

Ordinarily the doctor is using the term in its traditional sense of an unidentified agent of disease. Often he is in effect telling his patients that he has no idea what is the matter with them, but that whatever it is, it is not sufficiently serious to require them to go to hospital. With this they have usually been satisfied. A virus disorder, they feel, is a *real* illness; there is something physically the matter with them. Nobody can accuse them of being hypochondriacal or neurotic. Besides, they can also disclaim responsibility for being ill. They must have caught the bug (viruses are not excluded from the term, in spite of the doubts whether they are living creatures). 'We still think of human disease as the work of an organised, modernised kind of demonology, in which the bacteria are the most visible and centrally placed of our adversaries,' Thomas has complained, though such assumptions are 'paranoid delusions on a societal scale'.

Nothing, it seems, can banish these delusions, which survive in spite of these criticisms – and many more. The theory that infectious disease is primarily caused by transmission of an organism from one host to another is 'a gross over-simplification', G. T. Stewart, Professor of Epidemiology at the University of North Carolina, asserted in 1968; other factors that need to be taken into consideration are 'susceptibility, genetic constitution, behavior and socio-economic determinants'. Infectious disease does not have a single cause, Jeremiah Stamler reiterated five years later, 'not even where there is a micro-organism'. In a lecture honouring the memory of Theobald Smith – celebrated for his research into infectious disease around the beginning of the century, but a man always determined to emphasise the importance of the role of the terrain – Leon Eisenberg of the Harvard Medical School made the same point. Citing cases where streptococci were found in twenty per cent of some 1,600 cultures, 'What is noteworthy,' he feels, 'is that more than fifty per cent of all acquisitions were not associated with any illness.' The most accurate predictor of illness, in fact, 'was the stress the family members had been exposed to in the several weeks before the culture was made'. There are few infections which can invariably be traced to a cause – germ, virus, toxin – and which produce a reaction in the human host almost as predictable as, say, a phial of cyanide: botulism is one. But they are now rare. In most common infections, the crucial factor is the reaction of the host, related to genetic and constitutional endowment and to a great variety of environmental and psychosocial factors, ranging from nuclear fall-out to a broken love link.

About this there is, or should be, no mystery. The difficulty is simply to come to terms with the problems presented by the realisation that it is the terrain, varying elusively with each individual, that needs to be taken into consideration in research, prevention and treatment, rather than 'the bug that's going round'. The bug may not even be pathogenic, in ordinary circumstances: as Lewis Thomas emphasised, it may lead a blameless existence, until . . . Until what? Here lies the real mystery. If the bug is not the primary cause of infectious disorders, how can epidemics be accounted for? Common sense indicates that the transmission of, say, flu viruses from person to person in homes and offices the world over is chiefly responsible for flu. Yet it is now slowly coming to be realised that common sense has misled us. Epidemics are not, or not necessarily, spread in this way.

## Miasmas

That person-to-person transmission could not by itself account for flu epidemics was demonstrated in the 1890s by the pathologist Charles Creighton, in his massive survey of epidemic diseases. Flu, he insisted, is unique, 'the oldest and most obdurate of all the problems of epidemiology', because it does not follow the usual pattern. It is not transmitted in an ordinary way; it arises suddenly (as in Robert Boyle's description, 'I have known a great cold in a day or two invade multitudes in the same city with violent, and to many persons fatal, symptoms'). In looking for its source, Creighton argued, 'We are not to look for previous cases of the identical disease, but of something else of which it has been an emanation.' In other words, it did not spread out from foci of infection, as would be expected if it spread person-to-person. Its propagation was 'wave-like', as if an invisible pathogenic cloud rolled over the land. This was too close to the old assumption that epidemics were caused by miasmas – invisible clouds of noxious matter – to commend itself to bacteriologists. Creighton soon came to be regarded, where his work was considered at all, as the last defender of an outmoded superstition. The next attempt to revive the idea met with no more success.

Of all the diseases commonly attributed to miasmas, the one which best fitted the theory had been malaria. The term itself, derived from *mala aria*, foul air, reflected the assumption that the disease – as Thomas Sydenham described it in the seventeenth century – was the consequence of 'spirituous miasma impressed upon the blood' by residence in or near a marshy region. In 1880, however, a parasite assumed to be the cause of the disease was isolated, and shortly before the close of the century Ronald Ross showed how it was transmitted by the anopheles mosquito, a discovery for which he was awarded a knighthood and a Nobel prize. A two-pronged campaign was later launched to rid the world of the parasite. Wherever there was marsh or stagnant water near human habitation, it would be drained or treated with chemicals to prevent mosquitoes using it for purposes of reproduction. In the meantime, 'as proved by centuries of experience', Ross explained, 'chinchona bark, from which quinine is made, possesses the power of destroying the parasites and curing the infection'; not merely could it be used to treat the disease, it could also be taken as a prophylactic for prevention. Inexorably, therefore, the parasite's life-cycle would be disrupted, because such mosquitoes as remained, unable to draw infected blood from man, would themselves remain uninfected. 'I consider myself warranted,' Koch boasted in 1900, 'in stating that we are in a position, by means of this procedure, to make every malarious area, according to circumstances, wholly or nearly free from malaria.' To this day, it is commonly believed that this boast could be and should have been fulfilled if ignorant and lazy natives had not failed to adopt the required procedure, neglecting to take their prophylactic doses.

Yet this version was challenged by Professor Guido Cremonese of the Royal University of Rome in his *Malaria*, published in 1924. Not merely had the anti-malaria campaign failed; evidence had begun to appear which suggested to him that the reason for its failure was that its whole basis – interruption of the parasite's life-cycle – was mistaken. Why did epidemics occur in the spring, when there were no mosquitoes, and certainly no infected mosquitoes, around? Why, when the number of infected mosquitoes increased in the autumn, did cases of malaria decrease? How, then, Cremonese asked, could the phenomenon be explained?

The Malaria Commission of the League of Nations investigated, and reported some surprising findings. Where swamps and marshy areas in Italy had been drained to provide farm land, the canals and ditches were often 'more prolific breeding-places of anopheles than were the original swamps'; vast mosquito colonies had been found. Yet malaria had ceased to be a problem. In one district examined by the commissioners, the labourers employed on the reclamation project had suffered so badly from the disease that the project almost had to be abandoned, but although no effort had since been made to rid the area of the mosquitoes, which were still abundant, the incidence of malaria had subsequently become negligible. The common assumption had nevertheless remained that the only way to eradicate malaria was to interrupt the parasite's life-cycle. In the commissioners' opinion it was 'very desirable in certain circumstances to throw off the tyranny which that belief has exercised over men's minds during the last thirty years'.

The tyranny remained, as Elliot Fitzgibbon, an Irish engineer who had worked in the British colonies and made a careful study of the subject, observed in his *Malaria: the Governing Factor* in 1932. 'The reason,' he suggested, 'could be found in a remark in Sir Ronald Ross's *The Prevention of Malaria*: "unfortunately there are many people who seem to regard any new idea as a personal affront."' To argue that well-established methods of anti-malarial warfare were based on a false conception of the cause of the disease, Fitzgibbon feared, 'is to incur the odium and hostility of all such people as Sir Ronald Ross had in mind' – even more so if, as Fitzgibbon had come to believe, 'the now universally discarded miasmal conception was nearer to the truth'.

When and where the subsoil level of water is close to the surface-water-level, ran Fitzgibbon's theory, as it is in swamps and badly drained land, 'the intermediate products of the decomposition of organic matter are, as everybody is well aware, dangerously and sometimes rapidly and fatally poisonous to living human beings and other animals'. The common assumption had been that this was simply because they provided a breeding ground for mosquitoes. This, Fitzgibbon argued, was to fall into the fallacy of believing that, because the parasite and malaria were associated, the micro-organism must be the cause of the disease; it was more likely, he argued, that the parasite and the disease were both products of a common cause. It was not, after all, surprising that in a malarial region the parasite should be found in the glands of mosquitoes as well as in humans: 'What *is* surprising is that, if they are the cause of the disease, such parasites may also be found swarming in the blood of persons who do not and never did suffer from malaria.'

The evidence, Fitzgibbon thought, pointed to the essential correctness of the old miasma theory, and consequently the attempt to get rid of malaria by interrupting the parasites' life-cycle was futile. Instead, the aim should be to drain land where the subsoil water-level lay too close to the surface water-level; wherever such drainage was properly carried out, malaria would disappear, however many mosquitoes might remain. The mosquito, in other words, had been mistakenly crucified as the culprit, when in fact like man it was the victim. Lower subsoil water-levels, and neither mosquito nor man need fear malaria. Fitzgibbon's fear that his proposition would incur odium was, however, not fulfilled. His book appeared in the era when de Kruif could write that Koch was 'the man who really proved that microbes are our most deadly enemies'; anybody who took a different view was less likely to incur unpopularity than to be dismissed as a harmless crackpot.

The first concrete evidence that the accepted theory of epidemic transmission is misleading was provided by the results of the experiments at the Common Cold Unit in the late 1940s. When Sir Christopher Andrewes came to describe them in his book on the subject, he noted that research undertaken elsewhere appeared to justify Creighton's doubts about person-to-person transmission in connection with flu. The assumption had been that, when a new strain of virus appeared, it could be traced to a single source – Hong Kong, say. This was incorrect; the same emerging strain of flu had 'frequently been isolated from countries far apart at the same time'. In 1955, for example, similar strains of flu viruses had been identified in India, Ireland, and eastern America. In some cases, too, isolated individuals had simultaneously fallen ill with flu which was later traced to the same strain, as had happened in 1948 in the case of some Sardinian shepherds, living solitary lives far from the centres where they might have caught the disease from others.

In 1976 Louis Weinstein, described by the *New England Journal of Medicine* as 'a senior statesman of infectious diseases', remarked in a paper in the journal that the behaviour of the 1918 epidemic, in particular, had been inexplicable. 'Although person-to-person spread occurred in local areas, the disease appeared on the same day in widely separated parts of the world on the one hand, but, on the other, took days to weeks to spread relatively short distances.' Thus it was detected in Boston and Bombay simultaneously; yet in spite of the constant flow of traffic it took three weeks to get from Boston to New York. Similarly when the 'Hong Kong' flu arrived in 1968, though it was first reported in the United States in California – the most likely geographical location – it did not emerge, as could be expected, in one of its coastal cities, but in a small town in the desert. Thereafter it moved through the country in leaps, not along the main communication channels, but skipping out whole regions.

Yet at a conference held that year in France, attended by most of the world's leading authorities on flu, these peculiar epidemiological characteristics of the disease were not considered important enough to discuss. It has been left to two men who are not members of the medical profession to produce the evidence which invalidates the accepted transmission-theory in relation to flu and to other common infections, particularly those of childhood.

Sir Fred Hoyle, Professor of Astronomy at the Royal Institution, and Chandra Wickramasinghe, Professor of Applied Mathematics and Astronomy at University College, Cardiff, had been investigating the possibility that life reached earth in the form of bacteria deep-frozen in the tails of comets, when it occurred to them that if this were the case, micro-organisms might well still be raining down as miniature meteorites, and might be responsible for epidemics. Instead of simply presenting their hypothesis and waiting for medical scientists to test it, they decided that they would themselves first check the accepted theory. For this purpose they evolved a research project so simple that in retrospect it is extraordinary that it should not have been thought of before.

They used ready-made laboratories: boarding-schools. If person-to-person transmission were responsible, they argued, it ought to show up in the way disease spread: for example, from the person who first had it to others in his dormitory, after the usual two-to-three-day incubation period. With the co-operation of school authorities in the west country, who provided plans of dormitory lay-outs, and dates of the onset of flu for each pupil, they showed that the way in which epidemics have affected schools could not be accounted for by person-to-person transmission. From that moment, as they have recalled in their *Diseases from Space*, 'we knew that influenza is not a transmitted disease'. Further research along the same lines at other schools, including Eton, has confirmed their view, and whatever may be thought of their theory of micro-organisms floating in from space – a hypothesis for which there is still no hard evidence, in the form of bacteria 'netted' on their way down through the earth's atmosphere to start an epidemic – in the light of their findings person-to-person transmission cannot be accepted as the means by which such infections spread.

# 6

# Neuro-epidemics

Clues as to how infections spread may be found by examining the evidence about a category of epidemics which have been periodically reported throughout history, and which have struck from time to time in the present century, occasionally with devastating results: outbreaks in which the most prominent symptom is disruption of the nervous system.

The chief characteristic of neuro-epidemics (as for convenience they can be described) is loss of the control normally exercised jointly by the body's homeostasis operating at the unconscious level, with the conscious mind providing a check. Usually the initial symptoms are those which Hans Selye called 'the syndrome of just being sick': malaise, headache, backache and diffused pains; sore throat; nausea; feverishness. Sometimes suddenly, sometimes gradually – sometimes mildly, sometimes violently – the neuropathic symptoms emerge; tremors, tics, spasms, convulsions. These may be accompanied by emotional confusion: depression, outbursts of uncontrollable laughter or crying with no obvious cause, delusions, mania. Following the symptoms, or intertwined with them, there can be lethargy, muscle weakness, loss of feeling (as if parts of the body had been anesthetised) and in extreme cases catatonic rigidity or coma. In epidemics most patients will suffer from only a few of these indicators, often so mildly that at any other time they would be taken for flu. But a few patients may exhibit almost the full neuropathic range.

There are several varieties of epidemic. Some have been identified by the discovery of a germ or virus associated with them; others are recognised with the help of the results of laboratory tests, though these are usually pointers to, rather than clear-cut proof of, identity. In any case, the similarities are more striking than the differences.

*'The Sleeping Sickness'*

The most devastating of the neuro-epidemics of the twentieth century accompanied the wave of influenza towards the end of the First World

183

War. During the eighteenth century occasional outbreaks of an unfamiliar nervous disorder had occurred, whose chief characteristic was often a prolonged coma following the acute or positive stage. For over a century, however, there had been no sign of it until it reappeared in Austria in 1917. The general symptoms had by this time been given the name encephalitis – inflammation of the brain. It now came to be called encephalitis lethargica: the sleeping sickness (purists still insist it ought to be the 'sleepy sickness', to distinguish it from the tropical disorder which had prior claim, but 'sleeping' is the commoner version).

From Austria the sleeping sickness spread, much as flu was doing, to the rest of the continent of Europe, to Britain and to North America. The acute stage, which could manifest itself in a matter of seconds in an apparently healthy person, consisted of twitches, spasms, panting, staring eyes, and often manic behaviour, but what chiefly characterised the disease was that among the survivors (it was estimated that nearly five million people caught it, a third of them dying in the acute stage) many entered a trance state so deep that they would remain in the same position, sitting or standing or lying, for hours at a stretch. A few made no voluntary movement for weeks, even for decades.

No cause could be found for the disease. When Constantin von Economo managed to produce a culture which, when injected into monkeys, upset their nervous systems, it came to be assumed that the responsibility must lie with a virus, but no virus could be found. Immunisation proved impracticable, drugs ineffective. The epidemic gradually died away. Although isolated cases continued to be reported, by the close of the 1920s it had virtually disappeared.

## Poliomyelitis

By this time, however, the sleeping sickness was no longer the most dreaded of the diseases in its group: in the western world its place had been taken by poliomyelitis.

In the acute phase the symptoms included inflamed throat, aches in the head and back, vomiting, fever, muscle spasm and paralysis. It was chiefly characterised by the high proportion of young children who became its victims, hence its common name of infantile paralysis, and by the number of cases where the patients' muscles never recovered their strength.

Although occasional epidemics with the same symptoms had occurred in the nineteenth century, polio was not recognised as a major threat until 1916, when six thousand people died in an epidemic in the United

States, and of the nearly five times that number who survived, many were left partially paralysed. Whereas the crippled survivors of sleeping sickness were for the most part shut away in hospital wards, the shambling gait, partial paralysis and speech difficulties of polio victims were to make them a familiar sight in communities all over the western world. 'A polio epidemic kills a few of its victims immediately, and others after an interval of suffering,' as John Rowan Wilson put it in his compelling account of the campaign against the disease, *Margin of Safety*: 'The majority survive, often for scores of years, limping through life as a constant reminder to their fellows of the terrible visitation which occurred.'

## Neuro-epidemiology

What could be the explanation of these alarming neuro-epidemics? Inevitably they were attributed to viruses of a type which happened to assail the nervous system. Another possibility suggested itself to Smith Ely Jelliffe, a New York psychiatrist who studied some cases of sleeping sickness in the early 1920s. He observed 'an underlying mental unrest; a sort of physical excitement which might have shown itself in mild delirium if there were less blocking in the motor pathway'. In his pioneering *Rats, Lice and History* in 1934, Hans Zinsser, Professor of Bacteriology at Harvard, drew attention to a possible forerunner. 'In searching the literature for ancestral forms of infectious diseases of the nervous system,' he remarked, 'one cannot over-look a curious chapter of human affliction – namely, that dealing with the dancing manias spoken of in medieval accounts variously as "St John's dance", "St Vitus's dance" and "Tarantism".'

These epidemics are graphically described by the German historian J. C. F. Hecker in his *Epidemics of the Middle Ages*, a work which, though written nearly a century and a half ago, has yet to be supplanted. Breaking out towards the end of the fourteenth century, the epidemics soon affected most of Germany and some neighbouring countries. It was as if whole communities were engulfed in a wave of epilepsy, the victims panting, foaming at the mouth, and afflicted with strange contortions, like puppets in a crazy dance. They alternately laughed and cried, screamed and raved, and fell into comas. While under the influence they appeared to be insensible to all external sensory impressions, even to savage blows.

Allowing for the fact that by the 1920s people at the onset of such symptoms expected to be taken to hospital, whereas five hundred years

185

earlier they had been more inclined to dash out into the streets, there were obvious parallels. But it had come to be accepted that the dancing-mania outbreaks stemmed from mass hysteria, similar to that which still occasionally emerged at gatherings under the sway of an accomplished demagogue or hot-gospeller. By the 1930s it was assumed that organic diseases (the sleeping sickness and polio were taken to be in this category) must have some physical cause, which would rule out hysteria – even had it been considered a respectable diagnosis.

Zinsser was no rebel. He prided himself on his rigorously scientific and materialist standpoint (his attitude can be gauged by his derision of the popularity of the family doctor, 'so dear to the hearts of many of our reactionary contemporaries', which in Zinsser's opinion was the medical equivalent of muzzle-loading). Unlike many of his successors, though, Zinsser was not prepared to ignore evidence of a kind which did not fit prevailing dogma. He knew that the common assumption in northern Europe was that the dancers had been possessed by demons; hence the invocation of St Vitus and St John, who were supposed to be dedicated to protecting anybody affected in this manner. But along the Mediterranean the outbreaks were attributed to the bite of the tarantula spider – the notion that was to give the tarantella dance its name. And when, centuries later, it was found that the consumption of flour contaminated with ergot could produce the same symptoms, it was suggested that ergot poisoning might have caused the outbreaks.

Given the widespread nature of the epidemic, this was hardly a credible hypothesis. It might account for some of the outbreaks, but not all. In great part, Zinsser thought, they must surely have been 'the hysterical reactions of a terror-stricken and wretched population which had broken down under the stress of almost incredible hardship and danger'. For those who collapsed under the strain, there had been 'no road of escape except to the inward refuge of mental derangement which, under the circumstances of the time, took the direction of religious fanaticism'. The overwhelming majority of the outbreaks, therefore, could reasonably be attributed to 'purely functional nervous derangements'. But associated with the outbreaks, he thought, there must have been nervous diseases of infectious origin which followed the great epidemics 'in the same manner in which neurotropic virus diseases have followed the widespread and severe epidemics which accompanied the last war'. The explanation, he suggested, was that the sleeping sickness and polio are not caused by the depredations of new viruses. They probably represent 'a previously unknown biological relationship between virus and host'.

This was, in effect, Bernard's *terrain* idea, restated. But the role of the terrain, though not denied, was by this time regarded as minor. In any case, even to hint at a link between the neuro-epidemics and mass hysteria was unacceptable. Besides, one feature of the polio epidemics could be used to rebut Zinsser's theory. The first major outbreak had indeed been in 1916, but it had erupted in the United States, which was then still out of the war. And could it seriously be suggested that so noted a victim as the President, Franklin D. Roosevelt, had been a hysteric? The idea was absurd! The cause, surely, must be a virus. The virus must be found, and slain!

Roosevelt's career, John Rowan Wilson observed, made him 'a constant reminder of what polio could do'. A constant reminder, too, that it often struck members of well-off families, as if discriminating against the affluent. The combination of Roosevelt's prestige, the fears of the well-to-do, and a fund-raising campaign, 'The March of Dimes', the like of which had never been known before, led eventually to the production of the Salk and Sabin vaccines, providing effective immunisation and encouraging the hope that other such diseases could be similarly brought under control.

The hopes were not fulfilled, because polio in one respect turned out to be exceptional. Nobody had realised, Wilson recalled, 'that polio was not basically a disease of nervous tissue at all, but an intestinal infection which very occasionally might spread to the nervous system'. The belief was that the polio virus must earlier have been so common that children everywhere had acquired immunity to it from birth. Only when improved living standards brought better hygiene were the children of the well-off, in particular, deprived of this automatic immunisation, and consequently rendered more susceptible if they encountered the virus. The conquest of polio, therefore, represented an advance in the direction of finding ways to control intestinal infections, but it was of little significance in connection with the problem presented by neuro-epidemics.

Could Zinsser, then, have been on the right track when he suggested that neuro-epidemics should be regarded as the product of an interaction between pathogen and host? If so, the interaction mechanism should repay study. In his *Disease and the Social System*, published in 1942, Arthur Guirdham followed this trail. The only infections whose incidence was rising, he observed, were those of the central nervous system, and he questioned the wisdom of the accepted hard-and-fast distinction which orthodoxy made between their organic and functional (or mental) versions. 'We are a long way yet from discovering whether physical or nervous disease shall ensue, given the factor of strain and the presence of infective agents,' he warned, adding that although the infective agents were still regarded as the cause, in his view 'they are doomed in the future to be relegated to the status of mere precipitants'.

Such warnings from a young psychiatrist, however, appearing as they did in Britain in the gloomiest months of the war – just after the fall of Singapore and the near-rout of the Middle East forces by Rommel – were not likely to attract much attention. And when Guirdham returned to them in *A Theory of Disease* fifteen years later, emphasising the need to re-examine the links between the neuropathic disorders and the neuroses, his timing was again unlucky. The only type of neuro-epidemic that had been causing concern was polio, and his book appeared at the time when the mass immunisation campaign, using first the Salk and then the Sabin vaccines, had just begun to banish worry.

## Royal Free Disease

A number of outbreaks of neuropathy, however, had been reported, chiefly characterised by the fact that the victims usually all lived in an institution. In the same year a report about one of them appeared in the *British Medical Journal*. Its repercussions – less for what it said than for what it glossed over – have continued to reverberate ever since.

Periodically the medical journals had mentioned institutional epidemics of a type initially thought to be polio which had come to be described, a little lamely, as 'a disease simulating polio'. Patients suffered tremors, spasms, sometimes convulsions; muscle weakness followed, along with mental and emotional disturbance. Usually only people in a single institution would be affected, and the outbreaks were rarely either protracted or serious. In ordinary circumstances they would have been attributed, as indeed some were, to infection by an as yet undiscovered virus, which might be related to polio. But they showed a puzzling feature: a curious selectivity about their victims. When, for example, they occurred in a hospital, they tended to affect members of the staff, and particularly women, rather than patients, as they had done in the Los Angeles County General Hospital in 1934.

In 1955 there was a similar outbreak in the Royal Free Hospital in London. Out of nearly three hundred people affected, two hundred and fifty of them sufficiently seriously to be hospitalised, only a handful were patients, the great majority being women members of the medical, nursing and ancillary staff. Although every known test was employed to find an infective organism, none could be traced. When, two years later, the report of the formal investigation into the outbreak appeared, the authors had to admit that 'at present the aetiology of the disease remains

188

unknown, and the mode of transmission has not been elucidated'. The *Lancet* had earlier suggested that these institutional outbreaks had sufficient in common 'to suggest that this is a new clinical entity'; the *BMJ* now accepted this recommendation, suggesting that they should be classified as encephalomyelitis (inflamation of the brain and spinal cord), with the qualification 'myalgic', to indicate that there was muscular involvement.

Myalgic encephalomyelitis sounded imposing – even with 'benign' attached, as was sometimes the case, to indicate that lasting consequences of the kind familiar from polio and the sleeping sickness were very rare. But there was a growing source of embarrassment: outbreaks in schools, where the symptoms were very similar, even if less serious. Within three days, in 1956, thousands of schoolchildren in West Wales collapsed with the familiar symptoms – five hundred of them at one school in a single day. No cause could be found, and although at the time such outbreaks were automatically blamed on 'a virus', the manner and speed in which the symptoms spread not only within an institution, but also in several institutions at a distance from each other at the same time, meant that it would have to have been a virus of a kind never previously encountered.

Cautiously, Medical Officers of Health began to revive the almost forgotten diagnosis. 'I think it is a very strong possibility that mass hysteria is spreading from one school to another,' the Middlesbrough MOH told reporters, following a small wave of outbreaks in the autumn of 1965. 'It is unlikely in some cases that there has been a virus infection at all.' And an editorial in *The Times* reminded the profession that, although the blame was still being put on 'a virus', none had ever been isolated. Why, if it were a virus, should the incidence among girls be so much higher? 'So far as is known, viruses have no particular predilection for either of the sexes.' To suggest mass hysteria, the editorial admitted, 'is verging on *lèse majesté*, but it is a possibility that cannot be ruled out'.

*Lèse majesté* it might be, but with the evidence piling up from the investigations of the school outbreaks, the possibility of hysteria was becoming increasingly difficult to ignore. A year later the *British Medical Journal* carried a survey of some of them, in particular one in Blackburn. Although, in a last-ditch attempt to avoid having to commit itself editorially, the *Journal* entitled it 'An Epidemic of Over-breathing among Schoolgirls', the writers – Peter D. Moss, a Blackburn pediatrician, and Colin McEvedy, a psychiatrist at the Middlesex Hospital – made it clear that the only plausible explanation of the 'over-breathing' ('panting' or 'gasping' was the girls' own description) and its associated symptoms was mass, or epidemic, hysteria.

189

Ordinarily, Moss and McEvedy observed, such a diagnosis was made on the basis of excluding all other possibilities, but in their view this outbreak provided 'ideal material for an attempt to raise the dignity of hysteria as an epidemiological category'. From a careful examination of all the relevant evidence they had come to the conclusion that not merely were the alternative hypotheses, such as food poisoning or a gas leak, untenable, but also the outbreak had followed the course which could have been expected if emotional contagion, rather than any pathogen, was responsible. 'What became epidemic was a piece of behaviour consequent upon an emotional state: excitement or, in the latter stages, frank fear.'

McEvedy then switched his attention to the Royal Free outbreak, and with a colleague from the Middlesex Hospital, A. W. Beard, examined the available case-reports of the 1955 outbreak. Every possible diagnostic avenue had been explored, they reported in the *BMJ* in 1970, except one: the case for hysteria had not been examined. The *Lancet*'s editorial had claimed that the epidemic was clearly differentiated from polio and other forms of encephalitis 'and, need it be said, hysteria'. Yet re-examination of the case-notes of the patients, McEvedy and Beard pointed out, revealed more evidence pointing to hysteria than the hospital's own report had disclosed. For example, fits had been mentioned in the report only once, yet the case histories showed that in ten out of eighteen severe cases, convulsions had been observed, including one 'lasting about twenty minutes, consisting of throwing limbs about, foaming at the mouth, staring eyes'. There was little evidence, they concluded, of any organic disease: 'epidemic hysteria is a much more likely explanation.'

This diagnosis, they were careful to insist, should not be regarded as a slur on either the individuals or the institution involved. Inevitably it was so regarded, particularly by those women who, as students or nurses, had caught 'the pestilence', as they had called it. The recollections which the McEvedy/Beard paper aroused in one of them, Jane Eden, are revealing. The earlier symptoms, she recalled, had been swollen glands, shivering, aches, and a feverish feeling (which the thermometer belied, as it stayed obstinately around 98.4F). 'Of course, we could have gone to the physicians,' she explained; 'but as clinical students, we had racked our memories, looked up the textbooks and confirmed that the symptoms just did not fit any known disease.' So for weeks they gritted their teeth and 'tried to sleep off the inexplicable fatigue', because 'nobody wants to be labelled an hysteric and slung out when within spitting distance of Finals'. It had been bad enough to go through this ordeal at the time, she protested, without now having to put up with a couple of gentlemen who had never been near the hospital during the outbreak pontificating in the *BMJ* 'about it all being due to hysteria – which any doctor should know is the most dangerous diagnosis in medicine'.

Medical students, in other words, had been taught that to suffer from a hysterical disorder was disgraceful, so disgraceful that it would ruin their chances of qualifying. They had believed this, and they continued to believe it. So did their teachers, as they were soon to reveal. Jane Eden mentioned in her article that a group had been formed to study the syndrome scientifically. How 'scientifically' the inquiry had been conducted was to be shown at the symposium where its results were presented, held at the Royal Society of Medicine in 1978. Although fifteen papers were read, McEvedy and Beard were not asked to contribute. Such was the reluctance to face the possibility of epidemic hysteria that even those issues which might have dragged it in were tacitly avoided. Obviously the most interesting question in relation to the Royal Free outbreak, for example, was why it had afflicted so few patients, and so few male members of the hospital staff. One questioner remarked upon the oddity that the staff should have been the chief sufferers, whereas in polio it was the other way round. The chairman of the session could only suggest that being 'sedentary' might have offered some immunity, and the issue was dropped.

The possibility of hysteria, where it was referred to at all, was treated as a joke in poor taste. The most that any of the speakers were prepared to concede was that there might in some cases have been 'hysterical overlay' – a consequence of the disturbing nature of the symptoms. Amongst so many patients 'in a closed community, suffering from a disease of unknown prognosis', Nigel Compston of the Royal Free admitted, 'it would not be surprising if some patients exhibited emotional or even hysterical features'. But the disease itself was demonstrably organic. And at the end of the meeting a show of hands enabled the chairman complacently to claim 'there seems to be a practically unanimous belief that it is organic in origin'.

Nevertheless the dread spectre of epidemic hysteria was not entirely exorcised. Its presence had led speakers to vie with each other in producing evidence to prove that the outbreaks at the Royal Free and elsewhere constituted a single disease entity with, presumably, a single pathogenic source. Unluckily for this design, the discussion at the close left the meeting in disarray.

To the discomfiture of some of those present, the symposium had not been given the name to which they had become accustomed: 'myalgic encephalomyelitis'. Instead, it had been entitled 'epidemic neurosmyasthenia'. This alternative had been selected, the chairman explained, because it was the name of the disease in the United States. But 'myasthenia' means muscle weakness or fatigability, and that, as one speaker objected, 'in no way embraces the manifestations that we encountered at the Royal Free'. This view won general support. 'It seems to me,' the session's chairman observed, 'that there is a general preference for the term "myalgic encephalomyelitis".' So there was, among the British. But the leading US authority, Professor Shelokov, at the meeting declined to go along with it. Could it be, he wondered, that they were talking about different things? 'I, for one, no longer believe that it is really one disease.'

Worse followed. Not merely might there be more than one disease, Shelokov went on: there might be 'a variety of causes', in which case the symptoms that they had been discussing might be 'only the expression of a common final pathway of pathogenesis'. The chairman, disconcerted, turned to a different issue, and a few minutes later wound up the proceedings.

In two sentences, Shelokov had undermined the foundations upon which the whole concept of the new disease entity rested. Yet the *British Medical Journal*, in its editorial surveying the papers presented at the symposium, chose to ignore his contribution. 'Some authors have attempted to dismiss this disease as hysterical,' it recalled, 'but the evidence now makes such a tenet unacceptable' ('some authors', the source reference disclosed, were McEvedy and Beard, in their *BMJ* piece eight years before; now, they were unceremoniously jettisoned). Clear agreement prevailed, the editorial insisted, that myalgic encephalomyelitis (the American version, myasthenia, was also ditched) was a clinical entity, and 'the organic basis is clear'. Nothing was yet known about the cause of the outbreaks, but as they were still occurring, they should be studied 'by a collaborative team of neurologists, epidemiologists, virologists and immunologists'. One specialty was conspicuously absent; no psychiatrists need apply.


*Legionnaires' Disease*

By this time, however, a new variety of epidemic nervous disorder had appeared, with more sinister capabilities. Some argument had taken place over whether myalgic encephalomyelitis should have the 'benign' label attached; although nobody had died from it, and most of its victims made a full recovery, there had been a few cases where recovery had not been complete. Yet benign it certainly was compared to an epidemic in Philadelphia in the summer of 1976, where three thousand members (or relatives of members) of the American Legion had assembled to attend a convention at the Belleview Stratford Hotel. One hundred and eighty of them, most staying in the hotel, collapsed with a mystery disease, along with thirty-eight other people who were not at the convention but were living in the same block, and there were twenty-nine deaths.

The symptoms varied: they included general malaise, aching muscles, headache, and a feeling of alternating chilliness and feverishness. Among the many possible explanations put forward were nickel poisoning (because of a strike of sanitation workers, trash had been burned, including some nickel), and poison gas, pumped into the convention rooms by some maniac through the air-conditioning system. None of the hypotheses could be made to fit the established facts – not all the victims, for example, had entered the hotel. Accordingly the virologists began their investigations, initially scenting the possibility that the pathogen responsible might turn out to be a descendant of the 1918 strain of flu, returning in even more virulent form. But this time, for once, they were to be upstaged by the bacteriologists, who had observed that the symptoms of some of the victims, including high fever, chest pains and respiratory difficulties, resembled those traditionally associated with pneumonia, and in 1977 David W. Fraser and some colleagues in the Center for Disease Control at Atlanta formally staked their claim in the *New England Journal of Medicine*. Legionnaires' Disease, as it had come to be called, had been 'an explosive common-source outbreak of pneumonia caused by a previously unrecognised bacterium', and soon afterwards 'a gram-negative intracellular pleomorphic bacterium' was identified as the culprit.

For the general public, as for most doctors, this appeared to settle the issue. Legionnaires' Disease was a mystery no longer: the cause had been found, the syndrome identified. But it was not quite so simple, because pneumonia itself is not quite so simple.

Traditionally, pneumonia is 'the old people's friend'; it carries off those in whom the life force has sunk too low for permanent recovery ('A blessed escape from infirmities', as John Ryle put it). It used to be feared, though, because it also could strike at the young and outwardly healthy. They would have shiverings and chest pains, a rapid pulse rate and a high temperature; nothing could be done except to sponge them down and keep them quiet. After about a week the 'crisis' would arrive, which would settle matters. About one in ten patients could be expected to die; for the rest, recovery would follow, more or less rapidly according to their general condition.

When the pneumococcus was discovered in 1884, it was taken to be the cause of the disease. Half a century later, however, it was found that the pneumococcus was capable of changing its type (research into this transformation, in Sir Peter Medawar's view, led to the birth of molecular biology). Soon, 'the pneumococcus went the way of 'the' rhinovirus, as fresh variants were uncovered. 'Pneumonia remains ever-important,' the *British Medical Journal* recently warned in an editorial, 'because so many organisms may cause it: bacteria, viruses, fungi, chlamydia, and rickettsiae' – as well as 'recently identified fastidious bacteria'.

In one respect, the Legionnaires' Disease bacterium has certainly been fastidious. It has never been identified with any certainty; its presence and guilt have been largely assumed on the basis of the reactions of laboratory guinea-pigs. From time to time claims have been made that diagnostic specificity has been substantiated, but they have later been overturned. And although almost everything known about the disease, along with a great deal of speculation, was aired at an international symposium held in Atlanta in 1979, the papers read there by eminent authorities offered no clue as to why the episode occurred when it did, or why it took the form it did – a form which pneumonia had never been known to take. Yet in spite of this, Legionnaires' Disease is still being confidently diagnosed when cases which bear some resemblance to it are found in different parts of the world.

A few critics have pointed out weaknesses in the pneumonia theory. Surveying the evidence, Hywel Davies, formerly assistant professor of medicine in Denver, has argued that Koch's postulates have not been fulfilled. The bacterium has not been recovered from a high proportion of patients, and although it has been grown in cultures, inoculating susceptible animals with it has not necessarily reproduced the disease. The diagnosis in patients, too, is based on their immunological reactions, the diagnostic validity of which remains doubtful. If the bacterium is 'a virulent primary pathogen', why have there not been secondary cases among contacts? 'The demonology of bacterial diseases has been powerfully evoked in the saga,' Davies concludes. 'If I am correct in my conclusions, which are based entirely on data from the medical literature, the medical profession has been led by the nose into building a house of cards. One wonders what puff of wind, polluted or not, will blow it down.'

Davies's preferred explanation, however – that the Philadelphia patients succumbed to the ill-effects of a chemical used in the hotel – also does not fit the known facts. Members of the hotel staff would surely also have been among the victims, yet they enjoyed relative immunity: only one contracted the symptoms. And this in itself suggests that a type of selection process may have been at work, similar to that in other outbreaks where the casualties have been almost all from the same category – hospital staffs contracting it, but not patients; students, but not staff, and so on.

The confusion that can arise because of the assumption that the pathogen has been found was typified recently when *The Times'* medical correspondent, Tony Smith, criticised the British media for playing up the 'mystery disease'. Legionnaires' Disease, he asserted, 'is no longer a mystery'. Smith happened also to be the deputy editor of the *British Medical Journal*; two weeks later it included a contribution from an Italian bacteriologist, emphasising just how mysterious the disease has remained. 'Legionellosis', as he described it, is 'an ambiguous spectrum of illness', sometimes straightforward, sometimes 'multi-system'. Understanding of it is 'still rudimentary'; virtually nothing is known about the factors responsible, and even the histopathological findings 'vary considerably, and may be due to secondary infections, the results of therapy, or underlying disease'.

The most likely explanation of the mystery is that Legionnaires' Disease represents a variant of the encephalomyelitis/neuromyasthenia syndromes; as Shelokov suggested, 'the expression of a common final pathway of pathogenesis'. This, after all, is pneumonia's traditional role. If a pathogen is eventually positively identified it may turn out, like the polio virus, to be no more than a signpost to the particular path. As such, to know more about it may prove useful; but the more immediate need is to find the trigger to the outbreaks, and why some individuals are affected and others are not.

To try to banish the disease by getting rid of the pathogen would be a futile exercise. Research has revealed that 'Legionella pneumophilia', the presumed culprit, is to be found in many establishments that have no recorded cases of the disease – prompting the *British Medical Journal* to warn that in such circumstances its discovery 'should not at present be an indication for attempts at eradication'.

## Epidemic Hysteria

In this quest for an explanation of neuro-epidemics one possibility has been subjected to little systematic research: institutional outbreaks of the kind McEvedy and Moss described in the Blackburn school. In 1974 Richard Levine and colleagues from the epidemiology department of the Center for Disease Control, Atlanta, going back over the records, found over a hundred reports of such outbreaks from the nineteenth century, but only sixteen in English-language journals in the twentieth.

Since then they have been more commonly reported, which has led the *British Medical Journal* to surmise that they must have become more frequent. But the experience of two investigators, psychologists in the US Department of Health, Education and Welfare, suggests that they may always have been frequent but not as a rule reported. When in the early 1970s Michael Colligan and Michael Smith began to investigate outbreaks in industry, their contacts with occupational health professionals and representatives of labour and management convinced them that such incidents, far from increasing, had previously been occurring much more frequently than had been suspected.

They had received little publicity because in typical cases, where a number of workers suddenly become dramatically ill for no apparent reason, 'the investigative team is likely to consist of an industrial hygienist, a nurse or medical assistant, a physician, and possibly a toxicologist'. Their aim is to find a pathogen – perhaps a leak in some container giving out fumes. Only where nothing of the kind can be found, and where there also appears to be considerable tension in the work-force, is their report likely to mention the possibility that psychological factors may have contributed, and 'such a suggestion is always made with considerable caution'. By the time the report is completed, too, the affected workers will have recovered, the management will be anxious that the episode should be forgotten, and the investigative team will feel they have failed; so 'the final report is unceremoniously buried in the agency files'. Asked to address a conference of the American Footwear Manufacturers' Association on his researches, Colligan provided some case-histories and, during question-time at the end, asked if any of his audience had encountered similar outbreaks. Of the fifty representatives there, almost half indicated that they had.

Outbreaks at schools are still more rarely properly investigated. There is no obligation to report them, unless the epidemic is thought to be of a notifiable disease; usually they are put down to food poisoning or to 'a virus', and if no pathogen can be found, 'a mystery virus' will serve. Where mass hysteria is diagnosed, as in the case of an outbreak at a

196

Florida school described by Berton Roueché in the *New Yorker*, the diagnosis is unwelcome: not so much to the school authorities, who may be relieved that the original scare – say, about a poisonous gas – has been shown to be wrong, as to the parents (some of whom thought the Florida doctor was labelling their daughters as insane; fortunately for them he was six feet nine inches tall, which made a physical assault unlikely). Ordinarily such accounts, if they appear at all, are found only in local newspapers, or as a one-paragraph curiosity in the national press – 'Mystery School Illness', a *Sunday Telegraph* headline ran in 1977, going on to describe in a couple of sentences how it had caused twenty-four pupils in a school in Cornwall 'to roll on the floor and hold their heads'.

On the other hand, epidemics at institutions such as hospitals are usually carefully investigated, but again, as in the case of 'Royal Free Disease', all the emphasis is on the game of Hunt the Pathogen, the medical profession's grown-up version of Hunt the Slipper. Still, the controversy provoked by McEvedy and Beard has stirred up interest in the subject of unexplained epidemics, and medical and psychological journals have been more willing to consider papers arguing the case for mass hysteria – not by that name, as a rule, because it remains a dirty term, but as 'collective psychosis', 'mass delusion' or 'group pathology'. When outbreaks occur, too, employers have shown greater willingness, at least in the United States, to call in psychologists, in their case from the National Institute for Occupational Safety and Health, enabling them to collect data from workers who have been affected and from those who have not, in order to try to find the extent to which personality traits, life-style and circumstances can account for the difference, and in 1979 the Institute held the first-ever international conference on the subject in Chicago, with Colligan as chairman.

The most striking feature of the outbreaks is their consistency. The symptoms vary, but the pattern is the same. 'The episode generally begins,' Frieda L. Gehlen of the University of New Mexico has noted in a paper on 'Hysterical Contagion', with an individual exhibiting symptoms 'such as nausea, stomach cramps, uncontrollable trembling or twitching, dryness of mouth and throat, fainting, mild convulsions, or even temporary paralysis' – the classical symptoms of epidemic hysteria, and these symptoms spread to others.

Although the reports are not as yet sufficiently numerous to encourage confident generalisations, they suggest that the younger the age group involved, the less likely the symptoms are to appear serious. This even applied, McEvedy and Moss found, within the school in Blackburn. In a letter following their article on the Royal Free epidemic they

197

offered a generalisation which might, they thought, turn out to be useful, though it was 'not something we thought of, but something we found: the fact that whereas the disturbance was more easily elicited in the younger, it was more severe in the older'.

Ironically it is in junior schools, where the diagnosis is most commonly made and accepted, that the manifestations are least 'hysterical', in the colloquial sense; usually they consist of malaise, aches, fainting, dizziness, breathing difficulties. But the symptoms come on suddenly. Many children – mostly girls, where the sexes are mixed – feel ill within a few seconds of each other; there is fainting and 'over-breathing' or 'hyperventilating' – panting, as if from fear, and the symptoms are so similar that it looks as if the children are 'putting them on'. This makes the diagnosis of hysteria easier to reach than in adult institutions.

Where adults are involved, as in workshops, the symptoms may also bear only slight resemblance to classical hysteria. Often the chief symptom is one which can easily be blamed on the work the sufferers are engaged in: dermatitis, for example. Investigating two outbreaks in factories in a north of England town, Anne Maguire, called in as a dermatologist, found in both cases that they had started as a result of one woman complaining that she was the victim of an occupational skin disease. In both, the woman did in fact have a dermatological disorder, but not one connected with her occupation. In the other workers – nine in one case, sixteen in the other – the symptoms disappeared as soon as they accepted the dermatologist's findings that their employers were not responsible.

The evidence which Colligan and his co-workers have collected confirms that psychological rather than physical factors are frequently responsible for epidemics. In the cases investigated, rarely has anything been found which could account for the workshop outbreaks in terms of heat, noise, or noxious odours. The outbreaks appear to be a safety-valve, a means of letting off steam, getting rid of accumulated tensions. Those who succumb are more likely than those who do not to complain of boredom and of poor management-labour relations. Usually it needs an 'index case' as the epidemiologists call it, to act as catalyst by falling ill – sometimes, as in the Florida school case, with what is later diagnosed as a 'real' illness. The rest follow, their symptoms often being indistinguishable from those of the index case, but the symptoms vanish as soon as the scare subsides.

These episodes, Anne Maguire has suggested in her report in the *Lancet*, are of significance for society, as well as for doctors. In the two she investigated, several months of production for important export markets were lost because the workers involved took their symptoms to the shop stewards rather than to doctors. It was as if they had lost their sense of individuality, becoming 'only units in a system of groups'. They are also of significance in relation to the epidemics at the Royal Free and other hospitals. At the Royal Free, for example, the symptoms recorded, in order of most frequent occurrence, were headache, giddiness, pains in limbs, lassitude, inertia, neck pain, nausea, and 'subjective sensory phenomena' – much the same as in many a school outbreak. The chief difference was that the symptoms came on more gradually, in a few cases were distinctly more serious, and generally took longer to shake off than those commonly reported from schools or factories.

Again, however, the resemblances are more significant than the differences, a fact underlined by a recent account in the *Lancet* of an outbreak at a girls' school in Southampton. On the ground that there were 'no bizarre features resembling epidemic hysteria in schools' (a curious statement, as in the great majority of such epidemics there are no bizarre features) and that the outbreak was spaced out over a longer period (also not uncommon), the authors of the report presumed to assert that the outbreak had been a benign myalgic encephalomyelitis. Predictably this raised an anguished rebuttal from Melvin Ramsay of the Royal Free. With his colleagues he had tried to exorcise the spectre of mass hysteria, girls-school-style; now, here it was creeping back under the very designation that they had chosen to demonstrate and reinforce their case.

## Awakenings

The clue to what the victims have in common has been provided by Oliver Sacks in his remarkable book *Awakenings*, in which he describes his experience while working in the Mount Carmel Hospital, New York, with sleeping sickness patients, some of whom had caught the disease in the epidemic nearly half a century before. They had been turned into living statues, bereft of initiative, 'as insubstantial as ghosts and as passive as zombies', until the advent of the drug L Dopa. That L Dopa was indeed a 'miracle drug', Sacks remains ready to accept, but not the implication that its beneficent effects proved that the disease was exclusively organic. He has studied Jelliffe's writings in the 1920s, and recognised in patients many of the same indications of an emotional component.

The active symptoms, Sacks noted, appeared to be 'enactions of sudden *urges*'. On the passive side, too, not only the sensory motor system was disrupted: '*all* aspects of being and behaviour – perceptions,

199

thoughts, appetites and feelings, no less than movements – could also be brought to a virtual standstill.' It was as if some deep dissatisfaction with life had led the patients themselves off, yet not as a schizophrenic does, by shifting into another mental world, since they remained aware of what was happening around them. 'One thing, and one alone, was (usually) spared amid the ravages of this otherwise engulfing disease: the "higher faculties" – intelligence, imagination, judgment and humour.'

L Dopa restored them to activity, but not to health. How far they recovered the use of limbs and faculties depended on many other factors, chief among them the extent to which they could be induced to *want* to recover, and this in turn, Sacks concluded, related to 'that beautiful and ultimate metaphysical truth, which has been stated by poets and physicians and metaphysicians in all ages – by Leibniz and Donne and Dante and Freud: that Eros is the alpha and omega of being; and that the work of healing, of rendering whole, is, first and last, the business of Love'.

If recovery from the zombie condition imposed by the sleeping sickness depends upon being 'rendered whole', the possibility is worth exploring that what went wrong at the onset was some mind/body fracture. Initial susceptibility to the disease may well have been the same as for flu: a combination of physical weakness, following the years of privation, with war-weariness and the effects of strain on so many families of the long years when at any moment a telegram might arrive announcing the death of a loved one at the front. The sleeping sickness, on this hypothesis, might have selected those who were close to crack-up, but not necessarily through any character weakness – often, perhaps, for the positive reason that they had driven themselves too hard. For the present this can only be speculation, but it would help to explain why the victims of institutional outbreaks are not necessarily those who have a poor physical, mental and emotional record. Often it is the reverse.

The particular symptoms, if the hypothesis is correct, must depend partly upon the individual's genetic and constitutional make-up, and partly on whatever it is that gives an epidemic its specific character – different in the case of, say, Legionnaires' Disease and Royal Free Disease. If person-to-person virus-spread can be ruled out, as sometimes it has to be, the most likely explanation is that some process is at work to upset the nervous systems of members of a group, which can bring about a collective response in its victims. But *what* process? What is the nature of the infecting agent? Could it, for example, be released from a miasma: a pathogenic emanation, imperceptible to the senses and as yet unidentified by medical science?

*Group Pathology*

That epidemics may start and spread by some miasmic process is at first acquaintance hard to swallow. Yet the evidence produced by Hoyle and Wickramasinghe, coupled with the fact that institutional outbreaks cannot be fitted into conventional theories of disease-transmission except by the most dubious Procrustrean devices, suggests the need for a reappraisal of the miasma idea, with the possibility in mind that some unexplained force is at work, capable of transmitting diseases or, perhaps, transmitting the signal at which a disease process starts up in those who are in the catchment area, and who are susceptible.

Anybody entering this inadequately explored territory, however, encounters a trip-wire. The only recognised alternative to the accepted transmission theory is mass hysteria. As the Royal Free affair has demonstrated, it is unpalatable as a diagnosis of institutional outbreaks, and to suggest that it might be responsible for epidemics of flu excites only derision.

This objection, however, is the result of confusion arising out of the use of the term 'hysteria' to describe both a type of behaviour and the way in which, in certain circumstances, it appears to become collective – giving a group or a mob a common identity. The two meanings ought to be kept distinct, because the process by which a group is fused together does not necessarily dictate its behaviour, any more than the process by which TV pictures are broadcast determines the content of the programmes. The fusion may represent an evolutionary device, originally developed for very different purposes.

In *The Soul of the White Ant* Marais described the remarkable way in which termites function, as if directed by a guiding intelligence (although he was a dedicated disciple of Darwin, 'soul' came nearest to what he had in mind), capable of prompting each individual termite to perform its tasks, whether foraging, fighting, or building. Some of the work they carried out, he found, was of startling complexity, such as the building of an archway which fitted exactly, even when the termites engaged on the construction on one side were cut off from those on the other by a barrier which Marais interposed between them.

Mankind, Sir Heneage Ogilvie claimed in a lecture he gave in 1957, owes something to this evolutionary development. He put forward 'the wild, improbable but not impossible suggestion' that the human body and the termite colony ought to be regarded as different models derived from the same principle: 'The human body represents not a single individual, but the latest and not necessarily the final phase in the evolution of a polymorphic colonial animal.' If the theory is correct, it can come as

201

no surprise that people should still be capable, in certain circumstances, of shedding their individual identities and submitting to a group 'soul' – in Marais's sense – much as starlings, which behave as individual birds when they reach their feeding ground, function as a flock on their way there and back, whirling and swooping as if their movements are dictated by a single controller.

The solution to the mystery of how the 'group mind' works, the parapsychologist Whately Carington thought, will probably be found when more is known about the forces responsible for extra-sensory perception: he named this kind of group behaviour 'psychic integration'. But recently the discovery of pheromones has suggested a possible sensory component. In his stimulating *Tuning in to Nature* Philip S. Callahan, Professor of Entomology at the University of Florida, has explored the role of pheromones, free-floating scent molecules, in the insect communication system, and further research may show that they provide one of the missing links in our knowledge of the human communication system, too, enabling individuals to tune in to one another, facilitating harmony (or the reverse) on an unconscious level.

Ten years ago the Harvard psychologist Martha McClintock, following up a clue presented by research into the possible effect of pheromone communication on the oestrogen cycles of mice, set up a trial to find whether similar effects could be observed in women. She recorded the dates of menstruation of 135 female students in a dormitory of a suburban women's college; they showed a significant synchronicity of the periods of those who were either room-mates or close friends, even more significant in the case of those who were both, a phenomenon already observed by Mary McCarthy in *The Group*. It indicates, McClintock suggests, 'that in humans there is some interpersonal physiological process which affects the menstrual cycles'; commenting on the possibility that pheromones may turn out to be the messengers, the psychologist Tom Clark has surmised that they may also prove to explain how infections spread in schools and other institutions.

If infections can be transmitted in this way, much that seemed unaccountable becomes relatively simple to explain: in particular, why germs and viruses which are ordinarily harmless, giving their human host no trouble, can suddenly become a menace. The standard explanation is that reinforcements have been imported which have developed in, say, poorly refrigerated food; when the food is eaten, the micro-organisms it contains team up with those already in the body to overwhelm the body's defences. The weakness of this assumption, demonstrated by Pettenkofer in connection with cholera, has been demonstrated again in trials where volunteers have consumed quantities of dysentery bacilli in

202

conditions which, it is believed, would ensure that they caught the disease; very few did. Nevertheless, wherever there has been an outbreak of food poisoning, the blame has usually been put on whatever micro-organisms are found, and preventive measures have concentrated upon the need to keep down the number of bacteria, to the point of passing laws which have made it illegal to sell food with more than a specified amount of bacterial contamination. But as Anthony Sharpe of the Canadian Bureau of Microbial Hazards has pointed out, the risk to consumers is not proportionate to organisms in the food. What is important is the consumers' reaction, and about this little is known. It is here, Sharpe argues, that research is required. 'We need, initially, to concentrate on *people.*'

Sharpe, however, is thinking in terms of laboratory-type controlled tests concentrating not on the micro-organisms but on the human responses, to try to find 'the actual parameters of unwholesomeness to which human bodies respond'. If the body's response can be influenced by mood convection (to adopt the term Konrad Lorenz has used in connection with animal behaviour), such research could also have relevance for individuals. When a number of guests collapse at a banquet, one of them may indeed have been 'poisoned', either because he is particularly susceptible to the micro-organism involved, or through some allergic reaction, but the others may be the victims of their own alarm, as in the case of workshop outbreaks.

Mood convection could also explain the baffling episode of the 'margarine disease', skin eruptions accompanied by gastric trouble and pains, which afflicted tens of thousands of people in Holland in the summer of 1960. Most of the victims, it was found, had eaten a type of margarine which had recently been marketed with a new emulsifier; so close was the initial statistical correlation that the company stopped producing it, and resigned itself to paying compensation. Some investigators, however, rejected the attribution, pointing out that only about one in four of the people who had eaten the margarine had fallen ill; that people who had not eaten it had caught the disease; that far more women than men had caught it, and that it had earlier been marketed in Germany and the former Dutch colonial empire without ill-effects. In the end the evidence against the product was found to be so riddled with inconsistencies that the prosecution case collapsed.

Germs and viruses, on this hypothesis, should not necessarily be regarded as enemy invaders, or even as guerrillas. They may be a fifth column, to all appearances law-abiding citizens who are awaiting a given signal to go into action against the ruling authority. They may not even have that degree of menace; perhaps the analogy should be with looters, citizens who in normal times would do nothing criminal, but who are prepared to take advantage of any breakdown in law and order.

The advantage of this theory is that not merely does it accommodate all the known facts: it does so without doing too much violence to accepted beliefs. The role of germs and viruses is not challenged; it is merely changed. And if pheromone communication is provisionally accepted, it gets round the difficulty presented by any theory which would involve acceptance of extra-sensory faculties. Not that the existence of pheromones precludes the possibility that, as Guirdham has contended, one person might infect another on an extra-sensory plane, but the idea that the infection is transmitted by scent molecules is for the present less unwelcome. Although opinion polls have shown that a sizeable majority of academics and scientists accept the possibility of extra-sensory communication between people, the idea that it may provide an explanation for the spread of epidemics is unlikely to find favour. And because germs and viruses will still be involved – for whether they are fifth columnists or looters, they can still be blamed for the damage and the pain – the symptoms can be classifiable as 'real', rather than hysterical or neurotic (the symptoms of mass hysteria are, in fact, just as real as those of an organic disease – as the Florida doctor stressed, when telling Roueché about the school outbreak; but this is something which has tended to be forgotten).

Granted, for the sake of argument, that infections may be spread by pheromone (or extra-sensory) transmission, the question still has to be asked: What triggers the spread? Why do epidemics begin – and why do they end?

The most plausible hypothesis is that they represent a release mechanism. The fact that young school children are notoriously prone to attacks of epidemic diseases, particularly in boarding-schools, may be linked – Guirdham has suggested – to the problems of adjusting to institutional life. That people in closed institutions suffer from the bottling-up of tensions is notorious, finding expression in works ranging from Browning's 'Soliloquy in a Spanish Cloister' to Huxley's *Devils of Loudun*. Release of tension cannot account for all the outbreaks, however, or for the symptoms of all those involved: 'mood convection' can infect people who are not part of the group mainly affected, as in Philadelphia. Nevertheless, group or institutional identity deserves always to be considered as a possible factor in any outbreak.

That institutional stress ought to have been considered in relation to the epidemic at the Royal Free Hospital has since been disclosed unwittingly by one of the victims, Jane Eden, in her description of how it broke down previously existing barriers 'in a hierarchical set-up where the acquisition of post-nominal letters meant that, in public at least, you could not call your erstwhile best friend by her Christian name'. The victims found 'that the teaching hospitals aren't necessarily the best places to learn or practise medicine'; the general feeling had been 'we would never be quite the same again'.

The individual mind, this evidence suggests, may play a role not altogether removed from that of resident, normally quiescent micro-organisms: it can be affected only if receptive. Why some individuals are receptive, so that they succumb to flu or Legionnaires' Disease or any other infection, cannot be decided on the available evidence, though it is possible that research along Kissen's lines with TB could eventually throw up some clues. Such research would offer the prospect of a new way to prevent and treat infectious disease, as the neurologist Sir James Crichton-Browne urged, three-quarters of a century ago. The mind, he was certain, was capable of animating the body 'to a strength from which the noxious bacillus retreats baffled – yes, even though it is greedy there, and scents the fit soil, it does not find the climate'. His recommendation that the medical profession should make better use of the mind's resources to cure diseases of the body was already by that time un-fashionable, but it could now be ripe for revival.

# 7

# Neuropathology

The epidemic forms of diseases of the nervous system bear many resemblances to a range of neuropathic disorders which, though some are thought of as infections, are not ordinarily considered transmissible person-to-person. Some take an acute form: epilepsy, hydrophobia, meningitis, tetanus. Others follow a degenerative course: multiple sclerosis, myasthenia gravis, Parkinson's Disease. And others mysteriously come and go: shingles (herpes), glandular fever, migraine. Together they represent a category which has continued to baffle medical science.

'Whenever physicians congregate and engage in the inter-disciplinary banter which so often enlivens social intercourse in our profession,' Sir John Walton, Professor of Neurology at the University of Newcastle-upon-Tyne, has admitted, 'one often hears the old adage that "neurologists are interested only in diagnosis and not in treatment", or that "neurology is a specialty in which no treatment is available"'. Claiming that this is no longer true, he lists some of the 'remarkable advances in management of the commoner neurological disorders' which have emerged since he began to practise. The operative word, however, turns out to be 'management'; a discreet term commonly employed for whatever is done when no effective treatment is available. True, since he began to practise the introduction of the antibiotics and other drugs has brought about some improvement, notably in dealing with meningitis and neuro-syphilis. But in general the results of drug treatment have been disappointing, and such individual successes as there have been are tarnished either by their unwelcome side-effects, or by the need for patients to continue the dosage, as the symptoms return if treatment is interrupted.

Some of the 'advances', too, turn out to be nothing more than the fact that neurologists have learned sense from bitter experience.

Certain types of treatment which were once fashionable, such as surgery for Parkinson's Disease, have been quietly dropped. Claims for advances in the 'management' of any disorder must always be regarded

with suspicion because, at any given time, whatever form of management happens to be in vogue is assumed to be better than its predecessors. In recent years vitamins, steroids and many other drugs have been
successively hailed as deliverers from shingles, only to go out of fashion,
prompting a correspondent in the *British Medical Journal* to lament
recently that there is little more to offer the sufferer than 'analgesics,
sympathy and a liberal helping of hope'. The same prescription is all that
can be recommended for most neuropathic disorders. A succession of
new drugs appears which can be claimed to be more effective than their
predecessors, but the claims are rarely substantiated.

## *Multiple Sclerosis*

The most feared of the commoner forms of neuropathy is multiple
sclerosis. The symptoms of 'MS' vary from individual to individual; they
include weakness (sometimes paralysis) of a limb or part of a limb,
numbness and pins-and-needles, loss of control over muscle movements, lassitude, occasional vertigo and nausea, incontinence, blurring
of vision. It was first classified as a disease-entity distinct from what was
then loosely described as 'choreiform paralysis' – 'chorea' being the
name given to disorders involving loss of muscular control – by
Charcot, whose life's passion it was to sort out the neurological diseases
nosologically, thereby improving their status.

He identified MS largely thanks to his charwoman. 'In spite of her
costing him a small fortune in broken plates,' Freud was to recall,
Charcot kept her for years in his service; when at last she died, he could
prove in the autopsy 'that "choreiform paralysis" was the clinical expression of multiple cerebro-spinal sclerosis'. The autopsy evidence was
required because only after death could the disorder be positively
identified by the damaged condition of the myelin sheath which insulates
the nerve fibres. ('Patches of destroyed myelin are replaced by scar
tissue,' Thomas H. Maugh has explained in *Science*, 'and this interrupts
and distorts the flow of nerve impulses in much the same way that breaks
in the insulation of telephone cables, for example, can interfere with the
flow of information.') Inevitably the discovery of the damaged myelin
put the new clinical entity, MS, into the 'organic' category, and this in
turn was taken to mean that it must have a specific etiology, an organic
cause.

Research in MS has concentrated on looking for the cause ever since.
'Involvement of viruses in disease is of course a fashionable notion,' as
the *New Scientist* has noted, a touch sarcastically, 'and with the thrust of

academic virology behind it, there should be no surprise that multiple sclerosis has its candidate.' As the quarry has proved elusive, the search has recently been taken up by the immunologists, groping for links between MS and, for example, antigens. Quite often such links are found, and reported. Unluckily, they have served only to confuse the issue further. In one country, MS patients may consistently have a higher proportion of specific antigen in their systems than the population at large; in another, these proportions sometimes turn out to be reversed. Here again, the need for mutual succour has brought virologists and immunologists together in a marriage of convenience, the currently accepted formula being that MS is 'a virus-induced immune disease'. It is a union, however, that, in spite of a number of false pregnancies, has yet to be blessed with issue. Optimism has 'tended to diminish as neurologists have increasingly recognised the complexity of the condition', a recent survey has noted; 'at present, alleviation of inflammatory symptoms and supportive counselling are still the mainstays of management'.

The failure to find either cause or cure can be held to the discredit of the medical scientists only if they have neglected research into other possible causes or risk factors – as indeed they have. Some research has taken place into dietary links, and some into the epidemiology of MS, but the findings have only added to the mysteries. Why is it preeminently a disease of temperate climes? Why does it so often attack young people? Why should migrants stand the same chance of catching it as they would in their country of origin, no matter where they eventually settle – unless they emigrate as children, in which case their chances of catching it are the same as those of the inhabitants of the country of adoption? Clearly environmental factors must be involved; but where to look for them?

One obvious possibility is the presence of psychosocial risk factors. Multiple sclerosis, Charcot observed, was commonly related to long-continued grief and vexation, and periodically individual doctors have made similar observations. The result of the first tentative attempt at a controlled trial was reported in 1958 by G. S. Philippopoulos, Assistant Professor of Neuropsychiatry at the University of Athens, and colleagues from McGill University, to which he was temporarily attached. Aware of neurologists' common experience that emotional stress 'either immediately antedated the onset of the disease or led to relapse', they sought the answer to three questions. What kind of a person develops MS? How often does emotional disturbance precede the onset, or a relapse? And is there any MS-related 'psychodynamic constellation'? Working with forty patients, roughly divided between the sexes, they found that, in all but five, prolonged traumatic disturbance had preceded the onset of the symptoms – thus confirming Charcot's observation.

Only in four cases had the onset been linked to sudden acute trauma, but relapse was often associated with fresh sources of emotional disturbance. Although there was no clear-cut 'psychodynamic constellation', MS often followed an unhappy relationship with a parent, usually the mother, leaving a residue of anxiety. Not that the effects of childhood deprivation, or emotional stress in general, should be regarded as the cause of MS, Philippopoulos insisted; on the contrary, it was clearly multi-causal. They were only claiming that 'more often than is generally known, emotional factors play a part and may precipitate not only exacerbations and relapses of an established MS, but even its onset'.

If these researchers at McGill had discovered a *chemical* change related to the onset of MS, or to relapses, they would have sparked off frenetic research all over the world. But laboratory scientists cannot be expected to investigate anxiety, and neurologists have felt ill at ease with this psychosocial element. The research was backed by the Canadian Multiple Sclerosis Society, but it has not been followed up elsewhere, in spite of a recent reminder in the *Lancet* that, even if some abnormal auto-immune mechanism related to MS should be discovered, this would not in itself dispose of the need to investigate the psychological aspects of the disorder. 'Since the immunological response may change in bereavement and in various other kinds of stress, similar mechanisms may well be involved in the pathophysiology of MS,' the editorial points out. 'The possibility that psychotherapy may have some specific role to play in management deserves closer investigation and trial.' It is a possibility in which those MS fund-raising organisations dominated by neurologists and laboratory-orientated researchers have shown little interest. The only psychological aspect of the disease which has attracted much of their attention is how to help people cope with the emotional disturbance, which can be severe, consequent upon the diagnosis of MS.

This disturbance is so often severe largely because of the grotesquely misleading picture which the public has of MS, as a *British Medical Journal* editorial complained in 1972. An Office of Health Economics survey has since echoed the complaints. MS is taken to be 'a chronic crippling disease, characterised in the early stages by relapses and remissions, followed by a chronic progression to a bed-bound, incontinent, paralysed state, after which death ensues'. In fact this represents 'only one extreme of the spectrum, which relatively few people experience.

Much more common is the benign form of the disease in which relapses are mild and infrequent, permitting active life for many years.'

The responsibility for creating the misleading impression lies chiefly with the system by which patients with disturbing neuropathic symptoms are sent to a hospital for specialist diagnosis (or confirmation of a GP's diagnosis) and treatment. The consultant neurologist tends to see patients when their symptoms are in the acute stage; he sees them infrequently when their symptoms are in remission, and he may never see them again if their symptoms disappear. In other diseases such cases can be claimed as cures on the strength of the patients' not returning, but with MS, so firm is the assumption that it is incurable that when the symptoms disappear it is commonly assumed that the early diagnosis was mistaken, and this in turn tends to confirm the impression that the symptoms of real MS follow an inexorably destructive course.

So gloomy a prognosis has inevitably transmitted itself back to patients and their families. In a paper in the *British Medical Journal* on 'Common Psychological Problems in Multiple Sclerosis', Alexander Burnfield, a psychiatrist practising in Winchester, and Penelope Burnfield have described how emotionally unprepared some doctors are 'to cope either with the patient's problems or with their own feeling of inadequacy'. Often they shy away even from discussing the disease with the patient. Sometimes they will only tell a husband or wife, 'with instructions that the patient must not be told', which 'can place an intolerable strain on both partners, damaging their relationship'. It can also damage the doctor–patient relationship, when patients discover the truth – as, in the Burnfields' experience, they have often done: 'a few had read their medical notes on the doctor's desk; others had steamed open letters entrusted to them by their doctor; some had found out by accident from hospital staff who assumed that they already knew; and sufferers had occasionally diagnosed themselves after talking to other patients in a ward.'

What makes matters worse is that specialists tend to be driven by a compulsive need to make the diagnosis of MS at the earliest possible stage. As no effective treatment exists, this is of no benefit to the patient. Neurologists justify themselves by pointing out that it is desirable to know what is the matter, so that the patient will be spared further tests for other possible disorders, but at the time the diagnosis is first made, it is usually tentative. Statistical evidence about the incidence of MS is notoriously unreliable, because cases often have to be labelled 'probable' or 'possible' for years after the initial diagnosis; members of the MS Research Unit in Newcastle have recently pointed out in a letter to the *Lancet* that 'neurologists of great experience freely admit changing their initial diagnosis of MS'. Yet if they do change it, patients cannot be compensated for the suffering unnecessarily caused.

Unluckily, too, such is the pressure for early diagnosis that it infects newly qualified doctors in hospitals, so that, on encountering a case which displays some of the indications of the disease, they may be tempted to put 'MS?' in their notes, thereby adding another possible source of leakage and alarm to the patient. A few years ago a young woman who was being treated in a London hospital for unexplained paralysis and other neurologial symptoms actually overheard two doctors arguing whether she had MS or a brain tumour. It eventually turned out that she had neither. What she certainly had – as she tried unsuccessfully to tell the doctors – was an agonising emotional conflict; as soon as she reached a solution the symptoms vanished. The doctors, however, simply declined to believe that the symptoms could be psychosomatic. They were astonished that she should even suggest the idea. Yet her case suggests the possibility that, if stress can be a precipitant of MS-like symptoms, it may, if protracted, render them permanent.

Gradually the belief that MS must have a single pathogenic source is being eroded. It now seems clear, Thomas Maugh concludes after his survey in *Science*, that it is 'an exceptionally complicated disease that results from a complex interaction of genetics, environment, geography, viruses and the patient's immune system'. He laments that 'there is no clear picture of the entire disease process and no therapy for it'. A clearer picture and a therapy might emerge, however, if the link with emotional crises were to be more energetically explored, and the *Lancet*'s recommendation about psychotherapy were accepted. But with the neurologists in control, the prospects for such venturing are poor.

*Daniel Hack Tuke*

MS is at one end of the spectrum of neuropathic diseases in which the chief indicator is loss of muscular power; its chief companion in this category is Parkinsonism. In his *Essay on the Shaking Palsy* in 1817 the English physician James Parkinson described certain features – tremor, muscle weakness, 'a propensity to bend the trunk forward, and to pass from a walking to a running pace' – which provided a sufficiently recognisable picture for his name thenceforward to be attached to the disease, although other characteristics have since been added. The main symptomatic components, according to the Office of Health Economics' paper on the subject, are now accepted as 'shaking of the limbs or the head; slowness of, or even inability to initiate, movement; and muscular rigidity, leading to a characteristically bowed posture and immobile face'. It would be as much feared as multiple sclerosis were it not for the fact that it ordinarily afflicts the elderly, often being hardly distinguishable from what are commonly thought of as the symptoms of old age.

No cause has been found for 'idiopathic' Parkinsonism – the term idiopathic itself being a euphemism for 'unexplained'. But it can be the product of other illnesses, in particular the sleeping sickness; it can be induced by a variety of toxic substances, including medical drugs (it is a commonly observed side-effect of treatment in hospitals), and the symptoms can follow some severe physical or emotional shock. It often appears, in fact, to be a pathological version of the familiar symptoms of shock, which leaves people 'all-of-a-tremble' or sends them reeling. The symptoms take the form which could be expected if, after a shock, we lose the ability to recover, because our homeostatic system has been jolted out of order.

The same applies in cases of myasthenia gravis, where the muscles gradually cease to obey the instructions transmitted through the nervous system, culminating, in extreme cases, in the 'rag-doll syndrome'. According to a recent survey in the *Lancet* 'emotional stress, especially anger, increases symptoms, sometimes to a dangerous degree'. But patients, despite their awareness of this, 'resented being told that they were neurotic' – yet another example of the destructive consequences of the conditioning of doctors, and through them of patients, to regard neurosis as an indication of loss of self-respect and self-control.

Severe shock, though it may lead to collapse, can also have the opposite effect: voluntary control is lost, but far from leading to weakness, it galvanises the muscles into action of the kind that makes paralysed patients leap from their beds and run at the cry of 'Fire!', or in some emergency lift objects ordinarily far too heavy for them to lift. With epileptics it is as if the preparatory tension, the coiling of the spring, is carried out without any real need for it, so that eventually the nervous energy has to be discharged artificially in a fit. Their muscles go into spasm, their limbs flail around, their breathing becomes erratic, and they froth at the mouth. As the fit subsides, they go into a coma; when they come out of it, they may feel none the worse – sometimes much better, though there may be some mental confusion and loss of memory.

Although epilepsy can be identified by the particular pattern recorded on an electro-encephalograph, the symptoms are not substantially different from fits related to other diseases. Again, the outstanding feature of the convulsive symptoms of neuropathic disorders is their similarities.

The loss of control manifests itself in three main ways: regular contraction and relaxation, as in convulsions; irregular and excessive contraction, as in cramp; loss of power, as in paralysis. There are endless permutations, and it is possible to distinguish between different types, but the symptoms tend to straddle the diagnostic boundaries. Convulsions, for example, can occur as a by-product of many disorders, from tetanus and rabies to apoplectic strokes and brain tumours. They may be the consequence of poisons, 'nerve gas' or strychnine; they can occur in connection with the institutional neuroses and psychoses; they are one of the trade-marks of hysteria.

A little over a century ago Daniel Hack Tuke drew attention to this aspect of neuropathy in his *Illustrations of the Influence of the Mind upon the Body in Health and Disease*, which has some right to be regarded as the first textbook of psychosomatic medicine, although he did not use the term. In a long section on 'the influence of the emotions upon the voluntary muscles', packed with case-histories from the classics and Shakespeare as well as from medical textbooks, he showed how all the usual symptoms could be, and frequently had been, brought on by emotional as well as physical traumas. He was not arguing that mental or emotional disorder *caused* them: his thesis was that a breakdown in the mind's control allows them to happen. The normal equilibrium between the voluntary and the autonomic nervous systems, he claimed, 'is obviously more or less interfered with when the mind or brain is unable to exercise its accustomed force, or when it transmits a more than wonted impulse', allowing unrestrained action or inducing collapse.

Tuke's thesis was that, even where a cause could be established, such as the bite of a rabid dog, there could still be a powerful psychological element in the process, which determined whether or not the individual became ill as a result; he cited cases of individuals who had mistakenly believed that they had hydrophobia and who developed the symptoms, eventually dying from them. Admittedly the dominant causal feature can be of a kind which appears to be physiologically predetermined, as in Huntington's chorea, symptomatically linked to Parkinsonism but with a clear hereditary base, so that half the people in line for it because of their genetic background contract it. But this still leaves unresolved the question why the other half remain immune.

Tuke's work was soon forgotten, because he was swimming against the prevailing tide, which was flowing in the direction of a more precise diagnosis and specific etiology. Yet it has remained a commonplace that in their early stages, neurological disorders can be and frequently are mistaken for one another. Sacks has recalled that, when the sleeping sickness epidemic broke out, it was variously described as epidemic delirium, epidemic schizophrenia, epidemic disseminated sclerosis, atypical rabies, and atypical polio. In the Royal Free outbreak the initial fear was that polio had struck again; later the symptoms were attributed to glandular fever, and in some cases it was noted that they resembled multiple sclerosis. And at the time of the Philadelphia outbreak similar confusion prevailed, the diagnoses ranging from swine flu to psittacosis – 'parrots' disease'.

To the public the names given to neurological disorders tend to conjure up a much clearer picture of specific symptoms than to the neurologist who has to diagnose them. Tetanus, for example, means 'lockjaw', which sounds simple. Anybody reading Bernard Shaw's preface to *The Doctors' Dilemma* and coming across his assertion that he could remember hearing doctors 'deny the existence of hydrophobia as a specific disease differing from tetanus', will be inclined to think how primitive diagnosis then was. Yet recently the *Lancet* has admitted that the diagnosis of tetanus rests 'entirely on clinical acumen' because it can be so accurately mimicked by adverse reactions to drugs, or in certain psychotic conditions. The diagnosis 'glandular fever' has become something of a sick joke among neurologists, realising as they do that it has so often been used for lack of anything more specific. Even epilepsy, it is coming to be realised, is far from being straightforward diagnostically. 'It is one of the most fascinating diseases,' Philip Evans, Physician Emeritus at the Great Ormond Street Children's Hospital in London has remarked, 'common, various in cause and manifestations, changeable. It involves body and mind profoundly.'

The use of the term 'fascinating' is often revealing. Thomas McKeown has recalled that as a medical student he began to realise the existence of 'an inverse relation between the interest of a disease to the doctor and the usefulness of its treatment to the patient'. Neurology, in particular, attracted some of the best minds because its diagnostic problems were so fascinating; but for the patient with multiple sclerosis, Parkinson's Disease and most other serious neurological conditions 'the precision of diagnosis which was the focus of medical interest made not the slightest difference to the outcome', a point about which the neurologists, if they had any qualms, gave no indication of them, at least in the presence of students. According to R. E. Hope-Simpson, writing in the *Proceedings* of the Royal Society of Medicine, herpes is 'fascinating'; 'it arrives unpredictably, is readily diagnosed – a rare pleasure for most of us – and difficult to explain.'

One reason why an explanation of herpes has been lacking is that so often the doctors involved in treating it have tended to assume that neuropathies are caused by the germs or viruses linked with them. Yet these pathogens cannot be held responsible. The meningococcus, for example 'seems to have the characteristics of an implacable dangerous enemy of the whole human race,' Lewis Thomas has observed, 'but it is not so. When you count up the total number of people infected by the meningococcus, and then compare it with the number coming down with meningitis, the arrangement has a quite different look.' It is as if the meningococcus is itself infected by some other pathogen, and there is a range of suspects. According to Professor Ronald Illingworth 'meningitis can be caused by a wide variety of organisms', among them E. coli and other bacteria, streptococci, staphylococci, pneumococci, candidosis and herpes.

Resistance has continued, however, to the notion that one of the causes, or precipitants, of herpes may be some form of emotional stress. Yet over fifty years ago two doctors from the University of Vienna, Robert Heilig and Hans Hoff, found that they could induce an eruption of cold sores in patients by reminding them, under hypnosis, of emotionally-painful events. Cases have been recorded of individuals who have been able to predict the onset of symptoms because they follow situations in which hostility has been provoked. One, a soldier, reported to his medical officer that, given the opportunity, he could also prevent the sores appearing, by working off his feelings with hard work, or by getting drunk.

Since then, trials have shown that cold sores can be removed by psychotherapy or by auto-suggestion. When the discovery was made that ether inactivates the herpes virus in test-tubes, a controlled experiment was conducted at the University of Utah to see whether patients with cold sores benefited from ether treatment, and seventy-five per cent of them did. But seventy-seven per cent of the control group, who were given a placebo, also benefited; 'there was no noteworthy difference between groups given ether and placebo in progression of lesions, healing time, duration or intensity of pain, and duration or quantity of virus excretion.'

Herpes, Harold Wolff claimed in his *Stress and Disease*, 'is a classical example of a latent virus infection'; the virus is dormant in most people, but a few have 'flaring factors' related sometimes to the season, sometimes to the onset of other symptoms, and 'last but not least, to emotional upset'. If herpes' attacks may serve as a model, Herbert Benson has argued, 'even diseases directly attributable to specific viruses are related to psychological factors'.

How does the interaction between virus and emotional stress come about? The clue can be found in Hans Selye's theory of 'the General Adaptation Syndrome'. As a medical student he was struck by the fact that most patients in the early stages of their illness suffered from what he was to describe as 'the syndrome of just being sick' – malaise, coated tongue, diffuse aches, intestinal disturbances, fever, rashes and so on. These, his teacher explained, were 'non-specific' and consequently unimportant; the doctor's task was to watch for symptoms which could be diagnosed as a specific disease. Years later Selye was to present the idea that these non-specific symptoms represent the first stage of the body's reaction to an alarm, 'the bodily expression of the generalised call to arms of the defensive forces in the organism'. This is followed by the second stage of resistance, or adaptation, in which the defence forces rally to restore health. If the enemy proves too powerful, or the body's reserves too weak, a third stage follows: exhaustion, and death.

Exhaustion does not necessarily end in death. It may simply lead to an erosion of the ability to make a full recovery – a weakening of homeostasis. Neuropathic symptoms reflect this loss of control. Whether the outcome is MS or Parkinson's Disease is likely to be related to the individual's genetic and constitutional background, rather than to a specific infection. Again, Professor Shelokov's phrase, 'the expression of a common final pathway of pathogenesis' comes to mind. If so, neuropathic diseases ought to be considered not as disease entities, but as different manifestations of loss of homeostatic control.

If this hypothesis is correct, another fundamental mistake that has been made is in clinging to the assumption that hysteria is a separate disease entity. All neuropathies are hysterical, in a sense, because they all represent a breakdown of control over the nervous system. Cases where the breakdown can reasonably be attributed to emotional stress (or self-indulgence) can theoretically be classified as 'pure' hysteria: but in the great majority of cases not only is there no way in which the emotional and physico-chemical components can be prised apart, but also it is impossible to separate them – for example, by clinging to such concepts as 'hysterical overlay', as was done in the Royal Free to account for those symptoms which were too close to traditional hysteria for comfort. When they represent the final common pathway such distinctions become irrelevant. There is no way of deciding whether, say, the 'globus hystericus' – constriction of the throat muscles, long deemed a sign of hysteria – is a side-effect of an emotional release, as it is in crying, or part of the 'general neuropathic syndrome', as the Royal Free investigators tried to maintain in order to preserve their outbreak's organic virginity.

The futility of trying to separate the hysterical component has been most graphically demonstrated in connection with the sleeping sickness, as shown in Smith Ely Jelliffe's accounts. Jelliffe, who had studied

Freud, was startled to find explicit confirmation of Freud's theories of infantile sexuality. The inhibitions of formerly well-behaved children who caught the sleeping sickness would break down, so that they became 'salacious and lewd', sometimes so uncontrollably that they were sent to mental hospitals. With adults, however, the repressed urges were masked by what Freud had described as 'conversion hysteria', transformed 'not only into neurotic and psychotic behaviour, but into tics, "crises", catatonia and even Parkinsonism'. It was as if they had found a way to express their intense feelings indirectly, in physiological ways; 'they were gifted – or cursed – with a pathologically extravagant expressive facility of (in Freud's term) "somatic compliance"'.

It is not unusual for epileptics to display neurotic symptoms, and the mental disturbances associated with MS have from time to time been cited as a defence in court cases where a victim has been accused of a breach of the peace. Hysteria (or the symptoms commonly so designated), can be induced by any of a great variety of traumas, physical as well as emotional. When in 1848 an iron rod tore through Phineas T. Gage's skull, following an explosion, boring a hole through his brain, his intellect was miraculously unimpaired, but his doctor noted that 'the equilibrium or balance, so to speak, between his intellectual faculties and animal propensies seems to have been destroyed'; Gage became irreverent, 'indulging at times in the grossest profanity (which was not previously his custom)'. Was it that the part of his brain which had restrained his animal propensies had been destroyed; or was it the after-effect of the shock, perhaps coupled with the fact that from being an obscure working-man he had become a world-wonder? Or were both involved? There is no way of telling. Nor is there any way to be certain whether the hysterical symptoms displayed by some MS patients, or by some of the victims of the Royal Free outbreak, were physico-chemical or emotional or both. Where doctors are dogmatic on such issues, they are being as unscientific as bible-thumpers.

# 8

# Auto-immune Diseases

## Allergy

Of all the diseases of civilisation, those classified as allergic or 'auto-immune' are the most baffling because they are so pointless, so seemingly unnecessary. In allergy, the body's defences are called out to deal with an invader which is in fact harmless, like pollen, but which for some people acts as an allergen, provoking the sneezing and the streaming nose in an attempt to get rid of it. An auto-immune disease, M. H. Lessof of Guy's Hospital explained in a paper in 1962 – when the concept was still unfamiliar – 'is one in which a subject becomes immunised against his own body constituents, and tissue damage results'. As in practice it is often not possible to distinguish between allergy and auto-immunity, or even to be certain that the symptoms represent a breakdown of the mechanism rather than the intrusion of some disease agent, the story of allergy will serve as an introduction to diseases of immunity in general.

Historically speaking, allergy is a relative newcomer. Occasional references to allergic-type reactions have been noted: one of the Hippocratic writers, observing that some people can eat their fill of cheese and others cannot digest it, argued that there must be a constitutional difference, and 'in the latter case, they have something in the body which is inimical to cheese and disturbed by it', and the sixteenth-century physician and sage Jerome Cardan is credited with curing the young King Edward VI's asthma by the simple expedient of removing his feather pillows. But such tales are surprisingly rare. Not until the 1870s was what has come to be called hay fever traced to ragwort.

Shortly after the turn of the century the French psychologist and physiologist Charles Richet took the understanding of the process a step further. Experimenting with immunisation procedures, he found that laboratory animals which had tolerated one injection sometimes died following a second, although the dose was the same. Instead of providing protection against the disease, the first dose must have in some way alerted the body's defences so that they over-reacted. This 'anaphylaxis', the Austrian Clemens von Pir01quet realised, provided the explanation for what had come to be known as 'serum sickness', a sometimes fatal shock reaction in humans to immunisation; when further research showed that the substance did not need to be toxic to cause such a reaction, he coined the term, allergy – altered capacity to react – to describe it. Following up these clues the British physiologist Henry Dale found the explanation. The allergens entering the body, and the antibodies grappling with them, were liberating histamine in the course of their struggle, causing the effusions of mucus and the spasms. It was much as if an influx of tourists were to lead to a false alarm of an enemy invasion, causing troops to pour out into the countryside, disrupting normal life in the process.

Dale was awarded a Nobel prize, as Richet had been, and as the research had come so far, so fast, it seemed reasonable to expect that the next step would be the discovery of the keys to the way in which the body's homeostatic mechanism was being deceived, so that the false alarms could be turned off. But as has so often been the case, the researchers have chiefly found answers to the question 'What happens in the body when there is an allergic reaction?' They have been much less successful in their efforts to find out *why* the body should react to false alarms.

For a time the lack of progress was masked by what appeared to be a couple of major advances. One was the discovery that immunisation could be used to remove, or at least to reduce, vulnerability to pollen. Hay fever is the commonest of allergies, and pollen one of the hardest of allergens to avoid. But immunisation does not work in all sufferers, and when the pollen count turns out to be particularly high, it may not work at all. And although anti-histamine drugs provide some control over the symptoms, they have a sedative action which makes work difficult and driving dangerous.

The other discovery which raised hopes, for a time, was that by rubbing substances on to a patient's skin and making a pin-prick through them, it was possible to find what he was allergic to. The substance's guilt or innocence was demonstrated by whether or not a weal appeared, indicating an allergic reaction. Even if no way could be found to reduce sensitivity to an allergen, therefore, at least there might be some way to avoid it. But the value of this method of detection turned out to be limited. Most of the commoner allergens which it could be used to detect were either readily detectable without its help, or hard to avoid, or both.

## Auto-immune Disease

Over the past thirty years the centre of immunological interest has been shifting away from allergies to the broader field of disorders of all kinds which can be attributed to a breakdown in the body's homeostatic mechanism, and in particular those where the presumed cause of the reaction, the antigen, is not an outsider but one of the body's constituents, when Sir Macfarlane Burnet claimed in 1972 'Every pathologist and every academically-minded physician is aware that a growing number of sub-acute and chronic diseases are being spoken of as auto-immune,' if anything, he was underestimating the spread of the concept of auto-immunity or 'auto-allergy', a more self-explanatory term which for some reason – perhaps because it *is* self-explanatory and thereby lowers academic barriers – has not caught on. Increasingly, symptoms which were assumed to be caused by infections are being denominated immunological. Hardly a common disease remains that has not been claimed by the immunologists as their own.

For some years the immunologists met with passive, and sometimes active, resistance. Accustomed to the assumption that diseases are the consequence of invasion by pathogens, physicians did not take to the notion that what is really responsible is misguided action by the body's defence forces. Still, at least the immunologists were claiming that the body is reacting against some *thing*; the symptoms could still be classified as organic. And with research beginning to reveal the identities of the antigens which provoked the reaction, and of the antibodies rallying to master them, it even looked for a time not merely as if specificity could be maintained – one antigen, one antibody for each symptom, or even for each syndrome – but also that detection of the antibody would provide an infallible diagnostic label, so that disorders such as glandular fever, notoriously hard to diagnose with any confidence, could at last be pinned down.

Far from solving diagnostic problems, immunological research has succeeded only in complicating them. Lessof observed in 1962 that, already, researchers were being 'embarrassed by finding a plethora of antibodies, in a host of different diseases', and recently the *British Medical Journal* has echoed him in connection with glandular fever, where the variety of the antibodies involved, their transience, and their overlap with other diseases suggest that their detection 'may be a trumpet which gives an uncertain sound'. The same uncertainty is to be found in connection with many of the neuropathies; even when they are found there can be no certainty, as Lessof warned, that immunological changes are the cause, 'and not secondary reactions'.

As a result, diagnosis has continued to depend very much on the individual specialist, and upon his preconceptions as well as his diagnostic acumen. In a recent paper on skin allergies, for example, Paul Buisseret of Guy's Hospital Medical School has explained that he included urticaria (nettle-rash) only because 'nearly all doctors and most patients believe it is an allergy'; in his view, allergic urticaria is 'very rare'. Yet in a survey he cites of five hundred cases, no cause could be identified in ninety per cent of them, which makes it difficult to see how anybody can feel certain that they either are, or are not, allergic. Similarly some dermatologists take for granted that infantile eczema is an allergy, while others insist that it is not, leading to 'much confusion about etiology and management'.

Recently the confusion has been increased by the development of the school of thought which puts most of the blame for allergies on food. It has long been realised that people can become allergic even to everyday food, such as eggs or milk, but more and more culprits are being detected, notably gluten – proteins found in cereals. And some allergists, notably Richard Mackarness, have been claiming that food is responsible for many other everyday ailments, in addition to those which are recognised as, or suspected of being, allergic in origin – not only those disorders of the digestive system, the respiratory tract and the skin which used to be thought of as infections, but even neuroses and psychoses. For a time, his theory excited chiefly derision – and some active antipathy: Mackarness has recalled that some of his hospital colleagues 'used to turn and walk the other way when they saw me coming'. But tests have since shown that food does, in fact, play a much larger role in connection with allergy than had been realised.

The title of the book with which Mackarness launched his theory was odd: *Not All in the Mind*. Allergy sufferers, he had come to realise, were unpopular with the medical profession because so little could be done for them, and if a skin test presented no evidence of a culprit, they had often been given to understand that they were neurotic nuisances. Mackarness felt he was performing a service by releasing them from this stigma, and showing that their symptoms really are organic. This is still the aim of most allergists: they delight in demonstrating the existence of an allergen, and the more complex the task of finding it, the more satisfaction they obtain. But the reason why the body reacts to it remains unexplained.

In his *Allergy: Strangest of all Maladies* Warren T. Vaughan described a typical example of what such a search can entail: the case of bridge partners who began to find it difficult to continue to play at the same table. 'Although they were both charming people, an intense antagonism gradually developed', and it was eventually found that she was allergic to his dandruff. Buisseret has added an even odder case history: the story of a nine-year-old girl who suffered from a malaise whenever she went to school.

One weekend after a particularly severe attack, her doctor asked her if anything unusual had happened to her that week, and she told him that a school-friend's brother had teased her by flicking a blackboard duster at her, and then rubbing her face in it. This gave him an idea: might Natalie be allergic to chalk? Told to sit by an open window when she next attended school, she had no more trouble. This was fortunate for the girl, as it removed the suspicion that she might be neurotic, or even a malingerer. But it was then found that the chalk in use at the school was of a kind which did not produce dust. Further tests had to be made, until it was discovered that the allergen to which she reacted was part of the composition of the chalk.

The ability to unmask specific allergens has perpetuated the hope that some way will be found to check or reverse inappropriate immune reactions with the help of drugs, and periodically breakthroughs in this area are announced. In 1975 an immunologist at the University of California claimed that he had succeeded in synthesising a molecule which would perform that task. But as yet there has been no sign of any more effective form of prevention or of treatment. Even Burnet has admitted that 'by calling a disease auto-immune or auto-allergic nothing useful was necessarily being accomplished', and he was taking the words out of some critics' mouths – notably Sir George Pickering, who used to draw attention to the ominous resemblances of the auto-immune theory to that of 'auto-intoxication', fashionable between the wars, only to be comprehensively discredited later.

That many disorders are more plausibly accounted for by a breakdown of the body's defences than by the power of invading pathogens is not now in dispute. What remains a mystery is the reason for such breakdown, and here, research has been unavailing. But this may well be because most immunologists have been just as blinkered in their assumptions as have bacteriologists. Both have been conditioned to think in reductionist terms: to assume that the answers to their problems will be found in the laboratory. Admittedly this has not been Burnet's view; in his *Genes, Dreams and Realities* he argued that the future lay not in the laboratory but with the observational sciences, investigating environmental causes of disease. But for most immunologists the lure of the laboratory has proved too powerful. Their attention has continued to be focused upon the processes by which immunity is maintained or lost, which they believe will be found in some physico-chemical breakdown.

This assumption, as Sir Heneage Ogilvie pointed out, is illogical. He was ready to accept that many of the commoner disorders represent a breakdown of the central control mechanism: rheumatoid arthritis, for example, and ulcerative colitis. But why should the central control mechanism go wrong? To say 'endocrine imbalance' was merely to bring the inquiry back a stage: 'What is the cause of the imbalance?'

It is inherently unlikely that the composition of school chalk, or a bridge partner's dandruff, could be the cause of an allergic reaction. One obvious possibility is that they are simply the trigger mechanism, related to some stress arising out of school or bridge or perhaps a quite unrelated emotional conflict, the allergy representing an unconscious equivalent of the twitch or rictus which can accompany recollection of a past gaffe. The more open-minded specialists are aware of this, and keep an eye out for it. Bethel Solomons, a consultant dermatologist in London, recalls the case of a patient who came out in a rash every time he went home to the country for the week-end, which led to a long fruitless search for some rural substance as the offender. The rash, however, disappeared after the death of the man's wife, which left him free to marry the woman with whom he had been living during the week while he was working in the City.

## 'Smother Love'

In *Allergic Man*, published during the Second World War, Erwin Pulay made the point that his patients who suffered from allergies did not think of themselves as being ill. In recounting their symptoms, they would describe them as their 'state'. They were right, he submitted, to think in these terms. Allergy, he had come to accept, is a personality-related disorder, arising chiefly where there is an excess of sensibility. This hyper-sensitivity, he suggested, 'is a source of suffering not only to those about him but, above all, to his own self. He is in search of the inner harmony that he lacks, and seeks the peace of mind he can never find.'

In her *Mind and Body* Flanders Dunbar advanced a theory to account for that lack of inner harmony, particularly in connection with allergies such as asthma and hay fever: it represented 'a conflict about longing for mother love and mother care'. A child, she noted, may feel frustrated as a result of either too little or too much love. There may be a feeling of frustration 'as a result of too little love, or a fear of being smothered by too much', and with asthmatics it was 'smother love' which was usually the problem.

Although neo-Freudian interpretations of this kind soon went out of fashion, and the 'smother-love' notion did not lend itself easily to tests along the lines Kissen was pioneering, a few orthodox allergists have agreed that there is nothing improbable about the idea of allergy-prone people. As Harry Swartz, head of the allergy department of New York Polyclinic Hospital, pointed out in his book on the subject in 1963, fear, anger, anxiety and even more complex emotions share the same channels of communication through the nervous system as allergic reactions. He cited examples of the way in which alarm can trigger symptoms. In one, a doctor hung a chart which displayed the pollen count in his waiting-room, and found that when he faked the figure, raising it when in fact the pollen level had gone down, several of his patients reacted to the false count. In another experiment a woman who was allergic to roses developed the symptoms when one was offered to her, though it was an artificial bloom.

Suggestion has also been experimented with in treatment. Particularly when reinforced under hypnosis, tests have shown how effective it can be. A leading researcher into hypnosis in Britain, Stephen Black, has described how he took twelve subjects who were known to suffer from allergies, and injected them with the substance to which they were allergic, to ascertain their reactions. Under hypnosis they were told they would be given the same injection, but that they would not react to it. Eight of the twelve duly displayed no reaction; one of them retained immunity for nearly two months. In another experiment, serum was taken from a patient whose allergic reaction had been inhibited by suggestion under hypnosis, and injected into another patient with the same allergy. It provoked a reaction, showing that the hypnosis had not banished the physico-chemical component of the allergy, but had simply blocked the emergence of the symptoms.

The most remarkable instance so far reported of successful treatment of an allergy by suggestion under hypnosis was presented in the *British Medical Journal* in 1952, in a paper describing the case of a youth suffering from ichthyosis, a particularly virulent and intractable form of eczema which forms a black scaly layer on the skin, almost as if it were an epidemic of warts. It covered most of his body, and a variety of remedies had been tried without success. He had eventually been sent to the hospital in East Grinstead, where pilots badly burned in flying accidents during the war had healthy parts of their skin successfully grafted to repair their ravaged faces, as memorably described by Richard Hillary in *The Last Enemy*. It had been hoped that skin from the youth's chest, which was not badly affected, could be successfully grafted on to his hands, so covered with the horny casing that he was unable to use them, because they 'cracked, fissured and became infected'. The graft 'took', but a month later, the condition of his hands was as bad as ever.

As a last resort, it was decided to try suggestion under hypnosis. A. A. Mason, a senior registrar at the hospital, undertook to carry out the experiment. To guard against the possibility that overall improvement in the youth's condition could later be attributed to coincidence or to the delayed effects of earlier treatment, it was agreed that the initial suggestion would relate only to the skin on his left arm. He proved to be readily hypnotisable, and less than a week after the treatment was started the horny layer on his left arm began to soften, eventually falling away, the skin beneath revealing itself as almost normal in texture. Within ten days the area chosen was clear of the ichthyosis. The natural skin of the boy's body was gradually restored in the same way, and although parts of it were more resistant to the treatment, he was soon well enough to begin to lead a normal life. Previously he had had little schooling or social contact with other children, and was unemployable. A year after the treatment had been completed, the experimenters were able to claim that he had become happy and normal, and had secured a job.

Few cases respond so satisfactorily to hypnotic suggestion, partly because not every patient is sufficiently hypnotisable, partly – as experience in using it to help people give up smoking has endlessly shown – because it needs reinforcement in the form of the patient's own auto-suggestion. Much depends on the degree to which the patient's imagination can be stimulated, as Stephen Black realised from experimenters checking the effect of suggestion on blood flows. Neither hypnosis alone nor the direct suggestion 'you are hot' produced any significant effect, but 'you are hot because the house is on fire' did. In general, he found, 'The use of hypnosis as a research tool in both allergy and neurophysiology has shown the extreme delicacy of the informational mechanisms involved.'

The effects of hypnotherapy are usually short-lived, but this does not mean, as doctors sometimes try to maintain, that it is of little value. The effects of a drug, after all, wear off even more rapidly. The value of a session with a hypnotherapist is that it provides a convincing demonstration of the ability of the mind to override allergic reactions. This being recognised, allergists should have begun to explore ways by which the mind's potential can be more effectively exploited, with the help of autogenic training, meditation, yoga, or whatever method recommended itself: but few allergists have been interested in the psychosocial aspect. In any case, there are very few allergists as such. The great majority of patients diagnosed by their GP as having an allergy which he cannot handle are sent to somebody who specialises not in immunology, but in treating the particular symptoms they present: a rhinologist in cases of hay fever or asthma, a dermatologist in cases of skin rashes.

The absurdity of specialisation in this context is most obvious in connection with young children. It has long been a matter of common knowledge that 'infantile eczema' is frequently accompanied by asthma or hay fever. Yet an eminent London dermatologist admitted in 1977 that in thirty years of practice he had never heard of any conference to bring together members of his specialty and the rhinologists; none was held until 1979. To bring psychiatrists and psychologists into a gathering of this kind would present even greater difficulties, partly because of the continuing reluctance on the part of specialists to include emotional stress in their diagnostic repertoire; partly because of their mistrust of psychiatry. Yet if, as Harry Swartz insisted, psychological factors may produce allergic symptoms by creating an imbalance of the nervous system – 'many asthmatic children will respond to situations with asthmatic attacks of considerable severity rather than with temper tantrums', and examination in the course of the attack 'reveals all the typical findings of other attacks induced by foods or inhalants' – to leave the emotions out of consideration is absurd.

## Neuromimesis

At this point it is worth considering the question that has puzzled allergists: why should allergy appear to be so much more prevalent today than it was even a century ago? There are no statistics, admittedly, to confirm this impression, but if allergic reactions had been common in the nineteenth century, they would surely feature much more frequently in the correspondence, the reminiscences, and the fiction of the era.

One theory which has been put forward is that, other things being equal, the propensity to fall ill is inherently stable: if bacterial infections are brought under control, nature may restore the balance with another type of illness. It has even been suggested that this balance can apply to the site of infections. G. E. Breen, a lecturer in infectious diseases at University College Hospital, London, pointed out in 1967 that diphtheria, common before the Second World War, had been replaced by glandular fever as the commonest cause of membranous and persistent sore throat. This was a fact, Breen thought, which had not been sufficiently appreciated: 'Nature is said to abhor a vacuum, and the changing pattern of infectious disease certainly supports this view.'

Was there, then, a vacuum which allergy and auto-allergy arrived to fill? The textbooks and medical journals of a century ago reveal that there certainly was. One of the commonest, most intransigent and most widely discussed of disorders was labelled hysteria: not the convulsive type with which the term is colloquially associated, but a variety which, like allergy, was notorious for its ability to imitate everyday diseases so accurately that doctors had great difficulty in telling them apart.

Thomas Sydenham, with his unrivalled clinical acumen, had established this form of hysteria as a separate disease entity. It had already been realised that the symptoms of hysteria, in the traditional sense of the term, resembled those of epilepsy, apoplexy, and certain types of poisoning. Sydenham listed them: tremors, twitches, convulsions, pains in the head and back, nausea, a constricted throat (the 'globus hystericus'), coupled with immoderate senseless laughter and crying. But he added another version of hysteria, the symptoms of which were protean. No less remarkable than its frequency ('of all chronic diseases, unless I err, the commonest') was the variety of the forms in which it could appear: 'few of the maladies of miserable mortality are not imitated by it', he warned, and so accurate could the imitation be that, unless the physician was skilled and sagacious, he could easily be deceived into attributing the symptoms to the disease, 'and not to the effects of hysteria'.

One form of hysterical mimicry was particularly notorious: 'pseudo-

227

cyesis', or false pregnancy, in which all the traditional indicators appeared: morning sickness, suspension of menstrual periods, swelling of the belly and breasts. An English Queen, Mary, had been the victim of this strange trick, and William Harvey had described another such case in the treatise with which he supplemented his work on the circulation of the blood. The daughter of a close friend of his had experienced all the symptoms of pregnancy; after the fourteenth week she even 'felt the movements of the child within the uterus' and had prepared the cradle, 'before it became apparent that there was no foetus'.

That the symptoms of a great variety of diseases could be mimicked in this way had not been appreciated because, unlike Sydenham, most physicians learned their craft from ancient Galenic texts rather than at the bedside. Once recognised, however, hysteria of this kind came to be considered as an extremely common disorder, right down into Victorian times. It was one of the most intractable problems the doctor had to face, Sir James Paget – soon to become surgeon to Queen Victoria, and the unchallenged doyen of the profession – told his students: 'You hear of hysteric cough and hysteric aphonia, of hysteric dyspepsias and paralysis, of hysteric joints and spines.' And echoing Sydenham, he remarked that there was hardly any common disorder 'in which the mimicry of real disease is not sometimes so close as to make the diagnosis very difficult'.

Naturally confusion had often arisen because the same term, hysteria, was used to describe both 'hysterics' in its colloquial sense and hysterical mimicry. Coleridge, surprisingly, had urged that the imitative version should be given a separate identity; in his *Table Talk* he had suggested calling it 'mimosa', as it was 'capable of counterfeiting so many diseases, even death itself'. Paget favoured 'neuromimesis': although such cases were commonly described as hysteria, 'in many of them none of the distinctive symptoms of hysteria are ever observed, and from all of them it is desirable this name should be abolished'. So neuromimesis began to feature in diagnoses and in the textbooks.

## Charcot and Freud

But not for long. Neuromimesis was squeezed out, and soon all but forgotten, because of two developments, both, ironically, derived from theories which have since been shown to be fallacious.

The first was presented by Charcot. On the strength of his researches at the Salpêtrière in Paris he claimed to have discovered that hysteria was a neuropathic disorder, ordinarily following a regular course rather like a spun-out form of epilepsy, which could be demonstrated with the help of hypnosis. The hypnotic trance-state, Charcot argued, was simply induced hysteria. Hysteria was psycho-physical – by which he implied a kind of mind/body parallelism, replacing traditional dualism: every psychological change had its physico-chemical counterpart, and vice versa. In this respect, he argued, hysteria was no different from the other neuropathies – epilepsy, Parkinsonism, multiple sclerosis and the rest.

To Freud, who came to study under Charcot in 1885, this theory represented a massive advance in the understanding not just of hysteria, but also of its relationship to the whole family of nervous diseases. Hysteria, he recalled in his obituary of Charcot in 1893, had previously had an ill repute that extended not just to patients, but even to the doctors who treated them. 'Charcot's work restored dignity to the subject: gradually the sneering attitude which the hysteric could reckon on meeting when she told her story was given up.' She no longer risked being dubbed a malingerer, because Charcot had 'thrown the whole weight of his authority on the side of the reality and objectivity of hysterical phenomena'. As a result, 'the blind fear of being fooled by the poor patient, which had stood in the way of a serious study of the neurosis, was overcome'.

Freud was soon to be undeceived. It had already become apparent, even to him, that hysteria was not quite the simple neuropathy that Charcot thought he had proved it to be. His patients' hysterics had always demonstrated hysteria according to his specifications; but nowhere except at the Salpêtrière were the same symptoms found. Clearly Charcot's patients had merely demonstrated that their suggestibility was remarkably enhanced under hypnosis. Freud did his best to maintain that this did not upset the basic principle of psycho-physical parallelism. 'The relationship between the chain of physiological events in the nervous system and the mental processes is probably not one of cause and effect,' he argued. 'The former do not cease when the latter set in; they tend to continue, but, from a certain moment, a mental phenomenon corresponds to each part of the chain, or to several parts. The psychic is, therefore, a process parallel to the physiological, "a dependant concomitant".' He clung to this conviction for years; 'Anxiety, chemical factors, etc.,' he wrote to his friend Wilhelm Fliess in 1897, 'perhaps you may supply me with solid ground on which I shall be able to give up explaining things psychologically and start finding a firm basis in physiology.' But he added that, as he had nothing specific to work on, 'I must behave as if I were confronted by psychological factors only.' This decision was to prove crucial – his final split with conventional medical science, which terminated its brief flirtation with psycho-physical parallelism and reverted to a simpler materialist and organicist concept of disease. All diseases, it now came to be assumed, could soon be explained in terms of physics and chemistry. If symptoms were organic, neuromimesis could be ruled out. If they were functional or neuromimetic, they were not really diseases. Epilepsy, Parkinsonism, MS, meningitis and others qualified as neuropathies either because they had organic indicators or because it was assumed that an organic cause, on the lines of the meningococcus, would soon be found. Neuromimesis was excluded.

At the same time old-style hysteria, with its convulsions and dissociation, was also being re-categorised. Diagnostic craft had come to the rescue of the psychiatrists: Emil Kraepelin had introduced the idea that there were two separate and distinguishable forms of mental illness, dementia praecox (soon to be renamed schizophrenia) and manic depression. Theoretically hysteria might imitate either, or both, but because in practice the distinction could not be made, wherever convulsions and dissociation rendered their victims incapable of continuing to live in the community, psychiatrists tended to diagnose them as schizophrenia or as manic depression. Most of what remained of hysteria's former territory was eventually taken from it by Freud himself. A range of symptoms which had previously been regarded as either neuropathic or hysterical, from facial tics and slips of the tongue to serious and sometimes crippling obsessional actions, were the result, he claimed, of emotional conflicts aroused in early childhood, but repressed – battened down in the unconscious mind. When they tried to force their way up into consciousness, they were 'converted' by a form of censorship into the symptoms. Consequently they should be regarded as psychoneuroses – the term 'neurosis' representing his final attempt to cling to psycho-physiological parallelism.

Although behaviourists disagreed with Freud's interpretation, and orthodox psychiatrists shied away from his theories, shocked by his insistence on the sexual component of the repressions, it came to be generally accepted that such symptoms were neurotic rather than hysterical. This made little difference to patients; neurotic soon acquired the same derogatory connotation. But it meant that hysteria was left only with neuromimesis, which came to be thought of by the medical profession as little better than a confidence trick. When it was detected, doctors had little compunction in making the patient feel he was wasting their time, as there was nothing really the matter. As one of the leading authorities of the early years of the century, A. T. Schofield, put it, because disease 'has always a material basis, whether recognisable or not', the distinction between organic and functional or hysterical would soon become 'superfluous'.

## Neurasthenia

For a few years one rickety bridge between organic and functional remained: 'neurasthenia'. It owed its existence chiefly to the fact that some patients who should have been diagnosed as suffering from hysteria or neuromimesis were rich or influential enough for their doctors not to dare to offend them – Sir Edward Carson, for one, who, when Schofield's treatise appeared in 1908, was still in the running for the leadership of the Conservative Party. Carson periodically collapsed with what appear to have been hysterical breakdowns, but it was obviously unwise for his doctors to tell him so. For such patients neurasthenia – over-taxed nerves – was called into service, to do duty until the day when Schofield's prediction was fulfilled, and the appropriate organic explanation was found for every type of disorder.

Schofield himself pointed the way. 'Ninety per cent of neurotics are dyspeptic,' he claimed: 'we may well assert that a fertile cause of functional nerve disease are the toxins produced by indigestion.' Two years earlier, Bernard Shaw had satirised this idea in *The Doctors' Dilemma*, with the fashionable London surgeon Sir Cutler Walpole insisting that ninety-five per cent of the human race suffer from chronic blood poisoning because their 'nuciform sacs' are full of decaying matter. Shaw presumably had appendicitis in mind; the operation had become fashionable after it had been successfully performed on Edward VII. Appendicitis was at least occasionally traceable to toxic matter in the appendix; the belief that there were other foci of infection, almost an exact replica of Cutler Walpole's, was fantasy. Yet thousands of people with undiagnosed disorders were operated upon between the wars to have their focal sepsis dealt with by removing tracts of their gut, or their teeth, in the expectation that the symptoms would disappear. Or they could be told they had colitis, a similarly spurious diagnosis; or 'asthenia' (the 'neur' prefix was dropped, as too close to neurotic). As A. J. Cronin was to confess in his autobiography, the injections and tonics with which he treated asthenia, and the exorbitant fees he charged, made him successful because they gave bored society women a new interest in life.

Neurasthenia and focal sepsis eventually fell out of favour; but hysteria was not permitted to return. As Thomas Szasz recalled in *The Myth of Mental Illness*, even when confronted by its presence doctors were reluctant to admit as much in their diagnosis. A GP did not care to tell his patients that he considered their symptoms to be hysterical, partly because they would be angry, and might sue him if he turned out to be wrong; partly because he would look foolish, if he were wrong, in the eyes of his colleagues. He preferred to refer such patients to a specialist as undiagnosed; not to a psychiatrist, which would carry the hysteria (or neurosis) implication, but to a neurologist.

As a rule, only those patients whom doctors regarded as nuisances were diagnosed as hysterical and referred to a psychiatrist. Irritated, psychiatrists began to feel they were simply being used as a convenient refuse bin into which their physician colleagues could dump their diagnostic failures. 'The diagnosis of "hysteria" is a disguise for ignorance and a fertile source of clinical error,' Eliot Slater of the Maudsley Hospital, co-author of a standard psychiatric textbook and later described by William Sargant as 'England's greatest living psychiatrist', stated bluntly in 1964. 'It is in fact not only a delusion, but also a snare.'

Unluckily for Slater, hardly had he made this sweeping pronouncement when report after report began to appear of the outbreaks in schools and other institutions, culminating in the epidemic at the Royal Free Hospital, and leading *The Times*, in its editorial 'Vapour or Virus', to suggest the diagnosis of mass hysteria, even if 'in these days of scientific materialism it is verging on *lèse majesté*'. Sir Francis Walshe, who had also written a textbook of psychiatry and was a past president of the British Neurologists' Association, wrote in to express his pleasure at seeing the old term vapour coming into its own again; he had begun to wonder, he sardonically observed, whether the time might be coming when the health authorities at London Airport would be called upon to dismantle the central building 'in the search for the "virus" that induces "swarming", screaming and waving of arms and legs in adolescent girls whenever pop singers descend there', in which case modern medicine would 'have won its latest public triumph'. And in a polite but barbed article in the *British Medical Journal* a few weeks later he argued that, although the diagnosis of hysteria was neither easy nor popular, doctors ought not to shy away from it, in view of the historical evidence about such outbreaks, which could hardly all be diagnosed 'as organically determined or as conspiratorial mass-malingering'. They had been attributed to witchcraft or demoniacal possession, but 'armed – perhaps "hampered" would be the better word – with all the modern science of our time it is likely today that we should declare them to be due to some unknown and undiscoverable virus, and call the condition encephalitis'. This could very well happen, Walshe concluded, his tongue doubtless firmly in his cheek, as he must have known that encephalitis was at this time being put forward as the explanation of the Royal Free outbreak.

The neuro-epidemics have revived mass hysteria as a possible diagnosis; they have not rescued neuromimesis. Yet the indications are that the neuromimetic branch of hysteria has reappeared in the form of allergic and auto-allergic diseases.

The reason why this has not been appreciated is that allergy and auto-allergy are taken to be organic, whereas hysteria is regarded by definition as functional, the product of the patient's imagination. Again, this distinction is no longer tenable because research into biofeedback and placebo effect has made it impossible to think any longer in terms of the organic/functional division. That it should ever have come to be believed, let alone taught as orthodox medical dogma, that hysteria cannot produce organic symptoms is one of the mysteries of modern medicine. That intense mystical experience can create actual neuro-mimetic lesions has been observed on countless occasions in the form of the stigmata; and there have been a number of experiments in which the stigmata have been artificially induced in receptive individuals under hypnosis, as well as of demonstrations by people who are capable of the self-induction of a variety of symptoms (in *My Six Convicts* Donald Wilson described an encounter while he was a prison doctor with a convict who, among other strange feats, could reproduce at will the signs of the zodiac on his body). It requires no great leap of the imagination to recognise, in allergy and auto-allergy, neuromimesis sidling back into contention in a new guise.

If this hypothesis is correct, to continue to treat allergies as if they were the product of pathogens is a futile exercise. And it is hardly more sensible to track down the physiological process by which the symptoms are produced, in the hope of finding some way to interrupt it; in the light of history, neuromimesis is far too wily to be netted that way. Not just allergies, but the whole range of disorders which can be attributed to a breakdown in the body's auto-immune system need to be regarded and treated as self-induced – not, as hysteria in the colloquial sense so often is, from self-indulgence, but often from need. The symptoms are saying, in effect, 'enough is enough'. They act as fuse wires, 'blowing' because of a specific stressful event or an accumulation of loads, or through 'mood convection' providing the excuse of an epidemic of flu, or of a cold running through the office or the family. The symptoms are not, of course, desired consciously – or even semi-consciously, as in traditional hysteria. There need be no feeling of guilt attached to the diagnosis of an allergy, simply because it is self-induced. But it may be an indication that it is time to scrutinise life-style, to find whether habits – of eating, drinking, smoking, socialising, fantasising, or worrying – need to be changed.

233

# 9

# The Role of Illness

Neuromimesis can also fulfil another need. In *The Social System* Talcott Parsons pointed out that people who are ill are relieved from many responsibilities, so long as their illness is regarded as 'real'; this can represent a primary gain. They will also be looked after, helped to regain their health, with luck even be cosseted; such privileges can provide a secondary gain which the patient may come to enjoy. It is consequently easy for people to want to be ill, without being aware of it. Although they do not enjoy the actual symptoms, the discomfort and the suffering, unless they are masochists, the symptoms may be a small price to pay, particularly as, in general, the greater their severity the greater the gain, both primary and secondary. Hysteria and neuromimesis, not being regarded as 'real' illnesses, have offered no such benefit to patients. Yet it has only been in the last hundred years that they have been expelled, as it were, from the clinical club. Hysteria has a respectable ancestry, from earlier times; in tribal communities, in fact, it was revered, for reasons which suggest that it does not deserve its present-day disfavour.

## The Shaman Syndrome

Reports about shamans, witch doctors and medicine men, whether written by explorers, missionaries, colonial officials or anthropologists, display a striking consistency. The shaman's function was to provide information of the kind now described as psychic, and to obtain it he would enter into a trance – an altered state of consciousness. Sometimes it would be involuntary, sometimes self-induced, if necessary with the help of ritual and drugs. The type of trance varied according to the individual, but the kind most commonly described began with tremors and twitchings, culminating in convulsions, the shaman's eyeballs rolling, foam forming at his lips, strangled noises coming from the throat. This fit was believed to reveal that the shaman was being possessed by a spirit; at some point, if all went well, he would dissociate (as it would now be described) and begin to speak in a voice not his own, sometimes in a language not his own. In this state he was expected to have access to information of a kind the tribe required: where to find game or water: what was the matter with a sick child; how to ward off the unwelcome visitations of a sorcerer; how to propitiate the spirits. Eventually his possession would culminate in further convulsions, and he would sink into a coma.

To missionaries this behaviour came as no great surprise. They assumed that the devil was responsible, utilising 'possession' as a way to keep the wretched heathen under his sway. Colonial officials, when they arrived, were usually content to accept this interpretation, using it as an excuse to put down shamanism because the shaman's dominance so often appeared to offer a threat to their authority. By the time anthropologists began to study tribal ways, however, in the nineteenth century, the notion of diabolic possession had become unfashionable. Examining their evidence in the first volume of what, but for his death, would have been the greatest of the histories of medicine, Henry Sigerist noted their common assumption that shamans were suffering from a psychotic disorder. They differed about the precise diagnosis: 'most writers considered it hysteria'; some argued for epilepsy. One leading authority had insisted that the symptoms fitted best into the prevailing picture of schizophrenia – adding, however, the qualification 'in so far as they fit one of our pictures at all'. Shamanism was in fact much closer to Victorian spiritualism than to any form of mental illness – as Edward Tylor, later to become the first holder of a Chair in Anthropology at Oxford, was shrewd enough to realise.

In his *Primitive Culture* Tylor wondered whether 'the Red Indian medicine man, the Tatar necromancer, the Highland ghost-seer and the Boston medium' might share a faculty 'of the highest truth and import which, nevertheless, the great intellectual movement of the last two centuries has simply thrown aside as worthless'. Tylor could not bring himself to accept this; but at least he was open-minded enough to cast doubt on the conventional view that shamanism was a compound of insanity and fraud – the view which, thanks largely to Frazer and *The Golden Bough*, had become established. The essential point of shamanism was consequently missed until Professor Mircea Eliade picked up the threads again, that for a shaman his 'psychosis' was an asset – indispensable, indeed, to the tribe. Anybody who had fits, or other intimations of what were taken to be supernatural powers, would be encouraged, sometimes compelled, to make shamanism his vocation by training himself to release or induce them. And as a shaman he would also learn how to induce the syndrome in others with the help of artificial aids, rhythm and drugs, as a form of treatment.

In *The Mind Possessed*, William Sargant has described a number of healing ceremonies he has attended in different parts of the world, following the same pattern as those described by the explorers and missionaries who first reported tribal customs. In Kenya he watched while a witch doctor put patients into trance-states with the help of drumming; they began jerking and twitching as if in epileptic fits or orgasms. In some cases the 'spirits' possessing them began to speak through them, and eventually they collapsed into comas. The following day the witch doctor himself went into a trance, so that the spirits could prescribe for his patients. Their advice was much more impressive, Sargant jocularly observed, 'than the modern psychoanalyst giving his interpretations to the patient on the couch'; he had often been impressed both by the good sense of the shamans and the results of their treatments.

After watching similar ceremonies in Haiti, too, Sargant noted how quickly patients recovered. 'In our culture a person exhibiting repeated hysterical dissociative and trance phenomena would be considered nervously ill, but the same phenomena occurring in normal people in many African cultures leave very little nervous upset behind them; on the contrary they help relieve accumulated tension.'

The shaman syndrome, in other words, was regarded as a release mechanism, liberating certain faculties, natural healing forces among them. And there is a plausible explanation why such a shake-up was needed. Primitive man was evolving with startling rapidity from reliance on animal instinct to the use of reason and memory as guides. But in losing instinct, man lost a great deal. 'There is always a moment when a female pushes away an overgrown youngster coming to suckle,' as Doris Lessing has put it, 'or a bird tips a fledgling out of the nest.' With reasoning power in its fledgling stage, there remained much which instinct or intuition could have done better. Hence the need in tribal communities to allow instinct or intuition to come through. This process must have been erratic, but on balance it could have worked better than any therapy which nascent intellect could supply.

The process, though, had evolved. Some shamans, anthropologists found, did not display the familiar symptoms of the syndrome. The trance which they entered would often resemble sleep; when they came out of it, they would recount what they had seen or heard, much as today we recount dreams. It was as if they realised that for the purposes of their chief function, divination, the convulsions and the spirit possession were superfluous. Theirs was a more sophisticated technique of divination;

236

more efficient, too, because what poured out of a shaman who was possessed might be hard to interpret, might, in fact, be gibberish, or in some unknown tongue – just as sometimes occurred with mediums in Victorian seances. And eventually possession came to be regarded as an affliction, or worse: where induced for purposes of divination, it was taken to be witchcraft, as the story of Saul and the witch of En-dor reveals.

A combination of forces began to operate to bring the shaman syndrome into discredit. As consciousness became more dominant, dissociation must have become progressively harder to control, tending increasingly to resemble psychosis, so that the information emerging in the trance would often be irrelevant or unintelligible. With the rise of religions, too, illness came to be regarded as an indication of divine displeasure; to judge from the Old Testament, the Israelite shamans – the prophets – rarely tried to exercise healing powers. And when the new rationalism emerged in Greece the assumption that the syndrome was related to communication with the spirits or the gods, which had led to its being described as the divine, or sacred, disease, was called in question, because assumptions about the gods were being called in question. As one of the Hippocratic writers put it, 'I do not believe that the "Sacred Disease" is any more divine or sacred than any other disease.' On the contrary, 'it has specific characteristics and a definite cause'.

It was later to be assumed that the writer was referring to epilepsy. In fact he made it clear that he was describing the shaman syndrome: 'It is my opinion that those who first called this disease "sacred" were the sort of people we now call shamans' – the equivalent, he felt, of charlatans. And this was the view which was eventually to prevail: that convulsions, dissociation, and loss of control in general were symptoms of a disease. As it seemed chiefly to attack women, it was attributed to a uterine disorder, but – as in its epidemic form men were often caught up in it, too – it came to be thought of as a form of mania.

Yet in its earlier shamanic form, hysteria had that respectable past as a form of therapy, and this was to re-emerge, for a time, through the inspiration of the outbreak of mass hysteria at Pentecost, when Jesus's disciples 'were all filled with the holy spirit, and began to speak with other tongues as the spirit gave them utterance', at the same time losing control of their limbs, so that onlookers thought they must be drunk. For a time the syndrome again became, at least for Christians, not a disease but an aid to revelation. And not only to revelation – to health. Jesus's teaching had overturned the traditional Old-Testament-style attitude to disease: that as it was the Lord's will, there was no point in trying to find cures. On the contrary, Jesus insisted, every man had his cure within him: faith. By stimulating faith in others, too, he could heal them. For St Paul, in particular, the shaman syndrome was the essence of Christianity because it enabled the spirit – the holy spirit – to take possession, bringing to some the gift of healing, 'to another, the working of miracles; to another, discerning of spirits; to another, diverse kinds of tongues; to another, the interpretation of tongues'.

Without being aware of it, the early Christians had revived shamanism in very much the same form as it was used in tribal communities, for divination and for healing. The source, in their case, was assumed to be God, operating through the holy spirit, but the principle was the same. The advent of the Christian Church, however, with its authoritarian hierarchy, its dogmas and its ritual, made dissociation and possession again suspect. Popes and prelates conveniently forgot that Jesus had taken unlettered men as his disciples; when God wished to communicate with Christians, the new assumption was, He would naturally do it through educated and trained priests. Should individuals or groups become possessed, the chances were that it was the devil at work. Anybody who persisted in relying on the information obtained from possession risked suffering the fate of Joan of Arc, as heretic or witch or both.

Following the Renaissance, the pattern established by the Hippocratic writings was repeated. Fits, dissociation and possession, courageous individuals began to argue, should not be regarded as either divine or diabolic, but simply as a disease. The afflicted should be given sanctuary. Only where churches retained their grip, as in the Loudun outbreak and at Salem, were dissociation and convulsions still taken as evidence of diabolic possession.

Yet from time to time there were further reminders that the shaman syndrome could be therapeutic. The most striking examples were those reported in the strange and protracted epidemic at St Médard in the 1830s, following the burial there of the Jansenist François de Paris. Details of the symptoms of the mourners – the *convulsionnaires*, as they came to be called – were recorded by numerous eye-witnesses, and even allowing for exaggeration they leave no doubt that some of the *convulsionnaires* while in their trance states enjoyed a considerable measure of immunity not just from pain, but also from injury. '*La salamandre*,' as Marie Souet was soon called, could be suspended just above a blazing fire without being blistered; Gabrielle Moler could be beaten with mallets and jabbed with spikes without coming to any harm. To David Hume, so convincing were the reports, 'proved on the spot before judges of unquestioned integrity, attested by witnesses of credit and distinction in a learned age', that he felt compelled to cite them as the best available evidence for the reality of miracles, before going on to say that they must be rejected because of 'the absolute impossibility of the miraculous nature of the events'.


## Mesmerism and Homeopathy

In spite of the growing influence of sceptics on the Hume model, there seemed for a while to be a chance that the induced shaman syndrome would be revived as a form of therapy. It had been adapted for this purpose by the Catholic Church in the ritual of the exorcist, and at the time when Hume's treatise on miracles appeared the Swiss priest Johann Gassner was exploiting exorcism for healing, treating groups and eventually large crowds on the old convulsions/dissociation/coma model. Mesmer also used it with his patients, and when in 1784 his method was investigated by the Academy of the Sciences in Paris its eminent members – Benjamin Franklin, Lavoisier and Guillotin among them – though they were sceptical of Mesmer's theory that the sick were being cured by 'animal magnetism', had to admit that, however much they disapproved of inducing convulsions and dissociation in the way they had witnessed, the method seemed to work; many patients were cured of various disorders.

What if Mesmer had offered his shaman technique simply as a therapeutic device, without attaching it to an unacceptable theory? Conceivably physicians might reluctantly have accepted it. But infected as they by this time were with rationalism and materialism, his notion of animal magnetism was rejected, and his therapy along with it. The same fate was in store for homeopathy, introduced towards the end of the eighteenth century by Samuel Hahnemann. South American tribesmen, Hahnemann knew, used 'Jesuit's Bark' – quinine – to treat malaria. Yet when taken by a healthy person, quinine tends to produce symptoms like those of malaria. What we think of as the symptoms of an illness, Hahnemann reasoned, may in fact be the symptoms of the reaction to the illness. Running a temperature may be the sign that the body's defences have gone into action. If so, they should be helped with a drug which supports them, homeopathically – 'likes cure likes' – rather than an allopathic remedy, a drug designed to bring the temperature down.

For a century and a half the homeopathic theory has been rejected by orthodoxy. Yet it ties in well with Selye's stress theory, in which the first stage of the General Adaptation Syndrome, the syndrome of just being sick, is an alarm reaction. And it also fits A. T. W. Simeons' thesis in

*Man's Presumptuous Brain.* Neuropathic symptoms, Simeons showed, are of a kind common to all creatures who seek safety in flight or immobility. They are designed to ensure that, in the presence of danger, the instinct of hunger is over-ruled. 'The mouth drops open so that the teeth can no longer chew. The flow of saliva is shut off, making the mouth go dry. The oesophagus contracts, making swallowing impossible and producing the feeling known as "choking with fright".' In extreme danger, timid animals evacuate their bowels as a preparation for flight; man suffers from diarrhea. These are natural processes, but, Simeons warned, 'When such normal reactions occur in response to a sub-conscious fear, they are always interpreted by the cortex as an intestinal disorder, because no other explanation is forthcoming.' The syndrome of just being sick, then, along with the minor neuropathies, ought to be considered as an early-warning system, indicating that something is amiss and that the defences, alerted, are going into action. Allergy is part of the same process, but the defenders have been called out un-necessarily, or are over-reacting, as in migraine.

If this is accepted, what of the second stage of the General Adaptation Syndrome: the stage of resistance? Ought not this, too, to be re-assessed, in case what we think of as the symptoms of illness are in fact indications of a resistance campaign?

*The Stage of Resistance*

To a limited extent, orthodoxy has conceded this point. A high fever, it is acknowledged, can bring therapeutic benefits by killing off a range of pathogens, such as the spirochete of syphilis. In his book on malaria Elliot Fitzgibbon went so far as to surmise that if, as the evidence suggests, malaria is related to the subsoil water level, the parasite which the mosquito spreads, so far from being the cause of the disease, may be 'the beneficial agent of nature for dealing with the malarial poison in the human system' by stirring up the body to resist, with the help of fever, the destructive effects of the miasma. He might have added another piece of evidence: people who have caught malaria in the tropics are notoriously susceptible to 'bouts' of it when they return home. It is as if they are periodically flushing out their systems with the help of fever, having found this to be an effective prophylactic.

But there is more to the second, resistance stage. In it, neuropathy displays some symptoms which could be of immense value if we could understand the mechanism involved and find ways to exploit it: in particular, the extraordinary and as yet unexplained capacity to resist pain, and even injury.

Early in the seventeenth century the English physician Edward Jorden, criticising the way in which witches had been detected by being pricked with needles (certain parts of a witch's body were supposed to be immune from pain) pointed out that the fact that some people 'do not feel being pricked with a pin, or burnt with fire, etc.' was not unusual: 'in the palsy, the falling sickness (epilepsy), apoplexies and divers other diseases it is daily observed.' The *convulsionnaires* of St Médard were another example. There have been countless demonstrations of the ability of people who are in a deep hypnotic trance to feel no pain, and to show no sign of injury after, say, holding a finger in a candle flame. And recently the American William Neal has been giving demonstrations of auto-hypnosis, some of which have been filmed, showing a remarkable imperviousness to assault and battery.

Dissociation can also be an asset. We have too lightly forgotten that Socrates used to go into trance states, sometimes for hours at a time, to consult his 'daemon': the voice, as he thought, of the divine faculty. So entirely did he rely upon it, he told judges at his trial, that he did not propose to defend himself, because it had not instructed him to do so before he left home, or on his way to the court. In a paper on the relationship of religion to psychosis read to the International Congress of Social Psychiatry in 1964, Ronald Laing reiterated his argument that madness need not be all breakdown: it is also breakthrough, 'potentially liberation and renewal as well as enslavement and existential death'. We have lost touch, Laing felt, with our real selves, but 'the mind of which we are unaware is aware of us. It is we who are out of our minds.' If convulsions and dissociation of the kind which are labelled hysteria or encephalitis or epilepsy are a form which the second, resistance stage of the General Adaptation Syndrome may take, and are in essence the shaman syndrome resuscitated – the implications for orthodox medicine are disturbing. The standard assumption has been that fits damage the brain, even that the amount of damage done is determined by the duration of the fits. But there is no proof that the convulsions themselves do the damage. They may reflect an attempt to remove some threat, physical or psychological or both. If so, to try to treat them or to prevent them by allopathic means may be the very reverse of what patients need.

Some evidence suggests that this is the case. Epilepsy does not in itself greatly reduce life-expectancy; the chief danger is from injury sustained during fits, and it is primarily for this reason that anti-convulsant drugs are prescribed. They work symptomatically, but according to the *Lancet*, a study of the records of over 2,000 epileptic patients over the forty-year period between 1931 and 1971 has shown that the mortality rate of epileptics undergoing anti-convulsant treatment was 'greatly in excess of that of the general population', and that deaths from cancer were disturbingly common.

This at least should serve as a warning in the treatment of other neuropathies. Occasionally in migraine, more commonly in epilepsy, the build-up of tension to the explosive release appears to galvanise the imagination as well as the body, as Dostoevsky described in *The Idiot* – which, as his correspondence makes clear, he wrote from his own experience.

As a child, Prince Myshkin had been sent abroad for reasons of health 'because of some strange nervous disease, something in the nature of epilepsy or St Vitus' dance, some kind of convulsive spasms and twitchings'. But he had not been cured, and on his return to Russia still periodically suffered from them. The onset of the fits themselves was an ecstatic occasion: 'all his agitation, all his doubts and worries, seemed composed in a twinkling, culminating in a great calm, full of serene and harmonious joy and hope, full of understanding and the knowledge of the final cause.' And although the last moment before the fit seemed unendurable, in retrospect the Prince would tell himself that it did not matter whether the epilepsy was classified as a disease if the result, recollected in a state of health, 'turns out to be harmony and beauty brought to their highest point of perfection, and gives a feeling, undivined and undreamt of till then; of completeness, proportion, reconciliation, and an ecstatic and prayerful fusion in the highest synthesis of life'.

Other commentators have noted this link between fits and ecstasy. In his *Dissertation sur l'influence de l'éducation, des habitudes et des passions, dans les maladies nerveuses*, published in 1908, E. Calabre recalled the accounts of the way in which the Athenians were sent into raptures by Euripedes, 'and everybody knows how Corneille, Racine, Crébillon and Voltaire, stirring the soul of their audiences by their sublime works, have been able to produce fainting, spasms and even convulsions.' Fainting, spasms and convulsions are also a commonplace at revivalist and fundamentalist and pentecostal gatherings; the Quakers and the Shakers took their name from what happened at their services, when they were possessed by what they took to be the holy spirit.

That convulsions should be capable of serving a therapeutic purpose consequently becomes a less startling proposition, and recently a fascinating piece of evidence supporting their potential value has been provided by Norman Cousins, editor of the *Saturday Review*, describing how he cured himself with the help of convulsions induced by laughter.

The link between convulsions and laughter began to intrigue scientists in the nineteenth century. Darwin suggested that the squirming of a baby which is tickled is a defence mechanism designed to protect tender parts of the body from assault, but why, then, should tickling be associated with the pleasurable sensation of laughter? Herbert Spencer could think of no reason: 'The muscular actions constituting laughter are distinguished from most others by this, that they are purposeless.' In *The Act of Creation*, however, Koestler has advanced the hypothesis that children will laugh only if they perceive the tickling *as a mock attack*, a caress in a mildly aggressive disguise', even if it has 'no apparent biological utility'. It may, though, have acquired biological utility by providing a substitute for therapeutic convulsions. When we find something or somebody 'hysterically funny' and 'fall about laughing', or 'roll in the aisles', it can be an intensely exhilarating experience: a form of catharsis.

Norman Cousins explored laughter's biological utility when he fell ill following a visit to Russia in 1964. An initial feeling of malaise gradually worsened until he could hardly move his neck, arms, and legs. When his blood sedimentation rate reached 80 mm per hour he was taken to hospital, but it continued to rise until it was dangerously close to the point at which it becomes fatal: his jaws became almost locked, and his doctor, who was a close friend, felt compelled to admit to him that his chances of recovery were negligible.

Ten years before this, Cousins had read Selye's *The Stress of Life*. His last evening in Moscow, he remembered, had been an exercise in frustration; could it be that the stress had been responsible – perhaps along with something toxic he had eaten, or breathed in – for the collapse of his endocrine system? 'If negative emotions produce negative chemical changes in the body,' he asked himself, 'wouldn't the positive emotions produce positive chemical changes?' The positive emotions, for Cousins, were 'love, hope, faith, laughter, confidence and the will to live'. Of these, laughter was the only one which he could hope to generate artificially. He managed to get hold of a projector and some of the 'Candid Camera' TV programmes, which he had found hilarious. 'It worked. I made the joyous discovery that ten minutes of genuine belly laughter had an anesthetic effect and would give me at least two hours of pain-free sleep.' And with the help of further treatment along the same lines, with books as well as films, Cousins recovered.

It is only too easy to argue that his recovery may really have been due either to the abandonment of the drug treatment he had been receiving, the effects and side-effects of which had certainly contributed to his symptoms, or to coincidence. But Cousins had been sufficiently curious about his own theory to ensure that his blood sedimentation rate was taken before and after each laugh-in. 'Each time there was a drop of at least five points,' and although that was not substantial 'it held, and was cumulative'. And incongruous though the notion may seem that convulsions, whether induced by laughter, by grief, or by the reaction to a pathogen, are basically protective, they are understandable biologically as a device to 'shake off' threatened illness.

Why, then, have psychiatrists not thought along these lines? The answer is that they have, but they have made one crucial mistake. For the past half-century they have been experimenting with induced fits as a form of treatment. ECT is basically an induced epileptic convulsion. Hypnotherapy, drug abreaction (the use of 'truth drugs') and psychoanalysis are all ways of achieving dissociation in order to release repressed emotional tension. And continuous narcosis treatment represents an attempt to induce the coma stage. Little effort, however, has been made to involve the patients. The treatment is prescribed for them, but the essential element, voluntary or involuntary loss of control, is missing. The fits are artificial. They resemble the shaman syndrome, but they are not the real thing.

Psychiatrists admittedly have some excuse for keeping fits artificial. So long as involuntary convulsions and dissociation are equated in the public mind with madness, it is not easy to prescribe them, and both can be dangerous, if uncontrolled. Before muscle-relaxants were introduced cases of broken backs during ECT were not uncommon. Ronald Laing had admitted, too, that his technique of allowing a schizophrenic to plumb the depth of his psychosis, as it were, rather than try to bring it to the surface, proved far from foolproof: 'Alas, not everyone comes back to us again.' But this, he argues, is the result of our lack of a language in which to communicate with the real self, on its wanderings. Psychiatrists could at least be trying to learn to understand it better.

If convulsions and dissociation are the second stage of the General Adaptation Syndrome, other neuropathies represent the third stage: exhaustion – 'A kind of premature aging due to wear and tear', as Selye regarded it, 'a sort of second childhood which, in some ways, resembles the first.' Into this category fall Parkinsonism and MS. Certain observations about MS appear to bear this out – notably that patients who suffer acute attacks are known to have a much better prognosis than those whose symptoms emerge slowly and insidiously. 'Acute' in this context means that the patient is in the second stage, that his resistance movement is still functioning, and this factor improves his prospects of recovery. That older patients have a poorer prognosis, in institutional neuropathic outbreaks – as McEvedy found in schools, and as observed at the Royal Free – also fits the hypothesis. It is not their age which counts, so much as their level of responsibility – whether as six-formers or registrars and consultants in hospitals – and they may not care to ride with the symptoms; they are more likely to try to disguise them, as the medical students did at the Royal Free, for fear of being laughed at.

## Hysteria reassessed

Hysterical symptoms can help people to evade their responsibilities or indulge themselves at others' expense; this has been the main reason why they have picked up a bad reputation. Fantasists are hysterics: it is often impossible even for those who know them best to decide how far they are aware of their deception, and how far they are deceiving themselves: Dickens's Pecksniff is the prototype of the species. Tantrums – neuromimetic hysteria mimicking the neuropathic variety – come most easily to humour children who have found that making a scene wins a sweet, rather than a slap.

At the other end of the spectrum, however, are men and women of ability and integrity for whom hysteria provides a let-out only when they are taxed beyond endurance. That hysteria is not a sure sign of weak-mindedness and self-indulgence was first emphasised by Sydenham. Except for people who suffered from actual hallucinations, he claimed, hysterics were often persons of 'prudent judgment, who in the profundity of their meditations and the wisdom of their speech far surpass those whose minds have never been excited by such stimuli'. Two centuries later Sir James Paget echoed Sydenham's verdict: 'Nothing can be more mischievous,' he told his students, 'than a belief that mimicry of organic disease is to be found only or chiefly in silly, selfish girls.' He went further: it would be safer for them to expect to diagnose hysteria 'among the very good, the very wise, and the most accomplished'.

Breuer, who introduced Freud to the mysteries of hysteria and collaborated with him in his early research in this field, was of the same opinion. His patient 'Anna O', whose case history laid the foundations of psychoanalysis, was a walking compendium of hysterical symptoms, suffering from paralysis, muscle spasms, anorexia, sensory disturbances and a nervous cough, but for all her eccentricities, he insisted, she had a lively intelligence and a most attractive personality. Hysterics, in his experience, included 'people of the clearest intellect, strongest will, greatest character and highest critical power'.

If this is accepted, it helps to explain why women should have been more susceptible to hysteria than men. It is not because they were weaker-minded (though this might have accounted for epidemics where the element of self-indulgence was strong) but often because they knew very well that they were not.

Burton glimpsed this in his *Anatomy of Melancholy*, observing that hysteria was to be found in 'noble virgins, nice gentlewomen', rather than among women who had to work for their living, and this, he surmised, might relate to their socially-enforced idleness, as it was those of strong temperament who 'were violently carried away by this torrent of inward humours'. In 1853 a young country doctor, Robert Brudenell Carter – later to become celebrated as an ophthalmologist – took a similar line in his book on hysteria; it was only reasonable, he felt, 'to expect that an emotion which is strongly felt by great numbers of people, but whose natural manifestations are constantly repressed in compliance with the usages of society, will be the one whose morbid effects are most frequently witnessed'. And a few years later John Stuart Mill remarked, in *The Subjection of Women*, that they had 'greater nervous susceptibility', which could be more usefully employed; already, given some opportunities they had not had a half a century before, they were no longer displaying some formerly familiar morbid characteristics, 'as we see by the almost total disappearance of "hysterics" and fainting fits, since they have gone out of fashion'.

The good sense of these unorthodox views of hysteria was to be strikingly confirmed during the First World War. When the early fluid campaigning came to congeal into trench warfare, cases began to be reported with increasing frequency of soldiers suddenly collapsing, bereft of any power to move, or speak, and sometimes, more disturbingly, leaving their posts without permission and walking back through the lines, as if deserting. They would be picked up hours or sometimes days later, suffering from total amnesia about their past, though in other respects rational. Inevitably the initial suspicion fell upon sheer pretence. But it was soon realised that these were not the familiar battalion shirkers, who knew only too well the penalty for desertion. More often they were sensitive men who had driven themselves beyond the call of duty, until 'something snapped'. Naturally their commanding officers were anxious that they should not be punished, let alone shot for cowardice.

By this time the diagnosis of hysteria had become unfashionable, but, on the evidence, it was impossible to avoid the conclusion that these were cases of a disorder which, though rare, was sufficiently well known to have acquired an identification tag: hysterical fugue – 'fugue' sharing its derivation with 'fugitive', the assumption being that the sufferers were fleeing from reality. In its commonest form in civil life, they would be found wandering, or would present themselves at a hospital or a police station, having no idea who they were, or where they had come from – in their right minds, apparently, but with a total loss of memory. To have diagnosed hysteria in the case of soldiers, however, would have entailed a spell in a lunatic asylum, perhaps even a criminal lunatic asylum. The neurologists came up with the solution: 'shell shock'. The nervous system, it was claimed, could be damaged by blast. The disorder was consequently organic, and its victims would be referred to a hospital for nervous diseases.

## Playing Possum

The more fortunate among those who were diagnosed as shell-shocked found themselves being treated at the Craiglockhart Hospital near Edinburgh, in the charge of William Halse Rivers – 'that great and good man' as Siegfried Sassoon was to describe him, recalling his own treatment there in *Sherston's Progress* and *Siegfried's Journey*. Rivers was not merely a sympathetic psychiatrist who understood shell-shock; from his anthropological training he knew about the shaman syndrome. He had also (unusual at that time) read Freud's work on conversion hysteria without either becoming a disciple, as a handful of British psychiatrists had done, or rejecting him as a peddler of filth and an enemy alien, as most were doing. In the *Lancet* in 1917 Rivers praised Freud and his followers for having found a way by which 'hidden factors in the causation of disease may be brought to light', and in his *Instinct and the Unconscious* in 1920 he developed his theory that hysteria has a therapeutic function. Hysteria, he argued, is the way 'in which the sufferer regains happiness and comfort, if not health, by the occurrence of symptoms which enable him to escape from the conflict in place of facing it'.

There are two impulses involved, Rivers explained; one arising out of a desire to gratify natural tendencies, such as the sexual appetite, which are in conflict with society's mores; the other protective in intent, providing a warning of danger and, in some cases, assuming control in order to avert danger. This type of hysteria, Rivers believed, could be traced back in evolution to the process by which plants, insects and animals adopt a disguise as a means of support or self-preservation. Out of this, a further evolutionary development had produced what had come to be known as 'playing possum'. The opossum, when cornered, does not simply sham dead; to all intents, so far as predators are concerned, it *is* dead, as it does not react to blows or bites. Simple immobility, Rivers

247

reasoned, might become insufficient; 'If an animal capable of feeling pain or fear, in however crude a form, were to have these experiences while reacting to danger by means of immobility, the success of the reaction would certainly be impaired.' Complete *suppression* of fear and pain was needed, and this had been achieved by the opossum.

Playing possum, though it might deceive other animals, did not deceive man; hunters learned not to be taken in by the trick. In much the same way, doctors had learned not to be taken in by the human equivalent, hysterical paralysis or anesthesia. But before they had unmasked neuromimesis it had achieved one last fear. Hysterical fugue, Rivers realised, was a refinement of playing possum. For the strong-willed, strong-minded soldier in the trenches, determined to do his duty, simple physical paralysis was not enough; he would have been appalled at the notion that, although his limbs were in perfect working order, he had lost the power to make them obey his commands. So memory had to be expunged, too, removing all feeling of guilt for desertion.

Rivers, then, had restored hysteria's biological role as a protective device. But he had also shown that it could have destructive consequences when it misfired, as it did for an opossum pursued by a human hunter, or for a soldier who, unable to convince his superiors that he had not been guilty of desertion, was court-martialled and shot. This was only one of the destructive versions encountered during the war. Even more lethal was 'freezing on the joystick'.

When inexperienced pilots went into a 'tail spin' their reflex action was to put on the rudder against the direction of the spin, and pull back on the control column to lift the nose of the aircraft. But the aerodynamics of a spin were against them; the aircraft did not have sufficient flying speed for them either to lift the nose or to exercise directional control. The correct course, trainees were taught and shown, was to push the nose *down*, until sufficient flying speed had been attained for rudder control to become effective. All too often, though, if a spin occurred, the pilot 'froze', clutching the control column to his chest, unable to move, the possum-effect leading to his and the aircraft's destruction, unless, as in Hollywood films, somebody in the cockpit behind could knock him out with a handy spanner, and take over.

Panic is a hysterical reaction; it can be lethal when it deprives somebody of the power to move. It is the only credible explanation for the Moorgate tube disaster in London where the driver, instead of slowing down on entering the station, accelerated into the buffers at the far end. Equally it can be lethal when it deprives people of the power *not* to move – to enable them to remain calm in a fire, for example, rather than join in the stampede to the exits. That hysteria can produce irrelevant or dangerous reactions, though, is a reason not for continuing to refuse to take it seriously but for seeking a better understanding of its mechanism, in the hope of finding ways to control and exploit it. But two ingrained misconceptions make this difficult: that because neuromimetic symptoms are produced in some mysterious way by the imagination, they are not organic, and therefore not real illness, and that because they are not real, they deserve neither attention nor sympathy.

The assumption that neuromimetic symptoms are not organic arose at a time when the means to detect organic changes were primitive. To this day, they are ordinarily diagnosed as hysteria by the 'reprehensible practice', as Professor Trethowan has called it, 'of diagnosis by exclusion, rather than on positive grounds'. Medical scientists have not yet even looked for the positive grounds. When they do, it will doubtless be recognised that chemical processes exist in relation to neuromimesis, just as they do in relation to placebo effect. It is now firmly established, as Totman has pointed out in his *Social Causes of Illness*, that psychological states 'through their impact on the higher centres of the brain and the limbic-hypothalamic-pituitary-adrenal pathway', can 'tip some of the sensitive balances which govern the body's response to a vast number of diseases in which the immune system is involved', including not only allergies, but also infections, degenerative disorders such as arthritis, and cancer. To continue to think of psychological/functional illness as wholly distinct from organic illness is the clinical equivalent of flat-earthism.

Even more misguided is the continuing assumption that, if symptoms are hysterical or neurotic (the terms are still often interchangeable, when used pejoratively), what the patients need is a smart kick in the pants. 'As a result of the widespread impression that they are "neurotic",' Melvin Ramsay complained in his paper at the 1978 symposium on the Royal Free and other similar outbreaks, some of the victims had 'received scant sympathy or understanding from their doctors'. But the attitude of many of those who complained about the lack of understanding was just as misguided. They gave the clear impression that if the outbreak *had* been of hysteria, sympathy for the victims would have been misplaced.

That this attitude is not merely unfair for patients, but also dangerous for doctors, has recently been pointed out by Joyce Galbraith, a consultant psychiatrist in Birmingham. She had diagnosed a veterinary surgeon as suffering from depression, and suggested a break from his work. Impossible, he replied; it would be interpreted as a breakdown. How could he get over the shame? What if the surgery staff should hear! 'So what happens to sick doctors – especially those who are sick and sad in spirit?' Galbraith asked. 'From the terrifying statistics, doctors find it easier to take to drugs when depressed rather than admit their pain and have treatment.'

If this is representative of doctors' attitude to depression, it is even more true of their attitude to hysteria. As a result, they are loath to take advantage of research opportunities such as the one afforded by the Royal Free outbreak to try to find out how it works, not just in order to be able to treat it, but also to learn how it can bring freedom from pain and even from injury; to learn, in fact, how to exploit more effectively the still largely untapped therapeutic resources of the human imagination.

# 10

# The Role of the Medical Profession

If a synthesis is attempted of the criticisms of modern medical theory and practice – difficult because of their diversity – the general impression left is that the medical profession's chosen path, though providing some resounding triumphs, has ultimately proved to be a cul de sac. A great deal of what the profession does is valuable and essential, from the prescribing of antibiotics for infections which might otherwise prove fatal, to the forms of surgery so vividly described by Richard Selzer in *Mortal Lessons*. But the net value of orthodox medical treatment is far less than it was twenty-five years ago, and is declining.

Most of the commoner diseases which plague our civilisation – some affecting bone and muscle – rheumatism, arthritis, backache; some, respiration – asthma, bronchitis, emphysema; some, digestion – ulcerative colitis, gastritis, hepatitis – have resisted attempts to find a cure. In a few cases it has been possible to offer palliation with the help of drugs which tide the patient over, say, an attack of asthma. In others, where the body's homeostat has ceased to function properly, medical science has provided replacements – insulin for diabetics; artificial hip-joints; transplanted hearts or kidneys. For the rest, in spite of the proliferation of drugs designed to treat the commoner disorders, the record has been one of little progress. Drugs for backache and for headache come and go: the standby is still aspirin.

Such advances as there have been have fallen within a narrow range, Lewis Thomas has observed in his study of the impact of science and technology on medicine; since infectious disease was brought under better control, they have been for relatively uncommon illnesses. Looking back over forty years as a GP, on his retirement John W. Todd recalls that, although in the 1930s a great deal of the treatment which patients were given was useless, and some was absurd, he cannot see any striking improvement: 'Today, in spite of the therapeutic revolution, only a few patients can be much helped.' Surveying the evidence from the epidemiological standpoint, C. J. Roberts concludes that, whether judged by the mortality rate from common diseases or by the prevalence

251

of serious illness, 'the impact of technology on medicine has not been reflected in any substantial improvement in society's health'; impressive as many recent developments have seemed, 'there is a growing doubt about their ability to improve the natural history of many of the diseases to which they are applied.'

## The Mechanist Heresy

What, then, has gone wrong?

The turning-point came with the outcome of the long struggle for the possession of medicine's soul (and its pocket-book) between the vitalists, who believed that disease is the result of some disorder of the psyche, and the mechanists, who argued that it is the result of physico-chemical disorders. In the seventeenth century Borelli advanced the theory that disease would eventually prove to be accountable for on straightforward mechanical principles; if something goes wrong with the body, he claimed, it is for the same kind of reason that something goes wrong with a machine – grit in the works, insufficient lubrication, wear and tear. And during the eighteenth century, this view took over. The mechanists began to dominate the medical profession, vitalism falling into disrepute.

Inevitably, mechanist thought encouraged the development of nosography – the identification of diseases as entities, fitting into the pattern of disease as a whole; and of nosology – the application of diagnostic techniques to ascertain from which particular disease entity each patient is suffering. It also encouraged reliance on allopathic methods, treatments designed to counter the disease symptoms. And it led inexorably to concentration on the physical, organic diseases. Foucault has shown how this trend developed in eighteenth-century France, until in 1818 P. Rayer could enthuse about the 'entirely new period for medicine' that had opened up: 'The union of medicine and surgery and the organisation of the clinical schools have brought about an astonishing revolution that is characterised by progess in pathological anatomy.' In Britain the development took a little longer, with physicians for a time mocking such continental innovations as the stethoscope, but by the 1830s doctors were already concentrating upon those symptoms which, as Benjamin Brodie put it, displayed 'morbid growth or morbid change of structure, such as we find to exist in what are usually termed organic diseases'.

The essential truth of the mechanist theory appeared to be finally confirmed by Claude Bernard in the books and papers he published in mid-century. A problem before this had been to understand why, if man is a machine, he so often shows a remarkable capacity for running without the need for repairs. The answer, Bernard demonstrated, is homeostasis: man has a built-in mechanism designed to counter disease agents. Bernard did not deceive himself that this determinism, as he thought of it, was a complete answer. 'Admitting that vital processes rest upon physico-chemical activities, which is the truth, the essence of the problem is not thereby cleared up,' he warned. It could not have been simply chance which constructed each individual according to some pre-existing blueprint, producing the regulated activity 'which must never be neglected, because it is in truth the most striking characteristic of living beings'. How had that regulated activity come about in the first place? Bernard admitted that it was beyond scientists' powers to answer that question: 'Although we may think, or rather feel, that there is a truth which goes beyond our scientific caution, we are compelled to limit ourselves to determinism.'

Bernard's theory of homeostasis was enthusiastically embraced; his warning that it did not tell the whole story was forgotten. And by the time his *Leçons de physiologie experimentale* appeared in 1856, mechanism was being powerfully reinforced by Darwin, showing how chance operated in evolution, and by materialism. 'Divorced from matter, where is life to be found?' the physicist Tyndall asked the audience in his presidential address to the British Association in 1874. 'Whatever our faith may say, our knowledge shows them to be indissolubly bound.' Consciousness, T. H. Huxley asserted, is a by-product of the working of the body, as completely without any power to modify that working as the sound of a locomotive's steam whistle 'is without influence on its machinery'.

Although the mechanists were convinced that organic diseases must have organic causes, they still lacked proof. When Pasteur and Koch provided it, organicism – as it was sometimes described: it has since acquired other meanings – took a further step; each disease, it now seemed clear, must have its specific etiology. 'Etiology' left the door ajar: it signified that the terrain could play its part, as in the parable of the sower. But soon Pasteur's warning about the importance of the terrain was forgotten. Diseases were being attributed to a single cause – germ, virus, or toxin. Research began to be concentrated in laboratories; with the introduction of ever more sophisticated apparatus, it became progressively more reductionist, more involved with biochemistry, the emphasis eventually shifting from germs to viruses, and from viruses to molecular activity.

Over mental illness some doubt remained. It came to be widely assumed that the cause of the psychoses would eventually be found in the laboratory, but even the most dedicated organicist realised that it was less easy to be optimistic about the chances of finding a biochemical explanation for the neuroses. Still, this mattered little; psychiatrists were not taken seriously in the profession. In connection with *real* illnesses, organicism took over; 'functional' disease could be ignored.

By the 1920s, the mould had set. Only one thing was lacking: the 'magic bullets' which Ehrlich had predicted, specific drugs for specific diseases. With the discovery of the sulphonamides, penicillin, the antibiotics and cortisone, his dream appeared to have been fulfilled. Such was the triumph of mechanism that the term itself could be allowed to fall into disuse. Vitalism appeared so utterly discredited that the struggle was over, the distinction was no longer required. Doctors were 'armed with the therapeutic thunderbolts of Jove', Sir Derrick Dunlop could boast; they had seen in their lifetimes 'greater advances in medical treatment than have appeared in all previous aeons of time, and there is no saying what the majesty and splendour of its progress will be in the remaining years of this century'.

## Vitalism Revisited

Vitalism's cause had, however, been upheld by a few doctors courageous enough to tell their colleagues that the mechanist emperor was unclothed; among them was the engaging F. G. Crookshank. Like Rivers, he had become interested in the new school of psychoanalysis emanating from Vienna, though he leaned to the Adlerian rather than the Freudian school. 'All disease is disorder of function,' he wrote in 1927. 'If there is no functional disorder there is no disease, and the so-called organic changes that we find in some cases are just as much the effect as the cause.' Organic disease 'is what we say we cure, but don't; while functional disease is what the quacks cure and we wish to goodness we could'.

Three years later he returned to the attack. So powerful had the influence of organicism become, he complained, that he had begun to wonder why 'some hard-boiled and orthodox clinician does not describe emotional weeping as a "new disease" calling it "paroxysmal lachrymation", and suggesting treatment by belladonna, astringent local application, avoidance of sexual excess, tea, tobacco and alcohol, and a salt-free diet; proceeding in the event of failure to early removal of the tear glands'. Ludicrous though this sounded, Crookshank felt that 'a good deal of contemporary medicine and surgery seems to me to be on much the same level'.

Crookshank was a maverick, but in 1934 a similar view was put forward by the respected John Ryle, Regius Professor of Physics at Cambridge University. Diseases could and did occur in the absence of any organic cause, he insisted; they were just as real, and as painful, as those which could be detected with the help of 'objective' diagnostic methods. Each new aid – electrocardiographs, blood-analysing techniques, lumbar puncture and the rest – was hailed as evidence of progress, 'and as the employment of instruments is supposed to give a scientific accuracy to the observations, it is imagined that in this way medicine is becoming scientific'. The reverse was true. False mechanical and chemical concepts of the disease process were being created, leading to inaccurate diagnosis. 'By too great an anxiety to give our patients the benefit of modern investigations, and by a waning confidence in our own clinical ability, we may come to lose the astuteness and wisdom of our forebears.'

Ryle also reaffirmed the importance of the terrain. Preoccupied with the organic concept, he complained, and with the assumption that disease is initiated by bacterial action, 'we have too long delayed our study of the soil in which it thrives'. The pendulum, he thought, would swing again, away from mechanism. But mechanism was too well entrenched, and not even the evidence to illustrate the importance of the psychosocial element made much impression.

The first sign of cracks in the materialist foundations of medical science did not emerge until the 1950s, with the publication of Selye's stress theory of disease, and the findings of the epidemiological study of the risk-factors in connection with heart disease, both confirming the importance of the terrain's role. These could, however, be incorporated within orthodoxy's territory without too much heart-searching. Not so the discovery in the 1960s that it is possible to exercise mind control over the automatic nervous system, something which medical students had long been taught was impossible: it broke the organicist rules. More than that, it offered the prospect of a new approach to prevention and treatment such as lowering blood pressure by meditation rather than by drugs.

Early in the 1970s came another shock: the discovery that acupuncture worked. 'If one focuses on idiotic procedures enjoying a considerable popularity among the medical profession at one time or another,' Louis Lasagna contemptuously commented in The Doctors' Dilemmas in 1962, 'any number of lunacies could be cited.' As one of his citations he chose acupuncture. Ten years later a team of eminent American physicians, invited to China by Chairman Mao, returned to the United

States admitting that what they had seen had convinced them that acupuncture was not a ridiculous primitive superstition – a verdict soon confirmed by teams from other countries. And in the mid-1970s yet another fissure appeared in orthodoxy's foundations, with the discovery that placebo effect works through organic processes in the body.

That placebo effect worked well for a third or more patients in everyday disorders had been established in countless trials of drugs since the initial Evans and Hoyle experiment in 1933, and researchers, Stewart Wolf in particular, had shown that placebos had even more remarkable capabilities than had been realised. Wolf gave a patient ipecac, which had previously induced nausea and vomiting, telling her it would abolish her nausea; it did. It also had specific effects on her stomach as if it *were* an anti-nausea drug. 'Placebo effects which modify the pharmacologic action of drugs or endow inert agents with potency are not imaginary,' Wolf claimed in 1949, 'but may be associated with measurable changes at the end organs.' Orthodoxy found this hard to swallow. In spite of many further demonstrations of the power of suggestion, or auto-suggestion, it was only when endorphins – hormone messengers, described as natural opiates, capable of bringing dramatic relief of pain – were discovered in the 1970s that placebo effect was given a measure of materialist respectability.

One by one, therefore, the principles upon which medical science used to be based, the doctrines which have been dinned into generations of medical students, have been shown to be fallacious. Specific etiology, in particular, has been overthrown by the mounting evidence of the importance of the psychosocial element. The idol of materialism, already discarded by the physicists whose forbears worshipped it, can hardly be retained for much longer by the medical profession. The arbitrary division of diseases into organic and functional has been utterly discredited. Orthodox physiology and neurology have been shaken by the discoveries about acupuncture, suggesting that there are forces involved as yet unexplained by medical science. And waiting in the wings are many other therapies, from homeopathy to psychic healing, which researchers have just begun to explore with scientific techniques, sometimes with striking results.

## A New Model?

That a new medical model is needed has been the theme of a number of the critics of orthodox medicine – insiders, as well as the likes of Illich and Carlson.

The present model, designed to fit the beliefs and meet the requirements of a century ago, is 'fixed in a mold determined by medical and social circumstances that are quite different from those that exist today', William H. Glazier of the Albert Einstein College in the Bronx argued in 1973, in a long dissertation on the subject in the *Scientific American*. The same year, Oliver Sacks expressed a similar view, more forcibly, in his *Awakenings*: 'What we *do* see, first and last, is the utter inadequacy of mechanical medicine, the utter inadequacy of a mechanical world view.' From his experience of patients suffering from the sleeping sickness, Sacks had realised that they were living disproofs: 'They remind us that we are overdeveloped in mechanical competence, but lacking in biological intelligence, intuition, awareness; and it is this, above all, that we need to regain, not only in medicine, but in *all* science.'

According to McKeown, 'medical science and services are misdirected, and society's investment in health is not well used, because they rest on an erroneous assumption about the basis of human health.' The assumption has been that the body 'can be regarded as a machine whose protection from disease and its effects depends primarily on *internal* intervention', an approach which 'has led to indifference to the external influences and personal behaviour which are the predominant determinants of health'. 'All medicine is in crisis,' George Engel, Professor of Psychiatry at the Rochester, N.Y., School of Medicine, has claimed, because of its 'adherence to a model of disease no longer adequate for the scientific tasks and social responsibilities of either medicine or psychiatry'; it cannot be tinkered with, it can only be replaced by a new, 'biopsychophysical' model.

It is one thing, however, to accept that the old medical model has been shown to be irrelevant, another for doctors, even those who are sensitive or shrewd enough to recognise and admit its defects, to cope with the implications.

'I was schooled to believe,' Hugh Dudley, Professor of Surgery at St Mary's Hospital, London, has recalled, that organic disease was 'a clear-cut, repetitive syndrome which carried over from one patient to another'. Now that this belief has been shown to be fallacious, 'I should be taking detailed social psychological sexual histories to find out what deep-seated mental mechanisms are crying out for expression through the guts,' but 'the gaseous and the groaning rarely seem to have a credible background of this kind, or at least not one that I can elicit'. Dudley's solution is that he and his fellow-surgeons 'should be more honest about our inadequacies and concentrate upon what we can do', and in theory that is the obvious solution. But for most physicians and surgeons, the idea that the treatment of organic disorders ought to be relegated to a secondary, back-up role – with surgeons, for example, being considered as technicians, to be called upon only when all else has failed – would be unacceptable.

For many doctors, in any case, to be told they should concentrate upon what they *can* do would encourage them to maintain their conviction that real diseases are organic and can still best be treated by conventional means. This even applies in the case of some psychiatrists. Attending a Rockefeller Foundation seminar on health issues in 1977, George Engel heard speakers urge that, as one of them put it, medicine must 'concentrate on the "real" diseases and not get lost in the psychological underbrush'. The fact that the distinction between the two categories has been obliterated is still hardly appreciated, Engel observed, because the medical model 'has acquired the status of *dogma*'. A model can be changed when its limitations are exposed; 'a dogma, on the other hand, requires that discrepant data be forced to fit the model or be excluded'. As a result, there are still only two ways in which the psychosocial element can be assessed: 'the *reductionist*, which says that all behavioral phenomena of diseases must be conceptualised in terms of physico-chemical principle; and the *exclusionist*, which says that whatever is not capable of being so explained must be excluded from the category of disease'.

Even if the model's foundations have crumbled, doctors have continued to prescribe, surgeons to operate, teachers to instruct, as if nothing was the matter – nothing, at least, that medical science will not soon rectify with the help of new diagnostic aids, new drugs, and new forms of replacement surgery. The strength of the faith in the model can be seen in almost any medical textbook. The great majority of them take for granted the distinction between functional and organic. Some even maintain that virtually all disorders in their area *are* organic. In a standard work on orthopedics in use on both sides of the Atlantic, J. Crawford Adams – orthopedic surgeon at St Mary's in London, consultant to the RAF, production editor to the *Journal of Bone and Joint Surgery* – devotes only two paragraphs, in the course of nearly five hundred pages, to 'psychogenic or stress disorders', and they are included only, he emphasises, as a warning. There has been a tendency, he complains, when no cause can be found, 'to discount the genuineness of the symptoms and to ascribe them to "hysterical", "functional", or "psychogenic" factors, or simply to stress. This must be considered a dangerous policy that has led on countless occasions to the overlooking of a serious disease.'

Although medical students are now more often warned that so simplistic a view is no longer tenable, many consultants still share Adams's view that 'it is far safer to err on the side of disregarding possible factors than to overlook an organic lesion on the supposition that the symptoms are imaginary'.

Mechanist assumptions of this kind can also still be observed in every issue of the leading medical journals. Whenever an apparently new set of symptoms is encountered, as in the case of Legionnaires' Disease, the hunt immediately begins for *the* cause – physical or chemical. Its epidemics are studied primarily in the hope that, as the *British Medical Journal* has put it, more can be learnt 'about the biological characteristics of the causative organism'. The possibility that there is no causative organism, and that such organisms as are found in connection with the disease are simply its route-markers is rarely even mentioned.

Nostalgia for organicism and specific etiology can be seen even in the work of such a shrewd observer as Lewis Thomas. Aware that he can no longer offer them 'neat', he nevertheless does his best to maintain their supremacy. 'For every disease there is a single key mechanism that dominates all others,' he claims in his essay on medical lessons from history. If one can find it, 'and then think one's way around it, one can control the disorder'. He has to admit, however, that this belief is 'more like a strong hunch than a scientific assertion' – evidence of how powerful is the longing within the profession for the doctrinal certainties of the mechanist era.

And in this, the profession can still count upon very substantial support from the public. If orthodox medicine is losing ground it is chiefly on account of the soaring cost of treatment – in the US, at least – and its ugly side-effects, rather than from dissatisfaction with the model. In particular, resistance remains to the psychosomatic interpretation of illness. Should it be mentioned in the course of diagnosis, it is usually as unwelcome as the printed slip attached to a theatre programme announcing that an understudy is taking over the lead for the performance. The common assumption remains that it carries an implication of some weakness of character. Susan Sontag implies as much in her *Illness as Metaphor*, when she describes it as a 'powerful means of placing the blame on the ill'; patients who are told that they have themselves unwittingly been the cause of their disease are being 'made to feel that they have deserved it'.

The emotive term 'blame' is characteristically obtuse. Far from its being the idea in the minds of Dunbar, Selye, Kissen and the other upholders of the theory, their emphasis has always been on the need to regard stress-induced symptoms as no different from those induced by pathogens. That Sontagism remains the popular view, however, is obvi-

259

ous from the way in which people have continued to react to the proposition that their symptoms may be psychosomatic – with irritation, even with a sense of outrage. In one of his 'Annals of Medicine' series in the *New Yorker* Berton Roueché described a case of a woman who, after various tests and treatments had failed, was eventually diagnosed as suffering from Wilson's Disease, a rare disorder caused by a build-up of excessive copper in the blood-stream, which can cause schizophrenia-like symptoms. 'The thing that mattered most,' she told Roueché, 'the thing that put me in seventh heaven – was that I had a real disease. I wasn't a psychiatric case.' It is ironical that if, tomorrow, schizophrenia were traced to a similar deficiency or to a virus, patients suffering from it would automatically be upgraded in their own and their friends' estimation, though the symptoms would be precisely the same. Their disease would now be 'real', and they could hope to be treated, even if just as unsuccessfully, by a 'real' doctor, rather than by a mere psychiatrist.

As a result of this combined operation – the medical profession clinging to its dogmas, patients preferring to feel that they have no responsibility for their illnesses – the implications of recent discoveries of the mind over the body have hardly begun to be grasped. The significance of placebo effect, for example, is still largely misunderstood. As recently as 1974 a placebo was defined in a medical dictionary as 'an inactive substance or preparation given to satisfy the patient's symbolic need for drug therapy'. When research showed that placebos are *not* inactive – that they have organic effects – it might have been expected that their potential would be recognised and exploited, as Colin Brewer, a consultant psychiatrist, argued that it should in *World Medicine* in 1978, and Herbert Benson urged a year later in *The Mind/Body Effect* ('In its present disregard for the *positive* placebo effect, medicine has lost a valuable asset, an asset which sustained it for centuries; such a beneficial element should be reincorporated into medicine.') Far from being annoyed to be told that symptoms are functional or psychosomatic, patients ought to be delighted, because the diagnosis offers them the hope that auto-suggestion, in one of its forms, can be used to bring relief or even cure. But too often, patients continue to feel as did the woman Roueché described.

The organic aspect of auto-suggestion has not been welcomed. Like a poor but disreputable relation who has to be admitted to the household, it has been let in through the back door, and is being kept out of the way until it can be made respectably 'scientific'. The mechanics of placebo effect are being investigated less to find ways to enable patients to use auto-suggestion in, say, the control of migraine, than in the hope of synthesising the appropriate molecules so that they can be marketed as the latest wonder drug.

## Screening

The most obvious defect of the current medical system is the lack of interest it has shown in prevention. True, the need for more effective preventive measures is frequently urged in medical journals and by eminent members of the profession, but in practice little is done.

The only types of preventive medicine which have established themselves are immunisation and screening. In spite of some successes, notably against polio, the range of the diseases of civilisation from which immunisation provides protection is small, and screening all too often provides no protection, either because it discloses the existence of a disorder for which there is no effective remedy, or because it is not capable of detecting the onset of an illness in time for remedial action to be taken.

Unluckily, when screening became fashionable in the 1960s it was 'largely on the assumption', Archibald Cochrane recalled in his *Effectiveness and Efficiency*, 'that the discovery of any abnormality was worthwhile'. And when a more rational approach was adopted, screening being considered acceptable if there was hard evidence that it could 'alter the natural history of the disease in an appreciable proportion of the cases screened at a reasonable cost', it was found that few of the screening procedures met this standard. Some of them, in fact, have been criticised on the ground that they actually contribute to the disease process that they are designed to detect. Following continual warnings about the danger of indiscriminate use of X-rays, for example, a survey carried out by the British National Radiological Board revealed in 1980 that the risk of genetically-significant exposure had not been reduced, in spite of the introduction of shields for women's ovaries, because some hospitals were neglecting to employ them. 'How can the medical profession have got away with this sloppiness,' a *New Scientist* editorial asked, 'in a period of growing concern about the impact of radiation on people?'

The main defect of screening, however, is that too often it has been providing only the illusion of protection, as in the case of multiphasic, or comprehensive, screening, best known to the public in the form of 'annual check-ups'. These have been extremely profitable for the manufacturers of the gadgetry needed, particularly as industrialists have easily been persuaded that it is in their own interest to arrange for the check-ups, both to protect their executives and, should the protection fail, to protect themselves from being accused of callous reluctance to take precautions on their executives' behalf.

Yet the evidence of the value of such check-ups is flimsy. In the late 1960s and 1970s a team from St Thomas's Hospital, along with local GPs, carried out trials on over seven thousand Londoners between the ages of forty and sixty-four, randomly allocated to two groups; one was screened twice in two years and if necessary given whatever treatment was deemed appropriate; the other was left unscreened. Surveys conducted five years and nine years later showed no significant difference in the mortality rates of the two groups. In California, following trials, the Kaiser Permanente Organization reported similar findings.

Examining the evidence in 1978 Michael d'Souza, a Surrey GP, concluded that screening fails to identify the life-threatening diseases. One US study had shown that over half the people who died of cancer or heart attacks had been declared fit in their most recent annual check-up; that the treatments available after detection had proved to be largely ineffective. Tests, too, could be worrying when they disclosed a disease for which there was no effective treatment. Doctors should be more honest about the state of their art, d'Souza concluded, 'and bide our time until we can fulfil our promises'.

Even where screening can be effective, it may still not be cost-effective, as the experience of the introduction of the 'computerised tomographic scanner', a British device for photographing slices of the body, has shown. By providing an in-depth picture, the assumption was, it would revolutionise diagnosis, and within four years 750 of them had been sold – not in Britain as the NHS could not afford them, but in the United States, at a cost of around $700,000. To spread the payment load, the tendency was to use them as often as possible; this meant that running costs rose out of all proportion to the possible benefits. Yet when the National Academy of Sciences Institute investigated them in 1977 it was found that, although they had been in use for years, nobody had thought to assess their cost-effectiveness, or to ascertain whether they provided any real improvement over straightforward diagnostic acumen.

The present system of screening, C. J. Roberts argues, encourages the doctor to use it even when there is no clear evidence of benefit to those patients whose diseases are detected, although he may benefit financially, as GPs do if they perform certain screening procedures. The doctor may even use screening as an opportunity to advertise his services for personal gain, which he is not otherwise allowed to do. Or he may use it to advance his career with the help of some research project, without letting patients know this is the reason. Unless properly regulated, therefore, 'screening has the potential for being unethical (because it is an advertisement), for being immoral (because it may well inflate the hazards of non-compliance in order to achieve compliance), and for being illegal (because the advertisement of that which is immoral is potentially outside the law)'.

## The Drug Connection

It is never easy for any organisation whose members share a set of beliefs and attitudes to recognise that they are becoming irrelevant to the needs of the community. In the case of the medical profession it is made all the more difficult because it is sustained in many of those beliefs and attitudes by one of the most powerful commercial empires in the world: the pharmaceutical industry. The 'wonder drug' era from the 1930s to the 1950s forged an alliance between the profession and the industry. It has since led to the industry achieving an unprecedented and dangerous measure of control over the profession.

That the alliance should have been forged was understandable. 'The sense of wonder when antibiotics make light of such lethal diseases as pneumonia or meningococcal meningitis never leaves you,' a retired GP who qualified in the 1920s has recalled. 'To watch one young man or woman wake from the coma of cerebrospinal meningitis after sulphonamide therapy is enough to compensate for all the failures and frustrations of the years.' But the industry has exacted a formidable price from the profession for its assistance.

In the 'wonder drug' era the manufacturing companies found themselves with a market which was not only self-contained – they could devote almost their entire attention to the medical profession – but in sales terms almost open-ended, in that doctors were not called upon to spend their own money; their patients (or the tax-payer) were footing the bills. Doctors were inundated with promotional material: advertisements in medical journals, glossy brochures through the mail, sales talk from company representatives. Pfizer went one better, providing gifts and holidays for doctors. 'The company once rented 3,000 acres of marshland to entertain 700 physicians who enjoyed duck shooting,' Louis Lasagna recorded in *The Doctors' Dilemmas*. 'In Alabama, 460 doctors were treated to a fishing trip and barbecue, with the company supplying fishing equipment and boats and practically hooking the fish.' By the late 1950s the drug companies were annually spending $750m on promotion in the United States – more than three times the entire amount which was then being spent on medical education. A depressingly large proportion of the promotion, too, was misleading; some of it simply false, as the Kefauver Committee evidence showed.

The Committee's report, coupled with the thalidomide affair, led the industry to realise that it had been overplaying its hand. Promotion became more discreet. Doctors continued to have their holidays, but with a conference or symposium to occupy part of the time. Still, that was no hardship, as they could exchange views, gossip with their peers, and read papers which would later be published at the company's expense. By the 1970s the industry was laying out nearly $5,000 a year on promotion for each doctor in the country – over a billion dollars in all; again, a far larger amount than that spent on medical education. In Britain, the amount rose to well over £1,000 a year per doctor by the close of the 1970s.

Obviously the industry would not have been spending these sums unless it expected to profit. The profitable extent of the profession's patronage, even in Britain, where the structure of the NHS made the companies' task harder, was noted by David Owen when Labour Minister of Health; each GP, he calculated in 1976, had about £25,000 a year to spend on drugs, and each consultant £250,000, at the taxpayer's expense.

One of the prevalent illusions of doctors has been that they can take drug promotion or leave it alone. Doctors who say they ignore the advertisements in the medical journals, throw brochures unread into the wastepaper-basket and refuse to see company salesmen are a familiar species. But they are unrepresentative, as the industry's sales figures have continually shown. Some promotional schemes fail, just as they can fail for beer or biscuits, but sales tend to reflect the promotional effort put into them. In the industry, doctors are considered to have a low level of sales resistance – as, indeed, the low intellectual level of the drug advertisements in medical journals confirms. 'It frightens me,' the president of a drug firm has recently admitted, 'that the general medical community throughout the world is largely influenced by slogans, and its convictions are based on slogans.'

The training most doctors receive in pharmacology is derisory, but even if it were improved, it would be of little help to them in assessing the merits of a new drug. It is in the company's interest to try to achieve saturation-promotion when the drug is licensed, and this, as a rule, is all that doctors rely upon, as in all probability the reports of clinical trials have been published in specialist journals which most of them have not read. 'It seems incongruous,' the Lancet has lamented, 'that for months after a new drug is marketed, almost all the information reaching the doctor should come from the manufacturer and next to nothing from disinterested sources.' The few journals which are neither directly connected with the drug industry nor dependent upon it for their advertising revenue cannot hope to provide more than a small number of disinterested surveys, which are not widely read.

If there were any doubt about the superior pulling power of such promotion over the evidence from controlled trials, it was removed by the reception accorded to indomethacin, marketed as Indocid in the

United States and Indocin in Britain in the mid-1960s. It was 'the turning-point for many rheumatic patients', Merck's advertisements claimed; trials had shown that from a half to three-quarters of rheumatic patients had benefited, with reduced swellings, stiffness, and pain, and it was also claimed to be safer than its steroid predecessors. Immediately it became a best-seller. Eighteen months later two reports of trials of indomethacin appeared. One, in the *New England Journal of Medicine*, described how, in a controlled trial, it had done no better than aspirin. The other, in the *British Medical Journal*, showed that in another controlled trial it had performed no better than a placebo. A committee of medical specialists, according to the *Wall Street Journal*, 'blasted much of the research on which Merck based its claims', and President Johnson was reported as expressing his concern. But no action was taken, even when a mounting toll of side-effects was reported from the drug. Merck continued to promote it lavishly, and it remained a best-seller for a decade.

Naturally critics have argued that promotion of this kind ought to be stopped, or at least be brought under control. But this has alarmed the profession, because the first obvious target would be advertisements; really effective controls could simply lead to their withdrawal, the companies replacing them with more intensive operations by their salesmen. Scores of medical journals would disappear, and others be greatly reduced in size. As a result, it was not until 1977 that the Department of Health in Britain dared even to lay down that the advertisements should include contra-indications and adverse reactions, which the FDA had insisted upon for years.

To avoid the destruction of the medical journals, a variety of alternative ways to curb the propaganda flow have been suggested, such as 'monitored release' of new drugs – the drug being made available only to specialists or GPs participating in what, in effect, would be extended clinical trials – and 'post-marketing surveillance' – where the drug could be generally released, but prescribed only by doctors willing to make special arrangements to monitor the reactions and feed them back to the regulatory agencies.

Both these proposals have encountered the opposition of the industry. Monitored release, its spokesmen have claimed, would not permit a large enough sample of patients to give a clear idea of any problems in connection with the drug; post-marketing surveillance, although it would embrace a larger sample of patients, would be expensive. But the real reason is that the drugs companies, like any other branch of industry, need to maintain profits in order to survive, and to increase profits in order to flourish. The test procedures imposed by the regulatory agencies already necessitate a heavy expenditure of time and money; naturally they want to be free to sell their product, as soon as it is licensed, as profitably as they can. The best method is a massive promotional campaign the moment the product becomes generally available to doctors. To promote it in the monitoring stage would be wasteful; to await unrestricted general release might involve a sufficiently long list of side-effects and contra-indications to hinder the promotional campaign. Any form of licensing which delays unrestricted general release is consequently anathema.

## The Right to Prescribe

It might be expected that the medical profession would favour a system by which new drugs would undergo more extended trials by suitably qualified doctors. But the profession is still hooked on 'the right to prescribe' – the dogma that, once a drug has been licensed, any doctor should be permitted to prescribe it. This 'right to prescribe' dates from a period when there were few drugs, and their effects were reasonably well known. To imagine that any doctor, even the most highly trained of pharmacologists, is capable of assessing the merits and defects of the drugs now available is absurd. In 1979 the *Lancet* estimated that there were 15,000 drugs available on prescription in Britain. The year before, a committee set up to review medicines had noted that there were 950 major anti-rheumatic products, and well over a thousand psychoactive drugs.

Nevertheless the profession has clung to the right to prescribe as if it had been granted as a hereditary benefice. When in 1961 a lay member of a House of Commons Estimates Committee suggested that a solution to the problem of selecting doctors permitted to prescribe new drugs could be reached by a committee set up by the profession, Sir Bruce Fraser of the Department of Health replied that, on the contrary, it would be regarded as interference; 'the word "gross" would be added, I do not doubt, by the British Medical Association'.

## Drug Effectiveness

The fuss that the medical establishment has made about Laetrile might be taken as a sign that it is vigilant in its watch to protect the public from bogus drugs. It has not been vigilant, however, in its scrutiny of bogus prescription drugs for fear of limiting the doctors' right to prescribe, even when the evidence shows that the right is being widely abused. Only when the alternative is certain to be government intervention, as when the prescribing of heroin was restricted in Britain to designated clinics, has the profession given way.

Far from looking for ways to keep doctors from prescribing useless drugs, the establishment has watched with complacency the fumbling attempts of health ministers to do the job for them. In 1967 a Committee of Inquiry under Lord Sainsbury reported that over forty per cent of the drugs available on the NHS, in the view of a panel of experts which it had set up, were undesirable, obsolete or ineffective. In the same year, a permanent body was formed, founded by the Department of Health under Alastair Macgregor, Professor of Therapeutics at Aberdeen University, charged with monitoring drugs for effectiveness. It published a journal, *Proplist*, sent to all doctors twice a year, dividing the drugs its experts had tested into categories A and B; the Bs being drugs with 'an unacceptable lesser degree of efficacy or with an unacceptable greater toxicity than alternative preparations', or with other defects of any kind that rendered them unsuitable. Predictably, the pharmaceutical industry was hostile, but for GPs *Proplist* ought to have been a godsend. Yet three years later the Department recommended that the Committee should be wound up because doctors were paying so little attention to its findings, and when Edward Heath's new government took that advice, the medical establishment accepted the demise of the committee and *Proplist* with ill-concealed relief.

The American Medical Association, which had set up a council to monitor drug effectiveness, soon followed the British example, disbanding it ostensibly for reasons of economy. Economy was not the real reason, John Adriani, a former chairman of the council, complained; the AMA, becoming alarmed at the possibility that, if the pharmaceutical industry was irritated by the council's findings, it would withdraw its support, had 'abrogated its responsibility for providing factual information on drugs to the physician on the public's behalf'.

As a result doctors have been left with little guidance on drug prescribing. The few independent journals, such as the *Drug and Therapeutics Bulletin* published by the British Consumers' Association, tend to be studied only by those doctors who are careful in their prescribing habits. And although the flood of new drugs has recently abated, old ones remain in great numbers on the market to confuse doctors. An investigation by Ralph Nader's Health Research Group reported in 1978 that only about one in four of the new drugs approved by the FDA could be considered to have brought any therapeutic benefit, and although the British Department of Health set up a committee to review medicines in

1975, its own effectiveness was neatly sabotaged because it was denied the right to accept the verdicts of the Sainsbury or Macgregor Committees. When in 1979 it called upon the manufacturers of 219 drugs to withdraw them – less than one per cent of the total number of drugs available – most of the manufacturers elected to appeal against the decision, causing further delay. Pending the hearing of the appeals, the drugs were not named.

The only minor victory the consumerists can claim is that the *British National Formulary*, published jointly by the British Medical Association and the Pharmaceutical Society, is at last following *Proplist*'s example. Could the publishers not follow the lead of the World Health Organisation, the *Lancet* had urged in 1978, 'have the courage of their convictions, and advise us on the "best buys" in the British drug market'? Although they lacked that courage, in 1980 the decision was taken that in future, the *Formulary* would grade drugs as 'necessary' or 'unnecessary'. But no compulsion would be exercised on the manufacturers to withdraw the unnecessary drugs, or on doctors to cease prescribing them, and, as Martin Weitz has been able to show, nearly a hundred of the drugs which had been put in the Macgregor Committee's B category ten years before were still on the market, and still being prescribed, at a cost to the taxpayer of £6m a year.

### 'Me too'

The medical profession has also tended to take the industry's side, or at least not to come out against it, over what have become known as 'me-too' drugs. When a new type of psychoactive or anti-arthritic drug is successfully launched, the grant of a patent provides only a limited degree of protection to the company; by juggling with the molecular structure it is often possible for other firms to provide marketable variants. This causes confusion for doctors, and may put patients at risk from new side-effects; it has often been urged that such drugs should not be permitted unless the manufacturers can demonstrate that they are more effective and safer than the front runner.

Given the probability, amounting almost to certainty, that any new drug is bound to have some toxic effect, the *New Scientist* asked in 1977, 'should not the Committee now refuse to allow on to the market any new medicine with a known mechanism of action that does not represent a clear advance over an existing remedy with the same mechanism?' But the Committee has continued to concentrate on trying to ensure that new drugs are safe; whether they are effective, let alone whether they are more effective than drugs already available to treat the same symptoms, has not been of primary concern.

Recently the industry has been campaigning for a relaxation of the safety regulations. 'Take off the cuffs,' the newsletter put out by the Association of the British Pharmaceutical Industry has pleaded, with a picture of the manacles which, it claims, are shackling the industry. Naturally it is not suggested that patients would receive less protection; the pitch is that, because of bureaucratic red-tape interference, patients are not getting new drugs which would actually be safer and more effective than the ones currently available.

Milton Friedman took this line in his onslaught against the bureaucratic delays on progress imposed by the FDA. All right, he admitted, the FDA had protected women in the United States from consequences of thalidomide. But in terms both of cost and benefit and of human suffering, the delays which the FDA imposed before new drugs could be marketed were doing more harm than good.

What are these new drugs which would spare pain and suffering, if they could be marketed sooner? The industry's record in this respect for the past twenty years has been unimpressive. True, not a year has passed without some 'break through' being boasted about; but disillusionment has followed. And as the FDA was able to show in reply to Friedman's charges, the great majority of the drugs it had been called upon to sanction had shown no evidence, when tested, of being more effective than their predecessors.

## Consequences

The alliance between the pharmaceutical industry and the medical profession, immensely profitable though it has been for the industry, has been a malign influence on the profession because it has left doctors so heavily dependent upon drugs as their front-line therapeutic weapon. Individually, doctors may deplore this drug dependence; collectively, they have left themselves almost powerless to end it. Just how deeply they have come to rely on the industry has been demonstrated in a poll of doctors in Britain, conducted by the Association of the British Pharmaceutical Industry. Assuming that the sample was representative, it showed how doctors accept the vital importance of new drugs. In particular, GPs have been conditioned to regard drugs as their mainstay; without a continuing supply of new ones, they would feel bereft.

Yet there is a mass of evidence to show that doctors are not capable of protecting patients from the consequences of this addiction to medical drugs, one reason being that they have become so accustomed to patients' adverse reactions to the drug treatment that they have come to take them for granted, with depressing consequences which were illustrated by the Eraldin debacle.

Among the controls established after the thalidomide affair, one appeared to be eminently satisfactory. Each doctor was provided by the Committee on Safety of Medicines with 'yellow cards' on which he was asked to report any adverse reactions which his patients might suffer from drugs, the assumption being that such side-effects as were not observed during clinical trials would quickly be detected. Yet when reports that Eraldin caused corneal damage and other side-effects prompting ICI to send out a warning, only a single yellow card had been received by the Committee in connection with the side-effects of the drug. No sooner did the damage become generally known than scores of confirmatory findings began to come in from doctors who had observed the side-effects, but either had not related them to the drug, or had neglected to fill in and despatch the yellow cards.

Nor was this exceptional. Examining the figures, C. J. Roberts found that in the five years after the yellow cards had been sent out, the number returned showed that doctors were reporting only one suspected adverse reaction in every 20,000 prescriptions issued; on average, 'about one in every two years'. Many GPs had simply ignored the cards. And although a slight improvement was noticeable in the late 1970s, the proportion of adverse reactions not reported was estimated by W. H. W. Inman, a member of the Committee, as over ninety per cent.

Many doctors, too, are unwilling to emphasise a drug's risks to patients, for fear of unnecessarily alarming them. Others, who do provide a briefing, often put 'use as instructed' on the prescription, failing to realise that patients may not have taken in the instructions. A recent enquiry in Britain elicited the fact that patients had not properly understood what they had been told in connection with over half the drugs prescribed, and that nearly half of the patients in the sample, whether or not they claimed to have understood at the time, had later forgotten the doctor's instructions.

Even where doctors know about the dangers of a drug they too often fail to impress them upon patients. After the introduction of antibiotic tetracycline, it was found that in young children treated with it their teeth may become irreversibly discoloured or mottled. Yet a quarter of a century later companies were still making up 'pediatric drops', or syrups, designed to make it easier for parents to get young children to

271

take tetracycline, and staining was still common, varying 'from pale yellow through to purple, just like bruising', according to the chairman of the British Dental Association, 'and it can have a severely damaging psychological effect'. He blamed the companies; if they would stop putting tetracycline in syrups, 'doctors would stop prescribing them', and there was no need to prescribe them because other antibiotics are just as effective. The companies, as ever, replied that it was not their business to tell doctors what to prescribe.

Other examples exist of the danger of allowing companies to market drugs which taste attractive to children. The worst killer of all in Britain, according to the *British Medical Journal*, has been a fruit-flavoured drug for the treatment of bed-wetting. The BMA is sceptical about the value of the drug – or of any drug for this purpose. Yet some doctors, it complains, prescribe it 'almost as a reflex action'. Children could too easily get a liking for it as one four-year-old had just done – he had drunk a small bottleful, and died in hospital the next day.

The illusion persists, however, that doctors are the only people qualified to warn patients of the dangers of any drug prescribed. Obviously special warnings ought to be given where, say, the prescribed dose is not far removed from a fatal dose, as in the case of Distalgesic, a pain-killer where the margin is small. In Britain, the Committee on Safety of Drugs allowed the drug to be marketed, contenting itself with issuing a warning to doctors. In the United States the FDA held up the licence. In 1979 doctors from the Regional Poisoning Centre in Edinburgh reported that they had had to treat over a hundred cases of poisoning attributed to the drug. It was being advertised, they complained, as having the 'easy to swallow' shape, and patients were finding it all too easy to swallow one too many. A few days later, at an inquest in the north of England, the coroner heard how two women had died from overdoses, and although one of them had clearly intended suicide, the other had accidentally taken too much at a time.

A simple way out of the difficulty would be for the drug companies to enclose leaflets with their prescription drugs, just as they do with drugs which can be bought over the counter, but which would include warnings of all known hazards, from likely side-effects to the risk of exceeding the prescribed dosage. This proposal has met with firm resistance from the profession. The American Medical Association objects that such instructions are the responsibility of the doctor alone. Naturally the industry has been happy to agree. If firms were compelled to provide patients with the same lists of contra-indications and adverse reactions as they now have to provide for doctors, patients would be likely, on reading the warnings, to throw the pills away. 'We believe that patients

272

should be made more aware of the risks and benefits of drugs,' the Association of the British Pharmaceutical Industry virtuously claims, 'but the onus for doing this lies with the doctor. As manufacturers we do not want to interfere in the relationship between doctor and patient.'

## Balance Sheet

In *A Question of Balance: the Benefits and Risks of Pharmaceutic Innovation*, George Teeling-Smith of the Office of Health Economics (and also, recently, holder of a Chair at Brunel University) has put the case for the continued alliance between the industry and the medical profession. No longer, he has to admit, can we think in terms of drugs with no associated adverse reactions. But they still, he claims, bring enormous benefits. Assessment of their value 'is essentially a question of balance – and if we are not careful that balance is in serious danger of being swung too far against the development of those future new medicines which are needed to extend the dramatic therapeutic progress which has already been achieved in the past thirty years'.

His own selection of the successful drugs, however, shows little evidence of dramatic therapeutic progress. For him to cite the beta-blockers and cimetidine as major achievements, and to assume that the reduction of the number of patients in mental hospitals has been an unqualified benefit, is the measure of the extent to which the alliance has cemented itself by coming to believe in its own promotional material. The indications now are that the balance between the benefits and the disadvantages of drugs needs to be struck on the basis that little progress is likely to be made in providing more effective new drugs to treat the commoner disorders.

There is certainly a need for a new balance to be struck in assessing the usefulness of established drugs, but not of the kind which Teeling-Smith contemplates. For years there has been a tendency, when assessing the value of a drug (or of a type of drug), to make the assessment in terms of its success either in removing symptoms (so that the case can be marked as cured) or reducing mortality. The extent of the accompanying damage from adverse reactions has been brushed aside as unimportant, or ignored altogether. Thus when counting drug treatment of leukemia in children as one of the pluses for the industry, the figures given are usually simply for greater life expectation, without reference to what kind of life the children have led.

In 'You're the Boy with Leukemia, aren't you?' Bobby Millington described the effect of drugs on his own life shortly before his death at the age of sixteen: the nausea and vomiting ('of the oral tablets it is the steroids which are the worst; they act as both stimulant and depressant. The steroids retain the fluid in the body making the joints, gums, teeth and base of the spine continually ache'), and the occasional chemical burns from misdirected injections. Millington had taken drugs 'virtually non-stop week-in, week-out for six years', and until he came to write the article (found by his mother after he died) his relief at being thereby enabled to indulge in physical activity, football and cricket, had left him content. But eventually he had begun to wonder what mental effects the drugs were having on him. Again, the steroids were the worst; 'they make you feel like you've got to be constantly doing something and this, coupled with the fact that they keep you awake at nights, leads to a building-up in tension and depression which in turn leads to a breaking down of the mind'.

As leukemia is unpredictable in its course, it is impossible to tell what additional life-span Millington obtained from drugs, and no research has been done which would enable a comparison to be made between the results of drug treatment and those of alternative therapies. But even if it were accepted that drugs, and only drugs, can prolong life, the question whether the prolongation is likely to be sufficient to balance the adverse reactions always needs to be asked. And this is something which only individual patients can be expected to decide, given that they have received the briefing which they so rarely get. This they cannot expect, if it is given, if at all, by a specialist who is already convinced of the value of the drug as is presumably the case if he prescribes it.

## The Patient as Guinea Pig

When a specialist prescribes a drug without being convinced of its value it is ordinarily because he is engaged in a clinical trial; this brings up another of the problems which have arisen largely as a consequence of the profession's dependence upon new drugs. To test them adequately requires an endless supply not only of laboratory animals, needed chiefly as a precaution against toxicity (the positive evidence from animal tests is slight), but also of patients.

By the 1960s ambitious young doctors were beginning to realise that their prospects depended less on their personal capabilities at the bedside than on their ability to foster a good impression for the future by compiling a dossier of impressive-looking research papers. 'A whole new breed of doctors, spawned by hospitals and medical schools, is growing up with no other home than the large teaching hospital and its labs,' the Ehrenreichs warned in 1970; doctors who were the product of training in research rather than in clinical practice naturally gravitated back to teaching hospitals because 'that's where the grants are, the equipment, and the colleagues who make research fun and productive'.

The ethical issues raised by this type of research had already begun to cause concern. 'Modern medicine has provoked some serious moral questions not through malignant perversity, but because of the enormous momentum medical science has gained in the past few decades,' S. E. Stumpf, an academic philosopher from Vanderbilt University, Nashville, warned doctors in 1966. 'There is the nagging question: what are the permissible limits and the proper conditions of experimentation on humans?' That summer Professor Henry Beecher of the Harvard Medical School listed over twenty research projects which he thought unethical in the *New England Journal of Medicine*, and the following year M. H. Pappworth, a consultant physician working in London, set out to find what experimentation was actually being carried on. In *Human Guinea Pigs* he produced a horrifying record of the lengths to which human vivisection had been taken, with painful and hazardous procedures, often tried out on so-called 'volunteers' – prison inmates who were, in fact, being tempted by promised parole or earlier release.

Pappworth's book led to some soul-searching on the issue; ethical committees were established in hospitals to tighten up their safeguards. But the fact that an ethical committee is set up does not necessarily mean that it can exercise effective control. It may not even be convened. The forty-one ethical committees in Scottish hospitals were circularised recently to find out how they were working. Of the thirty-four that replied, only six had introduced formal procedures for monitoring research. Wide variations existed in their activity; some had had no meeting at all in the twelve months before receiving the questionnaire. Lay representation had hardly even been considered. 'In their present form,' the report on them concludes, they 'do not satisfy the interests of the public or the research worker.'

As technology advances, the pressure to relax ethical controls increases, the argument being that more lives will be lost in the long run if the research is held up. At the same time, the growing insistence both of the regulating authorities and of the medical journals that all trials of drugs should be rigorously controlled added to the problem of protecting patients, because if a trial is to be accepted as objective, it may not be possible to minister to the needs of individuals by, say, varying the dosage of a drug – short of taking them out of the trial. 'People who get into the grip, or on to the treadmill, of a modern, fully equipped and technically advanced hospital,' Bernard Towers, Professor of Pediatrics at the University of California, lamented in 1971, 'are liable, it seems to me, to be made to suffer all kinds of indignities, and worse – I mean, suffer actual harm – before they are "released".' But such indignities continue; in Britain the number of biochemical tests given has doubled every five years over the past two decades.

The more elaborate the trials system becomes, the more dependent it is on computers, and they too are a source of growing concern to doctors, because they impose their own tyranny. 'The complexity, ambiguity and richness of even the limited interviews I conducted,' the American social scientist Thomas Cottle, author of *Time's Children*, has lamented, 'contrasted markedly with the linear beauty and quintessential order of the data as it appeared all categorised and analysed in gorgeous printouts.' The effect of the computer 'was the constant separation of myself from the people I had studied – the very people whose utterances I had transformed into numerical co-efficients'.

In his *Doctors on Trial* John S. Bradshaw cites a number of criticisms of the resultant de-humanising of hospitals, including one by a doctor in the *Journal of the American Medical Association* in 1974, recording his experience as a patient. 'Nursing aides and assistants, technicians from the laboratory and dieticians came regularly and frequently to measure my blood pressure, weigh me, administer drugs, draw blood and talk about my diet,' he had found, but only once did a nurse visit him. 'Large hospitals have become disquieting places, as anyone who has been a patient there can testify,' another doctor wrote in the same issue. 'The patient is usually low man on the totem pole in an organization that is largely for the convenience of others.' And in a saddening indictment of a teaching hospital in Britain, Huw Morgan, a GP in Wales, has recalled how for the teaching staff, 'it seemed a positive advantage to be inhuman among the shining modern technology, the EMI scanners and computerised records'. Implicit in the system as it had developed was 'that the patients existed for the benefit of the research registrars' theses, the clinical demonstrations, and the new treatment trials', and though a few doctors were caring and humane, they were 'almost helpless against the howling gale of austere, depersonalised medical technology and "academic progress"'. One famous surgeon, 'a tin-god of the first order, aggressively browbeat a woman into having an operation she did not really want because, it seemed, he had not done it for a while and wanted the chance to perform'.

Recently the plight of patients has been made worse by the growing tendency to test combinations of drugs, making it more likely that patients will suffer adverse reactions. And this, in turn, has raised the issue as to whether it is now practicable to give full and fair briefing to patients when asking them if they will volunteer to take part in a trial. To do so it will be necessary to inform them that they may be part of the control group not receiving the treatment, and also to spell out all the possible side-effects.

When a large-scale, long-term trial of drug therapy for hypertension in Britain was announced in 1978 the implications worried the editor of the *New Scientist*, Bernard Dixon. Just how, he wanted to know, were the subjects to be briefed about the potential benefits of possibly receiving a drug and the unquantifiable risks of the therapy? 'Indeed, can the "guinea pigs" in such a trial be given a briefing that is ethically proper and yet does not render unjustifiably remote the prospect that unambiguous results will emerge?' The unpalatable fact is that few patients, given a really full and fair description of the results of past drug trials and their complications, could be expected to volunteer for one today.

The only way to make sure that the briefing which patients receive is full and fair would be to ensure that it is given by somebody who is not concerned in the outcome of the trials – a member of the hospital staff accredited, perhaps, for this purpose. Any such proposal would be bitterly resisted. The method of briefing patients has remained something which the experimenters prefer to put out of their minds, because it adds an uncomfortable subjective dimension to what, for them, ought to be an objective scientific procedure. At a gathering of clinical pharmacologists in 1979 a consensus was reached on the subject of how randomised controlled trials ought to be conducted which, the *Lancet* thought, provided 'an excellent defence, on scientific grounds (which is easy), and on ethical grounds (less so)'. The *Lancet*, however, was still not satisfied. 'If the patient is to surrender his right to participate in the treatment decision and his right to the doctor's clinical judgment, then we need a special system of informed consent.' This, surely, was an important issue, but the clinical pharmacologists had evaded it, deeming it 'not immediately relevant to the scientific/ethical issues considered'.

Hospital patients are at least given a choice whether or not they wish to take part in a trial, and given some indication of the possible risks. Patients of GPs have not enjoyed even this measure of protection, as a case brought before the General Medical Council in 1975 revealed. A doctor was struck off the register for falsifying the returns of a trial he had pretended to undertake for a drug company; it transpired that not merely were GPs being paid substantial sums to undertake such trials, but that they were under no obligation, except a moral one, to tell patients that they were taking part. 'I am quite sure,' the editor of *Clinical Trials Journal* admitted when questioned on the point by Oliver Gillie, the *Sunday Times* medical correspondent, 'that some drug trials published in my journal and in others are done without the patient's knowledge.'

The full extent of the suffering inflicted on patients in the course of experiments which have served only to discredit a new drug or combination of drugs also needs to be weighed in the balance when the benefits of drug treatment are being assessed. Usually it is noted only in passing, if at all, as when a third of the patients who were being tested with a drug to reduce blood pressure had to be taken out of the trial because they were suffering from severe adverse reactions – depression, disturbed liver function, impotence. No journal keeps a record of the effects of drugs which have failed to make the grade in clinical trials, or which later have had to be withdrawn: only the spectacularly destructive examples, such as thalidomide, are widely publicised. More than a slight improvement on the record of established drugs, which is all that can realistically be claimed for most new drugs, is necessary to compensate for the suffering that extensive trials can cause.

The need for effective checks on clinical trials becomes more urgent every year, owing to two developments which put patients increasingly at risk: the drug companies' need to keep up the profession's demand for their products, which is increasingly being met by the offer of new combinations of old drugs rather than new drugs – the testing of different combinations offering unprecedented scope for fresh trials – and the realisation that, as Archibald Cochrane has been reiterating, 'for controlled trials to be effective, large numbers need to be followed for several years'.

Such trials, Cochrane admits, are expensive, but some progress has been made. 'One has only to think of the magnificent "Atromid" trial, the series of trials on length of stay of coronary disease, and the on-going trial of intervention for slightly raised blood pressure.' One has only to think of two of those to realise the problems and the hazards of subjecting large numbers of people for many years: the ethical difficulties described by Bernard Dixon in his comments on the hypertension trial, and the eventual findings in the case of Atromid.

In the 1960s enthusiastic reports began to appear about the success of the drug clofibrate, marketed in Britain as Atromid, in lowering cholesterol levels in the blood; it was regarded as both effective and unusually safe, and so high did its reputation stand that cardiologists who declined to use it on the ground that the long-term effects were not yet known were sometimes accused by their colleagues of dereliction of their duty to their patients. But clofibrate happened to be a drug chosen by the World Health Organisation for an unusually protracted trial: patients were monitored not merely during the five-year trial period, but also for some years afterwards. The results were reported in 1980, and they revealed that the mortality rate from all causes for those patients who had been on clofibrate was twenty-five per cent higher than for the controls.

'Magnificent' the findings may have been as an illustration of the value of extensive and extended trials; but the implications are alarming. Suppose, for the sake of even greater statistical reliability, twice as many patients had been included in the clofibrate trial; the outcome, presumably, would have been that twice as many would have died prematurely, relative to the controls. The logical inference would ordinarily be that new drugs of this kind should not be licensed for general prescribing until after, say, five years' clinical testing and a further five years' monitoring. Were any such regulation to be introduced the drug companies would stop producing new drugs, and although in some ways this might well be on balance beneficial, it can hardly be what Cochrane had in mind.

## Promotion

As things stand, the pharmaceutical industry is becoming increasingly uneasy about its future, as its reaction to criticism often shows, and this uneasiness is shared by the research empire built largely with its profits. The result has been a rash of 'leaks' of projects which, the public is assured, offer the hope of breakthroughs if they are supported. The most notorious is the case of interferon.

279

The presence of a virus, immunologists have long assumed, alerts the body's immune mechanism. In 1957 Alick Isaacs of the National Institute for Medical Research in London, and the Swiss Jean Lindenmann who was attached to it at the time, extracted a substance from the human body incorporating this alarm reaction, which could be used to interfere with the ordinary processes by which viruses operate. It was a notable achievement, but there had been so many boasted virus-slayers before which had turned out to be of no value that it was not thought much of at the time. And for years afterwards the difficulty and expense of extracting and purifying interferon proved almost insuperable.

Still, research continued, and twelve years later – Isaacs having died in the meantime – interferon suddenly became front-page news with the discovery in pilot trials on cancer patients that it could sometimes slow down the growth of cancerous cells and the development of tumours. Headlines such as 'Race is on for Miracle Drug' began to proliferate, and in 1980 interferon ('IF', to scientists) won the accolade of a *Time* magazine cover story. It stressed the 'If' element: 'If longer-range tests show good results. If interferon can be manufactured in the massive quantities needed for effective treatment. If it proves not to have unexpected side-effects. Should these and other ifs become facts, IF will be an ideal cancer drug, for it is a natural substance produced in infinitesimal amounts by the body.' But other reports were less restrained; cancer specialists soon found themselves besieged with requests by patients for treatment with the new wonder drug, and the American Cancer Society launched one of its opportunist fund-raising drives. By 1980 the American drug companies had invested about $150 million in developing interferon, and the Society and the National Cancer Institute provided a further $15 million. Yet in May, a *New York Times* story headlined 'Studies put Interferon Cancer Use in Doubt' showed not merely that the doubts had emerged before the fund-raising drive, but that the American Cancer Society had been aware of them.

A few months later, following a gushing programme in the British 'TV Eye', series, a senior lecturer in oncology at the University of Glasgow, J. Gordon McVie, launched the most violent attack on the drug's promotion that had yet appeared. TV's *blind* eye, he complained in the *British Medical Journal*, had been turned on to 'the considerable evidence that interferon does not work; it does not prolong life; does not eradicate cancers; does not even partially shrink most tumours'. It also causes side-effects, and treatment with it costs a fortune. It might eventually work, he admitted, but the available evidence did not justify enthusiasm.

A fortnight later a report in the *Lancet* confirmed that there is good reason for caution. In a trial sponsored by Burroughs Wellcome the tumours of only two out of eighteen patients had shrunk after interferon treatment, and both had died soon after the treatment stopped. Side-effects included fever, hypertension and disturbed bone-marrow function. As the *New Scientist* pointed out, this does not offer much hope even for those advanced cancer patients who react well to the drug, as they will require massive doses, 'perhaps for the rest of their life, to keep the disease at bay'.

A letter in the *New Scientist* had also warned of another risk which had not attracted notice. Much had been made of the fact that interferon is a substance which occurs naturally in the body, the implication being that the body should be better able to tolerate it. But 'suppose that viruses developed resistance to interferon in the same way that bacteria have adapted to antibiotics?' If so, it might inadvertently deprive our bodies 'of what poor defences they already possess against viruses'. Could anybody, the writer asked, reassure him on this point? Nobody did.

What has made this fuss over interferon all the more ridiculous, as well as sad, is the medical profession's customary, almost paranoid hostility to claims for outsiders' cures for cancer, such as the various dietary regimes and Laetrile, on the ground that they arouse false hopes. The interferon publicity unjustifiably aroused the hopes of tens of thousands of cancer sufferers, some of whom have offered, and some actually given, large sums to be accepted on to the queue for interferon treatment.

## The Misdirection of Research

The vast sums lavished on research into interferon represent another of the disadvantages arising out of the pharmaceutical industry's dominance over medical research. Its need to ensure a continuing supply of new drugs has helped to keep research in its mechanist, organicist groove, by ensuring that this is the research area which will be most heavily funded out of the industry's profits.

Nearly forty years ago one of the philosophers of medicine, J. E. R. McDonagh, a former Hunterian Professor at the Royal College of Surgeons, warned in a letter to *The Times* that research into the causes of disease was carrying differentiation 'to such an extreme degree that there is a danger it may lead ultimately to chaos', because it was based on the fallacious assumption that viruses are the cause of disease, when in fact they are a symptom of a breakdown in the body's homeostasis. McDonagh was writing at a time when penicillin was just becoming available; it was confidently expected that some similar drug would be found to deal with viruses, and he was not taken seriously. Even when it gradually began to dawn on researchers that his theory might be correct, instead of looking around for psychosocial factors which might have some responsibility for disrupting the body's protective mechanism, they carried reductionism ever further with the help of more sophisticated gadgetery. Could it be an enzyme – a catalyst capable of inducing chemical changes – that is responsible for activating a virus? Unluckily it has turned out that enzymes are legion – 800 had been found by the mid-1960s; over 2,000 by 1980 – so that their role has become more, not less, confused.

For a time it appeared as if the immunologists might break the spell. 'Almost none of modern basic research has had any direct bearing on the prevention of disease or on the improvement of medical care,' Sir Macfarlane Burnet claimed in 1971; 'the contribution of laboratory science to medicine has virtually come to an end.' But after such preliminary sparring, the alliance between them and the laboratory scientists has been patched up, and has pulled immunology further away from direct concern with patients, towards the exploration of immune processes. The virologist has become aware that he may need auto-immunity to explain why viruses which are lying around doing no harm suddenly become dangerous, or vice-versa. And the immunologist needs viruses to prove that he is respectable – organically-orientated, not one of those dubious stress merchants. As the two now work in reasonable harmony, dividing the available funds between them, research is still concentrated in the hands of people dedicated to the 'almost metaphysical pursuit', as Sir Henry Miller described it, of molecular biology, ensuring that it continues to take precedence 'over the exploring of science in the interest of patients'.

The same argument always does duty: that in the long term, the research will be in the interests of patients, because it will elucidate disease processes. But often this is no more than an excuse to justify the pursuit of knowledge for its own sake. Even where the quest is for diagnostic certainty the emphasis is on the need to identify the disease, without much importance being attached to whether or not the identification will be of any benefit to the patient. There should be good evidence, C. J. Roberts argues, 'that earlier diagnoses will lead to a substantial improvement in prognosis', but all too often it merely establishes that the patient is suffering from a disease for which there is no known treatment.

If 'we all have cancer at 48', as Sir Heneage Ogilvie claimed, but most of us have some force which keeps it in check, simply to find a way to diagnose cancer, but not actually locate it, would bring no benefit, only worry. 'Imagine the mental distress of a person who discovers he has cancer,' Levitt and Guralnick have warned, 'but does not know where it is.' The distress would not only be suffered by the patient, as Mark Ravitch, a former professor of surgery at Johns Hopkins Medical School, intimated in a disturbing story which appeared in *Esquire* in 1967. It concerned a researcher who had found such a simple test, but had also found that it did not show from what form of cancer the patient was suffering. The article was in the form of a suicide note from the researcher, explaining how he had come to realise the misery he had inflicted on patients by endless futile laser tests designed to locate their cancers, adding to their mental torment of waiting, wondering when and where the tumour would appear.

This is not, however, an attitude widely shared among researchers. In an article on the cost-effectiveness of scanners, one researcher actually claimed that, even if no treatment is available for some fatal disorder they may disclose, 'surely the unlucky patient with his incurable disease is as entitled to have his hopeless condition diagnosed by the best and least disturbing procedure, as his more fortunate counterpart who can be cured'.

Recently some signs of impatience with this attitude have become apparent, notably in the World Health Organisation. Research could now profitably be switched from the pursuit of fresh knowledge, it has urged, to finding better ways to act upon what is already known. Even some members of the lay fund-raising organisations, normally subservient, have been showing signs of restlessness. When a question was asked recently in the House of Commons about what was being done for migraine sufferers, the Miniser for Health announced that the state-funded Medical Research Council was supporting research projects 'aimed at elucidating the biochemical and genetic correlates of migraine, and the identification and localisation of lesions of the vestibular system', and although none of these projects was directly concerned with development of a method for, 'all of them have indirect relevance to', the relief of the condition. But this same message had been given in 1960 'and every subsequent year', the editor of the Migraine Association's *Newsletter* lamented, adding, reflectively, 'Ask a silly question . . .'

## Pseudo-science

Until recently the assumption has prevailed that, even if reductionist research has not come up with the hoped-for solutions, it at least has been impeccably conducted. Now, it is coming to be realised that much of it has been doubtfully scientific. In his *Certainty and Uncertainty in Biochemical Techniques* (1972) Harold Hillman warned that the need to use electron microscopes to divine what happens in the living cell has created the possibility of serious error – a view he has repeated in a recent interview, in which he is reported as saying that the techniques essential to the preparation of specimens for the microscope 'so change the original material that what is seen or measured is merely an artefact, or largely an artefact, of the processes, not representative of the living cell'. The microscopists' reply was evasive. They had to admit that what they see may be an artefact, but they claimed they can make the necessary allowances for this in their interpretations. Can they? Hillman thinks not, and he has continued to challenge them.

More straightforward research, too, of the kind commonly conducted on patients in clinical trials, is very far from being as scientific as is claimed. The whole elaborate apparatus of controlled randomised double-blind trials is hopelessly flawed.

The full story of the way these trials developed is a curious one. Following the discovery half a century ago of the way in which placebo effect could influence the results of tests of new drugs, 'blind' trials were instituted in which the patients did not know whether they were receiving the drug or a placebo. When it was realised that the hopes and expectations of doctors about a new drug also influenced results, 'double-blind' trials had to be introduced so that neither those who were handing out the pills nor those who were taking them knew which was which until the results were decoded at the end of the trials. Even this procedure, however, could be faulted. One of the groups, it was pointed out, might happen to contain more 'placebo reactors' than the other, which would bias the results. The 'cross-over' was introduced: patients on the drug were switched to the placebo, and vice-versa, halfway through the trial.

It sounded foolproof; yet by a simple but ingenious ruse its pretensions were demolished. In 1962, Heaton Ward, a consultant psychiatrist in Bristol, described a trial made of a drug following the double-blind, cross-over pattern. The final results revealed that patients on the pills in container 'A' had done significantly better than those on the pills in container 'B', both before and after the cross-over, thereby confirming the superiority of the drug to the placebo – or so it was assumed. But at this point Heaton Ward confessed that halfway through the trial, unbeknownst to anybody else, he had switched the labels on the containers. As a result the patients who had been receiving the drug in the first half of the trial, and had been pronounced significantly the better for it, were still receiving the drug during the second half; yet in that period patients in the other group, though still on the placebo, did significantly better.

Had the trial been terminated at the halfway stage (as such trials sometimes are, when the results appear conclusive), 'there would have been no reason to suspect the validity of the statistically significant results'. But such was the strength of their conviction that the pills in container 'A' were working that it then influenced the results of the pills in container 'B'. 'We are fascinated,' Heaton Ward commented, 'by this apparent demonstration of the effect of inference and suggestion in influencing the observations and reporting of the nursing staff.' And it is hardly possible to stop nurses and doctors from seeing patients, observing whether they get better, and drawing their own conclusions about which pill is the drug, and which the placebo. In any case, particular side-effects often give the clue.

Further doubt has been cast upon the value of such trials by a psychiatrist, Peter Leyburn, in a paper 'A Critical Look at Anti-depressant Drug Trials', in the *Lancet* in 1967. Leyburn was tilting at Sir Henry Miller, who had just put his case for neurological, rather than psychiatric, diagnosis and treatment of depression. He claimed that he had had successful results with anti-depressants in ninety-seven per cent of cases. 'We can be reasonably certain that the taking of appropriate tablets will speedily transform suicidally depressive behaviours to normal.' How certain? Leyburn listed the results of recent trials of anti-depressants. One trial in 1965 had shown an anti-depressant to be 'an effective therapeutic agent'; another in the same year had shown that only fifty-two per cent of patients treated with it had shown improvement, compared to sixty-four per cent in the control group, on a placebo. In a trial in 1963 desipramine had been found to be more potent and quicker-acting than imipramine, with fewer side-effects; a further trial in 1965 had led to the verdict that, on the contrary, imipramine was 'to be preferred' to desipramine in the treatment of depression. In a trial in 1963 imipramine had been shown to be significantly more effective than amitriptyline; in a further trial in 1964 amitriptyline had been shown to be significantly more effective than imipramine. In a trial in 1965 trimipramine had been rated as significantly better than imipramine; in a further trial in 1967, no significant difference could be observed between the patients who had been on trimipramine and the control group on a placebo.

Even if it were to be conceded that the results of the standard double-blind controlled tests are as reliable as can be hoped for, their value depends upon the ability of the researchers to interpret them correctly, and, to judge from recent surveys, many do not. Out of sixty-two consecutive reports of trials in the *British Medical Journal* in 1977, investigators found – and unkindly reported in the *British Medical Journal* itself – thirty-two contained statistical errors, eighteen of them 'fairly serious'. In case the Americans might assume this simply reflected British (or *BMJ*) incompetence, the report of another survey has shown that the frequency of flaws in research design in papers in the *Journal of the American Medical Association* and the *New England Journal of Medicine* (as well as in the *Lancet*) was actually higher in the late 1970s than it had been thirty years before. Yet these are journals which pride themselves on insisting upon the highest standards before even considering papers for publication.

The reliability of clinical trials has also been put in doubt by the researches of Robert Rosenthal and others, showing the extent to which experimenter effect and expectancy effect can bias results even when precautions are taken to avoid them. Yet such trials have been proliferating, and the indications are that increasing numbers of patients will be asked to submit to them, because two powerful forces are at work to preserve them in their current form.

One of the forces is illustrated by a passage in Maynard Keynes's short memoir 'Dr Melchior: a Defeated Enemy', which offers an illuminating analogy. Even after the Germans surrendered in 1918 the allied blockade was maintained, partly, Keynes thought, owing to Lord Reading's uneasiness about the British public's reaction if the decision was taken to end it, but 'more profoundly to a cause inherent in bureaucracy'. The blockade had gradually been perfected, becoming Whitehall's finest achievement. 'Its authors had grown to love it for its own sake; it included some recent improvements, which would be wasted if it came to an end; it was very complicated, and a vast organisation had established a vested interest.' The feeling among researchers today is much the same: that randomised double-blind cross-over trials are as near perfection as scientific research in this area can hope to get; if they have to be abandoned, then the whole clinical research system is jeopardised.

The other force involved is ambition. The reason for trials will often be, as Mackenzie complained sixty years ago, that for any young doctor anxious to obtain a consultant post, they are the surest way. This is still true today. The projects may be flawed in design and inadequately controlled; the statistics may be suspect, and the interpretations misguided, but 'today the chances of promotion for any doctor,' Maurice Pappworth has sourly noted, 'are directly proportional to the volume of science fiction he has vomited'.

When promotion is achieved, it often carries the additional reward of research projects funded by one or other of the drug companies, an income as a company consultant or adviser, and various perks; 'a cosy relationship', as Peter Schrag has described it, as the beneficiaries 're-view each other's grant proposals, sit on the same committees, work on the same studies, write for each other's journals, attend the same meetings, and go to the same parties'. Because the relationship between the researchers and the industry is cosy, it is impossible to gauge the precise extent of the influence which the industry wields. When a doctor or a medical journalist contemplates writing a critical piece on the industry, or even about drug-prescribing habits in the profession, there is no way of telling, should he decide to modify it or not to write it, whether or not he has had his future prospects in mind. He may not know himself.

Researchers face a similar dilemma. The pressure to get new drugs licensed can lead to bias, conscious or unconscious, in interpreting the results of trials, and in deciding what information should or should not be provided to the regulatory authorities. For example, the 1980s opened with acclaim for the benefits of sulphinpyrazone, marketed as Anturan for the treatment of patients following a heart attack; trials had shown a seventy-four per cent reduction in sudden deaths during the critical first few months. When the figures were critically re-examined, it was found that some cases of patients who had died while on the drug had been excluded from the findings for 'minor protocol variations', and some deaths had in fact been wrongly classified in a way which favoured the claims for the apparent dramatic benefit of the drug. As the manufacturers, Ciba-Geigy, had not merely paid for the trials, but had also been involved in the collection and processing of the data – successive chairmen of the trials' operations committee had actually been company employees – Thomas Chalmers, president of Mount Sinai School of Medicine, New York, has suggested that unconscious bias could have affected the conclusions.

Depressingly often, when the side-effects of a drug lead to a court action, inquiry reveals that a drug company has not made full disclosure of its research results. In a recent action taken against Richardson Merrell, the manufacturers of the anti-nausea drug Debendox, evidence was given by a former FDA pharmacologist, Mrs Frances da Costa, who had been responsible for giving clearance to the drug. Had the company forwarded to her the results of a vital piece of research which had been done on rabbits, she claimed, she would certainly have demanded fresh trials, perhaps called for the drug's suspension.

In 1975 Professor Richard Smithells, a pediatrician at Leeds University, had on behalf of the company conducted a survey of three thousand women from Liverpool and Leeds for whom Debendox had been prescribed, comparing the results with a control group of 11,500 women for whom the drug had not been prescribed. Asked by the plaintiff's attorney if Debendox had at that time been available on prescription only, Smithells replied, yes. If it had been available off-prescription, he pointed out, his survey would have been useless, because the women in the control group had not been asked whether they had bought the drug over the chemist's counter. At this point the attorney produced evidence that Debendox had, in fact, been available over the counter in Britain at the time of Smithell's survey.

Smithells was also reminded of a grant which Merrell had given to his department, along with a payment of $1,500 for himself, after he had written a letter to the company in which he had suggested, 'it occurs to me that you may wish to acknowledge in some way our present activities, perhaps the more so if it turns out the way we both expect.' The company, he had suggested, might consider endowing a research fellowship in his department at Leeds University. 'I would not like you to think that in writing at this time I am threatening not to publish,' he had written. 'But I should appreciate any gesture Merrell felt inclined to make.' Merrell's gesture was $26,000. 'It is always good,' a company spokesman told the *Observer*, 'to have a friendly relationship with people like Professor Smithells.' When contacted by the *Observer*, Smithells declined to comment.

## The Regulatory Agencies

Some of these defects could easily be remedied if the regulatory agencies, the FDA and the Committee on Safety of Medicines, had government backing and the strength of purpose to insist upon radical changes. But neither of them wants to become involved in a fight with the profession – or, for that matter, with the industry. The Committee, in particular, has leant over backwards to reassure the drug firms that they are respected for what they have done. Its first chairman, Sir Derrick Dunlop, was an impassioned devotee of drug therapy; in his foreword to the *Textbook of Adverse Drug Reactions*, published in 1977, he claimed that, although in the early part of the century increased longevity was largely the result of improved hygiene, housing and nutrition, 'during the last 30 or 40 years it has been mostly due to modern medicines', evidently unaware that the trend towards increased longevity ceased thirty years ago, at the height of the 'wonder-drug' era, and began to go into reverse. Dunlop even accepted a post with a drug company on his retirement, in spite of the scandal a few years earlier, when a director of the FDA, with the reputation of being well-disposed to the industry, had made a similar move.

Since Dunlop's retirement the Committee's attitude has pleased the industry less. But most of the criticism of its ways still comes from those who feel that it is not doing enough to ensure the safety of new drugs – or to get them off the market quickly when, like Eraldin, they are found to be unsafe after they have been licensed. The FDA's record has been conspicuously better, and for that reason it has come under much more sustained attack from the industry. On balance, the industry in Britain is inclined to feel that the Committee is the lesser of two evils: if things go wrong with a licensed drug, its manufacturer can shelter behind the Committee's decision to award the licence. The main propaganda line has consequently been designed to impress on governments the mounting expense of finding, testing and marketing new drugs, in the hope that at least this will stop them listening to those critics who call for stricter – and more expensive – regulations: a shrewd policy, as with each passing year governments become more anxious not to increase the taxpayer's load, if they can help it.

## The Medical Journals

All these issues ought to be fully investigated, reported and discussed in the medical journals. But editors are caught in a journalistic version of the double-bind. On the one hand, to maintain their credibility they must appear to maintain their detachment, criticising where criticism is due. On the other, they are well aware of their dependence upon the pharmaceutical industry, without whose direct and (through advertisements) indirect support few of the scores of journals would survive, at least in their present form.

An unwritten and largely unspoken concordat had evolved whereby journals such as those of the American and British Medical Associations will report, say, adverse drug reactions, and give space from time to time to doctors complaining about promotional excesses (an Edinburgh doctor wrote in 1977 to complain that he had received some jumping beans with a company's promotional material, along with the comment, 'We can't promise to make your patients jump but your claudicants will be able to walk further'; surely, he suggested, the time had come 'to call a halt to such nonsense'). But the journals are careful to avoid investigations, designed to expose commercial skulduggery, of the kind which the *Sunday Times* undertook into the thalidomide affair. Investigative journalism is left to the mass media.

The double-bind leads inevitably to double-think. Periodically the *British Medical Journal* carries reports deploring the consequences of the over-prescribing and mis-prescribing of drugs, particularly of psycho-active drugs, sedatives, tranquillisers and anti-depressants, but also of antibiotics and steroids. If the lay media take up this cause, however, the *BMJ*'s attitude is of magisterial impatience, often coupled with praise for the pharmaceutical industry and insistence that there is no call for alarm. 'Recently the Cassandras of the national press have turned their attention towards various hazards,' the *BMJ* complained in 1977. The picture, it insisted, was less serious than had been alleged: 'While it is important to remain vigilant, the problem of drug-related deaths has yet to become a public health issue, and should be viewed in the light of the mortality arising in other types of human endeavour.'

A similar line is often taken when doctors support the campaign against the proliferation of 'me-too' drugs. Doctors who make this sort of criticism 'have no experience of and no comprehension of the world of commercial realities', Tony Smith, the deputy editor of the *BMJ*, has argued. 'The top 20 or 30 pharmaceutical companies in the world – the major innovators – can stay in business only so long as they remain profitable.' Recently the *BMJ* has even lent editorial support to the industry's contention that safety regulations, by pushing up the cost of new drugs and delaying their appearance on the market, have been depriving patients of useful and perhaps life-saving treatment. 'Drug lag bad: drug lack worse', an editorial has sloganised, arguing that the caution displayed by the FDA has meant that 'valuable drugs have been partially or wholly denied to the American people for long periods', and neglecting to mention that the American people had also been denied thalidomide, practolol, clioquinol and other disastrous drugs inflicted on patients elsewhere.

## Specialisation

The medical profession cannot be expected to regulate itself for the benefit of the community, and it has largely lost the power to do so, because it has conceded so much autonomy to specialists.

A warning of the dangers of increasing specialisation was given shortly after the First World War by Sir James Mackenzie. Mackenzie had done what was becoming increasingly hard to do: starting as a general practitioner he had become a consultant at the London Hospital, a Fellow of the Royal Society, and by 1919 he was the doyen of the profession in Britain. In *The Future of Medicine* he described what he regarded as the defects of medicine, and predicted with uncanny accuracy what would happen if they were not corrected; chief among them was specialism. 'I am convinced,' he wrote, 'that the conception of specialism today is a wrong one.' Helpful though it had been in some ways, 'instead of enlightening, it tends to darken understanding in a cloud of detail'.

The stock excuse for specialisation had been that it had become essential because the discoveries of medical scientists had rendered diagnosis and treatment too complex and recondite for any doctor to master in their entirety. What this meant in practice, Mackenzie knew, was that the specialist, instead of concentrating on the relatively simple, fundamental forces at work to create disease, became absorbed in the study of the infinitely varied *manifestations* of disease: 'What is now called progress is but the recognition of an additional number of these manifestations, and an ever-increasing difficulty in comprehending their significance.' The specialist was an expert in the detection of disease as soon as it had advanced far enough to present tell-tale indications, but this did not help to detect it before it had begun to do damage. He should be asking himself what had produced the indications. Failure to do so, Mackenzie feared, actually retarded clinical progress; too often the specialist was content with his diagnostic triumphs, and 'the glamour of his successes blinds him and the public'.

In 'The Physician as Naturalist', an address given twelve years later to the Cambridge University Medical Society, John Ryle took up the theme. 'I cannot but feel,' he observed, 'that of late, in the process of pursuing the small and special truths which relate to the causes and more intimate processes of disease, we have as a profession been falling into the error of neglecting the large and central truths which concern the nature of disease itself.' Four years later, in 1935, Alexis Carrel delivered a frontal attack on what he realised was a disastrous trend. He had earlier won a Nobel prize for physiology, but his *Man the Unknown*

291

was a plea for a new philosophy of medicine which would leave a place for psychological and even psychic forces. Specialisation, he warned, was a move in the wrong direction. 'Medicine has separated the sick human being into small fragments and each fragment has its specialist', and by the very fact of concentrating attention on one small part of the body, the specialist was ensuring that his knowledge of the rest would be so rudimentary that he would be 'incapable of thoroughly understanding even that part in which he specialises.'

Such warnings went unheeded, and have continued to go unheeded. By the 1970s only one doctor in five in the United States described himself as a general practitioner; the old-style family doctor 'who would listen to grandad's cough, check baby's rash and perhaps offer a little family counselling, all in one home visit,' the Ehrenreichs lamented in *The American Health Empire*, was 'vanishing along with memories of gramophones and Model T Fords'. In the year 1970 the American Medical Association gave formal recognition to no less than twenty-nine new specialties, making sixty-three in all.

In Britain the process was a little slower, partly because general practice was established as an integral part of the National Health Service. But the price which had to be paid was the severance of GPs' links with hospitals, where specialism took over. 'We are now in the ridiculous position,' Sir Heneage Ogilvie complained in 1953, 'where a well-trained and competent doctor is forced to refer his patient to a man of lesser ability but marked with the correct rubber stamp, in order that he may carry out treatment that he himself could do very much better.' In spite of the fact that the Department of Health, which has to authorise the creation of new specialist consultant posts, has often been loath to do so on grounds of expense, they have proliferated. 'There are currently 47 hospital clinical specialties,' the report of the Royal Commission on the National Health Service noted in 1979, '11 of them introduced in the last ten years.'

In the process, the general physician has been gradually squeezed out of his once leading role in hospitals, becoming 'an endangered species', as Professor D. N. S. Kerr of the University of Newcastle has put it. Forty years ago, he recalls, 'Newcastle boasted eight general physicians and one dermatologist.' Today 'it has seven cardiologists, seven neurologists, seven dermatologists, five endocrinologists, five haematologists etcetera etcetera'. The only cases which are likely to be referred to a general physician are those which the GP cannot categorise (or, if he can, feels it would be tactful to leave that responsibility to somebody else; other doctors' wives, for example, might resent being referred to a psychiatrist or a venereologist).

Specialisation has had all the unwelcome effects which its critics predicted, along with others they did not foresee. As Mackenzie and Ryle warned, medicine has concentrated upon the detection and treatment of individual diseases, rather than upon acquiring a better understanding of disease in order to prevent it; as Carrel warned, specialists have become progressively more blinkered. Even the Royal Commission on the National Health Service, although careful not to offend professional susceptibilities, noted in its 1979 report that when a specialty is created, 'those in the specialty become reluctant to perform non-specialised activities, while those who had previously cared for the kind of patients which the specialty has been promoted to serve may no longer see it as their responsibility to do so', and although the division and subdivision of specialties encourages expertise, 'It involves loss of flexibility in the manning of the service and tends to result in a fragmentation of patient care.'

The dangerous consequences of specialisation are most apparent in connection with patients who, as frequently happens, are obviously ill, but with no immediately recognisable cause. They find themselves shunted from specialist to specialist, with the psychiatrist at the end of the line. Rival specialists may even fight over patients; for instance, when gastro-enterologists treating stomach ulcers with cimetidine battle with surgeons who feel that the knife is more effective.

There have also been many cases reported of what has come to be known as 'syndrome shift', where the treatment by one specialist is apparently successful, and is registered in the records as such, but where the patient soon turns up with a different illness. Michael Balint used to cite the case of one patient who had collected over thirty specialists' reports and remained ill, though 'the surgeon who operated on his anal fissure, the orthopedist in charge of his crushed vertebrae, or the neurologist diagnosing his jerks, had closed his case as finally dealt with, possibly even successfully treated'.

In the long-term, too, another version of syndrome shift has significant implications for – or, rather, against – specialisation. 'In a restless and fretful age, which has largely lost the old simplicities of diet', Ryle recommended in 1932 that the best form of protection from a disease prevalent in civilisation 'is to furnish, as opportunity arises, sensible instructions to the community (and particularly to such families or individuals as manifest a constitutional or occupational predisposition to the disease) with regard to the evils of missed and bolted meals, of excessive smoking, and of the prevalent habit of attempting to combine the process of digestion with anxiety and affairs'. The disease in question was duodenal ulcer. It has often been observed that the incidence of

293

duodenal ulcers, until the 1950s regarded as *the* occupational hazard of the business executive, has declined, while that of heart attacks, which have now taken over in that capacity, has increased. If, as seems likely, they share a common etiology and common risk factors, to treat them as two wholly distinct disease entities, as specialists do, is illogical.

Perhaps the most serious of all the defects of specialisation, in view of the growing recognition of the importance of the psychosocial component in illness, is that the narrower the specialty's range, the more it tends to remove its doctors from diagnosing and treating their patients as people, taking into account their jobs, marriages, living conditions, and stress factors in general. 'All doctors, whatever their specialty,' a British Medical Association planning report urged in 1970, 'should possess some knowledge of the ways in which personality and social factors influence the response of their patients to disease and to its treatment and prevention.' But the BMA has power only to issue exhortations, and the General Medical Council, though in theory it has the power, is itself dominated by specialists. And as the medical profession is constituted, as soon as a specialty receives recognition and consultant status, it also acquires a considerable measure of autonomy, which its members are determined to preserve.

This in itself has unfortunate effects because, paradoxically, the greater the autonomy, the greater the tendency towards empire building. As resources within a hospital are limited, the specialty with the strongest claims – professional Chairs, research laboratories, wards, equipment and so on – is most likely to get its way.

'A diseased state of an organism, a society or a culture,' Arthur Koestler observed in *The Sleepwalkers*, 'is characterised by a weakening of the integrative controls and the tendency of its parts to behave in an independent and self-assertive manner, ignoring the superior interest of the whole, or trying to impose their own laws upon it.' The extent to which specialists have ignored the 'superior interest of the whole' was one of Carlson's themes in *The End of Medicine*. Inexorably, he pointed out, specialisation leads to a concentration of medical manpower and resources in affluent urban areas, because the practitioners need to work 'where the population is concentrated, to ensure a sufficient number of patients for their services'.

Inexorably, too, they draw in a retinue of specialised nurses, technicians and camp followers – Illich likened them to medieval fiefdoms with 'groups of medical pages, ushers, footmen and squires'. This in turn stimulates the demand for equipment and gadgetry, so that the specialist can show that he is impressively up-to-date. 'The major – and most expensive – part of medical technology as applied today,' Halfdan

Mahler of WHO has complained, 'appears to be far more for the satisfaction of the health professions than for the benefit of the consumers of health care.' According to a report by the US Office of Technology Assessment, published in 1980, the relative autonomy the medical profession has enjoyed, leaving it with the responsibility 'for regulating its own members and their use of technology', has simply meant that the technology has *not* been regulated. It has been developed and used with little attempt to assess either its effectiveness or its safety, such evidence as has been collected about it being fragmentary and sometimes contradictory.

When expensive equipment is installed, the natural tendency is to use it, particularly gadgets of the type designed for screening, because negative results can be registered as a plus both for the patient, who will be shown not to have any of a range of possible diseases, and for the doctor, who thereby eliminates as many suspects as possible. Eoin O'Brien, a consultant physician in Dublin, has given a disturbing account of the tests applied in his hospital to a lady in her seventies – in general healthy, but with mild breathlessness and palpitations – when she was admitted: 'urinalysis, urine microscopy, urine culture and sensitivity, hemoglobin, Erythrocyte sedimentation rate, blood film, white cell count and differential, serum B12 and folate, blood urea, serum creatinine, electrolytes, proteins, calcium and enzymes, alkaline phosphatase, chest X-ray, cardiac screening and echocardiography, and finally an electrocardiogram'. The excuses invariably given for conducting so many disparate tests are that it is wiser to investigate than to miss a diagnosis, because the reputation of individuals and hospitals depends on not making mistakes. But as a result, 'our clinical skills are atrophying,' O'Brien laments. 'We are not lacking in clinical ability; it's just that we do not happen to have common sense any more.'

He might have added that for every patient whose prospects are improved by the results of such tests, scores have to suffer varying degrees of discomfort and pain for a diagnosis that a good clinician could have made without them.

Every new test, too, establishes a vested interest among those concerned: the suppliers of the equipment or the drug; the laboratory workers; the pathologists; even, in many countries, the paramedical who carries out the test on the specialist's behalf. Naturally all concerned, when the empire has been established, are determined to maintain it, come what may. What can result is a new discipline, or the revival of an old one, threatening to make a previously established therapy obsolete. Professor Kerr of Newcastle has described what can happen in these circumstances. Because for many years radiotherapy was the chief non-surgical treatment for cancer, radiotherapists 'acquired large institutes, wards, clinics, staffs and a pattern of referral which gave them effective control'. But in the 1970s, chemotherapy became the growth area, and the indications are that in the 1980s it may be immunotherapy. These specialties call for a very different form of training. Obviously what is needed, Kerr argues, is a short course of radiotherapy for specialists who are going to concentrate on chemotherapy or immunotherapy. But as things stand, to qualify as radiotherapists they must start from scratch on the protracted course of training required, which equips them 'superbly for the medicine of ten years ago'.

The brutal fact is that specialists, having achieved such a measure of autonomy, are not voluntarily going to relinquish their empires. As McKeown has pointed out, they have no incentive to challenge the system in Britain; and they have still less to do so in America, where it has made them rich beyond their wildest dreams of avarice. The 1948 Act set a limit on British specialists' ability to exploit their status too greedily: even a millionaire, if he feels he is being rooked, may prefer to have treatment on the NHS. But in the United States the specialists have grabbed their opportunity to become the wealthiest of all the professions.

In 1937 the yearbook of the graduation class at Harvard Medical School included the results of the questionnaire which had been sent to alumni who had graduated ten, twenty and thirty years before. Sixty per cent replied, and the findings revealed, among other things, that the average income of all three, taken together, was between $5,000 and $10,000 a year. Coming across the yearbook forty years later, Lewis Thomas – one of the class of '37 – found that many of the comments in the section of the questionnaire left for 'remarks' were to the effect that practising medicine was not a way to make money. 'Forty-one years ago, that was,' Thomas sardonically comments. Now, money-making has become the name of the game.

## Medical Education

The specialists control not only their own affairs and their patients' treatment but also the education of medical students; this perpetuates the mechanist fallacy and all that stems from it. The more prestige a specialty holds, the higher the proportion of a student's time it can command. Around the foot of the ladder are psychiatry, pharmacology – in spite of the obvious importance of correctly prescribing drugs – and dermatology ('to most of us dermatology forms an embarrassing hiatus in our medical education,' a newly-qualified doctor has recently recalled; 'our knowledge is often limited to a few jumbled facts hastily learned on the eve of the final MB examination'). At the top of the ladder, the specialties of leading surgeons and physicians jostle for supremacy.

Inevitably the main emphasis is on hospital medicine. Although variations are found from school to school and from country to country 'there is no serious dispute about the basic concepts', McKeown insists; 'medicine is thought to be concerned with intervention in disease processes, mainly by investigation and treatment of established disease'. As the intervention is by physical, chemical and biological methods, the basic sciences are assumed to be physics, chemistry and biology – a preoccupation 'which leads away from consideration of the underlying causes of disease whose control is the essential basis of health'.

Medical schools have recently been persuaded to pay some attention to social science, but as it is even lower on the ladder than psychiatry, it has to be squeezed in whenever time can be found, competing with new medical specialties, each of which feels it has a more pressing claim on the student's attention. Not merely is he subjected to a course which is 'a ferocious assault upon his memory and stamina', Keith Norcross, an orthopedic surgeon in Birmingham, has complained; its content is determined less by the student's needs than 'by the power-politics and local interests within the medical school', and the same power-politics and local interests have extended their control by insisting upon ever-longer postgraduate courses. Each specialty, flaunting its 'science', forms a new college and incorporates established practitioners. 'It then invents an examination of contrived difficulty, and sets up an artificial training course.'

As research expands each specialty, old or new, has more information to absorb and to teach. To the names of bones and muscles to be learned, students now have to add the names of viruses and of the swarm of new microbiological entities. Each fresh discovery has to be provided with a name, and it has become even more difficult with, say, acids to

297

think up names which give some indication of the content. Where once it was possible to use simple terms like 'uric' there are now countless variants, such as 'hydroxyanthranilic' or 'alphaketobetamethyl'. Even if the specialist in charge of a department would prefer his students to learn about illness at the hospital bedside he cannot risk telling them that they need not worry their heads about the latest research findings, in case they should later be confronted with examination questions about them.

Writers of textbooks are under the same compulsion. 'If an author states in his preface that his book is intended for students,' R. S. Illingworth, Emeritus Professor of Child Health at the University of Sheffield, has observed, 'a good test of its suitability is a count of the number of conditions indexed which you have never seen after many years of experience.' One such textbook listed no fewer than 450 conditions which he had never encountered, and another included 'alcopara, lactodectus mactans, saccharopinuria, borreliosis, cimicocis, arabino-sylcytosine, betamercaptolactate cysteine disulfiduria, amylo 1,4 : 1,6 transglucosidase deficiency, the syndromes of Calcagno, Ganser, Gardner, Luder-Sheldon, Lucey-Driscott, Behr, Rothmund Thomson, and Ukari, adynamia episodia hereditaria of Gamstorf, pulicosis, Hailey Hailey disease, Kuf's disease, Batten Mayou's disease, Sandhof disease, Habberman's disease, Panner's disease and reduviid bugs. And the list carefully distinguished forminoglutamicaciduria types A and B.' Yet loss of appetite, nappy rash, circumcision, head-banging, or acute abdominal pain were not mentioned. As for the child who will not go to sleep, ten pediatric textbooks devote just four out of 12,000 pages to the problem, while devoting 'twenty-eight pages to mucopolysaccharidoses'.

The weirdest feature of medical education has been the way in which it has ignored the general disorders which a GP spends most of his time trying to treat. When the medical profession was formally established in Britain in 1858 its main objective was to bring some order into the prevailing chaos of medical schools, in order to provide standardised teaching throughout Britain. As the physicians and surgeons themselves controlled teaching in universities and hospitals, they simply continued to teach hospital medicine, making no provision for instructing intending GPs in their future work. It was consequently possible for a newly-qualified doctor to 'put up his plate' and start work as a GP, never having seen patients suffering from the everyday disorders he would be called upon to treat.

'I was not long engaged in my new sphere,' Sir James Mackenzie remarked in the *Future of Medicine*, recalling his entry into general practice in the 1880s, 'when I realised that I was unable to recognise the ailments in the great majority of my patients. They presented aspects of disease with which I was unacquainted.' Looking back, he had no doubt where the responsibility lay: with the Royal College of Physicians, which had been using its control over patronage not merely to make it impossible for medical students to learn about the ailments encountered in general practice, but also to ensure that anybody who did what Mackenzie had done, and went into general practice, could never be appointed to a teaching post. In addition they encouraged the young aspirant to such a post either to undertake research – 'the surest way of attaining his object' – or to take up an academic appointment. 'But one method he must not pursue – he must not attempt to qualify himself efficiently for such a post by the experience of general practice,' because the College 'practically requires of its members that while they may pursue almost any of the branches into which medicine is split up, they must not practise medicine in the only way by which a wide outlook may be obtained, and so render themselves fit and capable to become really effective teachers'.

Barely credible though it may sound, it was not until the 1970s that this system was finally broken and general practice became part of the curriculum. In the intervening period most teaching hospitals had continued to behave in much the same way as the army had, between the wars, with its devotion to cavalry training. Even now, most of the training which a prospective GP does in the field is added on after his teachers have finished with him in hospitals, rather than substituted for his often largely irrelevant hospital studies: partly because the specialists do not care to allow established teaching posts to slip from their grasp; partly because they need newly-qualified doctors to do the hospital donkey-work.

This has not escaped criticism. Individual doctors, some of them eminent, have echoed Mackenzie's comments, and a succession of committees of inquiry, including a Royal Commission, have recommended reforms designed to bring in a better-balanced curriculum. Yet the imbalance has increased because specialists continue to control the medical schools and to run them in their own interest.

Specialists' own interest does not merely dictate what is taught, and who qualifies. As specialists conduct the entry examinations, they naturally have promising specialist material in mind in making their choices, and this, in turn, compels schools to allow pupils who want to become medical students to specialise. That 'the influence of the modern medical school on liberal arts education in this country over the last decade has been baleful and malign, nothing less' sounds as if it might have been written by Illich; in fact the writer is Lewis Thomas. He blames admission policies which favour these 'premed' students, who have already taken pre-medical courses similar to the ones given to medical students after entry. As a result the students never acquire knowledge of 'how human beings have always lived out their lives', through acquaintance with the liberal arts.

The kind of boy or girl who is good at passing the examinations required for entry into medical schools is not necessarily the kind who is going to make a good doctor, particularly as a GP. The quality a GP needs today, the Headmaster of Greshams' School has observed in a letter to the *British Medical Journal*, is chiefly 'the ability to hear other people's negative emotions, without losing his kindliness, balance, sensitivity and judgment in the face of suffering'; if this is the case, 'why are GPs now recruited almost exclusively from those who gain their top A-level Grades in science'? And the entry examinations virtually decide who will become doctors. It is a common illusion, Horrobin has noted, that individuals 'are admitted to the medical profession at the time they receive their M.D. degree or its equivalent'; for the great majority, qualification is assured from the moment they are accepted as medical students. 'Frankly, it's a conspiracy against the public', Hugh Dudley claims. 'The finals are, except for the fewer than five per cent who are sacrificed to an ill-defined "standard", nothing more than the stamp of approval on what has gone before in the way of education and training.'

So manifestly absurd is the system, as well as being unfair by loading entry into the profession in favour of the children of well-to-do parents, that a few governments have felt compelled to pluck up their courage and intervene. In Germany a form of lottery has been introduced for selection purposes, and in Sweden the rule has recently been made that four out of five entrants should be mature students, with five years' experience of other work since leaving school. But the Swedes have unwisely left the curriculum in medical hands. By the time men and women have had five years' experience of other work they are apt to have lost the capacity to pass examinations of the kind to which medical students are subjected, and many of them fail to qualify. Any attempt at intervention along these lines would be unlikely to be contemplated, let alone introduced, in Britain or the United States. Tentative efforts are, admittedly, being made to attract a wider range of schoolboys. Some British universities have introduced a quota system designed to ensure that a proportion of the intake is from arts students, but this can make only a minor impact, so long as the medical training continues along traditional brain-washing lines.

It is unusual to meet a doctor who looks back on his training with approval. The old medical school is remembered with nostalgia, as are individual teachers, but not the curriculum. The most common complaint is that students are stuffed full of largely useless facts. 'It is obvious to anyone who can see beyond the end of his nose that no matter how complete and valid are the facts taught in a medical school,' Horrobin points out, those facts will not merely soon be partly forgotten; they will also 'cease to be facts, within a very short time, and within twenty years of graduation will be of little value'.

Such 'reforms' as have been introduced have led to no appreciable improvement, as Sir George Pickering, the former Regius Professor of Medicine at Oxford, discovered on a tour of inspection of British medical schools made on behalf of the Nuffield Provincial Hospitals Trust. Several, he knew, had been introduced in the 1960s and early 1970s: 'integration, topic teaching, the introduction of the behavioural and social sciences, and above all continuous assessment'. All they had done was provide some linkage between the teaching of the specialties.

With only two schools as possible exceptions, 'the students told us they were bored and frustrated, that they were treated as data banks, that they were there to learn what they were taught so that they could produce it for the next multiple-choice question paper.' They had entered their medical studies 'full of intelligence, energy and enthusiasm'; at the end they had tended to come out 'rather limp, and with minds that were certainly not more inquiring and more critical than they took with them on entry'.

Pickering had no doubt where to put the blame: on the growth of specialisation. The same faults had been criticised, he recalled, thirty years before, when he had been secretary to a Royal College of Physicians' committee which had examined medical education: and then, there had been only fourteen specialist departments, each under its professor, in the teaching hospitals. In the interim that figure had more than doubled, and each new professor 'feels it his duty to ensure that the student is properly instructed; that is to say, that he knows a large body of fact and the prevailing dogma'. None of the imcumbent professors, however, cares to give up any of his department's teaching time, so that each newcomer has to obtain his by adding it on to the already overloaded syllabus. At one medical school the new professors of geriatrics and of general practice both boasted to Pickering that they had managed to secure additional hours on top of the students' normal lecture time: as a result of continued accessions of this kind, coupled with established departments refusing to relinquish their *droit de seigneur*, the number of lectures had continued to increase until in one case, he found, at 'a famous school', they took up as much as thirty-six hours a week. As no career now attracts students of a higher academic standard 'it seems rather tragic,' Pickering concluded, 'that in their most impressionable years they are being pressed through a sort of sausage machine, designed to eliminate the worst doctors but incidentally probably also the best.'

Naturally each critic of the curriculum has his pet notions of how it ought to be changed, but two common themes emerge. One is the need for a greater emphasis on the psychosocial aspects of medicine. Students 'need not have more than a passing acquaintance with the specialties, except for midwifery, pediatrics and dermatology', Sir Heneage Ogilvie suggested in 1953, but they must be taught far more about the psychology of the normal, 'about industrial diseases, about minor maladies, about sex relationships, family planning and the day-to-day adjustments of married life'. 'Far too little attention has generally been paid hitherto to the study of the behavioural sciences (including psychology) and their application to medical care,' the Royal Commission on Medical Education noted in its 1968 report.

The second theme is that students should be encouraged to learn for themselves, rather than be required to listen to endless lectures, and to read an ever-increasing number of set books. 'It is not so much knowledge as the power to utilise knowledge that the student must acquire,' an editorial in the Lancet proclaimed in 1961. 'The rigid insistence on passage of all students through all departments should cease.' Students learn much, if not most, of their medicine despite their teachers, Owen Wade has argued. 'Our aim should be to reduce our teaching to a minimum and encourage and help our students to learn for themselves.' What is required, therefore, is a curriculum which gives the student 'a grounding in medical sciences and the basic skills of history-taking and clinical examination, develops the correct attitudes to patients and the community and its health problems, and teaches him how to continue to learn'. The major aim of a medical school in Horrobin's view should be to equip the student to learn how to select and process the mass of information available to him as a doctor, but as little or no attempt is made to provide this kind of training, 'the end result is a doctor whose education has most effectively atrophied the only characteristics which would enable him to remain competent throughout a lifetime'.

When it comes to suggesting ways to implement such ideas, however, the critics are at a loss, because the specialties enjoy a sufficient measure of autonomy to block reform. A typical example occurred a few years ago at Liverpool, when the students persuaded the authorities to reduce an anatomy course from two terms to one. The following year's students found that the actual course, and the lectures, had not been shortened;

they had merely been compressed into a single term. In theory a strong-minded dean of a teaching hospital could bang the specialists' heads together until they agreed to radical changes; in practice, few deans have the authority, let alone the power, particularly since the whole system receives backing from the top – as, for example, from Sir Douglas Black, President of the Royal College of Physicians of London.

In a recent lecture Black has argued for a strong medical profession as a counterweight to government power, and in elegant style has defended medical education from its critics, in particular McKeown. 'I believe his criticisms fail to take account of the changes over the past twenty years,' Black states. 'There must be few medical schools in this country which do not have pre-clinical courses in the behavioural sciences, and, in the clinical period, courses given by departments of social medicine, which should stress social and environmental determinants of health and disease and epidemiological approach.' But this is to ignore Pickering's observation that such courses, whatever they *should* be doing, have proved ineffective. And Black goes on to give the game away by saying that his 'extensive contacts with clinical teachers' encouraged him to rebut the critics. Naturally clinical teachers are satisfied with their status (even if not with their incomes). They are the last people to advocate reform.

If Black had spent more of his time listening to clinical *students*, he would have formed a very different impression. 'Like many others, I entered medical school full of humanitarian ideals,' Huw Morgan has recalled in *World Medicine*. 'I found, however, that a relentless war of attrition was waged against those noble concepts as the course progessed.' Even the 'reform' of 'continuous assessment' of students' work, rather than reliance on examination results at the end of their training, well intentioned though it was, had been exploited by specialists in order to exact still greater compliance and conformity.

Glyn Bennet, a psychiatrist in the Department of Public Health in Bristol, has made the same point in a disturbing chapter in his book, *Patients and their Doctors*. The doctors 'expect to be treated as something special. They expect to be able to park their cars where they will, or to have a telephone installed promptly'. And often the authoritarian attitude is displayed to students during the ward round. Bennet recalls that 'the greatest clinical neurologist of his day did not speak to his patients "on principle"; he saw himself as providing a service to the general practitioner, that was all'.

The consultant who discusses with his students the illnesses of his patients by their bedsides, as if the patients have no feelings, is also still a common institution. After Francis Chichester was admitted to a London hospital following an X-ray that had disclosed that he had cancer, he had not been told of the diagnosis when one of the leading British heart and lung surgeons arrived at his bedside, attended by a dozen students. 'This,' he told them, 'is a typical case of advanced carcinoma.' He proceeded to prod Chichester, and then to pick up his fingers, as if to show something in his fingernails, 'but flung them aside'. 'I came away feeling degraded, defiled and deeply depressed,' Chichester recalled. Sadly, such hospital bullies are by no means an extinct species.

The whole system of training medical students in hospitals, it is becoming clear, is an anachronism. They are accidents of history, as Donald Gould – a doctor who, as a medical journalist, has tirelessly campaigned against obscurantism in his profession, has urged in the *New Scientist*. The medical student should spend most of his time 'with family doctors, community physicians, high-street chemists, district nurses, and others concerned with the daily management of health and disease – *health* and disease'. It is absurd that the vocational part of a doctor's training, in which he actually learns how to deliver medical care, should not begin until after he has qualified: 'If we want to start *educating* our future doctors, then the sooner we get rid of all our medical schools, the better.'

## Medical Hubris

Until the close of the 1960s there seemed no reason for the medical profession to fear government intervention (except over remuneration). It stood too high in the public's esteem. But in 1970 a survey of its structure and management appeared which revealed just how inadequately it was in fact fulfilling its obligations: Professor Elliot Freidson's *Profession of Medicine*, winner of the Sorokin Award, given by the American Sociological Association to the author of a publication which has 'contributed in outstanding degree to the progress of sociology'.

Professions, Freidson observed, justify their autonomy on three main grounds: first, 'that there is such an unusual degree of skill and knowledge involved in professional work that non-professionals are not equipped to evaluate or regulate it'; second, that as professionals are responsible people, 'they may be trusted to work conscientiously without supervision'; and third, that the profession itself 'may be trusted to undertake the proper regulatory action on those rare occasions when an individual does not perform his work competently or ethically'. Surveying the evidence of the way the medical profession actually works, however, he found that its autonomy could not be justified on any of these counts.

Medicine's position today is akin to that of state religions yesterday, Freidson noted. 'It has an officially approved monopoly of the right to define health and illness and to treat illness.' It believes that it is fulfilling its obligations in return, but it is doing nothing of the kind. It is in fact 'rather ignorant of the actual behaviour of its members, and not equipped either to evaluate it or to regulate it'. The quality of its services is maintained only by setting minimum standards for qualification: 'There is virtually no other systematic method used to regulate performance, and the laying down of a qualifying standard is itself neither an active nor continuing method of regulation.' The 'profession' is in fact a trade union. It may be needed for the same reasons as are trade unions, but it is really no more 'professional' than they are; 'Indeed, so far as the terms of work go, professions differ from trade unions only in their sanctimoniousness.' By allowing and encouraging self-sufficiency, Freidson concluded, professional autonomy has bred self-deception and an attitude to its patients 'at best patronising and at worst contemptuous', leading it 'so to distinguish its own virtues from those outside as to be unable to even perceive the need for, let alone undertake, the self-regulation it promises'.

That this self-regulation is inadequately carried out in Britain, too, has long disturbed the more thoughtful members of the profession.

Until recently the General Medical Council's disciplinary committee came down heavily on any doctor found guilty of having sex with one of his patients, while declining to concern itself with doctors who were unfit to continue to practise by reason, say, of drug addiction or alcoholism. Suggestions that patients ought to be given some protection from such doctors were met with the British Medical Association's argument that this would infringe its members' legal rights. Similarly, accusations by junior hospital doctors that consultants were ducking their obligations – 'It is quite possible,' a report to the Commons Select Committee on medical education and manpower claimed in 1980, 'for a patient to be admitted to hospital, treated, operated upon and sometimes even discharged without ever having been seen by a member of the consultant staff' – have been met by bland evasions.

Such criticisms would ordinarily not have disturbed the profession so long as it felt secure in the public's estimation. But in the 1970s its popularity in the United States began to dwindle, partly because Freidson was followed by other critics, notably Illich and Carlson, but chiefly because doctors began making more money than was good for their image, provoking lawyers to find ways to level the professional score with the help of malpractice suits, which served to alert the public to the profession's deficiencies. There was also a growing sense that patients were being sacrificed to the demands of technology, with its proliferation of expensive and unwelcome tests, and of research projects. 'When patients begin to think that the doctor may be using the investigations that they themselves are being asked or made to suffer primarily for his own research,' Bernard Towers warned in 1971, 'or to those of the institute, or department or university or country to which he belongs, then resentment can become profound.'

In Britain disenchantment with the medical profession took longer to develop; doctors' earnings in the NHS could not match those in other countries, and technology was less in evidence. British patients, Towers observed, 'are very tolerant on the whole, and they have a fund of goodwill towards the medical profession'. He warned, however, that this could easily change 'if techniques are employed without any evident benefit to the subject (or should it be object?) which either cause pain, or are unduly time-consuming, or carry with them any more than the minimal risk associated with every interference with biological processes'. When during the 1970s many more such techniques were introduced, the British public reacted as Towers had predicted. In particular, patients became increasingly irritated by adverse reactions to drugs which proved ineffective, and patients who became hooked on tranquillisers and other psychoative drugs often blamed not themselves but the doctors who prescribed them. In the early 1970s opinion polls had shown that the British general practitioner stood high in the public's estimation; in 1980 a market research group found that the number of patients who trusted their GP had dropped from 52 per cent to 39 per cent in a single year.

During 1980 there was also a marked shift in the attitude of the British media to the medical profession. A survey of the media by the Guy's Hospital Unit for the Study of Health Policy in 1977 showed that the national newspapers, television and radio adhered to 'a single predominant framework' in relation to medicine, founded on the belief that 'the aims and practices of modern scientific medicine represent "excellence" in health care and are central to progress in health', and that 'the production and consumption of health services are the principal means of promoting better health' – more hospitals, say, being regarded as a good thing. The media, in other words, still accepted the medical profession's line. Three years later the change was striking. Newspapers and popular magazines were full of criticism of the profession (and of praise for alternative therapies, such as acupuncture); there was the fight between the BBC and the profession over the Panorama programme claiming that patients were being pronounced dead, so that their organs could be used for transplants without adequate precautions; and Ian Kennedy's Reith Lectures, following lines similar to those taken in the US earlier by Freidson and Carlson, were sharply critical of the profession.

This hostility has made it increasingly difficult for the profession to rely on ignoring attacks made upon it, as it has tended to do in the past. Illich's *Medical Nemesis*, for example, attracted some reviews but no attempt at rebuttal: 'The silence in the medical world,' David Horrobin had to admit in his *Medical Hubris*, 'has been deafening.' *Medical Hubris* is a conscientious attempt to break that silence, not by casting doubt on Illich's facts, which Horrobin has to admit were unassailable, but by querying his interpretations. Horrobin's own interpretation, however, is weakened by his assumption that the profession is capable of recognising its deficiencies and remedying them. He even argues that, where reform is necessary, it can be effected 'only by the doctors themselves' – by doctors, that is, who are 'sensitive to the criticism of laymen such as Illich'. But because, as he recognises, the vast majority of doctors are *not* sensitive to Illich's criticisms ('most of those who have heard of him are unremittingly hostile', often without having read his book) this is hardly a convincing thesis.

Even more remote from reality is Horrobin's contention that the existence of critics inside the profession 'indicates that the profession itself saw the danger very early on and has constantly striven to counteract it', even if not always successfully. The precise opposite is indicated: that the profession has tolerated occasional expressions of heresy chiefly because orthodox dogma has seemed so unassailable.

Now, the profession is less secure, but doctors understandably find it hard, as McKeown has observed, 'to accept that medicine is not vitally concerned with the major determinants of health'. Herein lies the main problem: that it is extremely difficult for a doctor to accept that much of what he does for his patients is irrelevant, and some of what he does is positively harmful. Occasionally a respected individual will wryly admit as much, as Franz Inglefinger used to while editor of the *New England Journal of Medicine*. 'Perhaps the role of the doctor as reliever rather than as healer should be accentuated to mitigate any disappointment that he cannot appreciably reorientate mortality and morbidity trends,' he once suggested, adding that by his estimate eighty per cent of diseases are self-limiting or not improvable, leaving only eleven per cent in which medical intervention is 'dramatically successful' – and nine per cent in which it is iatrogenic. But such humility is rare.

The obvious way to check the validity of those proportions would be to undertake some form of audit or 'peer review', but attempts to introduce one have been frustrated. The doctor, as Lesley Garner puts it in the introduction to her study of the National Health Service, 'has been educated to believe that his decision on medical matters is sacrosanct'.

The British Medical Association has declined to accept audit. In the United States a pilot study for a 'peer standards review' was set up, chiefly on account of worry about the rapidly rising cost of medical treatment, but it made no headway. As a result it remains possible for doctors to continue to delude themselves that medicine's recent record has been one of progress, marred only by the occasional mishap, enabling them to use the 'water under the bridge' argument when they are reminded of past setbacks – even to claim that the disclosures about drugs shown to be dangerous and subsequently withdrawn is evidence that the profession does not cover up its mistakes, but learns from them.

The belief in medical progress consequently lingers, ministered to by the pharmaceutical industry's promotion, which always gives the impression that the new drugs work better than their predecessors in clinical use. So they often do, thanks to placebo effect. When confidence in the drug of yesteryear begins to wane, so do its benefits, leaving its side-effects more glaringly obvious. Its successor may be no different, yet still give better results. As a result, for the past two decades the medical profession has had the impression that it is climbing, when in reality it has been on a treadmill.

This inability to admit that the mechanist era is over, reinforced by the specialist structure of the profession and by the influence and affluence of the pharmaceutical industry, makes it extremely unlikely that the profession will change its ways fast enough to serve the community's requirements. A growing number of doctors, particularly GPs, have become aware of the need for change, and their influence, along with that of the increasingly dissatisfied paramedicals, will doubtless spread. But meanwhile, the public will be left with the problem, for individuals often a serious one, of what to do and where to go when 'just what the doctor ordered' ceases to appeal.

# 11

# The Way Ahead

At this stage, one common belief needs to be exposed as a fallacy: that the root of medicine's troubles lies in the existence of a 'free' National Health Service.

That Shaw was right when he argued that it was absurd to give surgeons a pecuniary interest in cutting off legs has since been abundantly demonstrated. For all its many imperfections, the British National Health Service, in which surgeons and physicians are not paid 'per item of service', has two striking advantages over rival systems in the West. One is obvious: nobody is threatened with the loss of a life-time's savings if struck down through accident or illness when inadequately insured. Experience has shown, too, that the more serious the case, the less the difference in the type of medical care that prince or pauper, duchess or dustman, can expect to receive. The differences are mainly at the lower levels of hospital and general practice, in squalid out-patients' departments and slum surgeries, but these are often little better in countries without a national health service.

The other advantage is surprising: the NHS is easily the most cost-effective system. This is unacceptable to Milton Friedman's disciples; surely, they argue, comprehensive individual and family insurance cover ought to bring down costs to the taxpayer? So they might, in an affluent society, but experience in societies which are only part-affluent has been disillusioning.

The deficiencies of the American insurance system were set out by the Ehrenreichs in *The American Health Empire*. The existence of Blue Cross, Medicare and Medicaid meant that hospitals had 'a perpetual Santa Claus. Whatever the hospital wants by way of fancy new equipment, luxury accommodation, high-priced doctors (or even public relations men or full-time lobbyists) the third party will pay for.' It meant a vicious spiral: rising hospital costs were compelling people to pay more for their insurance cover, so that for more and more people health care was becoming a luxury.

Events have confirmed the Ehrenreichs' prognosis. In the 1950s the

310

United States spent 3.5 per cent of its Gross National Product on health care; by 1968 it had risen to 6.6 per cent; by 1975 to 8.5 per cent; by 1980 to 10 per cent. The Health, Education and Welfare Department calculated in 1980 that the average family had to lay aside almost $3,000 a year on provision for health care. The indications are that this outlay will continue to rise, fed, among other sources, from malpractice suits, which the public and the legal profession found to be a lucrative way of clawing back some of the money the medical profession was extracting from the community.

This has further pushed up costs, because doctors feel compelled to cover themselves by practising 'defensive medicine', involving numerous tests for their patients, the tests in their turn requiring expensive gadgetry as well as technicians to operate it. For Americans at the lower end of the middle-income group, the rise in the cost of insurance and/or treatment has been particularly devastating. As they cannot afford full insurance and do not qualify for Medicare or Medicaid, a serious illness can mean bankruptcy: in the late 1970s it was estimated that a quarter of the bankruptcies in the US were attributable to this cause.

In some countries many doctors scarcely bother to pretend that their profession is anything more than a lucrative way of twisting the patient's arm to pay for whatever treatment they choose to prescribe. Horror stories from patients caught out by an accident or emergency are legion. When Derek Wilson, the BBC's Argentine correspondent, was in hospital for a minor operation 'the surgeon suddenly appeared through the mist of sedation to ask for his cheque'. It was for 'a million', which Wilson took to mean old pesos – about £7. The surgeon, however, noticing his look of relief said, firmly, '*new* pesos' – more than £700.

Even in Canada, where the State picks up the bills, the difficulty of controlling doctors paid per item of service has led to soaring costs. If the payments are not meticulously checked, fraud is encouraged; if they are to be meticulously checked, a massive bureaucracy is required. Returning to Britain after working in Canada, a British GP recently warned colleagues thinking of emigrating there about the elaborate forms that had to be filled in for each item, and the constant surveillance kept by audit committees, reviewing committees, and prescribing committees. However careful such watchers are they cannot be expected to be able to judge whether, say, a tonsillectomy is necessary; endless scope remains for doctors to provide unnecessary forms of treatment.

Under the influence of monetarism, guided by a desire to reduce state spending on health and make individuals more responsible for their own health care, the Thatcher government in Britain decided to enlarge the private sector, even using the argument that as Britain spends less on health services than other European nations the injection of funds from the pockets of private individuals will benefit the NHS, by enabling hospitals that take in some private patients to purchase better equipment. That most private money tends to be poured into coronary care units and similarly wasteful channels is conveniently ignored, as is the fact that other European governments have openly expressed admiration for the British system (which they wish operated in their own countries). Italy, in fact, has recently abandoned an insurance-based health service for a tax-based one.

The more far-sighted medical journals have consequently sided with the Royal Commission on the health services, which rejected the idea of insurance financing health care in Britain. When the Thatcher government presented its proposals, the *Lancet* warned that the profession should treat them 'with the utmost suspicion'. Because the NHS determines doctors' earnings, 'it ensures that the modern disease of high commerce cannot become a corruptive force', *World Medicine* has claimed. 'Because it requires medicine for all, virtually on demand, it precludes, in large part, the gross expenditure of money and expertise on a few esoteric diseases.'

Cost-effective though the British system is by comparison with others, greater emphasis on prevention could increase its cost-effectiveness. Although Shaw's assumption that fewer operations would take place if surgeons were not paid for performing them was correct, tens of thousands of unnecessary operations are carried out every year in Britain because surgeons assume them to be necessary, or at least desirable; because the bias of medical training is towards acceptance that they *are* necessary, and to some extent because surgeons, being trained to perform them, continue to do so out of habit even when the evidence points to their uselessness.

The basic problem is that the medical profession is unable to recognise its limitations. In spite of the reminders by Dubos and McKeown, doctors tend to forget that it was the social reformers who were chiefly responsible for banishing the major epidemic disorders, the pharmaceutical industry arriving just in time, like Blucher at Waterloo, to turn defeat into rout. Led by the industry the medical profession has been doing what – to vary the military simile – the Royalist cavalry used to do under Rupert of the Rhine, pursuing the fleeing Roundheads with panache, but leaving Cromwell's infantry in possession of the field of battle.

Even those doctors who are aware of the profession's deficiencies tend to think that they can be, and are being, remedied by trial and error. No other profession, Archibald Cochrane claims, 'can approach our record of studying and publishing our errors and evaluating our work'. But as an epidemiologist, Cochrane understandably is thinking of his own specialty's achievements, which are indeed impressive. Yet, although it has eroded many accepted dogmas, it has largely failed to persuade the profession to accept the implications. The discovery he cites as his example – that people with a high level of blood cholesterol have been likely to die sooner if they have taken the drug Atromid – is of little value for the future unless the moral, that no drug of this nature should be pronounced safe on the basis of clinical trials until after a follow-up to find how patients fare later, is recognised and acted upon. There is little sign of that.

## Turning off the Tap

To expect governments to intervene decisively, in order to re-route health care away from treatment to prevention is futile. Even Marc Lalonde, who had more success than most health ministers in persuading Canadians to look at their life-styles – extracting money from the tobacco and alcohol companies for his prevention campaign, and pushing through measures designed to cut down the toll of accidents – was unable to get to the roots of his country's health problems. Governments devoted to the growth of the gross national product do not enthusiastically promote prevention, because it gets in the way; they are inclined to leave health to the medical profession, a tough adversary, whose reform would be tricky and expensive. As Carlson warned, too, the development of services designed to give the public better care or protection generates bureaucracies which, depending as they do on the maintenance of their services, themselves breed opposition to any attempt to re-allocate resources.

As a result we are left with a system well illustrated by a lecturer on the diseases of civilisation encountered by Lesley Garner, who showed a slide depicting two men mopping up a floor flooded by a constantly running tap: 'These men are experts in floor-mopping-up,' the lecturer explained. 'They have spent ten years of their life earning degrees in floor-mopping-up. They know everything there is to know about floor-mopping-up. Except how to turn off the tap.'

How, then, can the tap be turned off?

Carlson produced a string of ideas, including a vast expansion of health education, more research into health (as distinct from diseases), de-professionalisation, redeployment of health workers within the

313

system, social and environmental prevention campaigns, and a sustained attack on poverty. Given that neither the medical profession nor governments are likely to change their ways in the immediate future, only one of these is immediately practicable: de-professionalisation – or as Illich thought of it, 'laicisation'.

The process has in fact already begun, with the public turning from the profession in small but gradually increasing numbers. In the 1950s, 'fringe' or alternative medicine seemed moribund, but the thalidomide affair led to a revival of interest in nature cure, herbalism, homeopathy, osteopathy (in the United States the osteopaths had established themselves as almost the equivalent of medical doctors; elsewhere they were still on the wrong side of the tracks) and chiropractics. With the exception of the chiropractors, and in a few countries osteopaths, these groups were not sufficiently well organised to take advantage of the demand. It was not until, among other things, the advent of the Mahraishi and the Esalen influence led to greater interest in the role of the mind in health, and the medical profession capitulated over acupuncture, that they began to enjoy what has since developed into a boom, particularly in Britain, where the laws relating to medically-unqualified practitioners are less stringent than on the continent of Europe or in most American States.

From its inception in the 1850s the General Medical Council in Britain had laid down that for a doctor to refer patients to medically unqualified practitioners (other than a licensed medical auxiliary, such as a physiotherapist), or to collaborate with them, was an offence meriting erasure from the medical register – the fate of F. W. Axham, the doctor who administered anesthetics for the celebrated bonesetter, Herbert Barker. When in the 1920s Barker received a knighthood for his public services, such was the public's outrage at the GMC's refusal to reinstate Axham that the disciplinary weapon was not used again; it was none the less kept in reserve, until in 1977 it was quietly dropped. Many doctors, by this time, were known to be recommending patients with back-ache to try oseopathy or chiropractice; among those patients were cabinet ministers, tycoons, trade union bosses and even members of the GMC itself. The risk of an embarrassing contretemps was clear; by abandoning the regulation, this was averted.

Three years later the American Medical Association followed suit, for a different reason: it was being harassed by chiropractors under the anti-Trust laws. The AMA had been actively hostile to medically-unqualified practitioners, fomenting prosecutions against them and bitterly resisting attempts to relax State laws upholding the profession's monopoly, often with success. But gradually chiropractors had won the right to treat patients in all the States of the Union, and with the law behind them, they could counter-attack. Such was the unpopularity of the medical profession that the likelihood of the AMA winning court cases was diminishing, and the amount of damages awarded against it, greater. AMA membership, too, was declining, partly owing to internal scandals and dissensions. It could no longer afford the risk of fighting off its rivals, and therefore in 1980 it withdrew the ban on doctors collaborating with medically-unqualified practitioners.

This relaxation, it can be argued, points to a new spirit within the profession. The more likely interpretation, however, is that the profession is hoping to follow the course it took with the homeopaths, and later – in the United States – with the osteopaths: 'If you can't lick 'em, get 'em to join you.' The homeopaths were all but swallowed up in the process, and the osteopaths have become barely distinguishable from doctors; some chiropractors have been moving the same way. But there are now fresh rivals in the field, who will not so easily be seduced. In Virginia, Blue Shield has been held to violate the anti-Trust laws for refusing to reimburse clinical psychologists for treating patients, and people who are deserting the profession because of disenchantment with its treatment are no longer likely to switch to practitioners who ape doctors' clinical attitudes and methods.

A simple switch from one camp to the other, however, will not necessarily do much to introduce preventive medicine. Many more patients who emerge as refugees from orthodoxy will simply want treatment for their symptoms. How, then, can prevention be encouraged? The only route at present is for individuals to aim and campaign for it, through self-help – not to be confused with self-medication, already extensively practised, which tends to mean little more than purchasing off-prescription drugs of the same type as the doctor would prescribe. Self-help is more a matter of unlearning certain conditioned reflexes, such as the belief that constipation is a disorder which needs to be treated with purges. It is partly a matter of following the advice to be found in the Hippocratic writings, and in Juvenal's 'your prayer must be that you have a sound mind in a sound body': advice which remained standard until little more than two centuries ago. When the mechanists were on the point of taking over a few vitalists fought a rear-guard action – Calabre of the Hôtel-Dieu in his 1804 dissertation blaming emotional conflicts, along with sedentary habits, alcoholic excesses and the din and disorder of urban life for the respiratory disorders prevalent in Paris; sixteen years later J.-J. Virey making the point in his *L'hygiene philosophique* that what was needed was not better ways to treat illness, but some way to help people rediscover their instinct for health-giving

315

habits. But such voices were soon to be drowned in the mechanist, materialist floodtide.

'We have the medicine we deserve,' Carlson lamented. 'We choose to live recklessly, to abuse our bodies with what we consume, to expose ourselves to environmental insults, to rush frantically from place to place, and to sit on our spreading bottoms and watch paid professionals exercise for us.' But that is not quite correct: the element of choice is massively reduced by the commercial brainwashing with the processes, beginning with the parents but, through them, effectively palate-washing babies in their cradles. The main need is to link up with the organisations already campaigning, environmentalists and ecologists, to find ways to counter the forces promoting ill-health, and to compel local and national authorities to listen – or to lose more votes than they care to lose.

This means that it will not be a campaign against the medical profession, except when medical organisations or individuals persist in trying to divert resources provided by the public to meet their own needs, as they have so successfully done in the case of most of the major fund-raising bodies. When Christine Orton realised the extent of the suffering which had been caused by the use of topical steroids in the treatment of eczema, she urged the formation of a pressure group 'to find out exactly what doctors and drug manufacturers think they are doing', and within a few months the National Eczema Society had come into being with branches all round the country. But it quickly went the way of earlier organisations. To attract recognition and funds the organisers found it desirable to work with specialists. This had the additional advantage, Orton was to claim, that it prevented meetings from becoming 'moan-ins' by offering discussions with experienced professionals, 'or at least with someone who can see light at the end of the tunnel'. As a correspondent pointed out, replying to her in the *Guardian*, this was simply another example of the way in which organisations 'prompted by dissatisfaction with aspects of the professionally-run system for dealing with problems' end up by being 'co-opted into it in a dependent role'.

That this role can be changed has been shown by the emergence in Britain of Action Research for Multiple Sclerosis, a body set up as a result of frustration over the way that funds collected by the established MS body was largely controlled by specialist 'experts'. The members of the breakaway ARMS movement decided that they themselves would decide which research projects should receive funds, instead of leaving the decision to the jury of specialists. As a result the researchers who ordinarily could have expected funds, thanks to a specialist known to be interested in their work, found themselves called upon to justify, to a lay

316

group, what they were doing, and projects which previously stood no chance of acceptance because they were not sufficiently orthodox began to receive some support. The results might not be spectacular, but they were sufficiently promising for the established Multiple Sclerosis Society, orginally contemptuous and then patronising of its rival, to begin to alter its own policies, and to put some of its much larger resources behind projects initiated by ARMS.

Citing ARMS as an illustration, David Horrobin has put in a plea from his experience in Canada, and earlier in Britain, for lay organisations to take back the right to control the funds they raise, instead of leaving the distribution to the specialists – in particular, the cancer fund-raising organisations. 'Lay people should understand that there are no real experts in research on cancer or on any of the other diseases to which we do not have the answers,' he points out; 'the failure of cancer research to achieve substantial results and its failure to demonstrate why and how cancer develops, indicate that the so-called experts are *failed* experts.'

Specialists must be persuaded to recognise that the patient has a right to decide whether or not to accept their advice. Until very recently they have tended to assume that, if they diagnose breast cancer, say, and prescribe radical mastectomy, the patient will accept the operation. At present the patient has nobody to turn to for detached advice (the 'second opinion' is often from a specialist sharing the views of his colleague) on what the treatment entails, or what the alternatives may be; nor, as the system exists, is it possible to envisage an advisory service which would set out the paramedical possibilities, as well as those within orthodoxy's range. Such a service, if it comes, will have to be set up by some lay organisation.

GPs are likely to present fewer problems, particularly in Britain, where they can still retain a patient on their list even while recommending him to see an osteopath or an acupuncturist – or to leave his hated job and take a course in meditation. A growing number of GPs long for their patients to become more independent – more willing to seek advice about their life-styles rather than demand drugs. But so few GPs have any training, and some no aptitude, for this unaccustomed role of adviser that, having trained patients to be at the receiving end of drug prescriptions, they cannot easily reverse the process. Nevertheless, GPs are increasingly aware of the need to de-medicalise their attitudes and methods, even at the cost of losing those patients who do not want to have the responsibility for looking after themselves.

As Leon Eisenberg of the Harvard Medical School has emphasised in this thoughtful contribution, 'What makes Persons "Patients" and

317

Patients "Well"?', in the *American Journal of Medicine*, GPs are not being called upon to transmute the medicine they have been taught 'into a potpourri of psychotherapy, social work and contract law' – they are simply being reminded 'that the effectiveness of medical evaluation will be enhanced if the physician, in assessing patient problems, regularly includes a systematic inquiry into the social determinants of the decision to seek help'.

Perhaps the most important single step GPs could take would be to reverse the trend, apparent over the past half-century, to reduce the number of home visits to patients; some doctors actually pride themselves on their refusal to make home visits, on the ground that the time might be better spent in the surgery or consulting-room – not realising that, by their failure to take the home background into account, they are depriving themselves of information which may be essential to the understanding of patients' needs. Admittedly what they need may not be in the power of the GP to satisfy, but with experience he can direct them towards organisations or individuals who can help. And just how urgent is the need for such a shift of emphasis has been demonstrated in a remarkable survey carried out for the New South Wales Health Commission in Sydney, its report in 1979 representing, in the words of the Commission's director of research, 'an indictment of the way medical and health care agents are meeting the real needs of city dwellers', and probably of dwellers in any and every city of the west.

In the United States the growing shortage of GPs led in the early 1960s to the development of a new type of paramedical, the nurse practitioner – the affluent society's answer to the Chinese barefoot doctor. Opposition to licensing nurses with special qualifications to treat patients was gradually overcome, and their numbers have been rapidly increasing. Theoretically they still work under doctors' supervision; often, however, they build up what are to all intents independent practices – initially because they charge patients much less, later because they win patients' confidence. The risk, however, is that as they establish themselves they may begin to empire-build.

At this stage it is the public, rather than the profession, that needs to be guided and goaded into de-medicalising itself. The problems are formidable: how to persuade people to stop smoking and reduce the consumption of alcohol and sugar without imposing unwelcome or unacceptable restraints on the freedom of the subject; how to prevent ill-health from continuing to be inversely related to income levels; how to ensure that technological advance is not achieved at the expense of the community's well-being – and not just through pollution. Work deprivation, as Selye has warned, is a health hazard: 'let us start preparing right now not only to fight pollution and the population explosion, but also to combat boredom.'

For the immediate future, the most valuable weapon which the public possesses is the one provided by the research of Selye, Stewart Wolf, Harold Wolff and those who have followed in their course: that in so far as stress is a cause, precipitant or risk factor in disease, it is such not because of the impact of the stressor, but because of the reaction of the individual to the stressor. If people who are at risk, as Type As are, from heart attacks, can become aware of the danger, they can learn how to avoid the occasions of stress, or, better, how to modify their Type A personality by learning how to react less violently to stressors.

To do this, however, requires far greater willingness to recognise that such personality-type proneness and susceptibility to emotional stress are of fundamental importance in relation to illness of all kinds. It is still difficult to put across the fact that the term 'psychosomatic' does not mean that the symptoms are emotionally-induced – and certainly not that, as so many people still assume, that they are 'all in the mind'. It means simply that in the spectrum of disease – which runs from the almost exclusively physico-chemical, as following some catastrophe such as Hiroshima, to the almost exclusively psychological – the mind is interacting with the body, even if not to cause the symptoms, at least to make them more, or less, serious, and to make them last a longer or shorter time.

What is too often forgotten is that the mind operates in various dimensions and disguises. It can help to make people illness-prone, as with Type As. It can be a fuse-wire, as in Type B; or a defence mechanism which goes awry, as in some neuroses and psychoses; or an escape-hatch, as in neuromimesis; or a way out, as in some cancer cases. It may also be involved in the spread of infections, from flu to mass hysteria. Any of these, or more than one, can be a risk factor or a precipitant, and they represent variables which ought not to be disregarded, as they still are in prevention, diagnoses and treatment, or in research.

The mind must also be taken more seriously by those individuals who as writers, committee-members, or fund-raisers are, in effect, missionaries for self-help, not only for the right of the community to be protected from the relentless promotion of pathogenic products, and the right of the patients to exercise their judgment as consumers – the theme of Ian Kennedy's final Reith Lecture – but also for the need of individuals to accept responsibility for their health, within the limits our civilisation permits.

Vitalism, in fact, so long unfashionable, is ready for revival. The few

319

who swam against the tide should get credit they have been denied: Samuel Butler, with his Erewhonian concept of disease as a crime ('Prisoner at the Bar, you have been accused of the great crime of labouring under pulmonary consumption'); F. G. Crookshank; John Ryle (the more creditable, in that he was a pillar of the medical establishment) and the founders of psychosomatic medicine, whose research helped to turn the tide.

We have to learn from them that health, as René Dubos put it, is 'the expression of the manner in which the individual responds and adapts to the challenges that he meets in everyday life', challenges not just from the external world, 'since the most compelling factors of the environment, those most commonly involved in the causation of disease, are the goals that the individual sets for himself, often without regard to biological necessity'. Little though we can do about many of the pathogenic forces in the environment, from pollutants to unemployment, we can try to achieve a better understanding of ourselves through a liberation of instincts long dormant, and where necessary a change in our life-styles.

# Acknowledgments and Sources

'I am a chronic doctor-bore on social occasions,' I wrote a few years ago in the *Lancet*, on the only occasion that I have been invited to contribute to that doyen of medical journals, 'cheerfully passing up the opportunity to meet film stars or celebrities if I can corner a consultant.' That has remained true; and I cannot even begin to list all the members of the profession who have helped to provide and shape the material that I have included – often by their criticisms of my notions. I am not even going to name those, grateful though I am to all of them, who have read sections of the book, because some of them expressed strong disagreement with my views. I will content myself with thanking my proofreaders: Bernard Levin, who has performed that task heroically since we were colleagues on the *Spectator* twenty-five years ago, and Sir William Wood.

Well over a thousand medical journals are currently appearing in the English language; and, in 1980, three thousand medical books were published in Britain alone. My greatest debt is consequently to those journals which keep a watch over what is appearing elsewhere, and point to sources which could, otherwise, easily be missed. After reading a draft of this book one critic complained that my addiction to *World Medicine* was unfortunate as within the medical profession, it is 'not regarded as a reputable source'. So much the worse for the profession! *World Medicine*'s willingness to allow heretical opinions to be aired in its columns has made it invaluable to me.

I have tried to avoid jargon, using terms in their colloquial rather than their clinical sense, even at the cost of some precision. But with spelling I have tended to go along with the prevailing medical tide, which is usually a little ahead – for example, in the elimination of the diphthong. Where italics appear in quotations they are so in the original.

The name of the author of a quotation ordinarily appears in the text, and its source can be found either in the bibliography, where my aim has been to put the main works consulted, or among the source references. Where the text does not indicate sources, or where the reader may want more precise information than is available from the bibliography – the page number, for example, if a quotation comes from a book – these can be found in the source reference section; where that section lists only a name and a date, the title of the paper and the issue of the journal in which it appeared can be found in the bibliography. Where the source has been a personal communication, it is listed as 'p.c.'.

Abbreviations are of the following periodicals:

American Journals of: Cardiology, Epidemiology, Medical Science, Medicine, Obstetrics and Gynecology, Occupational Medicine, Public Health, Roentgenology.
Annals of: Internal Medicine, NY Academy of Science, Surgery.
Archives of General Psychiatry.
Brain/Mind Bulletin.
British Journals of: Clinical Practice, Hospital Medicine, Medical Psychology, Psychiatry, Surgery, Venereal Diseases.
British Medical Journal (BMJ).
Cancer; Cancer Treatment Review.
Circulation.
Comprehensive Psychiatry.
Drug and Therapeutics Bulletin.
General Practitioner.
Health Bulletin.
International Medical Tribune of Great Britain.
Journals of: American Medical Association (JAMA), Clinical and Experimental Psychopathology, Health and Social Behaviour, Hygiene, Immunology, Medical Education, Medical Science, National Cancer Institute, Obstetrics and Gynaecology of the British Commonwealth, Occupational Medicine, Psychosomatic Research, Royal College of General Practitioners, Royal College of Physicians, Royal Society of Medicine, Transpersonal Psychology.
Lancet.
Medical Clinics of North America.
Medical Journal of Australia.
Medical News.
Medical Officer.
Medical Press.
Modern Concepts of Cardiovascular Disease.
New England Journal of Medicine (NEJM).
New Scientist.
New Society.
New York Medical Journal.

Postgraduate Medical Journal.
Practitioner.
Prescribers' Journal.
Psychological Medicine.
Psychology Today (US and UK).
Psychosomatic Medicine.
Quarterly Journal of Medicine.
Science.
Scientific American.
World Health Organisation Bulletin, Chronicle.
World Medicine.

# Source References

viii Dubos, 1959, 28–9.
    Illich, 1977, 11
    Carlson, 1975, 1–2.
    *NEJM*, 24 Feb. 1977.
ix  NHS 30th anniversary survey: Draper, 1978, 5–20; Williamson/Danaher, 1978, 87.
x   Mahler, 1975, 829.
    McKeown, 1979, 131.
    Public opinion poll: Taylor Nelson Market Research Group.


## 1 HEART DISEASE

1  'Tantamount to professional negligence': Roberts, 1978, 67.
3  WHO: Press release Feb. 1969.
    Crew: Transactions of the Faculty of Actuaries, 1945.
    Framingham: Castelli (p.c.); Kannel, 1975, 1976.
5  Beecher: in Talalay, 1964, 81.
6  Dunbar, 1955, 126.
    Cincinnati researchers: Chambers/Reiser, 1952.
    Selye, 1956, 153–6.
8  Roseto: Wolff, 1968, 206–8; Pelletier, 1977, 100–1.
    N. Dakota: Syme, 1964.
9  Rahe, 1964, 1968, 1974, 1979.
    Miller, 1974.
    Benson, 1977, 56–64.
10  Inter-Society Com.: *Circulation*, Dec. 1970 (A. 82ff).
11  MER 29: Mintz, 1967, 242–6.
12  Allbutt: Ryle, 1948, 305–14.
    Mackenzie, 1925, 456–8.
13  Carruthers, 1974, 92–4.
    Eraldin: *BMJ*, Jan.–Dec. 1975; C. Doyle, *Observer*, 5 Sept. 1976.
14  Swedish trial: Berglund, 1978.
    Prague/Budapest trials: M. F. Oliver, EOCCD conference, 18 June 1979.
    Miller: cited in *New Scientist*, 23 Feb. 1978, 482.

McKeown: *Times*, 18 Sept. 1978.
*World Med.*, 14 June 1978, 52.
Nixon, *Lancet*, 24 Feb. 1979, 438.
15 *BMJ*, 28 July 1979, 245; July–Sept. 1979.
Bethesda trials: *JAMA*, 7 Dec. 1979, 2562–7.
16 Edinburgh survey: Armstrong, 1972.
Stamler, 1973, 10.
17 Bradshaw, *BMJ* 10 Feb. 1973, 349.
Cochrane, 1971, 53.
Tees-side: Colling (*et al.*), 1976.
18 Coronary or ordinary ward trial: Hill (*et al.*), 1977.
'Almost professional negligence': Roberts, 1978, 67.
Nixon, 1980 (p.c.).
19 By-pass ops rise: Hiatt, 1975, 237.
Ehrenreichs, 1971, 140–2.
20 Wertenbaker, 1980, 355.
21 *NEJM*, 11 Jan. 1973, 72–8.
*Chicago Trib.*, 29 April, 1976.
By-pass surgery investigations: Russek, in Norman, 1975; Preston, 1977, 30.
Preston, 1977, 227–56.
22 Veterans' trial: Murphy (*et al.*), 1977: *Sunday Times*, 23 July 1978.
23 Hiatt, 1977.
Hammersmith Hospital: Westaby (*et al.*), 1979.
Placebo surgery: Beecher, 1961; Dunkman, 1974, 818.
*Circulation*, 6 June 1980, 1269.
24 US consumption trends: Florey (*et al.*), 1978; Stallones, 1980.
Finnish trials: Tudge, *World Med.*, 1977, 47–51.
25 Cholesterol findings: *BMJ*, 2 Aug. 1980, 340.
Headline: *Daily Telegraph*, 27 June 1977.
Shillingford/McMichael: *Bulletin* EOCCD, 1978; *World Med.*, 13 Dec. 1978, 52.
26 *New Scientist*, 14 April 1977, 58.
27 Stanford: Farquhar (*et al.*), 1977.
28 *Lancet*, 6 March 1976, 544.
Kannel, *Archives Int. Med.*, 1979, 857–61.
Strain/personality type effects: Rosenthal, 1966, 19–20.
30 Friedman/Rosenman, 1974, 54–64.
32 Greens, 1977, 79ff.
34 Framingham and 'Type A': Kannel, 1976: *World Med.*, 4 Oct. 1980, 17; Lynch, 1977, 21–4.
36-7 Food and Nutrition Board investigation: Silcock, *Sunday Times*, 8 June 1980; Greenberg, *New Scientist*, 3 July 1980.
37 Questionnaire: Comroe/Dripps, 1976.
Yearbook: Harvey, 1978.
38 Sackett, 1974.

Roberts, 1977, 135.
Nixon, 1979.
*World Med.*, 2 June 1979.
40 Nottingham trial: Roland (*et al.*), 1979.
41 Nixon, 1979.
42 *Lancet*, 31 Jan. 1981, 257–62; 21 March 1981, 643.
Int. Federation: *BMJ*, 14 March 1981, 894–6.
43 *Lancet*, 30 Aug. 1980, 459.
L. Thomas, 1980, 511–13.
US operations: *Lancet*, 6 Sept. 1980, 511–13.
Nixon, 1980.
44 Transplant patient: ITN bulletin, 26 Oct. 1979.
Draper: *New Scientist*, 17 April 1980, 136–7; *Sunday Times*, 26 Oct. 1980.
45 Brighton experiment: C. Doyle, *Observer*, 14 Oct. 1979.
*BMJ*, O'Hanrahan (*et al.*), 1980.

## 2 CANCER

47 Ogden: *BMJ*, 9 Aug. 1958; Gordon-Taylor, 1959.
Jones: in Null/Houston, 1979, 2.
Nixon: Richards, 1978, 287–8.
48 Rauscher: Greenberg, 1974, 1975, 1977.
Dixon, *World Med.*, 12 March 1975, 41.
Institute's reply: *Science*, 4 March 1977, 847.
50 McKeown, 1979, 12.
51 Fisher, 1959, 1ff.
53 ASH: *Guardian*, 5 April 1977.
54 Young: *Guardian*, 22 Oct., 20 Dec. 1979.
*Observer*, 6 Jan. 1980.
55 Ministries: *Sunday Times*, 20 Feb. 1980; *Observer*, 6 July 1980.
*Guardian*, 22 Nov. 1980.
*Observer*, 17 June 1979.
56 *Sunday Times*, 29 Jan. 1978.
NCI investigation: *New Scientist*, 21 Dec. 1978, 917.
Cairns, 1978, 152.
57 Roberts, 1978, 160–1.
58 *BMJ*; Russell (*et al.*), 1979.
59 *BMJ*: Keynes, 1937.
60 Mastectomy varieties: Atkins, 1972; Carter, 1976.
Trials: *Int. Med. Trib. of GB*, 16 Nov. 1967; *Lancet*, 15 Feb. 1964, 367.
*JAMA*, 7th Oct 1974, 99–105.
Dao: in Kathari/Mehta, 1979, 49.
62 Senate Committee: 15 May 1976.
Institute and Society: *NEJM*, 28 April 1977, 1015; Greenberg, *New Scientist*, 19 May 1977.

NC Society: Thier, 1977; Cullition, 1977; Greenberg, *New Scientist*, 19 May 1971.
63 *Lancet*: Irwig, 30 Nov. 1974, 1307–8.
BUPA, *Times*, 24 Oct. 1980.
*BMJ*, 12 July 1980, 146.
*New Scientist*, 14 June 1979.
64 *Sunday Times*, 6 July 1980.
65 Marcus: *BMJ*, 17 Jan. 1981, 220.
Murley, *BMJ*, 21 March 1981, 194; Keynes, *BMJ*, 25 April 1981, 1392.
Armour, *World Med.*, 1 Dec. 1976.
66 British Columbia trial: Boyes (*et al.*), 1962.
Donaldson, *BMJ*, 16 Jan 1975, 195.
67 Robinson, *BMJ*, 9 May 1964, 1049.
Husain, *Int. Med. Trib. of GB.*, 10 Nov. 1966.
Nuffield investigation: A. Marcus, *Observer*, 6 Nov. 1968.
68 Diagnostic error: Spriggs/Husain, 1977; Cairns, 1978, 149; Kothari/Mehta, 1979, 42.
Cotton, *World Med.*, 5 April 1980, 21.
Cairns, 1978, 149, 156.
Cochrane, 1972, 27.
69 *BMJ*, 6 Sept. 1980, 629.
Roberts, 1978, 92.
*World Med.*, 23 March 1977.
70 Porritt, *Medical News*, 22 Oct. 1965.
71 Trials: *Int. Med. Trib. of GB*, 16 Nov. 1967; Murray, 1976; Baum (*et al.*), 1980.
*World Med.*, 12 Jan. 1977, 33–6; 15 June, 1977, 7.
72 Marchant, *World Med.*, 13 July 1977, 37–9.
Cytotoxic drugs: Zubrod, 1972: *BMJ*, 12 Aug. 1967, 433–4.
73 *NEJM:* Greco/Oldham, 1979.
*Lancet*, 12 Jan. 1980, 77.
74 Combination drugs: *BMJ*, 22 Nov. 1980, 1422.
75 Cairns, 1978, 153.
Peto: Tudge, *World Med.*, 8 Feb. 1978, 29; McGinty, *New Scientist*, 30 Aug. 1979, 649–51.
Levitt/Guralnick, 1979, 34.
76 Kothari/Mehta, 1979, 81.
*World Med.*, 6 Oct. 1979, 84.
77 Angell, *World Med.*, 18 Oct. 1978, 26.
78 Levitt/Guralnick, 1979, 204.
Devita: *New Scientist*, 24 July 1980.
79 Ehrlich, *Papers* (1957 ed.) ii, 561.
Burnet, 1957, 779–86, 841–6.
Watson: Greenberg, 1975; Kothari/Mehta, 1979, 12.
Burnet, 1979, 138; 1972, 2.
Currie, 1974, vi–vii.

80 *NEJM*, 30 March, 1974.
Environmental cancer: Lewin, *New Scientist*, 13 July 1978, 106–7.
Cancer conference: McGinty, 1977, 758.
81 McGovern: *New Scientist*, 22 June, 1978.
82 *BMJ*, 22 Dec. 1979, 1610.
83 Stevenson, 1961 (and p.c.).
Dixon, *World Med.*, 8 Feb. 1978, 27.
84 *Lancet*, 22 Sept. 1979, 619; 6 Oct. 1979, 727–8.
Richards, 1978, x–xi.
Strickland, *World Med.*, 21 Sept. 1977.
85 *ICRF* reply: *BMJ*, 19 Jan 1980, 178–9.
Cairns, 1978, 57.
87 Cooper: quoted in Sontag, 1977, 53.
Paget, 1876.
Parker: quoted in Pelletier, 1977, 137.
88 Chicago investigation: Bacon (*et al.*), 1952.
89 LeShan, 1977, 19–20.
Huxley, 1955, 64.
Eysenck (*et al.*), 1960.
90 Kissen, *Health Bulletin*, July 1960; *Medical Press*, 2 Aug. 1961.
91 Kissen, *The Medical Officer*, 24 Dec. 1965, 343–5.
Eysenck, 1965, 153.
Engel: *Medical News*, 21 Jan. 1966.
*Times*, 22 Aug. 1966.
*Lancet*, 26 Nov. 1966, 1173–4.
92 Kissen, *The Medical Officer*, 2 Sept. 1966.
Kissen, NY Conference: *Annals NY Academy of Science*, 21 Jan. 1966, 777.
Reaction to Bahnsons' paper: C. Doyle, *Observer*, 6 June 1976.
94 Pelletier, 1977, 135ff.
*Lancet*, 31 March 1979, 706.
95 Simontons, 1975; Carlson, 1975 (b), 59–69; *Quest*, 1977, 112; Sparks (*et al.*), 1978.
96 Greens, 1977, 111–12.
97 Burnet, 1972, 3.
Burch, 1976, 2.
Johns Hopkins: Thomas/Duszynski, 1974.
98 Curtis: in Stoll, 1979, 61.
Stoll, 1979, 3–7, 19–29.
Meares, 1977; Meares, *Lancet*, 5 May 1979, 978.
99 Warts: Eysenck, 1953, 215–16.
Fagan case: *World Med.*, 6 Oct. 1976, 20–1.
100 Chichester, 1964, 257–70.
Edwards (p.c.).
101 Carlson, 1975 (b), 61.
Sontag, 51 ff.

102  Levitt/Guralnick, 1974, 155.
     *World Med.*, 20 April 1926; 5 Oct. 1977; 16 Nov. 1977.
104  Pennsylvania researchers: Horne/Pickard, *Psychosomatic Medicine*, Nov.
     1979, 503–13.
     *BMJ*: B. M. Lee, 15 Dec. 1979, 1538–40
105  Devita: *New Scientist*, 24 July 1980.


3 MENTAL ILLNESS

106  Prudential case: *Sunday Times*, 29 Jan. 1978.
107  Clark/Cohen, 1979, 209.
     Szasz, 1962, 85.
     Koestler, 1974; Kramer, 1979.
111  *World Med.*, 16 Nov. 1977, 7.
     *BMJ*, 13 Oct. 1979, 884.
     *Lancet*, 27 Oct. 1979, 888.
     Gordon: *Guardian*, 10 April 1979.
112  'Properly selected cases': e.g. *World Med.*, 12 July 1978, 17.
     Schrag, 1980, 161–80.
113  *BMJ*: Barraclough, 1978.
     BBC: Gould, *New Scientist*, March 1981, 759.
     *Guardian*, 26 March 1981.
114  Ayd: quoted by Schrag, 1980, 112.
115  *BMJ*, 13 July 1957, 623–5; 27 Dec. 1958, 1386.
     Bishop of Chester: quoted by Shepherd, 1970.
     Tranquilliser statistics: Schrag, 1980, 34–8; O. Gillie, *Sunday Times*, 7
     Dec. 1975; Trethowan, 1979, 28.
     Rappaport: Schrag, 1980, 116.
116  *ABPI*: Wells, 1980, 3, 26.
     Rollin, *World Med.*, 21 May 1975, 55–60.
117  *BMJ*, 19 July 1980, 173.
     *World Med.*, 19 April 1978, 29.
118  Carlson, 1975, 117.
     Schrag, 1980, 56
     Shepherd, 1970.
     Side-effects: Schrag, 1980, 118.
119  Gardos: *Sunday Times*, 27 Oct. 1980.
     NIMH study: Brain/Mind Bulletin, 19 Nov. 1979.
     Harvard study: O. Gillie, *Sunday Times*, 7 Dec. 1975.
120  *BMJ*, 7 April, 1979, 919.
     Addiction: *New Scientist*, 12 April 1974; *JAMA*, 23 Aug. 1975, 673–7.
     ECT: Schrag, 1980, 148–9.
     *Lancet*, 16 Feb. 1980, 348–9.
121  Schrag, 1980, 237.
     Szasz, 1962, 84.
122  Szasz, 1962, 81–5.

Kallman; in Stevenson, *Harpers*, Aug. 1967, 62.
Delgado: Schrag, 1980, 170–3.
123 Kety, 1959; *BMJ*, 16 March 1963, 695–6.
124 OHE, 1979, 4–9.
Miller, 1967, 257–62.
125 Psychosomatic school: Alexander, 1957, 117.
Szasz, 1962, 9.
Stevenson, 1957.
126 Osmond, 1961.
127 Laing, 1965.
128 Carstairs, *BMJ*, 1 Jan. 1966, 49.
129 Morgan, *New Scientist*, 3 Nov. 1977, 306.
Mills, *World Med.*, 4 June 1978, 34–5.
130 Horrobin, 1980.
131 Engel, 1977.

## 4 IATROGENIC DISORDERS

132 Illich, 1977, 11, 41–2.
133 Cortisone: Roŭeché, 1958, 139.
134 Chloromycetin: Kefauver, 1961, 192–8; Harris, 1964, 95–105; *BMJ*, 8 April 1961, 1018–19.
135 *BMJ*, 30 Sept. 1961, 855.
Mintz, 1967, 247–56; Knightley (*et al.*), 1980, 247–56.
136 SMON: O. Gillie, *Sunday Times*, 22 May, 17 July 1978; O. Hansen, *New Scientist*, 23 Nov. 1978, 614–16.
137 Diabetes: Cochrane, 1971, 54–5; Simpson, *World Med.*, 13 Dec. 1978, 27–8.
Kern: *Am. Jnl. Med. Sci.*, 1957, 430.
Kefauver, 1961, 202–9.
139 Waring; Schering/ICI: O. Gillie, *Sunday Times*, 20 Nov. 1977.
*Guardian*, 7, 14–21 May, 18 June, 1975.
140 Chairman Eczema Society: *Sunday Times*, 27 Nov. 1977.
*Lancet*, 3 Sept. 1977, 487–8.
*BMJ*, 4 Oct 1980.
Queen's Award: *Daily Mail*, 21 April 1978.
Wolf/Wolff, 1947, 109ff.
141 Ryle, 1948, 117.
Guirdham, 1957, 33.
*NEJM*, 8 Dec. 1977, 1293.
*Lancet*, 9 Dec. 1978, 1237.
*World Med.*, 24 Feb. 1979, 21.
Teeling-Smith, 1980, 13.
142 Manchester evidence: *Lancet*, 1979, 1005.
Reed: J. Maurice, *Sunday Times*, 11 Jan. 1981.
Horrobin: *Lancet* 5 May 1979, 978; Press release, 1 Jan. 1981.

143  Valium: Tudge, *New Scientist*, 8 Jan. 1981, 80.
     Drugs remain a hazard: *BMJ*, 6 June 1981, 1814.
144  Wade, 1970, 66.
     *ADR Bulletin*, Feb. 1980.
     British GPs: Martys, 1979.
     *NEJM*, 29 April 1976, 1003–4.
     Registrar General: *World Med.*, 28 June 1980, 32.
145  Doll, *BMJ*, 7 April 1979, 919.
     Harvard, *Guardian*, 10 May 1979.
146  Limburg symposium: Dixon, 1978, 72–4.
     'Supergerms': O. Gillie, *Sunday Times*, 15 Oct. 1978; *Guardian*, 17 March
       1980.
147  Resistant strains: Tucker, *Guardian*, 24 July 1980; *Lancet*, 26 July 1980.
     Sargant: in Abse, 1978, 50–1.
     'Slipped discs': Inglis, 1978, 52–8.
148  Hiatt, 1975, 237.
     North, in Carlson, 1975, 12.
     Hysterectomies: *World Med.*, 14 June 1980, 7.

## 5  INFECTIOUS DISEASES

152  Sontag, 1978, 59–61.
153  Doyle: in Dubos, 1953, 105–6.
     BCG: Dubos, 1953, 160–4.
154  *WHO Statistics Report*, 1970, 8.
     BCG: *New Scientist*, 15 Nov. 1979, 499; *Lancet*, 12 Jan. 1980, 73–4.
     Medical Science: Dubos, 1953, 229–31; McKeown, 1979, 92–3.
     Pathogenicity: Dubos, 1953, 187–8; 1960, 75.
155  TB proneness: Dubos, 1953, 231–40; Lock, 1978, 53; Totman, 1979, 117.
     Consumption history: Kissen, 1958, 89–90.
     Osler: in Dunbar, 1955, 231.
156  Dubos, 1953, 219.
     Kissen, 1958, 1–17, 21–61.
157  Kissen, 1958, 65–86.
158  Dubos, 1953, 19.
     Kissen, 1958, 127–39; 1958, 203–8.
160  *Times*, 7 Feb. 1969.
     *Which?* Feb. 1980.
     Rhinoviruses: *Times*, 26 July 1961: *Med. News Trib. of GB*, 29 May 1972.
161  *NY Times*, 6 April, 8 June 1976.
     Fort Dix: Osborn, 1977, 30ff; *New Age*, Nov. 1977; *BMJ*, 8 March 1980,
       700.
     Pereira, *WHO Bulletin*, July 1978, 5–7.
162  Recent research; *Times*, 25 Jan. 1980; *New Scientist*, 7 Feb. 1980, 396–7.
     *BMJ*, 5 May 1979, 1164–8.
     Andrewes, 1956, 114.

164 Dixon, 29 June, 1977, 37.
P.O. trial: P. Taylor, *World Med.*, 7 Sept. 1977, 47–50; Dixon, *World Med.*, 1 Dec. 1979, 33; Smith/Pollard, 1979.
165 Totman, 1977, 55–63.
*New Scientist*, 28 Feb. 1980.
167 No satisfactory prevention: *Brit. Jnl. VD*, 1978, 422–32; *BMJ*, 8 March 1980, 668.
*MIMS*, 1 Feb. 1978, 104.
*BMJ*, 23 Dec. 1979, 1736.
Evans, 1979, 3–25.
Asscher: in Lock, 1979, 139–46.
168 Allergic reaction: Coutts (*et al.*), 1955; *BMJ*, 23 Dec. 1978, 1735–6.
169 Schofield, 1979, 32ff, 169–70; Turk, 1978, 170.
Young doctor (p.c.).
170 *World Med.*, 15 Nov. 1978, 47.
171 Pasteur/Bernard: Dubos, 1953, 227–8; 1960, 180; Selye, 1956, 205.
Pettenkofer: Dubos, 1951, 271–2.
172 Simeons, 1960, 2–3.
173 Guirdham, 1942, 118.
Gale, 96–7.
174 Dubos, 1959, 64, 89–90, 124, 131.
175 Thomas, 1974, 75–80.
*Time*, 17 Nov. 1961; *Daily Telegraph*, 21 Oct. 1965.
*Lancet*, 17 June 1967, 1314.
176 Thomas, 1974, 75.
Stamler, 1973, 36.
177 Thomas, 1974, 76–7.
178 Creighton, 1894, ii, vii, 40, 433.
Sydenham, 1050, ii, 96.
Koch: Fitzgibbon, 1932, 12–15.
179 Cremonese: Fitzgibbon, 1932, 45–7.
Commission: Fitzgibbon, 1932, 47.
Ross: Fitzgibbon, 1932, 7–16.
180 Fitzgibbon, 1932, 25–6.
Koch: de Kruif, 1930, 159.
Andrewes, 1956, 117–18.
181 Conference: Selby, 1977, *passim*.
Hoyle/Wickramasinghe, 1979, 71–99.

## 6 NEURO-EPIDEMICS

184 Sleeping sickness: Sacks, 1973, 8–13.
185 Wilson, 1963, 42.
Zinsser, 1960, 59.
Hecker, 1844, 81ff.
186 Ergot: Calder, 1961, 138.

Zinsser, 1934, 57–62.
187 Wilson, 1956, 44–5.
Guirdham, 1942, 95.
188 Guirdham, 1957, 47.
LA hospital: Lyle/Chamberlain, 1978, 711–17.
189 *Lancet*, 26 May 1976, 789–90.
*BMJ*, 19 Oct. 1977, 895–904; 927–8.
Welsh children: *Times*, 16 Nov. 1961.
MOH: *Mail*, 16 Oct. 1965.
*Times*, 16 Oct. 1965.
*BMJ*, 25 March 1967, 762.
190 Eden, *World Med.*, 15 June 1977, 25.
RCM symposium: Lyle/Chamberlain, 1978, 718–20, 730, 773.
192 Shelokov: Lyle/Chamberlain, 1978, 771–4.
*BMJ*, 3 June 1978, 1437.
193 Ryle, 1948, 265–7.
194 Medawar, 1980, xv.
*BMJ*, 1 March 1980, 591.
Claims unsubstantiated: e.g. Edelstein (*et al.*), 1973, 1172.
Atlanta symposium: Balows/Fraser, 1979, 489ff.
Confident diagnoses: e.g. *Lancet*, 2 Dec. 1978, 1173; *BMJ*, 14 July 1979, 81.
195 *Times*, 10 Sept. 1980.
*BMJ*, 4 Oct. 1980, 943.
*BMJ*, 14 Feb. 1981, 515.
196 *BMJ*, 18 Aug. 1979, 408–9.
Colligan/Stockton, 1978.
197 Roueché, *New Yorker*, 21 Aug. 1978, 63–70.
*Sunday Telegraph*, 17 July 1977.
199 *Lancet*, 22 Nov. 1980, 1122–3; 13 Dec. 1980, 1310.
Sacks, 1973, 3–27.
200 Eros: Sacks, 1973, 235.
202 Carington, 1945, 153–64.
Callahan, 1977, 59ff.
Clark, *World Med.*, 9 Feb. 1980, 39.
Pettenkofer: Dubos, 1959, 89–90.
203 *Med. News*, 3 April 1964.
204 Guirdham, 1957, 24.
Eden, *World Med.*, 15 June 1977, 25.
205 Crichton-Browne: quoted in Schofield, 1980, 295–6.

## 7 NEUROPATHOLOGY

207 *BMJ*, 6 Jan. 1979, 5.
Charcot: Szasz, 1961, 23.
*New Scientist*, 5 Oct. 1978, 23.

208 Virology/immunology: *Brit. Med. Bulletin*, Jan. 1977, 38.
Management: *General Practitioner*, 15 June 1979.
209 *Lancet*, 11 March 1978, 541.
*BMJ*, 12 Feb. 1972, 392; OHE, 1975, 20.
210 'Probable/possible': OHE, 1975, 9.
*Lancet*, 11 Aug. 1979, 310.
211 London hospital case (p.c.).
OHE, 1974, 4.
212 *Lancet*, 8 March 1980, 526–8.
213 Tuke, 1872, 191, 202–12.
Sacks, 1973, 8–13.
214 *Lancet*, 17 May 1980, 1066.
McKeown, 1979, xii.
215 Thomas, 1980, 93–4.
Illingworth, *World Med.*, 7 April 1979.
Heilig/Hoff: in Benson, 1979, 57.
Utah research: *JAMA*, 14 March 1980, 1059.
Wolff, 1968, 189.
216 Royal Free: Lyle/Chamberlain, 1978, 721, 772.
217 MS:/R. Lustig, *Observer*, 25 Feb. 1979.
Gage: Blakemore, 1977, 3.

## 8 AUTO-IMMUNE DISEASES

219 Allergy's history: Vaughan, 1942, 44ff.
220 *BMJ*, 10 May 1980, 1153.
Food allergy task: *Lancet* 15 Feb. 1978, 426–8.
221 Vaughan, 1942, 58.
222 California breakthrough: *Time*, 25 Aug. 1975.
Burnet, 1972–3, 2–3: Pickering (p.c.).
223 Ogilvie, 1957.
Solomons (p.c.).
Pulay, 1942, 80, 138, 193.
Dunbar, 1955, 185.
224 Swartz, 1963, 85.
Black, *BMJ*, 27 Feb. 1965, 562–7.
Black, 1964.
226 Swartz, 1963, 86.
227 Breen, *Med. News*, 3 Nov. 1967.
Sydenham, 1850, ii, 85.
228 Harvey: Hunter/MacAlpine, 1963, 32.
Hysteria common: Whyte, 1765.
Paget, 1873.
Coleridge, 1852, 81.
229 Freud, 1953, i, 9–23.
Fliess letter: in Clark, 1980, 97.

230 Schofield, 1908, 9.
231 Schofield, 1908, 55–72.
     Szasz, 1962, 95.
232 Sargant, *World Med.*, 20 April 1977, 81.
     *Times*, 16, 19 Oct. 1965.
233 Wilson, 1951, 280–94.

## 9 THE ROLE OF ILLNESS

234 Parsons, 1971, 436–7.
235 Sigerist, 1951, i, 141.
     Tylor, 1971, i, 141.
236 Sargant, 1973, 126–9, 160.
237 Hippocrates, 1978, 237.
239 Hume, *Essay on Miracles*.
240 Simeons, 1960, 89.
     Fitzgibbon, 1932, 25–6.
241 Jordan: in Hunter/MacAlpine, 1963, 71.
     Neal: Eagle, 1978, 107–10.
     'Fits damage the brain': e.g. *World Med.*, 10 March 1979, 43; *Lancet*, 17
       May 1980, 1065–6.
     Epilepsy life expectancy: Wells, 1980, 29; *Lancet*, 1 Sept. 1979, 458.
242 Dostoevsky (Penguin), 1978, 8, 29, 82, 258.
     Calabre, 1804, 65–6.
243 Darwin, 1872, 201.
     Spencer, 1891, ii, 458–86; Koestler, 1964, 79–81.
     Cousins, 1979, 27–48 (originally in *NEJM*, 23 Dec, 1976, 1458–63).
244 Selye, 1957, 31.
     MS: OHE, 1975, 20.
245 Sydenham, 1850, ii, 91.
     Paget, 1873.
     Breuer: Jones, *Freud*, 1953, i, 247–8.
246 Burton, 1948, 365.
     Carter, 1853, 21.
     Mill, 1869, 111–12.
247 Shell-shock: Rivers, 1920, 2.
     Sassoon, 1936, 20.
     Rivers, 1920, 127.
248 Rivers, 1920, 2, 55–63, 127–38.
249 Trethowan, 1979, 251.
     Totman, 1979, 96.
     Ramsay: in Lyle/Chamberlain, 1978, 720.
     Galbraith, *World Med.*, 12 July 1980, 570.

## 10 THE ROLE OF THE MEDICAL PROFESSION

251 Thomas, 1979, 165.
Todd, 1977, 47.
Roberts, 1977, 176.
252 Rayer: in Foucault, 1975, 124.
Brodie, 1837, 69–70.
253 Bernard: in Dubos, 1951, 199.
Huxley, T. H.; in G. R. Taylor, 1979, 4.
254 Dunlop, *World Med.*, 18 Oct. 1972, 52.
Crookshank, 1927, 88–9; 'lachrymation' in Dunbar, 1955, 53.
255 Ryle, 1948, 97, 201–2.
Lasagna, 1962, 9.
256 Wolf, *Jnl. Clin. Investigation*, 1950, 100–9.
257 Glazier, 1973, 13.
Sacks, 1973, 239–40.
McKeown, 1979, xv–xvi.
Engel, 1977, 129–35.
Dudley, *World Med.*, 9 Aug. 1980, 11.
258 Engel, 1977, 130.
Adams, 1976, 17.
259 *BMJ*, 2 Aug. 1980, 340.
Thomas, 1980, 168.
Sontag, 1979, 56–7.
260 *New Yorker*, 16 July 1979, 82–7.
Brewer, *World Med.*, 25 Jan. 1978, 61; Benson, 1979, 79–80.
261 Cochrane, 1972, 36.
*New Scientist*, 2 Oct. 1980, 2–3.
262 Scanner: *Sunday Times*, 24 Feb. 1980; *New Scientist*, 19 May 1977, 380.
Roberts, 1977, 96–7.
264 GP: *World Med*, 4 Oct. 1980, 35.
Lasagna, 1962, 135–6.
Kefauver, 1961, 155–221.
265 Promotion expenditure: Schrag, 1980, 122; R. Com. NHS, 1979.
Owen, *New Statesman*, 23 April 1976.
President: *BMJ*, 22 Nov. 1980, 1410–11.
*Lancet*, 9 Aug. 1975, 268.
266 Indomethacin: Pinals/Sumner, 1967; *BMJ*, 14 Jan. 1967, 69–75: Inglis, 1967.
Dept. Health: *BMJ*, 21 Feb. 1977, 574.
Monitored release: *New Scientist*, 20 Oct. 1977, 130; Teeling-Smith, 1980, 27; *Guardian* 11 Oct. 1980.
267 *Lancet*, 13 Oct. 1979, 781.
Fraser, 28 Feb. 1961.
268 Adriani, *Science*, 23 Feb. 1973, 776.

269 *Lancet*, 25 Feb. 1978, 424.
   *New Scientist*, 18 May 1978, 442–3.
270 *ABPI News*, July 1979.
   Friedman, *Science*, 23 February 1973, 179.
271 Roberts, 1977, 72ff.
   Inman: *New Scientist*, 17 July 1980, 218.
   'Use as instructed': *World Med.*, 12 July 1980, 7.
272 Tetracyline: P. Davies, *Guardian*, 3 Jan. 1978. *BMJ*, 17 March 1980, 705–6.
   Distalgesic: *BMJ*, 24 Feb. 1979, 551; *Guardian*, 13, 14, 21, 22 Feb. 1979.
   AMA: New Age, Nov. 1977.
273 Millington, *World Med.*, 28 June 1980, 40–3.
275 Ehrenreichs, 1971, 33.
   Stumpf, *Annals Int. Med.*, Feb. 1966, 450–6.
   Beecher, *NEJM*, 16 June 1966, 1354–60.
   Ethical committees: *BMJ*, 28 Feb. 1981, 719–20.
276 Cottle: in Jaffe, 1975, 22.
   Bradshaw, 1978, 203.
277 Dixon, *New Scientist*, 23 Feb. 1978, 482; *World Med.*, 4 April 1981, 91—2.
   *Lancet*, 4 Oct. 1980, 731.
278 *Sunday Times*, 27 July 1975.
   Cochrane, *Guardian*, 26 Nov. 1980.
279 Clofibrate 'dereliction of duty': P. Nixon (p.c.); WHO report, *Lancet*, 30 Aug. 1980, 489.
280 Headlines: e.g. *Observer*, 30 Dec. 1979.
   *Time*, 31 March 1980.
   *NY Times*, 27 May 1980.
   McVie, *BMJ*, 28 June 1980, 1613.
281 *Lancet*, 19 July 1980, 113; *New Scientist*, 24 July 1980; 21 Feb. 1980.
   MacDonagh, *Times*, 28 April 1944.
282 Enzymes: *New Scientist*, 12 June 1980, 330.
   Burnet, 1971, 218.
   Miller: in Pappworth, *World Med.*, 22 March 1980, 41.
   Roberts, 1977, 85.
   Ogilvie, 1957.
   Levitt/Guralnick, 1979, 35.
   'Unlucky patient', *World Med.*, 7 Sept. 1977, 9.
   WHO: *Sunday Times*, 23 July 1978.
   Newsletter: April 1980.
284 Hillman: Tucker, *Guardian*, 26 May 1980.
286 *BMJ*, Gore (*et al.*), 1977.
   Second survey report: *NEJM*, Fletcher (*et al.*), 1979.
287 Pappworth, *World Med.*, 22 March 1980, 41.
   Schrag, 1980, 123.
   Anturane: *NEJM*, 31 Jan. 1980; *Lancet*, 9 Aug. 1980, 306–7.

288 Debendox: St. Jorre, *Observer*, 20 Jan. 1980; Potter, *Sunday Times*, 24 Feb. 1980.
289 Edinburgh doctor: *BMJ*, 26 Feb. 1977, 574.
290 *BMJ*, 11 June 1977, 1492–3.
    Smith, *BMJ*, 22 Nov. 1980, 1410–11.
    'Drug lag': *BMJ*, 8 March 1980, 670.
291 Mackenzie, 1919, 44–5.
    Ryle, 1948, 12–13.
    Carrel, 1961, 46.
292 Ehrenreichs, 1971, 31.
    AMA: Carlson, 1975, 41.
    R. Com.: 1979, 215.
    Kerr, *World Med.*, 24 Feb. 1979, 19.
    GP: *World Med.*, 10 March 1979, 28–31.
293 R. Com., 1979, 215–6.
    Rival specialists: Pappworth, *World Med.*, 26 July 1980, 40; C. G. Clark, 1979.
    Ryle, 1948, 116–7.
294 BMA: Fitton/Acheson, 1979.
    Carlson, 1975, 41.
    Illich, 1977, 247–8.
295 Mahler, *Listener*, 4 Aug. 1977, 130.
296 Kerr, *World Med.*, 15 Dec. 1979, 19.
    McKeown, 1979, 152.
    Thomas, 1980, 143.
297 Dermatology: *World Med.*, 12 Jan. 1980, 12.
    McKeown, 1979, 148.
    Norcross, *World Med.*, 1 Dec. 1979, 63.
298 Illingworth, *World Med.*, 7 April 1979, 31–6.
    Mackenzie, 1919, 61, 120.
300 Thomas, 1980, 137–41.
    Headmaster: *Lancet*, 7 March 1981, 541–8.
    Horrobin, 1977, 73, 100–1.
    Dudley, *World Med.*, 6 Sept. 1980, 12.
    Germany/Sweden: *World Med.*, 21 April 1979, 30.
301 Pickering, 1978(b).
302 *Lancet*, 19 March 1961, 491.
    Wade, *World Med.*, 15 June 1977, 52–4.
    Horrobin, 1978, 100–1.
    Liverpool students (p.c.).
303 Bennet, 1979, 19, 133–46.
    Chichester, 1964, 262.
304 Gould, *New Scientist*, 9 April 1981, 107–8.
305 Freidson, 1975, 5, 137, 363–70.
307 Guys Hospital study: Best (*et al.*), 1977.
    Horrobin, 1977, iv, 1–7, 65–6, 88–9.

308 McKeown, 1979, 123.
Inglefinger, *NEJM*, 24 Feb. 1977, 449.
Audit/peer review: *BMJ*, 26 July 1980, 325; *World Med.*, 8 Sept. 1979.

## 11 THE WAY AHEAD

310 NHS: Roberts, 1978, 182; Garner, 1979, 179; *World Med.* 3 May 1980, 7.
Ehrenreichs, 1971, 131.
311 US system: Benson, 1979, 108; *World Med.*, 17 Nov. 1979, 49–50;
Ballantyne, *Guardian*, 13 Nov. 1979.
Wilson, *Listener*, 25 May 1979.
Canada: Richards, *World Med.*, 20 Oct. 1979, 36.
312 *World Med.*, 3 May 1980, 7.
313 Cochrane, *Guardian*, 26 Nov. 1980.
Lalonde, 1977.
Carlson, 1975, 131–2.
Garner, 1979, 153.
315 Blue Shield: *Brain/Mind Bulletin*, 21 July 1980, 3.
Calabre, 1804, 9ff.
Virey: in Dubos, 1960, 24–5.
316 Orton, *Guardian*, 11 April 1978; Jobling, *Guardian*, 20 April 1978.
317 Horrobin, press release, 1 Jan. 1981.
318 Selye, 1974, 88.
319 Dubos, 1959, 30.

# Bibliography

The publication date and place is of the edition I consulted: where there is an earlier edition it appears in brackets.

Abse, Dannie, *Medicine on Trial*, London, 1967.

Adams, J. Crawford, *Outline of Orthopedics*, London, 1976.

Alexander, Franz, 'Emotional Factors in Essential Hypertension', *Psychosom. Med.*, 1939, 1, 173–9.

Alexander, Franz, *Psychoanalysis and Psychotherapy*, London, 1957.

Alston, J. M., *Infectious Diseases*, London, 1967.

American Heart Association, *Coronary Risk Handbook*, Dallas, 1973.

Anderson, E. S., 'The problems and Implications of Chloramphenicol-resistance to the Typhoid Bacillus', *Jnl. of Hygiene*, April, 1975, 289–94.

Andrewes, Sir Christopher, *The Common Cold*, London, 1965.

Andrewes, Sir Christopher, *Viruses and Cancer*, London, 1970.

Armstrong, A. (*et al.*), 'Natural History of Acute Coronary Heart Attacks', *Brit. Heart Jnl.*, Jan., 1972, 67–80.

Ashley, David J. B., 'The Biological Status of Carcinoma *in situ* of the Uterine Cervix', *Jnl. Obstet. Gyn. Brit. C'wealth*, June, 1966, 372–81.

Atkins, Sir Hedley (*et al.*), 'Treatment of Early Breast Cancer', *BMJ*, 20 May 1972, 423–29.

Auchinloss, Hugh, 'Significance of Location and Number of Axillary Metastases in Carcinoma of the Breast', *Annals Surg.*, 1963, 37–46.

Bacon, Catherine L. (*et al.*), 'A Psychosomatic Survey of Cancer of the Breast', *Psychosom. Med.*, 1952, 14–16.

Bahnson, Claus B. (*et al.*), 'Psychophysical Aspects of Cancer', *Annals of the NY Academy of Sciences*, 21 Jan. 1966, 773, 1055.

Baldessarini, Ross J. (*et al.*), 'Tardive Dyskinesia', *Am. Jnl. Psychiatry*, Oct. 1980, 1163–72.

Balint, Michael and Enid Balint, *Psychotherapeutic Techniques in Medicine*, London, 1961.

Balows, Albert and David Fraser (eds.), 'International Symposium on Legionnaires' Disease', *Annals Intern. Med.*, April, 1979, 489–714.

Barnes, Glenda K. (*et al.*), 'Changes in Working States of Patients Following Coronary By-pass Surgery', *JAMA*, 19 Sept. 1977, 1259–62.

Barraclough, B. M. and N. A. Mitchell-Heggs, 'Use of Neurosurgery for Psychological Disorder in British Isles during 1974–6', *BMJ*, 9 Dec. 1978, 1591–3.

Barton, Russell, *The Institutional Neurosis*, Bristol, 1976 (1959).

Bartrop, R. W. (*et al.*), 'Depressed Lymphocyte Function after Bereavement', *Lancet*, 16 April 1967, 834–6.

Bateson, Gregory (*et al.*), 'Towards a theory of Schizophrenia', *Behavioral Science*, Oct., 1956, 251–5.

Baum, Michael, (*et al.*), 'Cancer Research Campaign Trial for Early Breast Cancer', *Lancet*, 12 July 1980, 55–60.

Baxter, S., 'Psychological Problems of Intensive Care', *Brit. Jnl. Hosp. Med.*, June, 1974, 875–85.

Beecher, Henry K., 'Surgery as Placebo: a Quantitative Study of Bias', *JAMA*, 1 July 1961, 1102–7.

Bennet, Glin, *Patients and their Doctors*, London, 1979.

Benson, Herbert, *The Relaxation Response*, London, 1977 (NY 1975).

Benson, Herbert, *The Mind-Body Effect*, New York, 1979.

Benson, Herbert and H. D. Epstein, 'The Placebo Effect', *JAMA*, 23 June 1975, 1225–7.

Berglund, G. (*et al.*), 'Coronary Heart-Disease after Treatment of Hypertension', *Lancet*, 7 Jan. 1978, 1–5.

Bernard, Claude, *Leçons de Physiologie Experimentale*, Paris, 1856.

Best, Gordon (*et al.*), *Health, the Mass Media and the NHS*, London, 1977.

Blacher, R. S., 'The Hidden Psychosis of Open Heart Surgery', *JAMA*, 16 Oct. 1972, 305–8.

Black, David, 'Medicine and the Mind', *Playboy*, April 1980, 121–2, 211–21.

Black, Sir Douglas, 'Medicine and Society', *Lancet*, 9 Aug. 1980, 304–6.

Black, Stephen, *Mind and Body*, London, 1969.

Black, Stephen, 'The Use of Hypnosis in the Treatment of Psychosomatic Disorders' (Conference Paper) London 1964.

Blackwell, B. (*et al.*), 'Hypertensive Interaction between MOI and Foodstuffs', *Brit. Jnl. Psychiatry*, 1967, 349–65.

Bomford, R. R., 'Changing Concepts of Health and Disease, with Particular Reference to Psychosomatic Medicine', *BMJ*, 21 March 1953, 633–9.

Blakemore, Colin, *Mechanics of the Mind*, Cambridge, 1976.

Bloom, B. S. and O. L. Peterson, 'End Results, Cost and Productivity of Coronary Care Units', *NEJM*, 11 Jan. 1973, 72–8.

Blythe, Peter, *Stress, the Modern Sickness*, London, 1975.

Borda, Ivan T. (*et al.*), 'Assessment of Adverse Reactions within a Drug Surveillance Program', *JAMA*, 26 Aug. 1968, 645–7.

Boyes, D. A. (*et al.*), 'Significance of *in situ* Carcinoma of the Uterine Cervix', *BMJ*, 27 Jan. 1962, 203–5.

Bradshaw, John S., 'Personal View', *BMJ*, 10 Feb. 1973, 349.

Bradshaw, John S., *Doctors on Trial*, London, 1979.

Brain, Lord, 'The Concept of Hysteria', *Procs. Royal Soc. Med.*, April 1963, 321–3.

Braunwald, Eugene, 'Coronary Artery Surgery at the Cross-Roads', *NEJM*, 22 Sept. 1977, 661–3.

Breast Cancer Symposium, *Brit. Jnl. Surg.*, Oct., 1969, 782–96.
British Breast Group, 'Screening for Breast Cancer', *BMJ*, 15 July 1978, 178–80.
Brown, Barbara B., *New Mind, New Body*, New York, 1975 (1974).
Brown, George and Tirril Harris, *Social Origins of Depression*, London, 1978.
Buisseret, Paul, 'Allergic Dermatoses and Similar Conditions', *MIMS*, Sept.–Dec. 1977.
Bunker, John P., 'A Comparison of Operations and Surgeons in the US and in England and Wales', *NEJM*, 15 Jan. 1979, 135–44.
Bunker, John P. (*et al.*), *Costs, Risks and Benefits of Surgery*, Oxford, 1977.
Burch, Philip, *The Biology of Cancer*, Lancaster, 1976.
Burnet, Sir Macfarlane, 'Cancer – a Biological Approach', *BMJ*, 6 April 1957, 779–86; 13 April 1957, 841–6.
Burnet, Sir Macfarlane, 'Somatic Mutation and Chronic Disease', *BMJ*, 6 Feb. 1965, 338–42.
Burnet, Sir Macfarlane, *Immunological Surveillance*, Sydney, 1970.
Burnet, Sir Macfarlane, *Genes, Dreams and Realities*, Aylesbury, 1971.
Burnet, Sir Macfarlane, *Auto-Immunity and Auto-Immune Disease*, Lancaster, 1972.
Burnfield, Alexander and Penelope Burnfield, 'Common Psychological Problems in Multiple Sclerosis', *BMJ*, 6 May 1978, 1193–4.
Cairns, John, *Cancer, Science and Society*, San Francisco, 1978.
Calabre, E., *Dissertation sur L'Influence de L'Éducation, des Habitudes et des Passions dans les Maladies Nerveuses*, Paris, 1804.
Callahan, Philip, *Tuning in to Nature*, London, 1977 (New York, 1975).
Canetti, Elias, *Crowds and Power*, London, 1962.
Cannon, Walter, *The Wisdom of the Body*, London, 1932.
Carington, Whately, *Telepathy*, London, 1945.
Carlson, Rick J., *The End of Medicine*, New York, 1975.
Carlson, Rick J., *The Frontiers of Science and Medicine*, London, 1975(b).
Carrell, Alexis, *Man the Unknown*, London, 1961 (1935).
Carruthers, Malcolm, *The Western Way of Death*, London, 1974.
Carter, R. Brudenell, *On the Pathology and treatment of hysteria*, London, 1853.
Carter, Stephen K. and R. L. Comis, 'Integration of Chemotherapy into Combined Modality Treatment of Solid Tumors', *Cancer Treatment Review*, 1976, 193–214.
Cassel, John, 'The Contribution of the Social Environment to Host Resistance', *Am. Jnl. Epidem.*, Aug. 1976, 107–23.
Cassells, Ward (*et al.*), 'Retirement and Coronary Mortality', *Lancet*, 14 June 1980, 1288–9.
Castelli, William (*et al.*), 'HDL Cholesterol and Other Lipids in Coronary Heart Disease', *Circulation*, May 1977, 767–72.
Chambers, W. N., and H. F. Reiser, 'Congestive Heart Failure', *Psychosom. Med.*, 1953, 39–60.

Christenson, William and L. E. Hinkle, 'Differences in illness and prognostic signs in two groups of young men', *JAMA*, 29 July 1961, 247–53.

Clark, C. G., 'The Influence of Cimetidine on Current Surgical Treatment of Peptic Ulceration', *Brit. Jnl. Clinical Practice*, 1979, 216–19.

Clark, Ronald, *Freud*, London, 1980.

Clarke, Edwin (ed.), *Modern Methods in the History of Medicine*, London, 1971.

Cochrane, A. L., *Effectiveness and Efficiency*, London, 1972.

Cohen, John and John H. Clark, *Medicine, Mind and Man*, Reading and San Francisco, 1979.

Coleman, Vernon, *Paper Doctors*, London, 1977.

Colligan, Michael J. and Michael J. Smith, 'A Methodological Approach for Evaluating Outbreaks of Mass Psychogenic Illness in Industry', *Jnl. Occup. Med.*, June 1978, 401–2.

Colligan, Michael J. and William Stockton, 'Assembly Line Hysteria', *Psychology Today*, Sept. 1978, 20–4.

Colling, Aubrey (*et al.*), 'Tees-side Coronary Survey', *BMJ*, 13 Nov. 1976, 1169–720.

Colling, Aubrey (ed.), *Coronary Care in the Community*, London, 1978.

Comroe, J. H. and R. D. Dripps, 'Scientific Basis for the Support of Biomedical Science', *Science*, 9 April 1976, 105–11.

Connolly, Joseph, 'Stress and Coronary Artery Disease', *Brit. Jnl. Hosp. Med.*, Feb. 1974, 297–302.

Constanza, Mary E., 'Sounding Board: the Problem of Breast Cancer Prophylaxis', *NEJM*, 20 Nov. 1975, 1095–8.

Corey, Lawrence (*et al.*), *Medicine in a Changing Society*, St. Louis, 1977 (1972).

Cousins, Norman, *Anatomy of an Illness*, New York, 1979.

Coutts, W. E. (*et al.*), 'Trichomonas Infection in the Male', *BMJ*, 8 Oct. 1955, 885–9.

Cox, Tom, *Stress*, London, 1978.

Crane, George, 'Clinical Pharmacology in its 20th Year', *Science*, 13 July 1973, 125–8.

Crane, George, 'Persistent Dyskinesia', *Brit. Jnl. Psychiatry*, 1973, 395–405.

Creighton, Charles, *A History of Epidemics in Britain* (2 vols.), Cambridge, 1894.

Crile, George, 'Results of Simplified Treatment of Breast Cancer', *Surg. Gyn. and Obstet.*, March 1964, 517–23.

Crookshank, F. G., *Migraine and the Other Common Neuroses*, London, 1926.

Crookshank, F. G., *Epidemiological Essays*, London, 1930.

Culliton, Barbara J., 'Mammography Controversy', *Science*, 14 Oct. 1977, 71–3.

Currie, Graham A., *Cancer and the Immune Response*, London, 1974.

Davies, D. M. (ed.), *Textbook of Adverse Drug Reactions*, Oxford, 1977.

Davies, Hywel, 'Legionnaires' Disease – an Organism or a Hotel Chemical Spray?', *World Med.*, 8 March 1980, 21–3.

343

De Kruif, Paul, *Microbe Hunters*, London, 1930 (New York, 1927).

Department of Health and Social Security, *Diet and Coronary Heart Disease*, London, 1974.

Department of Health and Social Security, *Inequalities in Health*, London, 1980.

Dixon, Bernard, *Beyond the magic bullet*, London, 1979.

Doll, Richard and A. Bradford Hill, 'Smoking and Carcinoma of the Lung', *BMJ*, 30 Sept. 1950, 739–48.

Doll, Richard and A. Bradford Hill, 'The Mortality of Doctors in Relation to their Smoking Habits', *BMJ*, 26 June 1954, 1451–5.

Doll, Richard and A. Bradford Hill, 'Lung Cancer in Relation to Smoking', *BMJ*, 10 Nov. 1956, 1071–81.

Donaldson, Malcolm, *The Cancer Riddle*, London, 1962.

Draper, Peter, *The NHS in the Next 30 Years*, London, 1978.

D'Souza, Michael, 'If Only You'd Come to Me Sooner', *World Med.*, 31 May 1978, 24–5.

Dubos, René, *Louis Pasteur*, London, 1951 (New York, 1950).

Dubos, René, *Mirage of Health*, New York, 1959.

Dubos, René, *Men Adapting*, Yale, 1965.

Dubos, René and Jean Dubos, *The White Plague*, London, 1953.

Dunbar, Flanders, *Mind and Body*, New York, 1955 (1947).

Dunkman, W. Bruce (*et al.*), 'Medical Perspectives in Coronary Artery Surgery', *Annals Int. Med.*, 1974, 817–37.

Dworkin, B. R. (*et al.*), 'Baroreceptor Activation . . . Implications for Hypertension', *Science*, 21 Sept. 1979, 1299–1300.

Eagle, Robert, *Alternative Medicine*, London, 1978.

Edelstein, Paul H. (*et al.*), 'Isolation of a New Serotype of Legionnaires' Disease Bacterium', *Lancet*, 2 Dec. 1978, 1172–4.

Ehrenreich, Barbara and John Ehrenreich, '*The American Health Empire*', New York, 1971.

Eisenberg, Leon, 'What Makes Persons "Patients" and Patients "Well"?' *Am. Jnl. Med.*, Aug. 1980, 277–86.

Engel, George L., 'The Need for a New Medical Model', *Science*, 8 April 1977, 129–36.

Engel, George L. and L. Salzman, 'A Double Standard for Psychosomatic Papers', *NEJM*, 4 Jan. 1973, 44–6.

Enstrom, J. E. and D. F. Austin, 'Interpreting Cancer Survival Rates', *Science*, 4 March 1977, 847–51.

Ernst, Frederick A. (*et al.*), 'Learned Control of Coronary Blood Flow', *Psychosom. Med.*, March 1979, 79–85.

European Organisation for the Control of Circulatory Diseases, *Report of Third Symposium*, Nov. 1978, Copenhagen, 1979.

Evans, Peter, *Cystitis*, London, 1979.

Evans, William and Clifford Hoyle, 'The Comparative Value of Drugs Used in the Continuous Treatment of Angina Pectoris', *Qly. Jnl. Med.*, July 1933, 311–38.

Evans, William, 'Anti-Coagulant Therapy in Coronary Occlusion', *Procs. RSM*, 1953, 318–23.

Evans, William, 'Addiction to Medicines', *BMJ*, 15 Sept. 1962, 722–4.

Everson, T. C., and W. H. Cole, 'Spontaneous Regression of Cancer: Preliminary Report', *Annals Surg.*, 1956, 366.

Eysenck, H. J., *Uses and Abuses of Psychology*, London, 1953.

Eysenck, H. J., *Sense and Nonsense in Psychology*, London, 1957.

Eysenck, H. J., *Smoking, Health and Personality*, London, 1965.

Eysenck, H. J. (*et al.*), 'Smoking and Personality', *BMJ*, 14 May 1960, 1456–60.

Farquhar, John (*et al.*), 'Community Education for Cardiovascular Health', *Lancet*, 4 June 1977, 1192–5.

Farrabee, Dale H. and Charles E. Roppel (eds.), *Questions and Answers?*, San Francisco, 1979.

Farrell, Frances, 'I have Breast Cancer', *World Med.*, 12 Jan. 1977, 33–6.

Ferris, Paul, *The Doctors*, London, 1965.

Finn, Ronald and H. Newman Cole, 'Food Allergy: Fact or Fiction?', *Lancet*, 25 Feb. 1978, 426–8.

Fisher, Ronald A., *Smoking: the Cancer Controversy*, London, 1959.

Fitton, Freda and H. W. K. Acheson, *The Doctor-Patient Relationship*, London, 1979.

Fitzgibbon, Elliot, *Marvels of Modern Medicine*, London, 1926.

Fitzgibbon, Elliot, *Malaria: the Governing Factor*, London, 1932.

Fletcher, Robert H. and Suzanne Fletcher, 'Clinical Research in General Medical Journals', *NEJM*, 26 July 1979, 180–3.

Florey, Charles (*et al.*), 'Changing Mortality from Ischemic Heart Disease in G.B., 1968–77', *BMJ*, 11 March 1978, 635–7.

Foucault, Michel, *Madness and Civilisation*, London, 1965 (Paris, 1965).

Frank, Leonard Roy (ed.), *The History of Shock Treatment*, San Francisco, 1978.

Frankel, Bernard L. (*et al.*), 'Treatment of Hypertension with Biofeedback and Relaxation Techniques', *Psychosom. Med.*, June, 1978, 276–93.

Fraser, David W. (*et al.*), 'Legionnaires' Disease', *NEJM*, 1 Dec 1977, 1189–97.

Freidson, Eliot, *Profession of Medicine: a Study of the Sociology of Applied Knowledge*, New York, 1975 (1970).

Freis, Edward, 'Medical Treatment of Chronic Hypertension', *Modern Concepts of Cardiovascular Disease*, April, 1971.

Freud, Sigmund, *Collected Papers*, New York and London, 1966.

Freud, Sigmund and Josef Breuer, *Studies in Hysteria*, London, 1956.

Friedman, Meyer (*et al.*), 'Serum Cholesterol, Blood Clotting and Stress', *Circulation*, 1958, 852–61.

Friedman, Meyer and Ray H. Rosenman, *Type A Behaviour and Your Heart*, New York, 1974.

Friedman, Milton, *Capitalism and Freedom*, Chicago, 1962.

Frumkin, Kenneth (*et al.*), 'Non-pharmacological Control of Essential

Hypertension in Man: A Critical Review', *Psychosom. Med.*, June 1978, 294–317.

Furnivall, P., 'A Personal Account of the Effects of the Modern Treatment of Carcinoma', *BMJ*, 26 Feb. 1938, 450.

Gale, A. H., *Epidemic Diseases*, London, 1959.

Garland, L. Henry, 'Studies in the Accuracy of Diagnostic Procedures', *Am. Jnl. Roent.*, July 1959, 25–38.

Garner, Lesley, *The NHS: Your Money or Your Life*, London, 1979.

Gehlen, Frieda L., 'Towards a Revised Theory of Hysterical Contagion', *Jnl. Health and Soc. Behavior*, March 1977, 27–35.

Gifford, R. H. and A. R. Feinstein, 'A Critique of Methodology in Studies of Anti-Coagulant Therapy', *NEJM*, 13 Feb. 1969, 351–7.

Glass, David, 'Stress and the Heart', *Psychology Today* (UK), April 1977, 21–3.

Godel, Roger, *Vie et Rénovation*, Paris, 1957.

Goldstein, P. H. (*et al.*), 'Isolation of a New Serotype of Legionnaires' Disease Bacterium', *Lancet*, 2 Dec. 1978, 1172–4.

Gordon, Barbara, *I'm Dancing as Fast as I Can*, New York, 1979.

Gordon, T. (*et al.*), 'High Density Lipoprotein as a Protective Factor against Coronary Heart Disease', *Am. Jnl. Med.*, May 1977, 707–14.

Gordon-Taylor, Sir Gordon, 'The Incomputable Factors in Cancer Prognosis', *BMJ*, 21 Feb. 1959, 455–62.

Gore, Sheila M. (*et al.*), 'Misuse of Statistical Methods: Critical Assessment of Articles in *BMJ* from January to March 1976', *BMJ*, 8 Jan. 1977, 85–7.

Greco, F. Anthony and Robert K. Oldham, 'Current Concepts in Cancer', *NEJM*, 16 Aug. 1979, 355–8.

Green, Elmer and Alyce Green, *Beyond Biofeedback*, New York, 1977.

Greenberg, Dan, 'The "War on Cancer": Official Fictions and Harsh Facts', *Science and Government Report*, 1 Dec. 1974.

Greenberg, Dan, 'Progress in Cancer Research – Don't Say It Isn't So', *NEJM*, 27 March 1975, 707.

Greenberg, Dan, 'On the Cancer Front', *New Scientist*, 8 Sept. 1977, 623.

Greer, S. and Tina Morris, 'Psychological Attributes of Women Who Develop Breast Cancer: a Controlled Study', *Jnl. Psychosom. Research*, April 1975, 147–53.

Greer, S. (*et al.*), 'Psychological response to Breast Cancer', *Lancet*, 13 Oct. 1979, 785–7.

Greer, S., 'Psychological Enquiry: a Contribution to Cancer Research', *Psychological Med.*, Feb. 1979, 81.

Grindle, Michael J. (*et al.*), 'Psychosocial Outcome after Coronary Artery Surgery', *Am. Jnl. Psychiatry*, 12 Dec. 1980, 1591–4.

Grinker, Roy, *Psychosomatic Research*, New York, 1961 (1953).

Guirdham, Arthur, *Disease and the Social System*, London, 1942.

Guirdham, Arthur, *A Theory of Disease*, London, 1957.

Guirdham, Arthur, *The Nature of Healing*, London, 1964.

Gunderson, E. K. E. and R. H. Rahe (eds.), *Life Stress and Illness*, Springfield, Ill., 1974.

Gutstein, William H. (*et al.*), 'Neural Factors Contributing to Atherogenesis', *Science*, 27 Jan. 1978, 449–51.

Halliday, James L., 'Psychological Factors in Rheumatism', *BMJ*, 30 Jan., 6 Feb. 1937, 213–17, 264–9.

Hammond, E. C. and D. Horn, 'Relationship Between Human Smoking Habits and Death Rates', *JAMA*, 7 Aug. 1954, 1316–28.

Hammond, E. C. and D. Horn, 'Smoking and Death Rates', *JAMA*, 8 March, 15 March 1958, 1159–72, 1294–1308.

Harris, Richard, *The Real Voice*, New York, 1954.

Harper, R. M. J., *Evolutionary Origins of Disease*, Barnstaple, 1975.

Harter, Herschel R. (*et al.*), 'Prevention of Thrombosis in Patients by Low-Dose Aspirin', *NEJM*, 13 Sept. 1979, 577.

Harvey, W. Proctor (*et al.*), *The Year Book of Cardiology*, Chicago, 1978.

Heaton-Ward, W. A., 'Niamid in Mongolism', *Jnl. Mental Science*, Dec. 1962, 865–70.

Heaton-Ward, W. A., 'Psychopathic Disorders', *Lancet*, 19 Jan. 1963, 121–3.

Hecker, J. F. C., *The Epidemics of the Middle Ages*, London, 1844.

Heller, Tom, *Restructuring the NHS*, London, 1978.

Hiatt, Howard H., 'Protecting the Medical Commons: Who is Responsible?', *NEJM*, 31 July 1975, 235–41.

Hiatt, Howard H., 'Lessons of the Coronary By-Pass Debate', *NEJM*, 29 Dec. 1977, 1462–4.

Hill, J. D. (*et al.*), 'Comparison of Mortality in a Coronary Care Unit and an Ordinary Medical Ward', *BMJ*, 8 July 1977, 81–3.

Hippocrates, *Writings* (ed. G. E. R. Lloyd), London, 1978.

Holden, Constance, 'Cancer and the Mind: How are They Connected?', *Science*, 23 June 1978, 1363–8.

Holmes, T. H. and R. H. Rahe, 'The Social Readjustment Rating Scale', *Jnl. Psychosom. Research*, 1967, 213–18.

Hope-Simpson, R. Edgar, 'The Nature of Herpes', *Procs. Royal Soc. Med.*, Jan. 1965, 8.

Hopkins, Philip, 'Psychiatry in General Practice', *Postgraduate Med. Jnl.*, 1960, 323–30.

Horne, R. L. and R. S. Pickard, 'Psychosocial Risk Factors for Lung Cancer', *Psychosom. Med.*, Nov. 1979, 503–13.

Horrobin, David F., *Medical Hubris: a Reply to Ivan Illich*, New York and Edinburgh, 1977.

Horrobin, David, 'A Singular Solution for Schizophrenia', *New Scientist*, 28 Feb. 1980, 642–4.

Hoyle, Fred and Chandra Wickramasinghe, *Diseases from Space*, London, 1979.

Hughes, Sally S., *The Virus: a History of the Concept*, New York, 1977.

Hunter, Richard and Ida Macalpine, *Three Hundred Years of Psychiatry, 1535–1860*, London, 1963.

Hurley, Rosalinde and John de Louvois, 'Candida Vaginitis', *Postgraduate Med. Jnl.*, Sept. 1979, 645–7.

Hurst, J. W. (*et al.*), 'Value of Coronary By-Pass Surgery', *Am. Jnl. Cardiology*, August 1978, 308–29.

Hurwitz, Natalie and O. L. Wade, 'Intensive Hospital Monitoring of Adverse Reactions to Drugs', *BMJ*, 1 March 1969, 531–6.

Huxley, Julian, *Biological Aspects of Cancer*, London, 1958.

Illich, Ivan, *Limits to Medicine: Medical Nemesis*, London, 1977 (1976).

Inglis, Brian, 'Psyche Submerged', *Lancet*, 10 Dec. 1966, 1307–10.

Inglis, Brian, *Drugs, Doctors and Disease*, London, 1965.

Inglis, Brian, 'The Profitable Rise and Fall of a Wonder Drug', *Sunday Times*, 2 July 1967.

Inglis, Brian, *The Book of the Back*, London, 1978.

Inman, W. H. W., *Monitoring for Drug Safety*, London, 1980.

Irey, N. S., 'Deaths Due to Adverse Drug Reactions', *JAMA*, 6 Jan. 1975, 22–3.

Irwig, L. M., 'Breast Cancer', *Lancet*, 30 Nov. 1974, 1307–8.

Jaffe, Denis T. (ed.), In Search of a Therapy, New York, 1975.

Jacobs, Michael R. (*et al.*), 'Emergence of Multiple-Resistant Pneumococci', *NEJM*, 5 Oct. 1978, 735–40.

Jarrett, W. F. H., 'High Incidence of Cattle Cancer', *Nature*, 20 July 1978, 215–17.

Jelliffe, Smith Ely, 'Encephalitis Lethargica', *NY Med. Jnl.*, 6 March 1920.

Jelliffe, Smith Ely, 'Multiple Sclerosis and Psychoanalysis', *Am. Jnl. Med. Science*, May 1921, 666.

Jelliffe, Smith Ely, 'The Hysteria Group' (in Tice, 1924, 329–59).

Jelliffe, Smith Ely and William White, *Diseases of the Nervous System*, London, 1935.

Jenkins, C. David, 'Psychological and Social Precursors of Coronary Disease', *NEJM*, 4, 11 Feb. 1971, 244–54, 307–17.

Johnson, Walter, *Diseases of Young Women*, London, 1849.

Kannel, William B., 'Some Lessons in Cardiovascular Epidemiology from Framingham', *Am. Jnl. Cardiology*, Feb. 1976, 269–82.

Kannel, William B. and P. Sorlie, 'Hypertension in Framingham' (from *Epidemiology of Control of Hypertension*, ed. Oglesby Paul, Miami, 1975.)

Kefauver, Estes, *Report on Drug Industry*, Washington, 1961.

Kelly, Michael, 'Steroids: Drugs of Addiction', *Jnl. Chronic Diseases*, May 1964, 461–4.

Kety, Seymour, 'Biochemical Theories of Schizophrenia', *Science*, 5, 12 June 1959, 1528, 1590.

Keynes, Geoffrey, 'Conservative Treatment of Cancer of the Breast', *BMJ*, 2 Oct. 1937, 643–7.

Kirklin, J. W., 'Evaluating the Results of Cardiac Surgery', *Circulation*, Aug. 1973, 232–8.

Kissen, David M., *Emotional Factors in Pulmonary TB*, London, 1958.

Kissen, David M., 'Personality Characteristics in Males Conducive to Lung Cancer', *Brit. Jnl. Med. Psychology*, 1963, 27–30.

Kissen, David M., 'Relationship Between Lung Cancer, Cigarette Smoking – inhalation and Personality', *Brit. Jnl. Med. Psychology*, 1964, 203.

Kissen, David M. and H. J. Eysenck, 'Personality in Male Lung Cancer Patients', *Jnl. Psychosom. Research*, 1962, 123–7.

Kissen, David M. and Laurence LeShan (eds.), 'Psychosomatic Aspects of Neuplastic Disease', London, 1964.

Kleinman, Joel (*et al.*), 'The Effects of Changes in Smoking Habits on CHD Mortality', *Am. Jnl. Public Health*, August 1979, 795–82.

Knightley, Phillip (*et al.*) (Sunday Times Insight Team), *Suffer the Children*, London, 1980 (1979).

Koestler, Arthur, *The Act of Creation*, London, 1964.

Koestler, Arthur, 'Can Psychiatrists be Trusted?' (in *The Heel of Achilles*, London, 1974.

Kothari, Masui L. and Lopa E. Mehta, *Cancer*, Boston and London, 1979.

Kramer, Morton, 'Cross National Study of Diagnosis of the Mental Disorders', *Am. Jnl. Psychiatry*, April 1979 (supplement).

Laing, R. D., *The Divided Self*, London, 1959.

Laing, R. D., *The Self and Others*, London, 1961.

Laing, R. D., 'Schizophrenia and the Family', *New Society*, 16 April 1964.

Laing, R. D., 'Results of Family-Orientated Therapy with Hospital Schizophrenics', *BMJ*, 18 Dec. 1965, 1462–5.

Lalonde, Marc, 'Beyond a New Perspective', *Am. Jnl. Public Health*, April, 1977, 357–60.

Langdon-Brown, Walter, *Thus We Are Men*, London, 1938.

Langlands, Allan O. (*et al.*), 'Long-Term Survival of Patients with Breast Cancer', *BMJ*, 17 Nov. 1979, 1247–51.

Lasagna, Louis, *The Doctors' Dilemmas*, London, 1962 (New York, 1962).

Ledingham, J. G. G. and B. Rajagopalan, 'Cerebral Complications in the Treatment of Accelerated Hypertension', *Qly. Jnl. Med.*, 1979, 25–41.

Lee, B. N., 'Has the Mortality of Male Doctors Improved with the Reductions in Their Cigarette Smoking?' *BMJ*, 15 Dec. 1979, 1538–40.

LeShan, Lawrence and R. E. Worthington, 'Some Psychological Correlates of Neoplastic Disease', *Jnl. Clin. and Exptal. Psychopathology*, 1955, 81–8.

LeShan, Lawrence, 'Personality as a Factor in the Pathogenesis of Cancer', *Brit. Jnl. Med. Psychology*, 1956, 49–56.

LeShan, Lawrence, *You Can Fight for Your Life*, New York, 1978 (1977).

LeShan, Lawrence, 'Psychological States as Factors in the Development of Malignant Disorder: a Critical Review', *Jnl. Nat. Cancer Institute*, Jan., 1959, 1–18.

Lessof, Maurice H., 'Auto-Immune Disease' (reprinted from Guy's Hospital *Reports* 1962, 276–88).

Levi, Lennart, *Society, Stress and Disease*, New York, 1967.

Levine, Richard J. (*et al.*), 'Outbreak of Psychosomatic Illness at a Rural Elementary School', *Lancet*, 21 Dec. 1974, 1500–3.

Levitt, Paul M. and Elissa Curalnick, *The Cancer Reference Book*, New York and London, 1979.

Lewison, Edwin F., 'An Appraisal of Long-Term Results in Surgical Treatment of Breast Cancer', *JAMA*, 14 Dec. 1963, 975–8.

Leyburn, Peter, 'A Critical Look at Anti-Depressant Drug Trials', *Lancet*, 25 Nov. 1967, 1135–7.

Liljefors, I. and R. H. Rahe, 'An Identical Twin Study of Psychosocial Factors in CHD', *Psychosom. Med.*, 1970, 523.

Lock, Stephen and Tony Smith, *The Medical Risks of Life*, London, 1976.

Lock, Stephen (ed.), *Today's Treatment*, London, 1979.

Logan, W. P. D., 'Cancer of the Breast: No Decline in Mortality', *Lancet*, December, 1975, 462–71.

Loranger, Armand (*et al.*), 'Intellectual Impairment in Parkinson's Syndrome', *Brain*, 1972, 405–12.

Luthe, W., *Autogenic Training*, New York, 1965.

Lyell, Alan, 'Management of Warts', *BMJ*, 24 Dec. 1966, 1567–9.

Lyle, W. H. and R. N. Chamberlain (eds.), 'Epidemic Neuromyasthenia', *Postgraduate Med. Jnl.*, Nov. 1978, 705–44.

Lynch, J. L., *The Broken Heart*, New York, 1977.

McClintock, Martha K., 'Menstrual Synchrony and Suppression', *Nature*, 22 Jan. 1971, 244–5.

McEvedy, Colin and A. W. Beard, 'Royal Free Epidemic of 1955: a Reconsideration', *BMJ*, 3 Jan. 1970, 7–10.

McGinty, Lawrence, 'Controlling Cancer in the Workplace', *New Scientist*, 22 Dec. 1977, 758–61.

Mackarness, Richard, *Not All in the Mind*, London, 1978.

Mackarness, Richard, *Chemical Victims*, London, 1980.

Mackenzie, James, *The Future of Medicine*, Oxford, 1919.

Mackenzie, James, *Diseases of the Heart*, Oxford, 1925 (1908).

McKeown, Thomas and C. R. Lowe, *An Introduction to Social Medicine*, Oxford, 1966.

McKeown, Thomas, *The Role of Medicine: Dream, Mirage or Nemesis?*, Oxford, 1979.

McLachlan, Gordon and Thomas McKeown (eds.), *Medical History and Medical Care*, London, 1971.

McMahon, F. Gilbert, *Management of Essential Hypertension*, New York, 1978.

McNeill, William H., *Plagues and People*, Oxford, 1977 (New York, 1976).

McPherson, Klim and Maurice S. Fox, 'Treatment of Breast Cancer', (in Bunker, 1977, 308 ff).

Magill, T. P., 'The Immunologist and the Evil Spirits', *Jnl. Immun.*, Jan. 1955, 1–8.

Maguire, Anne, 'Psychic Possession among Industrial Workers', *Lancet*, 18 Feb. 1978, 376–8.

Mahler, Halfdan, 'A De-mystification of Modern Technology', *Lancet*, 1 Nov. 1975, 829–33.

Malleson, A., *Need Your Doctor be So Useless?*, London, 1973.

Mann, George V., 'Diet-Heart: End of an Era', *NEJM*, 22 Sept. 1977, 644–50.

Marmot, M. H., 'Epidemiological Basis for the Prevention of CHD', *WHO Bulletin*, 1979, 331–47.

Martys, Cedrick R., 'Adverse Reactions to Drugs in General Practice', *BMJ*, 10 Nov. 1979, 1194–7.

Mason, A. A. (*et al.*), 'A Case of Congenital Ichthyoform Erythrodermia Treated by Hypnosis', *BMJ*, 23 Aug. 1952, 422–3.

Mather, H. G. (*et al.*), 'Acute Myocardial Infarction: Home and Hospital Treatment', *BMJ*, 7 Aug. 1971, 334–8.

Mather, H. G. (*et al.*), 'Myocardial Infarction: a Comparison Between Home and Hospital Care for Patients', *BMJ*, 17 April 1976, 925–9.

Maugh, Thomas, 'Multiple Sclerosis', *Science*, 18, 25 Feb. 1977, 667–9, 768–81; 11 March 1977, 969–71.

Meares, Ainslie, 'Atavistic Regression as a Factor in the Remission of Cancer', *Med. Jnl. Australia*, 23 July 1977.

Meares, Ainslie, 'Meditation: a Psychological Approach to Cancer Treatment', *Practitioner*, Jan. 1979, 119–22.

Melville, Joan, *Phobias and Obsessions*, London, 1977.

Melzack, Ronald and Patrick Wall, 'Pain Mechanisms: a New Theory', *Science*, 19 Nov. 1965, 971–9.

Meyler, L., *Side-Effects of Drugs*, Amsterdam, 1966.

Millar, J. H. D., *Multiple Sclerosis*, Springfield, Ill., 1971.

Miller, Henry, 'Depression', *BMJ*, 4 Feb. 1967, 257–62.

Miller, Henry, 'Historical Influences on Medicine' (in McLachlan/McKeown, 1971, 223–40).

Miller, Jonathan, *The Body in Question*, London, 1978.

Miller, Neal, E., 'Applications of Learning and Biofeedback' (in Freedman [*et al.*], *Comprehensive Textbook of Psychiatry*, Baltimore, 1974).

Miller, Theodore, 'Psychophysiological Aspects of Cancer', *Cancer*, Feb., 1977, 413–18.

Mintz, Morton, *By Prescription Only*, Boston, 1967.

Morgan, Huw, 'Medical Education: a Traumatic Experience', *World Med.*, 22 Sept. 1979, 21–3.

Morgan-Jones, A., 'The Nature of the Coronary Problem', *Brit. Heart Jnl.*, 1970, 583–91.

Morris, J. N., *Uses of Epidemiology*, London, 1975 (1957).

Morris, J. N. (*et al.*), 'Incidence and Prediction of Ischemic Heart Disease in London Busmen', *Lancet*, 10 Sept. 1966, 553–9.

Morris, J. N. (*et al.*), 'Diet and Heart: a Postscript', *BMJ*, 19 Nov. 1977, 1307–14.

Moss, Peter D. and Colin McEvedy, 'An Epidemic of Overbreathing Among Schoolgirls', *BMJ*, 26 Nov. 1966, 1295–9.

351

Mulcahy, Risteard, 'How rational is Our Treatment of Coronary Heart Disease?', *World Med.*, 20 Oct. 1976, 39–40.

Murphy, Marvin L. (*et al.*), 'Treatment of Chronic Stable Angina', *NEJM*, 22 Sept. 1977, 621–7.

Murray, J. G. (*et al.*), 'Management of Early Cancer of the Breast', *BMJ*, 1 May 1976, 1035–8.

Myers, F. W. H., 'Hysteria and Genius', *Jnl. Soc. Psychical Research*, April 1897, 50–9.

Nathanson, Neal and A. Miller, 'Epidemiology of Multiple Sclerosis', *Am. Jnl. Epidem.*, June 1978, 451–61.

National Institute of Health Consensus Development Panel, 'Adjuvant Chemotherapy in Breast Cancer', *BMJ*, 13 Sept. 1980, 724–5.

New South Wales Health Commission, *Psychosocial Problems of Sydney Adults*, Sydney, 1979.

Nixon, Peter, 'Questionable Dogma', *World Med.*, 3 Nov. 1979, 51–2.

Nixon, Peter, 'The Responsibility of the Cardiological Mapmaker', *Am. Heart Jnl.*, Aug. 1980, 139–43.

Norman, John, C. (ed.), *Coronary Artery Medicine and Surgery*, New York, 1975.

Null, Gary and Robert Houston, 'The Great Cancer Fraud', *Penthouse*, Sept. 1979.

O'Brien, Eoin, 'Six Years Shalt Thou Labour', *World Med.*, 24 March 1979, 26–7.

Office of Health Economics, *Skin Disorders*, London, 1973; *Parkinson's Disease*, 1974; *Multiple Sclerosis*, 1975; *Schizophrenia*, 1979.

Ogilvie, Heneage, 'The Practitioner and His Hospital Service', *BMJ*, 26 Sept. 1953, 707–11.

Ogilvie, Heneage, 'The Human Heritage', *Lancet*, 6 July 1957, 35–40.

Oliver, M. F. and G. S. Boyd, 'Some Current Views on the Etiology of Coronary Artery Disease', *Brit. Heart Jnl.*, 582–3.

Orchard, Trevor J., 'Epidemiology in the 1980s: Need for a Change?' *Lancet*, 18 Oct. 1980, 845–6.

Ornstein, Robert E., *The Nature of Human Consciousness*, New York, 1974.

Osborn, June (ed.), *Influenza in America*, 1918–76, New York, 1977.

Osmond, Humphrey, 'Models of Madness', *New Scientist*, 28 Dec. 1961.

Paget, James, 'Nervous Mimicry of Organic Diseases', *Lancet*, 11 Oct. 1873, 511–13.

Paget, James, *Lectures on Surgical Pathology*, London, 1876.

Pappworth, M. H., *Human Guinea Pigs*, London, 1967.

Parsons, Talcott, *The Social System*, New York, 1951.

Patel, Chandra and W. R. S. North, 'Randomised Controlled Trial of Biofeedback in Management of Hypertension', *Lancet*, 19 July 1975, 93–5.

Paul Oglesby (ed.), *Epidemiology and the Control of Hypertension*, Miami, 1975.

Pearce, Ian, 'A Holistic Approach to Cancer' (unpublished paper, May 1978).

Pelletier, Kenneth R., *Mind as Healer, Mind as Slayer*, New York, 1977.

Pendergrass, Eugene P. 'Host Resistance and Other Intangibles in the Treatment of Cancer', *Am. Jnl. Roentology*, May 1961, 891–6.

Perduzzi, Peter and Herbert Hultgren, 'Effect of Medical and Surgical Treatment in Stable Angina Pectoris', *Circulation*, Oct. 1979, 888–900.

Peterson, J. E. (*et al.*), 'Hourly Changes in Serum Cholesterol Concentration', *Circulation*, 25 May 1962, 798–803.

Philipoppoulos, G. S. (*et al.*), 'The Etiologic Significance of Emotional Factors in the Onset and Exacerbation of Multiple Sclerosis', *Pychosom. Med.*, 1958, 458–74.

Pickering, George, 'The Significance of the Discovery of the Effects of Cortisone on Rheumatoid Arthritis', *Lancet*, 15 July 1950, 81–4.

Pickering, George, *Hypertension*, Edinburgh and London, 1974.

Pickering, George, *Quest for Excellence in Medical Education*, London, 1978.

Pickering, George, 'The Medical Straitjacket', *World Med.*, 29 Nov. 1978.

Pinals, Robert and Frank Sumner, 'Relative Efficacy of Indomethacin in Rheumatoid Arthritis', *NEJM*, 2 March 1967, 512–14.

Polanyi, M., *The Logic of Liberty*, London, 1951.

Powles, T. J. (*et al.*), 'Failure of Chemotherapy to Prolong Survival in a Group of Patients with Metastatic Breast Cancer', *Lancet*, 15 March 1980, 580–2.

Pulay, Erwin, *Allergic Man*, London, 1942.

Rahe, R. H. (*et al.*), 'Social Stress and Illness Onset', *Jnl. Psychosom. Research*, 1964, 35–44.

Rahe, R. H., 'Life-Change Measurement as a Predictor of Illness', *Procs. Royal Soc. Med.*, Nov., 1968, 1124–6.

Rahe, R. H. and M. Romo, 'Recent Life Changes and the Onset of Myocardial Infarction and Coronary Death in Helsinki', (in Gunderson/Rahe, 1974, 105–20).

Rahe, R. H. (*et al.*), 'Brief Group Therapy in Myocardial Infarction Rehabilitation', *Psychosom. Med.*, May 1979, 229–41.

Ramsay, A. Melvin and Ronald Edmond, *Infectious Diseases*, London, 1978 (1967).

Randall, Keith J., 'Cancer Screening by Cytology', *Lancet*, 30 Nov. 1974, 1303–4.

Rawles, J. M. and A. F. Kenmure, 'The Coronary Care Controversy', *BMJ*, 20 Sept. 1980, 783–6.

Raymond, M. J. (*et al.*), 'A Trial of Five Tranquillising Drugs in Psychoneurosis', *BMJ*, 13 July 1957, 63–6.

Rhodes, Philip, *The Value of Medicine*, London, 1976.

Richards, Victor, *The Wayward Cell: Cancer*, Berkeley, Calif., 1978 (1972).

Riddell, Sylvia A., 'The Therapeutic Efficiency of ECT', *Archives Genl. Psychiatry*, 1963, 546–56.

Rivers, W. H. R., *Instinct and the Unconscious*, Cambridge, 1920.

Rivers, W. H. R., 'Medicine, Magic and Religion', *Lancet*, 22 Dec. 1917, 919–23; 29 Dec. 1917, 959–64.

Roberts, C. J., *Epidemiology for Clinicians*, London, 1978 (1977).

Roland, J. M. (*et al.*), 'Effect of Beta-Blockers on Arrythmias', *BMJ*, 1 Sept. 1979, 518–21.

Roman, T. N. and J. P. A. Latour, 'The Effect of Early Diagnosis on Survival Statistics in Carcinoma of the Uterine Cervix', *Am. Jnl. Obst. Gyn.*, 15th March 1967, 739–49.

Rosedale, Neville, 'Trichomonal Vaginitis is not a Venereal Disease', *World Med.*, 13 July 1977, 33–4.

Rosenhan, D. L., 'On Being Sane in Insane Places', *Science*, 19 Jan. 1973, 250–8.

Rosenthal, Robert, *Experimenter Effects in Behavioural Research*, New York, 1966.

Rose, G., 'Epidemiology of Ischaemic Heart Disease', *Brit. Jnl.Hosp. Med.*, March 1972, 285–8.

Roueché, Berton, *The Incurable Wound*, New York, 1957.

Royal College of Physicians, 'Prevention of CHD', *Jnl. Royal Col. Phys.*, April 1976, 213–75.

Royal College of Physicians, *Smoking and Health*, London, 1962; *Smoking and Health Now*, London, 1971; *Smoking or Health* London 1977.

Rubenstein, Edward, 'Diseases Caused by Impaired Communication among Cells', *Scientific American*, March 1980, 78–87.

Russell, M. A. H. (*et al.*), 'Effect of GPs' Advice Against Smoking', *BMJ*, 28 July 1979.

Ryle, John, *The Natural History of Disease*, London, 1948 (1936).

Sackett, David L., 'Cardiovascular Diseases', *Lancet*, 16 Nov. 1974, 1189–91.

Sacks, Oliver, *Awakenings*, London, 1973.

Schindel, Leo, *Unexpected Reactions to Modern Therapeutics*, London, 1957.

Schneider, R. A., 'An Experimental Study of Life Situation and Emotion and the Clotting Time and Relative Viscosity of the Blood', *Am. Jnl. Med. Science*, 1951, 562–73.

Schofield, A. T., *Functional Nerve Diseases*, London, 1980.

Schofield, C. B. S., *Sexually Transmitted Diseases*, Edinburgh, 1979 (1972).

Schrag, Peter, *Mind Control*, London, 1980 (New York, 1980).

Schultz, Johannes and Wolfgang Luthe, *Autogenic Training*, New York, 1959.

Selby, Philip (ed.), *Influenza*, London and New York, 1976.

Selye, Hans, *The Stress of Life*, London, 1957 (New York, 1956).

Selye, Hans, *Stress Without Distress*, New York, 1974.

Selzer, Richard, *Mortal Lessons*, London, 1981.

Shapiro, A. K., 'The Placebo Effect in the History of Medical Treatment', *Am. Jnl. Psychiatry*, 1959, 298–304.

Shapiro, David (*et al.*), 'Effects of Feedback and Reinforcement on the Control of Human Systolic Blood Pressure', *Science*, 7 Feb. 1969, 588–90.

Shapiro, Sam (*et al.*), 'Evaluation of Periodic Breast Cancer Screening', *JAMA*, 28 Feb. 1966, 731–8.

Shapiro, Sam (*et al.*), 'Evidence on Screening for Breast Cancer', *Cancer*, 1977, 2772–82.

Sharpe, Anthony N., 'Germ of a New Food Microbiology', *New Scientist*, 13 Dec. 1979, 860–2.

Shaw, G. Bernard, *The Doctor's Dilemma*, London, 1911.

Shaw, K. M. (*et al.*), 'The Impact of Treatment with Levodopa on Parkinson's Disease', *Qly. Jnl. Med.*, 1980, 283–93.

Shepherd, Michael, 'A Critical Appraisal of Contemporary Psychiatry', *Comprehensive Psychiatry*, July 1971, 302–20.

Shepherd, Michael, 'The Use and Abuses of Drugs in Psychiatry', *Lancet*, 3 Jan. 1970, 31–3.

Sigerist, Henry, *A History of Disease* (vol 1), London and New York, 1951.

Sigerist, Henry, *Man and Medicine*, London, 1932 (New York, 1931).

Sikora, Karl, 'Does Interferon Cure Cancer?' *BMJ*, 27 Sept. 1980, 855–7.

Simeons, A. T. W., *Man's Presumptuous Brain*, London, 1960.

Simonton, O. Carl and Stephanie Simonton, 'Belief Systems and Management of the Emotional Aspects of Malignancy', *Jnl. Transpersonal Psychology*, 1975, 29–47.

Skey, F. C., *Hysteria*, London, 1867.

Skultans, Vieda, *English Madness*, London, 1979.

Slater, Eliot, 'Diagnosis of "Hysteria"', *BMJ*, 29 May 1965, 1395–6.

Slater, Eliot, 'Health Service or Sickness Service?' *BMJ*, 18 Dec. 1971, 734–6.

Smith, Anthony, *The Body*, London, 1968.

Smith, J. W. G. and R. Pollard, 'Vaccination Against Influenza: a Five Year Study at the Post Office', *Jnl. Hygiene*, Aug. 1979, 157–70.

Smithers, D. W., 'Cancer: an Attack on Cytologism', *Lancet*, 10 March 1962, 493–9.

Sneddon, Joan, 'Myasthenia Gravis', *Lancet*, 8 March 1980, 526–8.

Sokolov, Maurice and B. McIlroy, *Clinical Cardiology*, Los Altos, Calif., 1978.

Sontag, Susan, *Illness as Metaphor*, New York, 1978 (1977).

Sparks, T. Flint (*et al.*), 'The Psychological and Physiological Factors of Cancer', *Institute of Noetic Sciences Bulletin*, 1978.

Special Correspondent, A, 'Adaptation to Stress', *BMJ*, 9 Aug. 1958, 382–4.

Spencer, Herbert, 'The Physiology of Laughter', (in *Essays*, London, 1891).

Sprague, H. B., 'Emotional Stress and the Etiology of Heart Disease', *Circulation*, 1 Jan. 1958.

Spriggs, A. I. and O. Husain, Cervical Smears, *BMJ*, 11 June 1977, 1516–18.

Stallones, Revel A., 'The Rise and Fall of Ischemic Heart Disease', *Scientific American*, Nov. 1980, 43–90.

Stamler, Jeremiah, 'Epidemiology of Coronary Heart Disease', *Med. Clinics of North Am.*, Jan., 1973, 5–46.

Stamler, Jeremiah (*et al.*), 'Dietary Cholesterol, Fat and Fibre, and Colon-Cancer Mortality', *Lancet*, 13 Oct. 1979, 782–5.

Stevenson, Douglas Lang, 'The Evolutionary Origins of Cancer' (paper read at Symposium, 'New approaches to cancer', Royal Society of Medicine, 23 Nov. 1979).

Stevenson, Ian, 'Schizophrenia: Our Worst Mental Illness', *Atlantic Monthly*, Aug. 1957.

Stewart, G. T., 'Limitations of the Germ Theory', *Lancet*, 18 May 1968, 1077–81.

Stokes John B. (*et al.*), 'Hypertension Control', *NEJM*, 20 Dec. 1973, 1369–71.

Stoll Basil (ed.), *Risk Factors in Lung Cancer*, London, 1976.

Stoll, Basil (ed.), *Mind and Cancer Prognosis*, London, 1979.

Storr, Anthony, *The Art of Psychotherapy*, London, 1979.

Swartz, Harry, *Allergy*, London, 1963.

Sydenham, Thomas, *Works* (ed. R. G. Latham), London, 1850.

Syme, S. L. (*et al.*), 'Some Social and Cultural Factors Associated with the Occurrence of CHD', *Jnl. Chron. Diseases*, 1964, 277–89.

Szasz, Thomas, *The Myth of Mental Illness*, London, 1962 (New York, 1961).

Talalay, Paul (ed.), *Drugs in Our Society*, Baltimore and London, 1964.

Tarassoli, M., 'Health in a Developing World', *JAMA*, 16 Dec. 1974, 1527–9.

Tate, Helen C. (*et al.*), 'Randomised Comparative Studies in the Treatment of Cancer in the UK', *Lancet*, 22 Sept. 1979, 623–5.

Taylor, Lord, 'Violence and Unreason in Everyday Life', *World Med.*, 21 Feb. 1981, 88–98.

Teeling-Smith, George, 'What Price Screening?', *World Med.*, 6 April 1977, 43.

Teeling-Smith, George, *A Question of Balance*, London, 1980.

Thiel, H. G. (*et al.*), 'Stress Factors and the Risk of Myocardial Infarction', *Jnl. Psychosom. Research*, Jan., 1973, 43–57.

Thier, Samuel O., 'Breast Cancer Screening', *NEJM*, 10 Nov. 1977, 1063.

Thomas, Caroline B. and Karen Duszynski, 'Closeness to Parents and the Family Constellation in a Prospective Study of Five Disease States', *Johns Hopkins Med. Jnl.*, May, 1974, 252–70.

Thomas, Lewis, *The Lives of a Cell*, London, 1974.

Thomas, Lewis, *The Medusa and the Snail*, London, 1980.

Thomson, H. J., 'Consent for Mastectomy', *BMJ*, 25 Oct. 1980, 1097–8.

Tice, Frederick (ed.), *Practice of Medicine* (ten vols.), Hagerstown, Maryland, 1924.

Tinbergen, Nikolaas, 'Ethology and Stress Disorders', *Science*, 5 July 1974, 20–7.

Todd, John W., *Health and Humanity*, Oxford, 1970.

Todd, John W., 'Then and Now', *World Med.*, 16 Nov. 1977, 37–47.

Todd, Lord, *Report of Royal Commission on Medical Education*, London, 1968.

Toffler, Alvin, *Future Shock*, New York, 1970.

Totman, Richard, *Social Causes of Illness*, London, 1979.

Totman, Richard (*et al.*), 'Cognitive Dissonance, Stress, and Virus-Induced Common Colds', *Jnl. Psychosomatic Research*, 1977, 55–63.

Towers, Bernard, 'The Influence of Medical Technology on Medical Services' (in McLachlan/McKeown, 1971).

Treadwell, B. J. L. (*et al.*), 'Side-Effects of Long-Term Treatment With Corticosteroids', *Lancet*, 23 May 1964, 1121–3.

Trethowan, W. H., 'From Straitjacket to Soma', *World Med.*, 16 June 1979, 26–7.

Trethowan, W. H., *Psychiatry*, London, 1979.

Tudge, Colin, 'Preventive Medicine – California Style', *World Med.*, 17–21.

Tuke, Daniel Hack, *Illustrations of the Influence of the Mind Upon the Body in Health and Disease*, London, 1872.

Turk, J. L., *Immunology in Clinical Medicine*, London, 1975.

Tylor, Edward, *Primitive Culture*, London, 1871.

Vaillant, G. E., 'Natural History of Male Psychologic Health', *NEJM*, 6 Dec. 1979, 1249–54.

Vaughan, Warren T., *Allergy: Strangest of All Maladies*, London, 1942.

Veith, Ilza, *Hysteria*, Chicago, 1970 (1965).

Wade, O. L., *Adverse Reactions to Drugs*, London, 1970.

Wade, O. L., *The Lost Discipline*, Birmingham, 1972.

Walshe, Francis, 'Diagnosis of Hysteria', *BMJ*, 18 Dec. 1965, 1451–4.

Walshe, W. H., *Nature and Treatment of Cancer*, London, 1846.

Walton, John, 'The Nerve to Treat', *World Med.*, 8 Sept. 1979, 19–20.

Watts, Geoffrey, 'ECT', *World Med.*, 28 Jan. 1976, 27.

Weinstein, Louis, 'Influenza, 1918: a Revision', *NEJM.*, 6 May 1976, 1058–60.

Weiss, Edward, and O. S. English, *Psychosomatic Medicine*, Philadelphia, 1957 (1943)

Wells, Nicholas (Office of Health Economics), *Medicines: 50 Years of Progress, 1930–80*, London, 1980.

Wertenbaker, Lael, *To Mend the Heart*, New York, 1980.

Wheatley, David, 'Influence of Doctors' and Patients' Attitudes in the Treatment of Neurotic Illness', *Lancet*, 25 Nov. 1967, 1133–5.

Whitby, L. G., 'Screening for Disease', *Lancet*, 5 Oct. 1974, 819–21.

White, Leon S., 'How to Improve the Public's Health', *NEJM*, 9 Oct. 1975, 773–4.

White, Paul Dudley, 'The Psyche and the Soma', *Annals Intern. Med.*, 1951, 1291.

White, Susan J. (*et al.*), 'Anti-Convulsant Drugs and Cancer', *Lancet*, 1 Sept. 1979, 458–60.

Whyte, Robert, *Observations on Hysteria*, Edinburgh, 1765.

Williamson, John D. and Kate Danaher, *Self-Care in Health*, London, 1978.

Wilson, Donald P., *My Six Convicts*, London, 1951.

Wilson, John Rowan, *Margin of Safety*, London, 1963.

Wittkower, Eric and R. A. Cleghorn, *Recent Developments in Psychosomatic Medicine*, London, 1954.

Wolf, Stewart, 'Psychosocial Forces in Acute Myocardial Infarction and Sudden Death', *Circulation*, 1969 (supplement).

Wolf, Stewart and Harold G. Wolff, *Human Gastric Function*, New York, 1947.

Wolff, Harold, *Stress and Disease* (revised and edited by Stewart Wolf), Springfield, Ill., 1968.

Ziegler, Philip, *The Black Death*, London, 1969.

Zinsser, Hans, *Rats, Lice and History*, London 1960 (New York, 1935).

Zola, Irving K., 'Communication, Diagnosis and Patient Care', *Jnl. Med. Educ.*, Oct. 1963, 838.

Zubrod, C. Gordon, 'The Basis for Progress in Chemotherapy', *Cancer*, 1972, 1474–9.

Zuckerman, Lord, *Cancer Research*, London, 1972.

# Index